AF527548

A Photographic Field Guide to the

BIRDS OF THE HIMALAYAS

and South Assam Hills

Om Books International

First published in 2024 by

Om Books International

Corporate & Editorial Office
A-12, Sector 64, Noida 201 301
Uttar Pradesh, India
Phone: +91 120 477 4100
Email: editorial@ombooks.com
Website: www.ombooksinternational.com

Sales Office
107, Ansari Road, Darya Ganj,
New Delhi 110 002, India
Phone: +91 11 2326 3363, 2326 5303, 4000 9000
Fax: +91 11 2327 8091
Email: sales@ombooks.com
Website: www.ombooks.com

ISBN: 978-81-19750-00-9

Printed in India

10 9 8 7 6 5 4 3 2 1

A Photographic Field Guide to the

BIRDS OF THE HIMALAYAS

and South Assam Hills

CONTENTS

INTRODUCTION

Amur Falcon

Asian Fairy Bluebird

Red-billed Chough

Eyebrowed Wren Babbler

Himvan, Himvat, and Himadri and all other names used to describe the range associate it with eternal snow. 'Himalaya' means the 'abode of snow'. In a memorable verse in the *Kumarasambhava*, the famous Sanskrit poet Kalidasa compares the Himalayas to a gigantic measuring rod striding the earth between two oceans.

This great range contains huge deposits of ice and snow and encompasses about 15,000 glaciers, which store about 12,000 cubic km (3,000 cubic miles) of fresh water and its glaciers include the Gangotri, and Yamnotri, Khumbu glacier (in the Mt Everest region), and Langtang and Zemu glaciers (in Sikkim).

The Himalayan range is often broken into several zones such as the Trans-Himalaya, the Tethyan Himalaya, the Higher Himalaya, the Lesser Himalaya and the Sub-Himalaya. It also includes the Shiwalik range. In the west, these ranges come together to form the Hindu Kush and the Karakoram ranges. While to the east, they end at the Indochinese Peninsula.

Interestingly a vast shallow sea, the Tethys, existed where the Himalayas stand today. The submerged landmasses on either side started pushing towards each other, giving birth to these nascent mountains. This was a relatively recent occurrence in the geographical time frame, so the Himalaya is considered a young and fragile land formation. Scientists speculate that the whole process took five to seven million years. Fossil finds at heights of over 8,000 m (26,000 ft.) support these theories. The Himalayas have risen 2,000 m (6,600 ft.) in the past 20,000 years and continue to rise at the rate of 7.5 to 10 cm a year.

The world's mightiest mountain range boasts of 14 peaks and hundred of summits over 7,000 m (23,000 ft.) high. It stretches to 2,700 km (1,700 miles) across an area between Assam and Kashmir. In the east, Namcha Barwa stand sentinel; the western extremity is guarded by the majestic Nanga Parbat. Other imposing peaks, in the Himalayas include the K2, Kanchenjunga, Makalu, Dhaulagiri, and Annapurna – all of whose summits are above 25,000 ft.

The snow-capped, frost-crusted peaks have posed a challenge not only to the physical prowess of adventurers, they have also inspired sublime metaphysics and lyrical poetry. There are innumerable references to this King of Mountains, the glistening divinity, and the noble soul. The earliest is in the *Rig Veda*. Singing the praise of the supreme deity, the poet sages refer to the Himalayas: 'It is to He to whom belong these celestial mountain ranges.' These sages also describe its stretch as, 'the expanse of the two arms of the great being'. The epics *Ramayana* and *Mahabharata*, and the *Puranas*, describe this as the region where the Gods dwell, and the landscape is evoked beautifully in classical works. The *Skanda Purana* notes, 'As the sun dries the morning dew so does the mere sight of the Himalayas dissipate the sins of man.'

The Himalayas are the source of many great rivers of the Indian subcontinent. The Indus or Sindhu (the river rising out of a lion's mouth) rises in the Trans-Himalayan Tibetan Plateau, as does the Brahmaputra (India's only 'male' river). The Ganga and the Yamuna, with their countless colourful Himalayan tributaries, are inexorably intertwined with local myths and legends. The rivers of the Himalayas drain into two large river systems. The western rivers combine and flow into the Indus Basin, with the Indus itself forming

Black-breasted Parrotbill

Eurasian Sparrowhawk

Lord Derby's Parakeet

the northern and western boundaries of the Himalayas. It begins life in Tibet when the Sengee and the Gar rivers meet and flow northwest, passing through India on to Pakistan and finally the Arabian Sea. In its journey, it is joined by many tributaries including the Jhelum, Chenab, Ravi, Beas and the Sutlej that collectively give the name Punjab or the land of five rivers.

The eastern rivers, the primary of which are the Ganga, the Yamuna and the Brahmaputra and their countless tributaries flow into the Brahmaputra Basin in Assam. The mighty Ganga and the Brahmaputra meet in Bangladesh before joining the Bay of Bengal in the Sunderbans, the world's largest estuary.

Although the Himalayas can be traced to the Arakans and Arunachal in the east, its majesty is truly encountered only when we reach Nepal, Bhutan and Sikkim. The 8,682 m (28,483 ft.) – tall Kanchenjunga overshadows all else in Sikkim. This beautiful mountain is considered sacred by Hindus and Buddhists alike and its name translates as the 'Treasure of Five Jewels'. It is the third-highest mountain in the world.

Sikkim is situated to the south of Tibet and east of Nepal. Many of the most famous mountains in the Himalayas lie in Nepal, including Mount Everest, which holds the record as the world's highest peak at 8,848 m. Known as Sagarmatha in Nepalese and Chomolungma in Tibetan, it is named after the famous British Surveyor-General of the Survey of India – Sir George Everest. Many attempts were made to conquer it and many lives were lost in the process. Finally in 1953, New Zealander Sir Edmund Hillary and his Nepalese Sherpa Tenzing Norgay, made it to the top using the Southeast ridge route. Since then, the ascent to this mighty peak has been the dream of all climbers.

Neighbouring Bhutan also shares in the grandeur of the Himalayas. The entire country is a close basin between two parallel and deeply intersecting ridges. It is the catchment area of the Teesta River and its affluents. After travelling through Sikkim, the Teesta goes in to the Brahmaputra.

Uttarakhand lies in the central sector of the Himalayas, its boundaries are marked by the Kali River in the east and the Sutlej in the west. One-third of the land here consists of barren rocks, ridges and wild gorges. The 7,890 m (25,885-ft.) – high Nanda Devi is the highest peak here followed by Kamet, Trishul and the Panchachuli mastiff. Nanda Devi is the beloved Goddess of the people in Kumaon and Garhwal. Veteran mountaineers have gone into raptures over this moving sight, which has been described as 'the white-robed vision, hanging from heaven, which pulsates like a star with purity.'

Golden-throated Barbet

Hoary-throated Barwing

Greater Flameback

Red Crossbill

Eric Shipton and HW Tilman discovered the Nanda Devi Sanctuary, and were of the view that such scenic beauty was too profound for human conception. Himachal Pradesh lies further west, and the Kinnaur Kailash in the Kinnaur district is the most famous peak in this region. The Dhauladhar range may not boast of many high peaks but it exudes a quaint charm of its own.

The beautiful valley of Kashmir and the alpine meadows of Pahalgam and Gulmarg have been well trodden by travellers for centuries. The Trans-Himalayan region proper is encountered in Ladakh, the northernmost part of the Indian Himalayas. It is bounded to the north by the Kunlun and Karakoram mountains and to the south by the Zanskar ranges. Mountains run parallel to each other in the southeast and northwest. The famous Silk Route passed through Leh, meaning 'oasis'. Until recently, caravans rested here before and after negotiating dangerous passes. The highest pass traversing through the Karakoram is at 6,628 m (18,464 ft.). The confluences of the Indus River and Shyok, Zanskar, Nubra and the Dras rivers are in Ladakh, where the landscape is almost lunar and the climate extremely arid. It is here that the Himalayas begin to taper down and merge into the Hindu Kush, skirting the heartland of Asia.

As can be imagined, the Himalayas have diverse vegetation and can roughly be divided into the following types:

Red-headed Trogon

Montane Grasslands and Shrublands

Many Alpine shrubs and grass meadows are found between 10,000 and 16,000 ft. where the summers are relatively mild but the winters can be very harsh. The lower shrublands are often dominated by a variety of rhododendrons and other shrubs. This is the home of the Snow Leopard, Himalayan Tahr and several species of Pikas.

Temperate Coniferous Forest

The vegetation in the northeast, consists of coniferous forests between the elevations of 8,000 and 14,000 ft. Located in the inner valley area, these forests are protected from the monsoons by huge mountain ranges. The trees include pine, hemlock, spruce, and fir. Animals found in this region include red pandas, takins, and musk deer.

Eurasian Magpie

Temperate Broadleaf and Mixed Forests

The middle elevations of the eastern region are both broadleaf and conifer. These forests receive many inches of annual rainfall, mostly during summer. In addition to oaks and maples, plants like orchids, lichen, and ferns also grow in the area. The birdlife is incredible and many mammals thrive here including the recently described Golden Langur.

Tropical and Sub-tropical Broadleaf Forests

This low-lying strip consists of the Himalayan sub-tropical broadleaf forests. A wide range of plant life exists due to varied topography, soil types, and rainfall levels. The forest types include sub-tropical dry evergreen, northern dry mixed deciduous forests, moist mixed deciduous forests, sub-tropical broadleaf forests, northern tropical semi-evergreen forests, and northern tropical wet evergreen forests.

Where the treeline ends, the *buggyals* (alpine meadows) begin to unfold like a green, velvet carpet. Frank Smythe, who explored the Nandankanan – famous the world over as the Valley of Flowers – confessed that he had not seen a more beautiful flower than the Blue Poppy growing wild, watered by the melting snow. Other Himalayan flowers of rare beauty are seen in abundance. These meadows have been aptly described as the Eden of Flowers. Up here, lilies and potentillas change the landscape dramatically from a barren wasteland to a heavenly pasture within a short distance.

Black-faced Laughingthrush

It is difficult to imagine today that these Himalayan slopes were densely wooded, more than a century ago. ET Atkinson, in his *The Himalayan Gazetteer*, has mentioned coniferous forests, which reminded him of 'unbroken masses' swelling like waves of the sea over many miles, and presenting a scene of magnificent grandeur unknown elsewhere. Whilst the Himalayan forests are not as lush as the rain-fed South Indian forests, they do attain an impressive magnificence in the still unspoilt upper regions.

Wildlife in the terai comprises tigers, elephants, deer, wild boar, crocodiles and pythons. At great heights dwell more exotic species like the elusive Snow Leopard, the sure-foot Bharal or Blue Sheep and the diminutive Musk Deer.

Black-headed Shrike Babbler

Birds with colourful plumage like the pheasants and tragopans are seen in the eastern, central and western segments. It is surprising that many of these species have survived, given the ruthless destruction of their habitat. However, there is no room for complacency. Most are perched precariously on the verge of extinction.

The biggest threat to the birdlife in this region is deforestation which remains a major cause of concern. The latest satellite imagery makes for depressing reading. Forests have been reduced to only 5% of the landmass. Till recently, the Himalayan forests were relatively untouched but the policy to replace these originals with pine plantations does not augur well for several species of the Himalayan flora. The mass planting of the exotic 'Dhupi' tree in the hills of North Bengal by the British has also led to the complete extinction of native conifers. The desire of rapacious forest-based industries has led to the conversion of natural forests into never-ending timber 'mines'. This is due to serious depletion of the plains-based forests, which have rapidly been urbanised or converted into agricultural lands.

Forest fires, often set by local grass-cutters affect ground nesting birds including many endangered pheasant species, like the Western Tragopan. Traditional hunting, particularly in the northeast area, where several thousand birds are killed per annum for food, remains a matter of grave concern.

Grey-winged Blackbird

Green-backed Tit

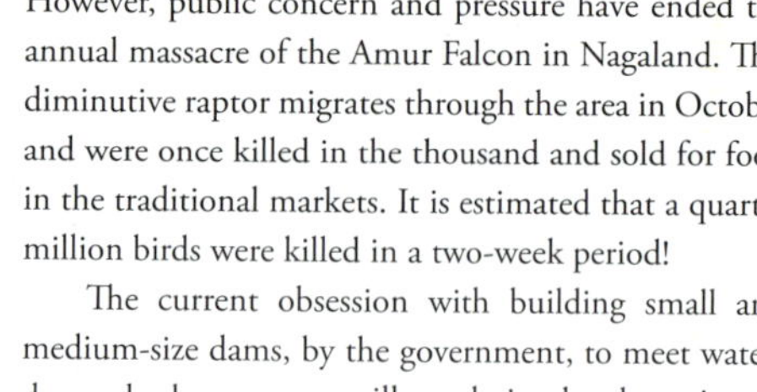

However, public concern and pressure have ended the annual massacre of the Amur Falcon in Nagaland. This diminutive raptor migrates through the area in October and were once killed in the thousand and sold for food in the traditional markets. It is estimated that a quarter million birds were killed in a two-week period!

The current obsession with building small and medium-size dams, by the government, to meet waters demands downstream will result in the drowning of over 60% of its most primordial forests.

Though the South Assam Hills are not considered a part of the Himalayas, but birds of this region have been included due to their similarity with their counterparts there, though of a different race. Even within this small area, there are considerable differences particularly in some wren-babblers and laughingthrushes. These fabled hills, primarily carved out of Assam, consist of Meghalaya, Nagaland, Manipur and Mizoram. Hunting and Jhoom (slash and burn) cultivation remain the biggest threats.

Black-headed Bunting

Gould's shortwing

The maps in the book give the range of the species in the subcontinent. The red areas indicate resident birds. The blue areas denote non-breeding winter visitors.

Chinese Pond Heron

SNOW PARTRIDGE

Lerwa lerwa Phasianidae

Size 38 cm

Voice Loud call, similar to Grey

Range Resident; the Himalayas, 2,500–5,000 m

Habitat Alpine meadows; scrubby hillsides; rhododendron; fern undergrowth

Rather plump bird with prominent bright red bill and legs. Upperparts blackish-grey and finely barred with rufous and white. Underparts dark chestnut, broadly streaked white and deep chestnut breast. Upper half of legs feathered and spurred. Dark tail also barred with white, white tip to tail. Sexes alike, but male has blunt spur on tarsus. Juvenile has mottled underparts and less prominent barring. Found in small groups of about six to eight, and upto 30, in non-breeding season. Nests on ground under rock ledges. Feeds on lichens, mosses and shoots. Nests well concealed on hillsides under rocks.

TIBETAN SNOWCOCK

Tetraogallus tibetanus Phasianidae

Size 51 cm

Voice Noisy. Call an accelerating bubbling, a whistle and loud *cur…lee*

Range The Himalayas

Habitat Rocky ridges; slopes and meadows above snowline

Largish partridge with strong, short, red legs. Distinguished from other snowcocks by extensive white underparts with heavy blackish streaks on sides and flanks. Adult has overall heavily streaked plumage, pale grey-buff upperparts streaked with dark grey. White forehead, ear-coverts and throat. White cheeks, chin, throat and breast, with some irregular dark grey-patches on upper breast and foreneck; dark grey bands on sides of neck and breast. Dark grey crown and upperparts; grey wing-coverts streaked white; white secondaries; reddish-brown rump and tail. Underparts white with black barring. Short tail with pale brown uppertail-coverts. Sexes alike, but female slightly smaller and duller.

HIMALAYAN SNOWCOCK

Tetraogallus himalayensis Phasianidae

Size 55–72 cm

Voice Noisy; cock utters loud whistle of several notes

Range Resident; the Himalayas; Kashmir to Kumaon and W Nepal; 3,800–5,500 m in summer; moves lower to 2,200 m in winter

Habitat Alpine meadows; rocky country above treeline

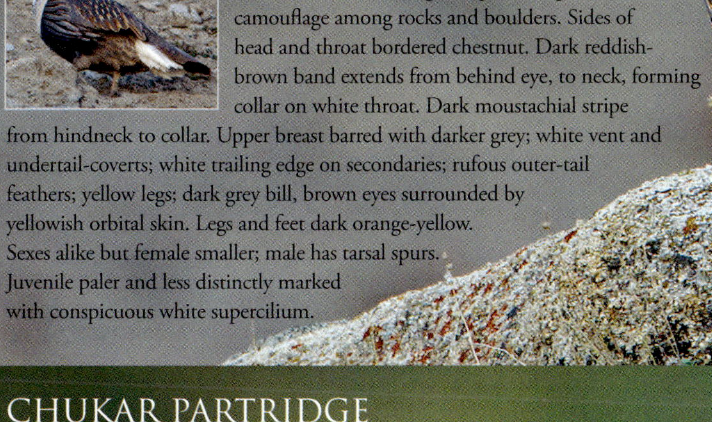

Largish bird, overall grey, black-and-white with some chestnut streaking that provides good camouflage among rocks and boulders. Sides of head and throat bordered chestnut. Dark reddish-brown band extends from behind eye, to neck, forming collar on white throat. Dark moustachial stripe from hindneck to collar. Upper breast barred with darker grey; white vent and undertail-coverts; white trailing edge on secondaries; rufous outer-tail feathers; yellow legs; dark grey bill, brown eyes surrounded by yellowish orbital skin. Legs and feet dark orange-yellow. Sexes alike but female smaller; male has tarsal spurs. Juvenile paler and less distinctly marked with conspicuous white supercilium.

CHUKAR PARTRIDGE

Alectoris chukar Phasianidae

Size 38 cm

Voice Male utters a loud chuckle, of upto a dozen notes

Range Resident; W Himalayas to C Nepal; about 1,200-5,000 m

Habitat Scrub and rock-covered hills; cultivation

Plumpish, medium-sized partridge, overall greyish-brown with distinct black band running from eye to base of neck; whitish-buff face and throat; grey head and breast. Upperparts grey-buff, black gorget across forehead and eyes, white cheeks and throat. Flanks prominently barred black-and-white with tinge of buff; tail and lower back dark grey; buffish belly; chestnut outer-tail feathers; bright red bill and legs. Sexes similar, but female smaller with smaller knob on legs. Juvenile smaller and mottled brown-and-grey, with slight brown barring on flanks. Small groups forage on open barren grounds.

BLACK FRANCOLIN

Francolinus francolinus Phasianidae

Size 34 cm

Voice Male utters a loud 3- to 6-noted crow

Range Locally resident; N subcontinent, along foothills; south to N Gujarat and C Madhya Pradesh; an eastern race *melanotus* occurs east of Nepal in Duars

Habitat High grass, cultivation; prefers wetter areas along canals and rivers

Handsome, jet-black bird with stub-tail. Upperparts and flanks spotted white and fulvous; white-patch on cheeks; chestnut collar, belly and undertail-coverts; brownish-red legs. Black tail has narrow white bars. Female similar to male, but paler with wider brown bars on lower back, white cheek-patch and chestnut collar missing, small nuchal patch. Singly, or in small parties in high grass and edges of water; secretive; fast runners on ground. Nests in grass-lined depression in bare ground.

♀

SWAMP FRANCOLIN

Francolinus gularis Phasianidae

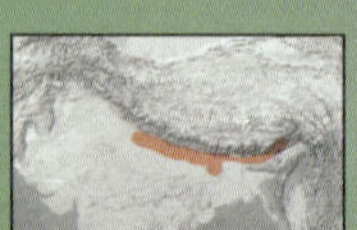

Size 37 cm

Voice Calls include vocal and loud *kyew…kyew…kyew…kaa…kaa* and *chukeroo…chukeroo…chukeroo*. Alarm a loud *kaw*

Range Globally threatened; breeding endemic resident restricted to Nepal, N India and Assam

Habitat Tall grasslands; swamp; sugarcane fields

Largest francolin with unusually long legs. Brown crown, beige supercilium and thin brown eye-stripes that extend to neck; upper throat and upper neck rusty-brown. Back and wings have mix of black and brown feathers with white flashes on the chest, chestnut flight feathers and outer-tail. Underparts brown longitudinally streaked with white. Blackish bill and dull brownish-red legs. Sexes alike, but female smaller and lacks spurs. Male has darker legs. Shy, seen in pairs or small groups near rivers and jheel edges in tall wet grasslands. Comes into open ground or cultivation to feed. Nests on a pad in shallow water amongst reeds.

TIBETAN PARTRIDGE

Perdix hodgsoniae Phasianidae

Size 31 cm

Voice Calls include strong, repeated *scherrrreck* and a high *chee…chee…chee*

Range Common breeding resident: N India, Nepal, Bhutan

Habitat High altitude semi-desert and rocky slopes with scattered low scrub

Medium-sized terrestrial bird of high altitude. Striking black-and-white facial markings contrasting with rufous nape. White throat and supercilium; black cheek patches; chestnut hind-collar and flanks, brown back, blackish belly. Underparts pale buff barred black on breast and belly; white lower belly. Rufous tail visible in flight. Female similar to male but duller. Juvenile a featureless buff-brown. Flies for short distances, glides downhill when disturbed. Feeds in pairs or small groups of 10-15, mainly on seeds, shoots and insects. Nests in grass-lined depression near rocks or scrub.

RUFOUS-THROATED PARTRIDGE

Arborophila rufogularis Phasianidae

Little-known bird with distinct head and throat pattern; white half-collar and broad chestnut breast-band, rufous-orange ear-coverts, throat and foreneck; black spots on ear-coverts and neck sides. Sexes alike. Habits little known but said to breed on a cushion of grass under rocks in forests. Feed on insects, seeds, berries, shoots and invertebrates. *A. r. rufogularis* and *A. r. intermedia* are two subspecies found in the foothills of the Himalayas.

HIMALAYAN QUAIL

Ophrysia superciliosa Phasianidae

Presumed extinct, this mysterious quail was last recorded in 1890 and has not been seen since then. Old accounts record that it moved in small coveys and rarely left its habitat of long grass and brushwood on steep hillsides. Known only from the Kumaon and Garhwal regions of Uttarakhand.

MANIPUR BUSH QUAIL

Perdicula manipurensis Phasianidae

Small darkish grey quail with dark olive upperparts, finely marked with black; white eye-patch; golden-brown underparts with black cross-shaped markings; rich buff belly and vent, whitish loral patch, faint eyebrow. Male has chestnut forehead and throat. Not seen recently but said to be very secretive, keeping to dense cover. Habits and flight similar to other bush quails. Endemic. Confined to Assam, Manipur, Meghalaya and Nagaland. Globally threatened.

CHINESE FRANCOLIN

Francolinus pintadeanus Phasianidae

Easily confused with the female Black. Male has orangish-buff crown; white cheek-patch and white throat separated by black stripe. Strong moustachial stripe divides white throat from white ear-coverts. Overall body plumage mottled black-and-white. Little is known about this species in India but said to be a scarce breeding resident in SE Manipur. Few recent records. Sexes similar, although female paler in colour and lacks spurs.

WHITE-CHEEKED PARTRIDGE

Arborophila atrogularis Phasianidae

Medium-sized bird, identified by black mask and throat; throat both black and white; barred upperparts like Common; grey flanks instead of rufous streaks. Rare resident of E Himalayas, NE India and Bangladesh; inhabits bamboo thickets and forest undergrowth.

HILL PARTRIDGE

Arborophila torqueola Phasianidae

Size 28 cm

Voice Call a mournful whistle *po…eer…po…eer…*, the second syllable slightly longer

Range The Himalayas, east of Garhwal

Habitat Dense jungle undergrowth in hill country

Plump, medium-sized game bird with black barred brown upperparts and grey underparts with chestnut, white flank streaks. Male has bright chestnut head with white-streaked black eye-stripe, throat and neck, and white gorget. Female smaller, less colourful with brownish head and no white neck-collar. Secretive, prefers to run if disturbed. Expert flier through trees. Roosts in trees at night, huddled together. Nests on ground. More heard than seen.

♀

MOUNTAIN BAMBOO PARTRIDGE

Bambusicola fytchii Phasianidae

Size 35 cm

Voice Calls *che…chirree… che…chirree*

Range Resident: S Assam Hills

Habitat Rocky scrub and thickets on dry hillsides

Smallish bird with long tail. Characteristic black-and-white eye-stripe; buffish-white supercilium; distinctive patterning on the head; buff ear-coverts, throat and foreneck; rufous spotting on creamy-white breast, mantle and scapulars; strong blackish, heart-shaped spotting on flanks; displays rufous in primaries and sides of tail in flight. Sexes alike. Spends considerable time in undergrowth, feeding on seeds, berries, shoots, buds, grains, insects and worms. Secretive and difficult to flush.

3LOOD PHEASANT

'thaginis cruentus Phasianidae

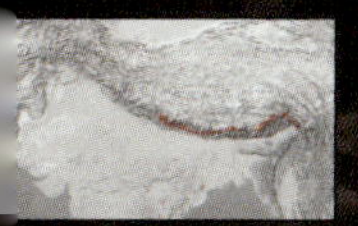

Size 38 cm

Voice Call a long-drawn squeal

Range High Himalayas, east of C Nepal

Habitat Steep hill forests

Dissimilar to other pheasant species, resembling partridge in size and shape. White crest; black stripe above and below the eye; red orbital skin. Upperparts white-streaked grey. Pale buff upper breast, rest of underparts, greyish-white streaked with red. Tail streaked with grey and buff. Female even brown with grey nape and crest. Colour varies according to race. Feeds on ground, scratching for food.

♀

cruentus

tibetanus

3LYTH'S TRAGOPAN

Tragopan blythii Phasianidae

Size Male 68 cm; Female 59 cm

Voice Call a loud *hwaa…ouwaa…ouwaa*. Also *gock…gock…gock*

Range Globally threatened; rare breeding resident; Bhutan, S Assam Hills

Habitat Montane forest undergrowth on steep slopes

Large, brilliantly coloured game bird. Bare yellow facial skin with black band extending from base of bill to crown. Unmarked red head, rusty-red neck and breast. Pale blue horns. Upperparts brownish red with many white ocelli. Grey-red lower breast belly faintly spotted. Pinkish-brown legs; white-spotted red flanks. Female uniform brown with black buff

♀

SATYR TRAGOPAN

Tragopan satyra Phasianidae

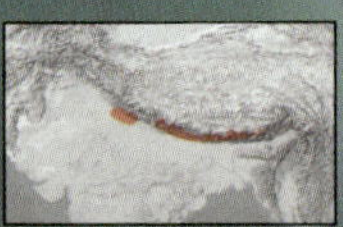

Size Male 68 cm; Female 59 cm

Voice Call a loud mournful *guwaa… guwaah…guwaah*. Also, a *wak…wak* alarm

Range Scarce, very local breeding resident from Uttarakhand to Arunachal Pradesh. Relatively common in Bhutan

Habitat Montane forest undergrowth particularly on slopes or in ravines

Found in oak forests with an understorey of bamboo and rhododendrons or mixed coniferous and deciduous forests. Also found in rocky areas or gorges with small flowing streams.

WESTERN TRAGOPAN

Tragopan melanocephalus Phasianidae

Size Male 71 cm; Female 60 cm

Voice Call notes rather goat-like *waa…waa …wan…*; unmistakable once heard

Range W Himalayas, from W Pakistan, through Kashmir to Garhwal; rather uncommon and little-known over its entire range

Habitat Dense forest undergrowth; ringal bamboo

Male has black crown, red hindneck and cheeks; green throat; reddish-orange breast; grey-brown upperparts and black and red underparts, both heavily spotted with white. Female greyish-brown with white spots. Very skulking, but appears in open areas early morning or late evening. Male displays horns and lappets on head when breeding. Mostly vegetarian. Feeds on fresh leaves, bamboo shoots, acorns, berries, seeds and insects.

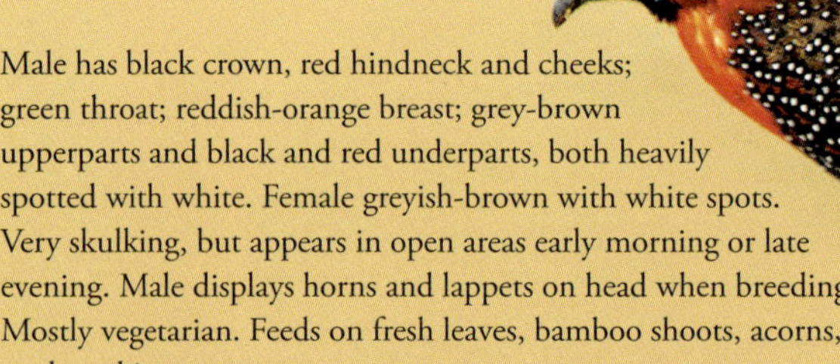

TEMMINCK'S TRAGOPAN

Tragopan temminckii Phasianidae

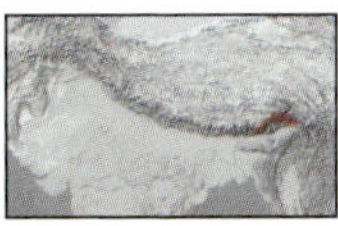

Size Male 64 cm

Voice Call a loud, moaning *whoah*, gets louder, longer

Range Rare resident: E and NE Arunachal Pradesh

Habitat Deep forested hills

Medium-sized, extremely bright-coloured pheasant similar to Satyr. Upperparts orange, densely covered with cream ocelli; brilliant blue face surrounded with black; black-and-white spotted brown wings and uppertail-coverts and darker tail. Red underparts have grey spots. Black bill and pink legs. Female brown with white spots; has brown-and-blue circular eye skin.

KOKLASS PHEASANT

Pucrasia macrolopha Phasianidae

Size Male 61 cm; Female 53 cm

Voice Call a loud *khok...kok... kok...kokha...*; vocal around dawn and dusk, but intermittently through the day

Range The Himalayas, hills of NE India; lower in winter. Several races

Habitat Steep forested hills; nullahs

Silvery grey and brown bird with distinct backswept crest and elongated tail. Black head; white cheek-patches; bright orange breast; male has deep green head and ear tufts; golden-brown crest. Underparts chestnut; silver-grey flanks; dark pointed tail. Female paler with shorter crest. Feeds in pairs on steep slopes on seeds, insects and berries. Very shy and timid; running or flying when disturbed. Interesting display of courting male. Nests on ground; spends nights roosting on trees, or under rock overhangs.

HIMALAYAN MONAL

Lophophorus impejanus Phasianidae

Size Male 72 cm; Female 63 cm

Voice Call a wild whistling, *coooor…lew*, much like Curlew's

Range The Himalayas

Habitat High forest; glades; snow patches. Not uncommon

Sturdy bird with long luminous green crest. Male has overall iridescent purple-blue upperparts with chestnut tail and wings. Underparts, face and foreneck brown-black; patch of metallic purple behind ear-coverts. Rear neck coppery-yellow changing to green on mantle; purple shorter tail-coverts and longest tail-coverts iridescent green. Female brown with black-and-white throat. Confiding; seen flying down hill at great speed.

♀

SCLATER'S MONAL

Lophophorus sclateri Phasianidae

Size Male 68 cm; Female 63 cm

Voice Call a shrill, harsh cry

Range Arunachal Pradesh

Habitat Fir forests with dense undergrowth

♀

Medium-sized bird similar to Himalayan but with blue and bronze colouring on head. Upperparts range from larger iridescent purplish-green to metallic green, blue, purple and black with white back patches; velvety-black underparts. Lacks the spatulate crest. Female dark brown with white throat and tail-tip.

RED JUNGLEFOWL

Gallus gallus Phasianidae

Size Male 65 cm; Female 42 cm

Voice Characteristic crow of male, shriller version of domestic. Other cackling sounds

Range The Himalayas, E Kashmir; E and C India, south to Narmada

Habitat Sal forests mixed with bamboo and cultivation

Both sexes resemble domestic bantam breeds. Male vibrant red-orange with combination of glossy blue-green, rich dark red, maroon-red, fiery orange, rufous and blackish brown feathers; deep red crown and neck; metallic green tail with long, drooping central feathers distinctive. Female has bright chestnut forehead, supercilium continuing to foreneck; reddish-brown plumage, vermiculated with fine black and buff. Seen in small parties, often several hens accompanying a cock; shy and skulking; emerges in clearings and on forest roads; flies up noisily when flushed.

KALIJ PHEASANT

Lophura leucomelanos Phasianidae

Size Male 65 cm; Female 60 cm

Voice Loud crowing by male. Chuckling calls on disturbance

Range The Himalayas, NE hill regions; foothills across country

Habitat Forest undergrowth; open clearings; terraced cultivation; vicinity of hillside habitation

Male glossy black above, with steel-blue gloss; glossy tail, ending in sickle-like feathers; whitish edges to rump feathers; bare, scarlet around eyes; long, hairy white crest; brownish-grey underbody; lanceolate breast feathers. Female reddish-brown, scalloped paler; brown crest and bare scarlet patch around eye; brown tail, smaller than male's. Several races over the Himalayas and NE India; male varying in colour from glossy black to black and grey or white; crest black in other races. Pairs or small gatherings; spends day on ground, gleaning on forest roads and clearings during early mornings and late afternoons; good flier; roosts in trees at night.

♀

hamiltonii

melanota

leucomelanos

lathami

CHEER PHEASANT

Catreus wallichii Phasianidae

Size Male 118 cm; Female 76 cm

Voice Noisy before dawn and at dusk. Call a loud, distinct sounding *ehir…pir…ehir…pir*. Other cackling calls

Range The Himalayas between NW Pakistan and C Nepal

Habitat Grass-covered steep rocky hillsides with scattered tree cover

Male grey-brown; buff bar-tailed pheasant with long crest and red facial skin; large and very long-tailed; long backswept crest and red face; plain pale-grey upper neck. Male more boldly marked than female with black barring above and on white breast. Female smaller and more brown with greyish-brown rump. Feeds on roots, tubers, bulbs, seeds, insects and worms in pairs or groups on ground. Very wary and runs swiftly for cover when disturbed; hurtles downhill if flushed. Nests on ground. Roosts in trees.

MRS HUME'S PHEASANT

Syrmaticus humiae Phasianidae

Size Male 90 cm; Female 60 cm

Voice Distinctive crowing. Also utters cackling notes

Range S Assam Hills

Habitat Steep rocky slopes

Large pheasant with graduated tail barred black-and-brown. Male has greyish head, red facial skin, yellowish bill; metallic blue neck, upper breast and upper mantle and mainly chestnut underparts. Female brown with whitish throat and white-tipped tail. Little known. Recently recorded only in Mizoram. Globally threatened and seldom seen.

GREY PEACOCK PHEASANT

Polyplectron bicalcaratum Phasianidae

Size Male 64 cm; Female 48 cm

Voice Call a loud, guttural *hoo*

Range Sikkim to Arunachal Pradesh

Habitat Dense undergrowth in tropical forests

Small greyish-brown pheasant with short tufted crest and long broad tail. Male has striking iridescent purple and green ocelli, rimmed in white on mantle, wing and uppertail-coverts and tail; bare pink or yellow facial skin, white throat, and grey iris, bill and legs. Female similar though smaller and less ornamented. Found singly, in pairs or family groups. However, rarely seen, though not uncommon.

GREYLAG GOOSE

Anser anser Anatidae

Size 74–84 cm

Voice Domestic goose-like single-note honk, often uttered several times, loud and ringing. Typical geese gaggles when feeding

Range Winter visitor; most common in N India, across the Gangetic Plains to Assam, Odisha; S to N Gujarat; Madhya Pradesh; rarer south

Habitat Jheels; winter cultivation

Large goose with bluish-grey plumage with pale fringes to feathers; large darker head; thick long neck; thick pink bill, pink legs and feet; white uppertail-coverts; pale belly dotted black. Sexes alike, though male larger than female. Black-speckled belly, absent in juvenile. Feeds on grass, on grassy islets and shore meadows. Occasionally feeds in the water on algae. Gregarious and wary. Nests on heaps of plant material, lined with feathers.

BAR-HEADED GOOSE

Anser indicus Anatidae

Size 75 cm

Voice Nasal, quiet honking

Range Breeds only in Ladakh within Indian limits; winter visitor

Habitat Rivers; large jheels

Silvery-grey and white bird with two horseshoe-shaped, brownish-black bars on back of white head. Body overall grey; dark hindneck and lower flanks; yellow legs, black-tipped yellow bill, white neck-stripe along back of neck, white tail-coverts and grey tail. Juvenile has black cap and lack head stripes. In flight, the silvery-grey forewings contrast with the dark flight feathers. Feeds on grasses, roots, stems and other plant matter. Very gregarious.

RUDDY SHELDUCK

Tadorna ferruginea Anatidae

Size 66 cm

Voice Call a loud, goose-like honking, on ground and in flight

Range Breeds in Ladakh; winter visitor, all over India; less common in the south

Habitat Around freshwater, salty and brackish lakes and rivers in open country, avoiding areas with dense, tall vegetation

Distinct rusty orange colouring with lighter head and white face. Stubby black bill; buff neck; rump, tail, primary and secondary feathers black. White wing-coverts conspicuous in flight; legs and feet black. Black collar on neck present in breeding bird. Female similar to male, but smaller, with more white on the face, no collar and buff wash on upperwing-coverts. Juvenile similar to female but duller and with more brown back. Pairs or small parties; nocturnal feeder; rather wary; rests on riverbanks, sandbars, edges of jheels during day; prefers clear, open water.

♀

breeding

FALCATED DUCK

Anas falcata Anatidae

Size 45–55 cm

Voice Male utters a crisp low-pitched whistling note; female a rough *quack*

Range Very scarce but, regular winter visitor

Habitat Freshwater lakes; ponds; rivers and marshes that are surrounded by forests

Striking duck with large head. Male has green head and high, chestnut crown; black-bordered white throat and neck and black-and-white speckled breast. Rest of the body grey with black rear and yellow vent patch. Elongated black and grey scapular wings, diagnostic. Female barred brown all over and has greyer head. Seen singly, or in small groups. Wary.

♀

EURASIAN WIGEON

Anas penelope Anatidae

♀

Size 50 cm

Voice Male has a haunting *wheeo* whistle; female a gruff bark

Range Common winter visitor throughout. Most numerous in N India

Habitat Jheels, marshes and large rivers where there is access to short grass or cereals for grazing

Medium-sized, plump, large-headed and short-necked duck. Breeding male has grey backs, white bellies and pink chests, rusty red head with buff forehead, tail predominantly black. White shoulder patch; stubby, greyish-blue bill with black tip. Male in eclipse resembles female. Female dull, mottled greyish-brown. Juvenile very similar to female. Both sexes show white belly, long, pointed wings and pointed tail in flight. Very gregarious, often mixing with other ducks.

♀

MALLARD

Anas platyrhynchos Anatidae

Size 60 cm

Voice Call a loud, wheezy *yheeep* of drake; female quacks loud, loudest when alarmed

Range Very small numbers breed in some of Kashmir's lakes. Winter visitor: N, C India. Rare in Deccan and further south

Habitat Marshes; lakes; swamps; rivers; streams; ponds

Large heavy-looking duck said to be the ancestor of most domestic ducks. Male has long, grey body and black stern. Head and neck are glossy deep green; white neck-ring and dark purplish-brown breast; whitish underparts; yellow bill. Diagnostic blue patch on top of wings bordered white; two curly feathers on tail. Female and eclipse male mottled brown; orange bill. Both sexes have orange feet and bluish-purple speculum, edged with white.

INDIAN SPOT-BILLED DUCK

Anas poecilorhyncha Anatidae

Size 65 cm

Voice Call a loud, duck-like *quack*

Range Resident; all over India, to about 1,800 m in Kashmir; local migrant in some areas

Habitat Wetlands; freshwater vegetation; covered jheels; reservoirs

Overall grey bird with paler head and neck; black bill with bright yellow tip. Whitish wings with black flight feathers below; whitish head; upperparts blackish-brown, feathers edged paler; black cap, dark, broad eye-stripe; green-blue speculum bordered above with white; coral-red legs and feet. Male has black bill tipped yellow; red spot on base of bill. Sexes alike. Juveline more brown and duller than adult. Pairs or small parties seen on marshy land, wet cultivation, or upending in shallow water.

GARGANEY

Anas querquedula Anatidae

Size 40 cm

Voice Male's mating call a distinctive crackling call

Range Abundant winter visitor

Habitat Narrow or well-sheltered, and shallow standing freshwaters, merging into grasslands, floodlands, or other wetlands

♀

Small, slight duck with large grey bill and flat crown. Dramatic broad, white supercilium crossing to the back of mottled brown head and curving downwards to neck; grey flanks; brown breast and spotted brown stern; white underparts; silvery-blue forewings seen in flight. Female similar to Common Teal, but paler, more patterned head, mottled brownish and distinct eye-stripe; pale supercilium; loral and chin spots and larger bill. Gregarious and social, seen often with other species.

♀

COMMON TEAL

Anas crecca Anatidae

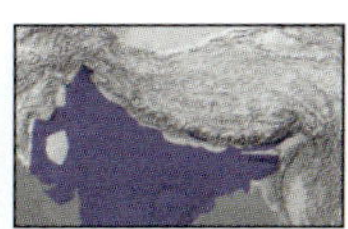

Size 34 cm

Voice Call a *krit...krit...*. Also, wheezy *quack*

Range Entire subcontinent in winter months

Habitat Jheels; marshes; village ponds. Often hunted

♀

♀

Small pale-grey duck with chestnut head. Underparts finely streaked dark grey; creamy patch on chest has fine black spots. Dark russet-red head with bottle green eye-stripe bordered white. Both sexes display dark green, black-and-white wing-bar in flight. Female mottled dark and light brown; pale belly; black and green wing speculum. Most common migratory duck. Swift flier.

PINK-HEADED DUCK

Rhodonessa caryophyllacea Anatidae

Unmistakable. Long-bodied and long-necked, with slightly tufted head in the male, and peculiar stiff-necked posture. Adult male has chocolate-coloured body; deep pink head and hindneck. Female and juvenile duller, appearing much like dark female Red-crested Pochard with pinkish tinge to the head. Presumed extinct.

RED-CRESTED POCHARD

Netta rufina Anatidae

Size 55 cm

Voice Silent

Range Rather scarce winter visitor throughout lowlands

Habitat Well-vegetated large rivers and lakes

Large duck with deep orange-crested head and red bill. Black neck and breast; pale flanks; brown back and black stern. Female lighter brown with pale cheeks and darker crown, dark bill. Juvenile darker with multicoloured belly. In flight, both sexes display broad white wing-bars. Nests near slow-moving rivers and clearings of open water with shrubs. Feeds actively early morning and late evening. Feeds on aquatic plants and animals by diving and upending.

♀

COMMON POCHARD

Aythya ferina Anatidae

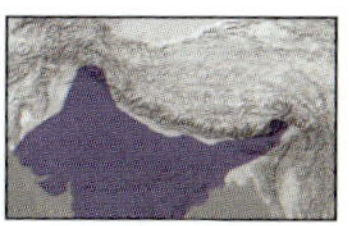

Size 45 cm

Voice Rather quiet. Female sometimes purrs in flight

Range Common winter visitor throughout lowlands. Less common in east

Habitat All types of open water including village ponds

Stocky, medium-sized with rich reddish-brown, wedge-shaped head, black breast, stern and tail. Grey body; large black bill with broad grey band; red eyes. Female more brown with pale cheeks and flanks. Both show black bordered grey wing-bars in flight. Feeds by diving or dabbling, on aquatic plants, aquatic insects and small fish. Gregarious; forming large flocks in winter, often mixed with other diving ducks.

BAER'S POCHARD

Aythya baeri Anatidae

Size 41-46 cm

Voice Mostly silent

Range Winter vagrant mostly to NE India and Bangladesh

Habitat Large rivers; lakes

Dark grey to black head, neck and back, with light brownish-red and white sides. Head can be seen to have dark green sheen on it in sunlight, and at all times, white eyes contrast strongly with surrounding feathers. White band on upperwing can be seen in flight, but not when wings are folded at rest. Female can be distinguished by difference in colour between head and brown breast, and more domed head. Juvenile similar to female, except for light brown head.

FERRUGINOUS DUCK

Aythya nyroca Anatidae

Size 40 cm

Voice Usually silent, although female sometimes makes *burring* sound in flight

Range Scarce and local winter visitor throughout lowlands. Commonest in NW India. Rarely in large numbers

Habitat Well-vegetated jheels, rivers, canals and ponds

Small, compact diving duck with peaked head. Both sexes are mahogany brown, darker on back and head. Large triangular patches of white under the tail. Male brighter, russet-brown; sharp white iris. Long white wing-bars and belly visible in flight. Not as gregarious as other diving ducks. Usually keeping in small groups. Cautious and wary.

TUFTED DUCK

Aythya fuligula Anatidae

Size 45 cm

Voice Rather quiet. Male has high bubbling note; female croaks

Range Fairly common winter visitor throughout lowlands. Less common in E and S India

Habitat All kinds of open water including reservoirs

Round-bodied, medium-sized diving duck with round head and very obvious head tuft. Male glossy black with broad white flanks, while female dark brown with paler flanks; white under the tail, occasionally visible in flight. Both sexes have yellow irises and black-tipped grey bills. Feeds during day by diving.

GREATER SCAUP

Aythya marila Anatidae

Size 40–50 cm

Voice Mostly silent

Range Rare winter visitor

Habitat Coastal bays; lagoons and estuaries. Winters on inland lakes

Larger and bulky duck with no crest. Iridescent greenish-black head; barred, grey back; light blue-grey bill; black breast and rump. Female overall brownish with white collar. Feeds mainly by diving; spends days swimming around waterbodies. In large flocks outside breeding season. Gregarious. Few details about this duck are known in the subcontinent.

GOOSANDER

Mergus merganser Anatidae

Size 58–72 cm

Voice Male has a deep *kruu…kra* call; female a shorter *praha* note

Range Rather scarce. Breeds in the Himalayas and NE mountains. Winters on N rivers

Habitat Rests on rocks. Flight path usually follows the river course

Large, slender duck with streamlined body, big head and long, narrow, reddish-orange, serrated bill. Breeding male has glossy green domed head; bushy, mane-like feathers on back of neck; white lower neck, breast, belly and flanks; bright red feet and legs; pinkish tint to underparts; white patch on inner wing. Female has brown head and shaggy crest; grey and cream underparts. Juvenile similar to female, but duller with whitish throat, paler head and creamy-yellow bill. Feeds solely on fish by repeated diving. Often swims with head submerged to locate prey.

LITTLE GREBE

Tachybaptus ruficollis Podicipedidae

non-breeding

breeding

Size 23–29 cm

Voice Shrill trilling notes. Occasional click

Range Subcontinent, upto 2,000 m in Kashmir. Resident in most areas

Habitat Reasonably large waterbodies in lowlands, with plenty of vegetation

Very small grebe, with short neck; short, straight beak; plump, rounded body. Black head, nape, breast and back; dark reddish-brown cheeks, throat and neck; dark brown flanks. Diagnostic small yellow patch at base of pale-tipped, black beak. Dark green legs; reddish-brown iris. Juvenile paler than adult, with dark cap, nape and back; yellowish-brown cheeks, neck sides and flanks, and reddish-brown lower neck and chest. Feeds on small fish, insects, crustaceans, shellfish and molluscs by diving or dabbling. Hard to spot as mostly concealed in vegetation. Floating nest built near shoreline, attached to aquatic plants or branches of waterside bushes; territorial, solitary nester. Performs a variety of elaborate courtship display.

GREAT CRESTED GREBE

Podiceps cristatus Podicipedidae

Size 46–51 cm

Voice Call includes loud, guttural croaks when breeding

Range Scarce breeder in N mountains and Gujarat. Winter visitor to N lowlands

Habitat Large, deep open bodies of freshwater, rivers, lagoons, lakes, swamps, reservoirs, saltfields, estuaries and bays

Medium to large-sized, graceful bird with long neck, long bill and distinctive black double crest. Black crown; white face; black line from base of bill to eye; dark brown wings with prominent white-patches; satiny-white underparts; dark olive-green feet prominent in flight. Breeding adult of both sexes has reddish-orange head plumes, tipped black. Sexes similar, but female slightly smaller than male. Juvenile can be distinguished by blackish stripes on cheeks. Both male and female take part in elaborate courtship display. Dives for fish, insects and invertebrate larvae, chasing prey underwater by propelling feet.

non-breeding

breeding

BLACK STORK

Ciconia nigra Ciconiidae

Size 95–100 cm

Voice Voiceless

Range Scarce winter visitor mainly to N India

Habitat Prefers undisturbed, open forests and woodlands, upto 2,000 to 2,500 m

Similar to White, but sturdier with wider wings. Long neck, bill, and legs; short tail; black upperparts with varying green and purple gloss; white breast and belly; scarlet red bill and legs, brighter in breeding and more brownish in non-breeding. Flies with neck and legs extended; white triangles on underwings visible in flight. Sexes alike, though male larger. Juvenile, less brightly-coloured. Secretive.

juvenile

GLOSSY IBIS

Plegadis falcinellus Threskiornithidae

Size 60 cm

Voice Usually silent

Range Fairly common, but local breeding resident subject to wandering. Most frequent in N and W India

Habitat All types of shallow freshwater, particularly with floating vegetation

Dark wading bird with long legs and decurved bill. Breeding adult chestnut with green and purple gloss; naked, grey, facial skin; pale blue lines bordering the front part of face; brown eyes and bill; grey legs with red knee joints. Flies with neck and legs outstretched. Nests on ground, in reeds or low shrubs. Feeds in shallow water or marshy wetlands on small fish, aquatic insects, molluscs, frogs, and food sifted from water surface.

juvenile

LITTLE BITTERN

Ixobrychus minutus Ardeidae

Size 25–35 cm

Voice Call a distinctive *kohr*

Range Very local breeding resident, mainly in Kashmir and Assam. Scattered records from elsewhere, mainly N India

Habitat Reed beds near rivers and jheels

♀

Small heron with dark back and cap; buff-white neck and wing patches. Male has small green crest; yellowish-green bill and iris. Upper breast and sides have tufts of elongated black feathers. Buffy-white undersides streaked brown; white underwings; greyish-green legs. Solitary and crepuscular.

juvenile

YELLOW BITTERN

Ixobrychus sinensis Ardeidae

Size 35–38 cm

Voice Occasionally, a sharp *kark*. Male's breeding call a quiet *uu…uu*

Range Rather local breeding resident mainly in NE India, Bangladesh, Sri Lanka and Indo-Gangetic Plains. Monsoon breeding visitor to NW India

Habitat Reed beds and wet scrubs near rivers, jheels and wet paddy

Small bittern with dull yellowish-brown upperparts and whitish underparts streaked darker from chin to belly. Short neck; longish bill. Crown, short crest and nape black marked with buff; orangish-brown on side of face, head and neck; deeper rufous on hindneck, greyer on forehead and supercilium; white undertail- and underwing-coverts; black tail. Female has brown streaking on crown, neck, and breast. Juvenile similar, but heavily streaked brown below, and mottled buff above. Solitary; hunts quietly in reed beds and undergrowth. Solitary but breeding densities can be quite high. Usually seen in feeding flights.

juvenile

CINNAMON BITTERN

Ixobrychus cinnamomeus Ardeidae

Size 36-38 cm

Voice Male's breeding call a loud *kok...kok*

Range Rather local breeding resident mainly to eastern coast, NE India, parts of the Indo-Gangetic Plains, Bangladesh and Sri Lanka

Habitat Reeds in marshes

juvenile

Solitary and crepuscular bittern, overall cinnamon in colour with darker crown. Sides of face, mantle, back and tail paler and tinged with pink; underparts rich buffy-brown with dark reddish-black central streaks down the middle from chin to belly. Chin and throat whitish. Flanks pale cinnamon; vent and undertail-coverts pale buffy-brown. Female has more brown crown and mantle, more streaked neck, while immature darker and more boldly streaked.

BLACK BITTERN

Dupetor flavicollis Ardeidae

Size 58 cm

Voice Characteristic booming call mainly heard during breeding season, at day or night

Range Scarce breeding resident

Habitat Reed beds with bushes and bushy margins of canals, rivers and jheels

Medium-sized heron with diagnostic yellow neck-stripe. Male has dull black upperparts; buff streaks on the throat; rufous-streaked, black and grey belly. Female paler than male, with more yellowish wash on underparts. Immature more streaked; upperpart feathers have buff fringes. Nests on bed of sticks on branch overhanging water. Feeds on frogs, reptiles, fish and invertebrates. Crepuscular, solitary and extremely secretive. May fly quite high to feeding sites.

MALAYAN NIGHT HERON

Gorsachius melanolophus Ardeidae

Size 47 cm

Voice Usually silent

Range NE India; S Western Ghats; Nicobar Islands. Winter visitor to Sri Lanka

Habitat Subtropical and tropical swamps, streams, marshes; especially regions with high rainfall

Reddish-brown heron with streaked underparts, black underwings, black crown and variable bluish lores; reddish-brown sides to head and neck; stout dark bill. Sexes similar, but male may have dark crest. Juvenile greyish-brown with black-and-white spots and streaked underparts. Immature greyish-brown above with black-and-white spots; underparts buff with brown spots and bars. Rarely seen. Nests in forest trees and bamboos.

BLACK-CROWNED NIGHT HERON

Nycticorax nycticorax Ardeidae

Size 58-72 cm

Voice Call a harsh raucous *quak quak*, mostly in flight

Range Locally common breeding resident throughout lowlands

Habitat All wetland types including paddy and mangroves

Stocky heron with short neck and legs. Black cap, upper back and scapulars; grey wings, rump and tail; stout, black bill; blood-red iris; pink legs in breeding; creamy-white underparts. Sexes alike. Juvenile buff-spotted and streaked brown. Social; nests colonially on trunks or forks of branches.

juvenile

juvenile

INDIAN POND HERON

Ardeola greyii Ardeidae

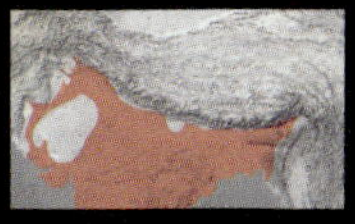

Size 45 cm

Voice Call a harsh *croak*, usually when flushed

Range Common resident throughout subcontinent

Habitat Marshes; jheels; riversides; roadside ditches; tidal creeks

breeding

Small heron, commonest of family in India; thick-set and earthy-brown in colour, with dull green legs; bill bluish at base, yellowish at centre with black tip; neck and legs shorter than in true egrets. Difficult to sight when settled; suddenly springs to notice with flash of white wings, tail and rump. In breeding, buffy-brown head and neck; white chin and upper throat, longish crest; rich maroon back; buff-brown breast. In non-breeding, streaked dark brown head and neck; grey-brown back and shoulders; more white in plumage. Sexes alike. Found around water, even dirty roadside puddles; ubiquitous in the plains; found in hills upto 1,200 m; remains motionless in mud or upto ankles in water, or slowly stalks prey. Hunts alone; roosts in groups with other pond herons.

non-breeding

CHINESE POND HERON

Ardeola bacchus Ardeidae

Size 42-45 cm

Voice Rather silent. Call a hard *croak* in flight, at dusk or when flushes

Range NE India; Andaman Islands

Habitat Wetlands; shallow water; fresh or saltwater; also ponds

Breeding adult has slaty-black mantle and scapulars. Dark brown head, neck and breast; slaty-patch in lower breast; white wings and belly. Legs and feet pinkish in breeding; yellow bill with black tip, pale blue on base of upper mandible; yellow lores and eyes.

non-breeding

GREY HERON

Ardea cinerea Ardeidae

Size 100 cm

Voice Call a loud *quaak* in flight

Range Mostly resident; subcontinent; breeds upto 1,750 m in Kashmir

Habitat Marshes; tidal creeks; fresh waterbodies

Long-legged, long-necked bird of open marshes. Ash-grey above; white crown, neck and underparts; black stripe after eye continues as long, black crest; black-dotted band down centre of foreneck; dark blue-black flight feathers; golden-yellow iris at close range. Sexes alike. Mostly solitary except when breeding; occasionally enters shallow water; usually stands motionless, head pulled in between shoulders, waiting for prey to come close; characteristic flight, with head pulled back and long legs trailing.

WHITE-BELLIED HERON

Ardea insignis Ardeidae

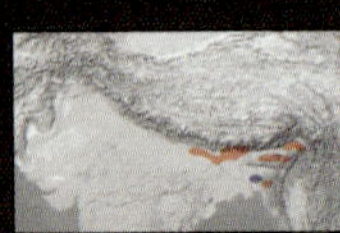

Size 127 cm

Voice Call a loud croaking *bray*

Range Small pockets in Bhutan, Assam and Arunachal Pradesh. Exceedingly rare and little known. Seldom seen

Habitat Undisturbed forested streams; rivers; marshes

Large, darkish grey, long-necked heron with white throat, belly and vent. Scapulars, foreneck and upper breast streaked white; large black bill, black legs. Breeding adult has greyish-whitish nape plumes and elongated grey breast feathers with whitish centres. Juvenile more brown, with smaller plumes. Similar to Grey, but larger. In flight, white belly and underwing linings diagnostic. Shy and rarely seen. Forages alone or in small groups. Feeds mainly during day on fish, frogs and reptiles.

STRIATED HERON

Butorides striata Ardeidae

Size 45 cm

Voice Call a Redshank-like *tewn…tewn*

Range Uncommon resident, south of the Himalayas

Habitat Secluded pools. Found in mangroves, intertidal flats

Small, squat heron with longish drooping crest. Upperparts slaty-grey, washed green; underparts grey with pinkish tint; green wing feathers outlined with yellow; yellow eye has deep grey surround; deep green forehead; short legs, grey head and black crown. Orange feet in breeding. Juvenile darker, more heavily streaked and mottled. Characteristic hunched posture with head tucked into body.

PURPLE HERON

Ardea purpurea Ardeidae

Size 78–90 cm

Voice Usually silent. Occasionally, a harsh *croak*

Range Mostly resident

Habitat Marshes and lakes with extensive reed beds. Prefers more open wetlands with fringing vegetation outside breeding season

Slender-necked, lanky bird with slaty-purple upperparts, black crown with long, drooping black crest; rufous rear neck with prominent black stripe along length; white chin and throat; deep slaty-grey and chestnut below breast; almost black on wings and tail; pale yellow eyes; yellow bill; orange-yellow legs and feet. Crest and breast plumes less developed in female. Juvenile more brown and lacks crest; duller in colour and narrow steaks in neck and underparts. Solitary; crepuscular; extremely shy but master of patience; freezes and hides.

juvenile

CATTLE EGRET

Bubulcus ibis Ardeidae

Size 50 cm

Voice Mostly silent except for some croaking sounds when breeding

Range Resident; subcontinent, upto 1,800 m in outer Himalayas. Rare in NW and NE India

Habitat Marshes; lakes; forest clearings; also, fields

Small snowy-white heron with characteristic hunch and relatively short legs and thick neck. Breeding adult white with orange-buff feathers on crown, neck and back; bright red bill, lores and legs; yellow eyes. Non-breeding adult very similar to Little, but told by yellow beak and from other egrets by size. White plumage, sometimes with pale reddish-buff wash. Sexes alike. Juvenile resembles non-breeding adult, has blackish bill, legs and feet. Eyes pale yellowish. Immature has black leg and bill. Very social. In large flocks; follows livestock, also farm equipments like tractors to catch insects that are disturbed. Nest of sticks in bushes or trees.

breeding

non-breeding

breeding

GREAT EGRET

Casmerodius albus Ardeidae

Size 94-104 cm

Voice Occasional *croak*

Range Resident, local migrant; not common but widespread across country

Habitat Marshes; jheels; rivers; tidal estuaries

Large, almost entirely white heron with contrasting black feet and long, black legs. Black tip to bright yellow bill; greenish-yellow patch between bill and eye; long S-shaped neck prominent in flight. Breeding adult displays beautiful plumes extending from back to beyond tail. In courtship display, bird spreads plumes into a fan shape. Juvenile similar but without plumes. Feeds actively at dawn and dusk, waiting motionlessly to catch prey.

INTERMEDIATE EGRET

Mesophoyx intermedia Ardeidae

Size 80 cm

Voice Usually silent

Range Locally common breeding resident throughout lowlands and the coast

Habitat Wetlands; the coast

As its name implies, intermediate in size between Great Egret and smaller white egrets. Overall striking white bird with dark legs and thickish, yellow bill. Breeding adult may have reddish or black bill, greenish-yellow gape skin, loose filamentous breast trails and back plumes, and dull yellow or pink upperparts. Sexes similar. Stalks prey in shallow water, including flooded fields. Feeds on fish, frogs, crustaceans, and insects. Nests in colonies with other herons, normally on platforms of sticks, trees, or shrubs.

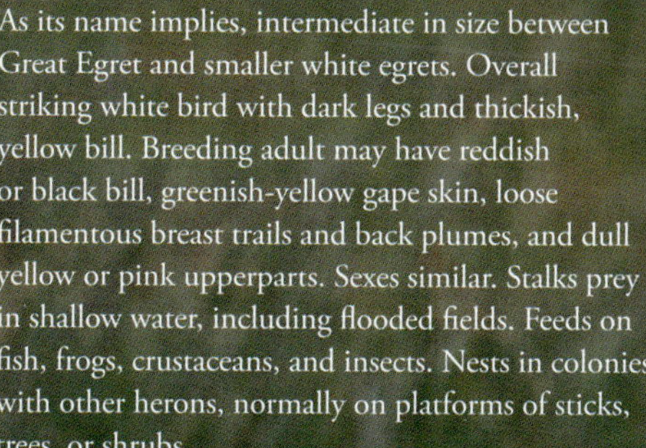

breeding

LITTLE EGRET

Egretta garzetta Ardeidae

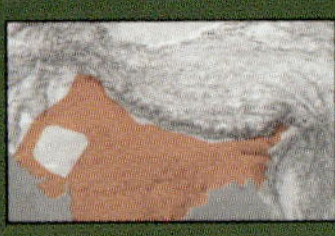

Size 65 cm

Voice Occasional *croak*

Range Fairly common breeding resident; subcontinent, upto 1,600 m in the outer Himalayas

Habitat Margins of coastal and inland water habitats, preferring open areas with shallow freshwater

Striking and elegant heron distinguished by pure white feathers, long sinuous neck, long, black legs and dark, pointed bill. Breeding adult has two long, nape plumes and light feathery plumage around breast and back. Juvenile similar in appearance to non-breeding adult, but has less striking colouration on feet and around eyes.

breeding

LITTLE CORMORANT

Phalacrocorax niger Phalacrocoracidae

Size 50 cm

Voice Vocal, low roaring sounds near nest and roost

Range Subcontinent, south of the Himalayas

Habitat Village tanks; jheels; lakes; rivers and coastal areas

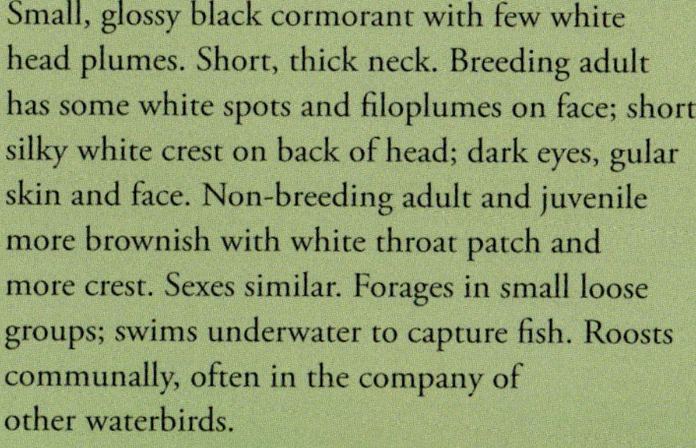

Small, glossy black cormorant with few white head plumes. Short, thick neck. Breeding adult has some white spots and filoplumes on face; short silky white crest on back of head; dark eyes, gular skin and face. Non-breeding adult and juvenile more brownish with white throat patch and more crest. Sexes similar. Forages in small loose groups; swims underwater to capture fish. Roosts communally, often in the company of other waterbirds.

juvenile

INDIAN CORMORANT

Phalacrocorax fuscicollis Phalacrocoracidae

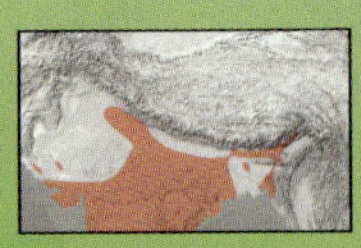

Size 63 cm

Voice Harsh croaks at nest

Range Throughout the region. Locally common breeding resident

Habitat Large freshwater wetlands; marshes; estuaries; brackish tidal creeks and mangrove swamps

Small to medium-sized slender cormorant mainly black in breeding season, with white neck plumes and whitish throat. Silvery wing-coverts; longish tail; white ear tufts, white-flecked feathers on neck, blackish gular pouch and no crest. Non-breeding adult more brown, with no ear tufts or white plumes and more yellow gular pouch. Sexes alikes. Juvenile more brown and lacks neck plumes. Gregarious, often found in larger bodies of water and rivers. Feeds in shallow water.

GREAT CORMORANT

Phalacrocorax carbo Phalacrocoracidae

Size 80 cm

Voice Usually silent

Range Resident in most areas; subcontinent

Habitat Jheels; lakes; mountain torrents; occasionally coastal lagoons

Sexes alike. Breeding adult has black plumage with metallic blue-green sheen; white facial skin and throat; bright yellow gular pouch and white thigh patches; silky white plumes on head and neck. Non-breeding adult has no white thigh patches; gular pouch less bright. First year juvenile dull brown above, white below. Aquatic. Not gregarious outside breeding season; usually one or two birds feeding close by; dives underwater.

breeding

breeding

DARTER

Anhinga melanogaster Anhingidae

Size 90 cm

Voice Calls include loud croaks and squeaks

Range Subcontinent, south of the Himalayan foothills

Habitat Freshwater lakes; jheels

Long, snake-like neck, pointed bill and stiff, fan-shaped tail. Black upperparts, streaked and mottled with silvery-grey on back and wings; chocolate-brown head and neck; white stripe down sides of upper neck; white chin and upper throat; entirely black below. Juvenile brown with rufous and silvery streaks on mantle. Bird of deep freshwater; small numbers scattered along with Little. Highly specialised feeder, entire structure of bird modified for following and capturing fish underwater. Swims low in water with only head and neck uncovered; chases prey below water with wings half open, spearing fish with sudden rapier-like thrusts made possible by bend in neck at 8th and 9th vertebrae, which acts as spring as it straightens. Tosses fish into air and swallows it head-first. Basks on tree stumps and rocks, cormorant style.

immature

PIED FALCONET

Microhierax melanoleucos Falconidae

Size 20 cm

Voice Low, chattering call. Utters a shrill scream

Range Resident; E Himalayas and NE India

Habitat Forest clearings; tea plantations; wooded foothills

Smallest falcon in the world, only slightly larger than sparrow. Upperparts glossy black and underparts white, with black mottling on breast. Some have thin white line across base of cere, above eyes and down to breast giving the appearance of white face with large black eye patches. White spots on inner wing and narrow white bars on innertail.

COLLARED FALCONET

Microhierax caerulescens Falconidae

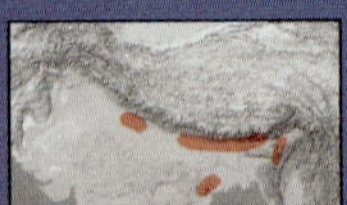

Size 18 cm

Voice Call a shrill whistle *killi...kill*

Range Scarce breeding resident: Himalayan foothills, Nepal

Habitat Clearings in, and edges of, broadleaved tropical forests and plantations

Very small pied falcon, with bold white supercilium and collar. Slaty-grey cheeks and crown; double-toothed bill, shortish wings, barred tail; underwings white with black bars; strong half-feathered legs, and powerful feet. Sexes similar. Juvenile has brownish-orange forehead and supercilium. Perches on top or edges of trees or bushes, frequently bobbing head and slowly moving tail up and down. The more northeasterly Pied Falconet, *M. melanoleucos,* is larger, black-and-white with no collar.

COMMON KESTREL

Falco tinnunculus Falconidae

Size 32–39 cm

Voice Infrequent clicking sound. Also *kee-kee-kee*

Range Resident; local migrant; several races

Habitat Open country; cliffsides

Overall light chestnut brown falcon, with dark spotting on upperparts and buff underparts with narrow blackish streaking. Ash-grey crown, neck sides and nape; prominent black malar stripe; white tip to grey tail with black subterminal band. Bright yellow cere, feet and eye-ring; dark bill. Female has more black spots and streaking on pale rufous upperparts and pale buff underparts. Juvenile similar to female, but broader streaks on underparts and yellow parts paler. Solitary or in pairs; often hovers when hunting.

AMUR FALCON

Falco amurensis Falconidae

Size 26–30 cm

Voice Call a high-pitched *kew… kew…kew* at roost

Range Scarce passage migrant (mainly in autumn) between NE Asia and SC Africa

Habitat Open country; often near water

Small, slender falcon with long, pointed wings. Male overall dark grey, with rusty-cinnamon lower abdomen and thighs; white underwing, prominent in flight; bright orange-red legs and facial skin; orange base to beak; white claws. Female similar in size to male, with cream or rusty underparts, streaked and barred; grey upperparts; slaty-grey head with cream forehead; barred tail with dark tip; white cheeks and throat; dark eye patch and moustache. Juvenile similar to female, but paler, with rusty-brown or buff-edged feathers. Very sociable.

EURASIAN HOBBY

Falco subbuteo Falconidae

Size 33 cm

Voice Call a hurried *ki ki ki ki*

Range Breeds in the Himalayas; scarce passage migrant mainly in the NW India. Scattered records throughout lowlands

Habitat Open, wooded country often over or near water

juvenile

Small, slender falcon with long square-tipped tail. Upperparts and crown slaty-grey; creamy buff underparts heavily streaked black; chestnut thighs and vent; underwings and undertail barred; pale throat and cheeks; dark moustache; thin white line above eye. Sexes alike. Juvenile more brownish and mottled; creamish thighs and vent, and bluish-grey to greenish legs and facial skin. Aerial feeder, pursuing bats and small birds. The rarer Oriental Hobby, *F. severus*, is even darker with chestnut underparts.

ORIENTAL HOBBY

Falco severus Falconidae

Size 27–30 cm

Voice Call includes a shrill trill of 3- to 4-notes

Range Resident to the Himalayas, NE India

Habitat Forested, hilly country

Small, robust falcon with slaty-grey upperparts; deep black head and cheeks; rich chestnut underparts, paler on throat. Long, pointed wings; short, powerful bill with 'tooth' on sides; black teardrop-shaped patch on sides of head. Juvenile has rufous breast, streaked black and some mottling on back. Fast flying birds attaining high speed as they dive from high altitudes to knock out birds; eats on wing or on perch. Nests in holes in trees or in nest of another species; in trees, building ledges or cliffs.

PEREGRINE FALCON

Falco peregrinus Falconidae

Size 42 cm

Voice Variety of calls including loud, harsh, persistent chatter, used against intruders

Range Resident; all over India, to about 3,000 m in the Himalayas; not found in semi-arid regions

Habitat Mostly rugged, mountainous areas; cliffs

calidus

One of the fastest fliers, the Peregrine is fairly large; stocky falcon with pointed wings and relatively short, square tail. Upperparts bluish-grey; underparts reddish-brown with variable dark spotting and barring; barred underwing and tail; pale throat and cheeks; broad, dark moustachial stripe. Yellowish-orange facial skin and legs; bluish beak, tinged yellow at base and black at tip. Sexes similar, but female substantially larger. Juvenile more brown with heavily streaked underparts, and blue-grey or greenish legs and facial skin.

peregrianator

OSPREY

Pandion haliaetus Accipitridae

Size 55-58 cm

Voice Short, nasal scream. Calls rarely

Range In parts of the Himalayas, between about 2,000-3,500 m. Winter visitor all over India

Habitat Lakes; rivers; coastal lagoons

Large bird whose long wings have characteristic bend at carpal joints. Underparts sharp white, with dark brown patches at carpal joints and mottled dark brown necklace. Dark eye-stripe; dark brown back; pale blue-grey feet; black beak. Female heavier and darker with more defined necklace. Solitary, or in scattered pairs; circles over water; hovers characteristically; dives with feet dangling; often splashes into water; carries fish on to perch.

JERDON'S BAZA

Aviceda jerdoni Accipitridae

Size 48 cm

Voice Calls include a *kip... kip... kip* and *keeya...keeya* during breeding. Also *pee...ow*

Range Rare breeding resident to hills of NE India, Bangladesh. Also, Sri Lanka and S peninsular hills

Habitat Evergreen forests and plantations; crepuscular

Medium-sized raptor characterised by short, stout legs and feet and well-developed talons; unfeathered lower tarsus and thin white-tipped black crest usually held erect; brown upperparts; rufous barred underparts; three black tail-bands tipped white. Long, paddle-shaped wings reach almost till tail-tip. Sexes alike. Perches well concealed in tall trees. Feeds on snakes, lizards, frogs, and insects. Insects captured by sallying from perch.

BLACK BAZA

Aviceda leuphotes Accipitridae

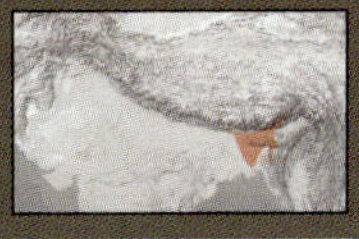

Size 32 cm

Voice Vocal in flight and when perched. Utters soft, quavering, plaintive or whistling notes

Range Uncommon resident; Kerala and some parts in adjoining Karnataka; NE India, east of E Nepal

Habitat Evergreen forests; clearings; streams; foothills

Small raptor with black head, neck, upperparts and tail. Black head with long, black crest; black throat; dark blue-grey cere; snowy white breast-band bordered black and chestnut; rufous belly barred with buff. Secondary flight feathers show chestnut and white patches; chestnut markings on lower back, scapulars and greater wing-coverts. Black vent, undertail-coverts and thighs. Groups of several birds often perch on same tree. Feeds on large insects, lizards, tree frogs, and occasionally small mammals, bats and birds.

ORIENTAL HONEY-BUZZARD

Pernis ptilorhynchus Accipitridae

Size 65 cm

Voice Call a high-pitched, long-drawn *weeeeeu*…

Range Resident and local migrant; subcontinent to about 2,000 m in the Himalayas

Habitat Forests; open country; cultivation; vicinity of villages

Highly variable buzzard. Upperparts greyish-brown; grey head, underparts range from cream to blackish-brown and marked and streaked; slender head; longish neck distinctive; tail rarely fanned; crest rarely visible; pale underside of wings barred; broad dark subterminal tail-band; two or three more bands on tail; tarsus unfeathered. Scale-like feathers around eyes and forehead protect from stings of wasps, bees and hornets the bird preys upon. Specialises in feeding on larvae and honey of bees and wasps.

BLACK-WINGED KITE

Elanus caeruleus Accipitridae

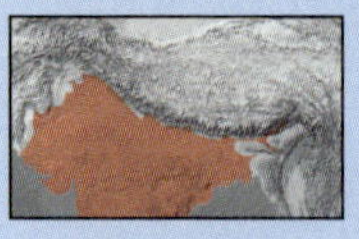

Size 32 cm

Voice Generally silent. Call a weak *weeet...weeet... weeet* when agitated

Range All over India, to about 1,500 m in the outer Himalayas

Habitat Open scrub and grass country; light forests

Striking bird of prey with pure white head and breast and ruby-red eyes surrounded by black-patches. Grey crown, back of neck and upperparts; black-patch on upper edges of wings. Juvenile similar but with more brown upperparts and dusky streaks on crown; yellowish-brown breast and head. Solitary, or in pairs; sits on exposed perch or flies over open scrub and grass country; mostly hunts on wing.

BLACK KITE

Milvus migrans Accipitridae

Size 47-60 cm

Voice Call a loud, musical whistle

Range Resident; subcontinent upto about 2,200 m in the Himalayas, co-existing with Black-eared in some localities

Habitat Mostly neighbourhood of humans

Medium-sized raptor; overall very dark brown plumage with light brown and rufous markings, particularly on head, neck and underparts. Light brown bar on shoulder; tail forked and barred darker brown; edges of wings appear 'fingered', dark brown eye; black bill with yellow cere. Sexes similar. Juvenile lighter brown with less pronounced fork in tail.

WHITE-TAILED EAGLE

Haliaeetus albicilla Accipitridae

Size 90 cm

Voice Call a loud *klee*...*klee*...*klee*

Range Rare winter visitor: India, Pakistan. Records throughout

Habitat Large rivers and lakes; only rarely on coast in this region

Impressive-sized bird with broad club-ended wings. Relatively short, wedge-shaped tail; large head and beak. Feathers mottled shades of brown with paler head and neck and pale areas on both upperwing and underwing. Reddish-brown tail feathers, and pale stripes running down to tail-tip. Immature has brown tail and very dark head. Head and neck protrude in flight, edges of wings appear 'fingered'. Hunts for fish, mammals and birds.

LESSER FISH EAGLE

Ichthyophaga humilis Accipitridae

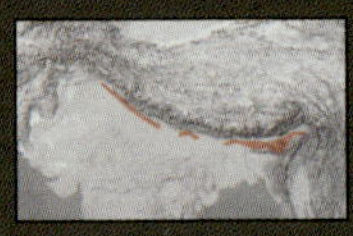

Size 64 cm

Voice Loud excitable shrieks include wavering *kleeeuee*

Range The Himalayas; SW India

Habitat Forested streams; lakes

Medium-sized bird; overall grey-brown plumage. Blunt, broad wings; featherless legs. Similar to Grey-headed but smaller and has brown breast, white thighs and belly and grey tail with slightly darker subterminal tail-band. Short, rounded tail; long neck and small head; large, curved talons specialised for catching fish. Juvenile similar to adult, but has brown eyes as opposed to yellow in adult, has more brown head and neck, more brown upperparts, and pale mottling on underwing-coverts. Feeds on fish, snatched from water.

GREY-HEADED FISH EAGLE

Ichthyophaga ichthyaetus Accipitridae

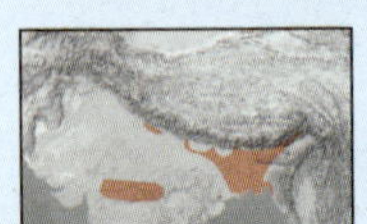

Size 61-75 cm

Voice Calls include *awh-awhr* and *chee-warr* repeated

Range Resident; from E Delhi to Assam; south through the peninsula

Habitat Lakes, rivers in forested country

Striking bird with relatively small head, longish neck and powerful, grey beak. Upperparts brownish-grey and white underparts. Rounded tail; sandy-yellow eyes; long, black talons; relatively short legs; and tail with broad, black terminal band. Female larger and heavier than male. Juvenile has white belly mottled with brown.

juvenile

BEARDED VULTURE

Gypaetus barbatus Accipitridae

Size 125 cm

Voice Usually silent. Sometimes, a deep croak

Range The Himalayas, W to E, 1,000–5,000 m. Soars higher

Habitat High mountain slopes

Large, majestic vulture, with enormous wings that enable it to soar easily above the mountains. Long, diamond-shaped tail distinctive in flight. Creamy-yellow head; black eye patches that extend below bill; short, narrow bill; black bristles under chin creating a 'beard'. Neck and underparts rusty-orange; back, wings and tail dark grey-blue to black. Juvenile patchy brown. Known for its unusual habit of dropping bones on to rocks to smash them open and get at the marrow.

SLENDER-BILLED VULTURE

Gyps tenuirostris Accipitridae

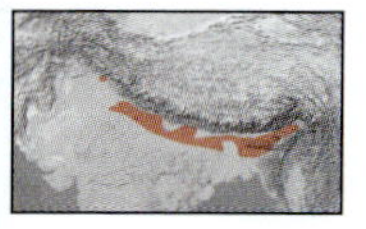

Size 93-100 cm

Voice Cackling screeches

Range Resident; lower Himalayas, from NW India through Nepal; NE India and Ganges delta

Habitat Similar to White-rumped. Cities; towns; villages. Globally threatened

Overall greyish-brown vulture, with sharply accentuated dome. Rather scruffy, ill-kempt appearance. Generally slimmer and more elongated body than Indian. Slender snake-like neck; thin elongated dark bill; dark cere with pale culmen; bare head and neck with wrinkled skin; dark eye-ring; Underparts streaked pale. White thigh-patches visible in flight. Dark underside to flight feathers. Juvenile similar to adult, but with whitish downy feathers on nape and upper neck.

HIMALAYAN VULTURE

Gyps himalayensis Accipitridae

Size 125 cm

Voice Cackling screeches at carcass site

Range The Himalayas, between about 600-3,000 m; forages much higher. Recorded over 5,000 m

Habitat Barren, high altitude country; around mountain settlements

Bulky vulture with huge wing span. Soft white downy feathers on head and upper neck; sandy-brown upperparts and ruff on lower neck; short, square black tail; buffy-white coverts; dark brown flight feathers. Tawny underparts streaked white; large heavy yellow bill, yellow eyes; fleshy pink legs. Sexes similar. Juvenile dark brown with whitish streaks; brown neck; black beak. Wary and shy; takes flight if disturbed while feeding. Soars solitary, or in small flocks over mountain slopes and cliffs.

GRIFFON VULTURE

Gyps fulvus Accipitridae

Size 100 cm

Voice Quiet. Grunts and hisses when feeding

Range Common breeding resident to W Pakistan hills, N India and Nepal to E Sikkim. Winters widely in lowlands of Pakistan and NW India, south to Gujarat and Madhya Pradesh

Habitat Mountains and semi-desert, wandering into nearby dry plains in winter

Large, carnivorous scavenger, with impressive creamy-white ruff. Plain pale reddish-brown upperparts; white head and neck; yellow bill; dark flight feathers on rest of wings and tail; pale underwing-coverts with bands of white. Juvenile has very pale upperwing feathers and grey bill. Breeds colonially containing 15 to 20 pairs. Builds nest on cliff-face, preferably in protected ledge or cave. Usually in pairs or small groups, often with other vultures.

RED-HEADED VULTURE

Sarcogyps calvus Accipitridae

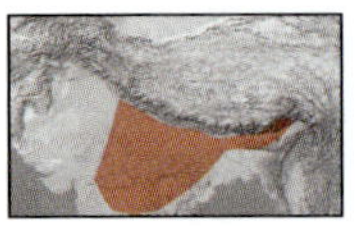

Size 85 cm

Voice Call a hoarse *croak*

Range Scarce resident; all over India, upto about 2,800 m in the Himalayas

Habitat Open country; village outskirts

Medium-sized, bulky vulture with wing span of over two metres. Unmistakable with its black feathers and bald red head. Two lappets attached to neck; thin, white margin on underside of wings at base of remiges; white patches on thigh. Sexes similar, male has white or yellow eyes while female has dark. Juvenile overall paler with more mottled plumage and dark eyes. Usually found alone, or in breeding pair.

CINEREOUS VULTURE

Aegypius monachus Accipitridae

Size 115 cm

Voice Usually silent

Range Mainly scarce winter visitor; N mountains, river valleys

Habitat Open country, ranging widely and solitary while singly looking for carcass, often near rivers. Dominant over other species at carcass

Large bird with long and broad parallel wings that have prominently indented trailing edge and splayed wing-tips. Short, wedge-shaped tail; bare, buff head; dark eyes; dark facial mark; whitish legs; chocolate brown plumage and ruff; bluish neck; blackish throat and large, dark eye-patches. Powerful horn-coloured bill; pale blue cere. Juvenile has blackish face, black bill and pink cere; and often fluffy tuft on back of head. Nests on small trees growing out of cliffs.

SHORT-TOED SNAKE EAGLE

Circaetus gallicus Acciptridae

Size 65 cm

Voice Call a loud *kee yo*

Range Scarce breeding resident in lowlands, more common and widespread winter visitor except in NE India, Bangladesh and Sri Lanka

Habitat Open country with preference for scrubby grasslands

Large, long-winged eagle with large head, relatively small beak and long, bare legs. Upperparts, head, throat and chest brown; white underparts, marked with dark bars and blotches. Dark flight feathers of tail marked with three to four dark bands; bright yellow eye and grey legs. Sexes similar, female heavier with slightly longer tail. Feeds on snakes, usually eaten whole.

EURASIAN MARSH HARRIER

Circus aeruginosus Accipitridae

Size 55 cm

Voice Usually silent

Range Winter visitor; common; subcontinent, south of the Himalayan foothills; most common in N India

Habitat Marshes; jheels; wet cultivation

Large broad-winged harrier, with sexes dissimilar. Male overall dark reddish-brown with buff-yellow streaks, more dense on breast; dull rufous head and breast; silvery-grey wings, tail; black wing-tips visible in flight; legs, feet, iris and cere yellow; black bill. Female and juvenile uniform chocolate brown; throat, crown and shoulders have yellowish wash; lack grey tail and wing-patch.

juvenile

juvenile

♀

juvenile

CRESTED SERPENT EAGLE

Spilornis cheela Accipitridae

Size 65-75 cm

Voice Call a loud whistling scream *keee...kee...ke...*

Range Subcontinent, to about 3,000 m in the Himalayas

Habitat Forested country

Medium-sized eagle with brown upperparts and light brown underparts. Wing-coverts and scapulars heavily streaked and mottled; black flight feathers with broad bands; black crown and nape; brown crest barred white; rusty orange thighs and belly barred and mottled white; short, broad wings; bright yellow eyes. Fans crest when alarmed. Solitary, or in pairs; flies high over forests and swoops down on prey.

juvenile

EASTERN MARSH HARRIER

Circus a spilonotus Accipitridae

Variable harrier with blackish upperparts, streaked paler. Rest of wing grey with black wing-tips and white front edge; grey tail; rump and underparts white; tail has dark bars. Similar to Pied, but larger. Sexes similar, but female larger. Juvenile dark brown; buff head and pale underwing patch. Hunts, glides low over open ground, searching for prey with wings held in shallow V-shape and often with legs dangling.

HEN HARRIER

Circus cyaneus Accipitridae

Size 40 cm

Voice Usually silent

Range Winter visitor to mainly Pakistan, the Himalayas and N India

Habitat Open country, grasslands and cultivation in plains and foothills

Slender, medium-sized raptor with flat owl-like face and broad wings. Long, rounded tail; sharp, hooked bill. Upperparts grey; underparts whitish; black wing-tips, dark trailing edge to wing; black-banded tail; white patch on rump, conspicuous in flight. Female brown, with black bands on tail; whitish underparts streaked brown. Juvenile also brown, but more buffy and less streaked. Roosts gregariously on ground. All Northern Harriers have white rump-patch obvious in flight, with wings held in V-shape.

PALLID HARRIER

Circus macrourus Accipitridae

Size 40-48 cm

Voice Usually silent

Range Widespread winter visitor. Unrecorded in parts of NE India and W Pakistan

Habitat Open country in plains and foothills; semi-desert; grassy slopes; cultivation; scrub-covered plains and marshes

Slender bird with narrow wings and tails. Light grey upperparts, dark wedges on primaries, pale grey head and underbody; lacks black secondary bars. Female has distinctive underwing pattern; pale primaries, irregularly barred and lacking dark trailing edges. Immature male may display rusty breast-band and juvenile facial markings.

PIED HARRIER

Circus melanoleucos Accipitridae

Size 45-49 cm

Voice Usually silent

Range Resident: Manas and adjoining areas in Assam. Winter visitor over parts of E India and erratically in parts of C and S India

Habitat Grassy areas; cultivation; reedy edges of jheels

Slim and long-winged raptor, overall white and grey. Black head, back, throat and breast; grey tail, wings; black primaries; black band across median coverts. Female dark brown above; pale white nape-patch, rump; pale buffy-rufous below; marked underside of flight feathers. Juvenile has pale marking on head, rufous brown underparts, dark upperwings; pale patch on primaries, white uppertail-covert patch. Solitary, or in pairs.

CRESTED GOSHAWK

Accipiter trivirgatus Accipitridae

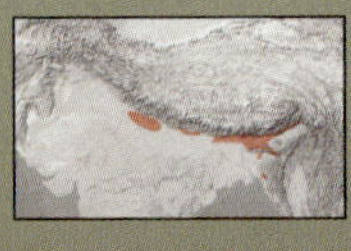

Size 42 cm

Voice Call a high-pitched scream *ke… ke…ke…ke*

Range Fairly common breeding resident

Habitat Forests

Large dark brown hawk with diagnostic black mesial-stripe from chin to breast. Long, brown tail has four wide black bands; brownish-black head with slight crest; black neck and white throat. White undertail; breast vertically streaked rufous; belly marked with horizontal dark brown bands. Iris, legs and feet yellow. Watches prey from perch, capturing it in rapid attack.

SHIKRA

Accipiter badius Accipitridae

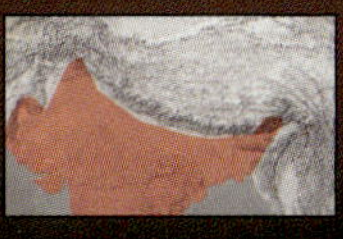

Size 35 cm

Voice Call a loud, drongo-like *titew…titew*

Range Subcontinent, upto 1,600 m in the Himalayas

Habitat Light forests; open country; neighbourhood of villages. Also in cities

Adult male has uniform grey upperparts, with faint rufous half-collar. Dark grey primaries tipped black. Underparts white, with narrow black streak from chin to throat centre; greyish red face and neck sides; breast and belly finely barred chestnut; grey tail has five dark bands and dark tip. Underwings rufous to buff; orange to red eye; yellowish-orange legs. Female larger, more slaty-brown and boldly barred.

♀

juvenile

BESRA

Accipiter virgatus Accipitridae

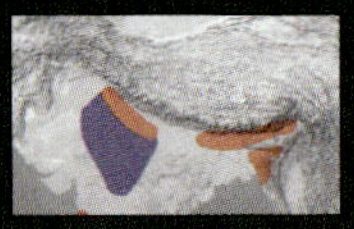

Size 32 cm

Voice Quite noisy. Call a high-pitched *chew…chew…chew*, when perched and in flight

Range Scarce breeding resident: The Himalayan foothills, Nepal, NE India, Western Ghats, Sri Lanka. Winters in N plains

Habitat Forests; open woodlands

Medium-sized raptor with short broad wings and long tail. Similar to Shikra, but darker and distinct dark vertical throat-stripe. Upperparts dark bluish-grey and whitish underparts barred rufous. Female larger and more brown. Juvenile has dark brown upperparts and white underparts barred brown with barred tail.

EURASIAN SPARROWHAWK

Accipiter nisus Accipitridae

Size 35 cm

Voice Rather quiet. Call a rapid *kew…kew…kew…kew* when nesting

Range Fairly common breeding resident

Habitat Open wooded country, including cultivation. Probably overlooked

Smallish sparrowhawk with long legs and short, rounded wings. Upperparts dark grey with pale underparts finely barred reddish-brown. Hooked beak; pale line above eye; white chin-patch. Female significantly larger, with darker, more brown upperparts and white underparts barred. Juvenile similar to female, but more brown upperparts, with rusty feather margins, broader barring on underparts; yellow iris. The Himalayan resident, *A.n. melaschistos*, is blackish-grey above.

NORTHERN GOSHAWK

Accipiter gentilis Accipitridae

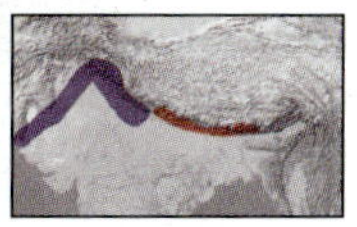

Size Male 50 cm; Female 61 cm

Voice Usually quiet. Pairs call a chattering *yek...yek...yek*; female a high *kee...aw*

Range Scarce winter visitor

Habitat Often soaring high over oak and coniferous forests

Large, powerful bird with short, strong wings and long tail. Upperparts brown-grey; black cap on head; distinct white supercilium; orange-red eyes; light grey underparts, finely barred on breast; throat, vertically streaked. Female has more brown upperparts and less-defined markings on breast. Juvenile brown above and pale buff to whitish below, with heavy streaking. Usually solitary, or in pairs.

HIMALAYAN BUZZARD

Buteo b burmanicus Accipitridae

Size 51-57 cm

Voice Call a loud *peee...ooo* similar to that of *buteo buteo* but clearer, higher-pitched

Range Resident and winter visitor to the Himalayas. Winter visitor to NE India

Habitat Mountains; cultivated slopes

Recently split from Common to which it is very similar. Resident but numbers augmented in winter.

UPLAND BUZZARD

Buteo hemilasius Accipitridae

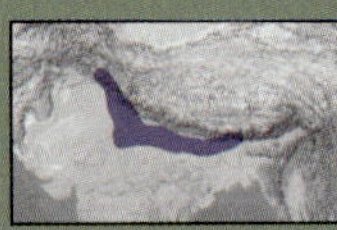

Size 70 cm

Voice Call a nasal *pee…ou*

Range Scarce, probably breeding resident of N mountains, but status unclear

Habitat Open, often rocky country, frequently soaring

Very large buzzard with pale head, and broad, brown moustachial streak. White edge to head, culminating in white patch on nape. White chin and brown throat. Upperparts light brown edged pale rufous; white spotting on uppertail-coverts; brown tail with two or three bars towards tip; black primaries. Underparts whitish, washed rufous; rusty-red underwing-coverts; upper breast, flanks blotched brown; brown thighs have pale bars. Greenish-yellow cere; yellowish-grey legs and feet. Feeds mainly on rodents.

GREATER SPOTTED EAGLE

Aquila clanga Accipitridae

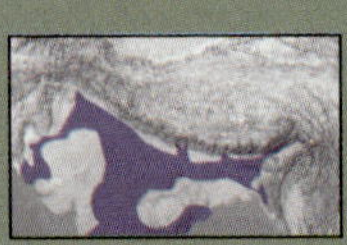

Size 62–74 cm

Voice Call a loud, shrill *kaek… kaek…* often from perch

Range Globally threatened. Breeds in parts of NW India; spreads south in winter

Habitat Tree-covered areas in vicinity of water

fulvescens

Large eagle with massive wing span. Adult almost entirely blackish except for some white in wings and base of tail. Immature has broad white bars on wings and white rump. Huge wings hold out straight from body when soaring. Seen mostly in open country, near freshwater. Often perches on low trees. Regularly seen on carcass; impressive master of the air.

BLACK EAGLE

Ictinaetus malayensis Accipitridae

Size 69-81 cm

Voice Rather quiet. Call a loud *kee… kee…kee* when courting

Range Local breeding resident to N hills from E Punjab to Myanmar border, Bangladesh, and hills of Eastern and Western Ghats, Sri Lanka

Habitat Hills; mangrove forests

Almost entirely black eagle with yellow cere and yellow feet. Brown eyes; yellow-grey beak tipped black; white patches at base of primary feathers; extended primary feathers; long wings reach tail-tip at rest. Wings held in shallow V-shape with long upturned fingers when gliding. Juvenile has dark brown crown, nape, back, and wings, speckled buff-yellow; tail barred with grey; heavily streaked underparts. Normally seen soaring alone, or in pairs over canopy.

INDIAN SPOTTED EAGLE

Aquila hastata Accipitridae

Size 59-67 cm

Voice Very high-pitched cackling call

Range N subcontinent; largely unrecorded in Pakistan

Habitat Wooded areas interspersed with cultivation in lowlands. Globally threatened

Medium-sized eagle with short, broad wings and short tail. Adult overall brown. Broad head with wide mouth. Flesh gape extending to middle of eye. Upperparts medium-brown; uppertail-coverts light brown barred white; large creamy spots on median coverts. Wings angled down at shoulder. In flight, shows rounder wings, lighter and slimmer than Greater Spotted. Seizes prey from ground whilst quartering over areas within, or near forests.

TAWNY EAGLE

Aquila rapax Accipitridae

Size 70 cm

Voice Loud crackling notes; high-pitched call

Range Sporadically over parts of the country; *nipalensis* is a winter visitor

Habitat Open country; vicinities of villages; towns and cultivation

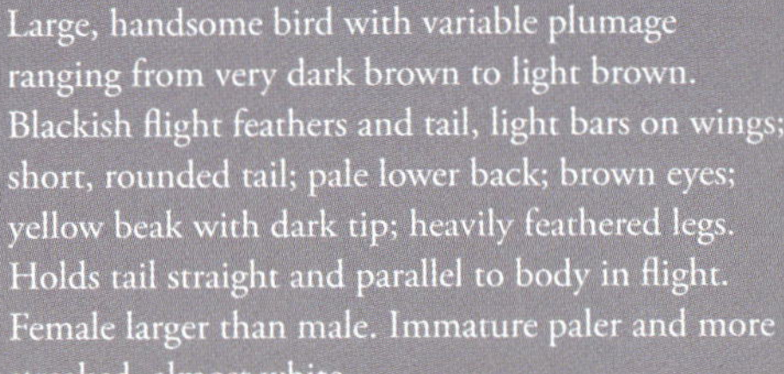

Large, handsome bird with variable plumage ranging from very dark brown to light brown. Blackish flight feathers and tail, light bars on wings; short, rounded tail; pale lower back; brown eyes; yellow beak with dark tip; heavily feathered legs. Holds tail straight and parallel to body in flight. Female larger than male. Immature paler and more streaked, almost white.

juvenile

STEPPE EAGLE

Aquila nipalensis Accipitridae

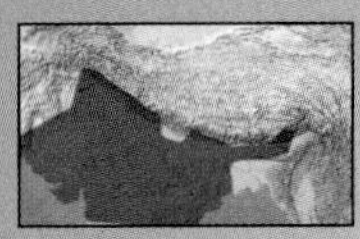

Size 80 cm

Voice Usually silent

Range Fairly common winter visitor

Habitat Lightly wooded and open country. Also villages and towns

Adult overall dark brown, with well-defined bars on flight and tail feathers; pale-tipped secondaries; reddish-brown patch on nape of neck; long, wide gape; small head; pale throat; dark iris; yellow legs. Juvenile resembles adult, but paler brown, with characteristic broad white band running along underside of wing.

juvenile

GOLDEN EAGLE

Aquila chrysaetos Accipitridae

Size 90 cm

Voice Usually silent

Range Scarce breeding resident of N mountains. Rarely wandering to plains in winter

Habitat Mountains above treeline and near steep cliffs; open country in plains

Huge bird of prey with very long wings and long tail. Almost entirely dark brown with massive bright yellow talons. Golden or reddish-brown head, nape and neck; dark-tipped tail; protruding head and neck; legs, densely feathered. Flies in V-shape with wings lifted. Solitary, or in pairs. Captures prey on or near ground, locating it by soaring, flying low over ground, or hunting from perch.

BONELLI'S EAGLE

Aquila fasciata Accipitridae

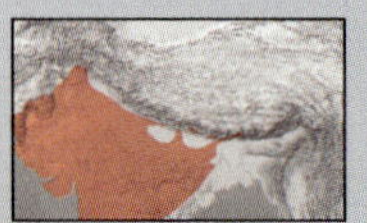

Size 70 cm

Voice Call a shrill scream of 3- to 6 notes

Range All over India, sporadically from about 2,400 m in the Himalayas

Habitat Forests

Large brown-and-white eagle with short, rounded wings and long tail. Dark brown back and wings; white belly and underparts mottled brown; white trailing edge to wing; black terminal band; grey patch at carpal joint; long, feathered legs; yellow-orange eyes; yellow feet and cere. Juvenile has pale chestnut underside and hazel eyes.

BOOTED EAGLE

Hieraaetus pennatus Accipitridae

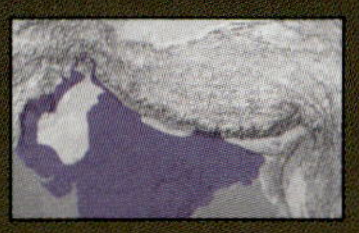

Size 52 cm

Voice Call a loud scream of several notes

Range Breeds in the Himalayas

Habitat Open forests; scrubs

pale morph

dark morph

Has two distinct colour phases. In lighter phase, head paler as uppertail and upperwing-coverts. Buffy white wing linings, underbody and tail with blackish flight feathers distinctive. In darker phase, chocolate-brown below. Pale-banded tail makes it easily identifiable in flight. Often seen alone, or sometimes in pairs hunting in concert. Often roosts together at night.

pale morph

RUFOUS-BELLIED EAGLE

Lophotriorchis kienerii Accipitridae

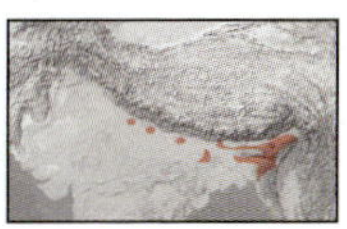

Size 60 cm

Voice Normally silent, but has plaintive scream when breeding

Range Rare breeding resident: Western Ghats, Sri Lanka, Nepal, Bangladesh, NE India and the Himalayan foothills

Habitat Humid forests

Medium-sized raptor with black hood and short crest. Black upperparts; white to rufous throat and chest; rufous belly and legs streaked black; brown, square tail; undertail barred black-and-white; barred wings; white base to primary feathers; red-brown eyes; yellow cere and feet; feathered legs. Juvenile has dark brown upperparts, brown crown and nape, and two black eye-patches; white underparts and grey tail with dark, narrow barring and white tip. Normally seen soaring over canopy.

CHANGEABLE HAWK EAGLE

Nisaetus c limnaeetus Accipitridae

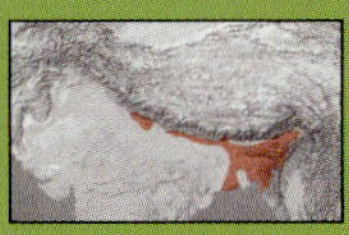

Size 70 cm

Voice Similar to Crested, but slower

Range The Himalayan foothills; NE India, Andaman Islands and Bangladesh

Habitat Well-wooded country

Recently split from Crested Hawk to which it is very similar. Mostly distinguished by its prominent crest. Also, lacks dark morph. Tail more heavily barred. Usually solitary, or in pairs; soars infrequently.

MOUNTAIN HAWK EAGLE

Nisaetus nipalensis Accipitridae

Size 72 cm

Voice Call a high whistling *peeo… peeo* during breeding season

Range Locally common breeding resident: N mountains, Western Ghats and Sri Lanka

Habitat Upland forests

Large brown-and-white raptor with brown upperparts, rufous head and black, pale-tipped crest. Belly and underwing-coverts barred dark brown; tail has three bands and grey-brown from above and white below. Juvenile dark brown with buff to tawny underparts, barred tail and white legs. Broad wings with curved trailing edge, held in shallow V-shape in flight.

juvenile

RUDDY-BREASTED CRAKE

Porzana fusca Rallidae

Size 22 cm

Voice Rather quiet, but makes soft crake calls, sometimes accelerated into trill

Range Scarce breeding resident, local migrant: Most often recorded from N Pakistan, Nepal, Bangladesh, Sri Lanka and Western Ghats

Habitat Secretive; crepuscular and thus easily overlooked. Well-vegetated marshes; jheels and riverbanks

Medium to small, uniformly reddish-brown crake. Upperparts brown; deep chestnut forehead, forecrown and sides of head; pale throat, deep red underparts and white-barred black undertail-coverts; bright pink legs and feet. Sexes similar, but female paler. Juvenile more brown with faint white barring on underparts.

BLACK-TAILED CRAKE

Porzana bicolor Rallidae

Size 25 cm

Voice Call a low, hoarse *hraaa… hraaa…waak…waak; keck…kik;* then an extended trilling

Range Isolated pockets in Nepal, Bhutan, Assam and Arunachal Pradesh. Often found in high altitudes

Habitat Forests and dense undergrowth surrounding paddy fields; marshy streams; pools in or near forests, secondary growth

Small, red-legged, jungle-dwelling crake with sooty-grey head, neck and underparts, whitish chin, rufous-chestnut mantle and wings; charcoal-black rump, vent, tail and undertail-coverts. Pale green bill, sometimes with red base. Red iris. Generally shy.

BLACK-NECKED CRANE

Grus nigricollis Gruidae

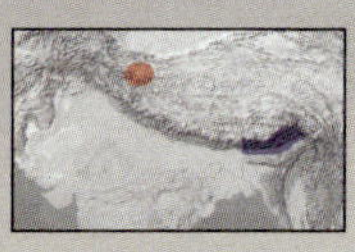

Size 150 cm

Voice Loud, trumpet-like call, higher-pitched than Sarus's

Range Breeds only in Ladakh within Indian limits; possibly in parts of Arunachal Pradesh

Habitat High-altitude marshes; lakesides; open cultivation

Ash-grey crane with black head, neck; dull-red lores, complete crown; small white patch around eye; black wing-tips, drooping plumes; whitish underparts. Sexes alike. Female slightly smaller. In pairs or small flocks; upto 100 birds seen together in Bhutan, where much revered by locals. Barely three to five pairs breeding in Indian region (Ladakh). Dancing displays commence around March, flies high during afternoons, calling loudly.

juvenile

IBISBILL

Ibidorhyncha struthersii Charadriidae

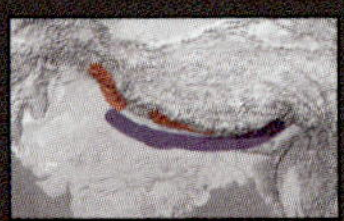

Size 41 cm

Voice Call a high *ti...ti...*, *kluklu; wicka...tik...tik*

Range Rare breeding resident in N mountains; moves lower in winter

Habitat Pebble beds in fast-flowing rivers, blending well among stones

Grey wader with white belly, crimson, long downcurved bill, black face and black breast-band. Short orange legs. Upperparts sandy-grey with short white wing-bars. Head, neck and breast lavender-grey with white-edged black crown and face, white and black breast-bands. White below. Juvenile has grey bill and pale face. Usually solitary, or in small groups. Wary, but loyal to favoured spots. Bobs when alarmed. Feeds on invertebrates by probing and turning over stones.

BLACK-WINGED STILT

Himantopus himantopus Charadriidae

Size 35 cm

Voice Calls include shrill notes in flight, very tern-like. Noisy when breeding

Range Resident and local migrant all over India, south from about 1,800 m in W Himalayas

Habitat Marshes; salt pans; tidal creeks; village ponds; also riversides

Characterised by long, red legs and black-and-white plumage. Jet-black mantle has greenish iridescence; rest of plumage glossy white. Underparts white, sometimes with pale pinkish wash on breast. Pointed wings. Female dark brown with black spots on head; duller overall in winter. Gregarious; seen in large numbers, often along with other waders in wetlands; long legs enable to enter relatively deep water; clumsy walk; submerges head when feeding.

♀

juvenile

NORTHERN LAPWING

Vanellus vanellus Charadriidae

Size 31 cm

Voice Characteristic shrill call has given rise to the imitative local name *peewit*

Range Rather scarce winter visitor mainly to N lowlands

Habitat Wet grasslands; jheels; river margins; fallow

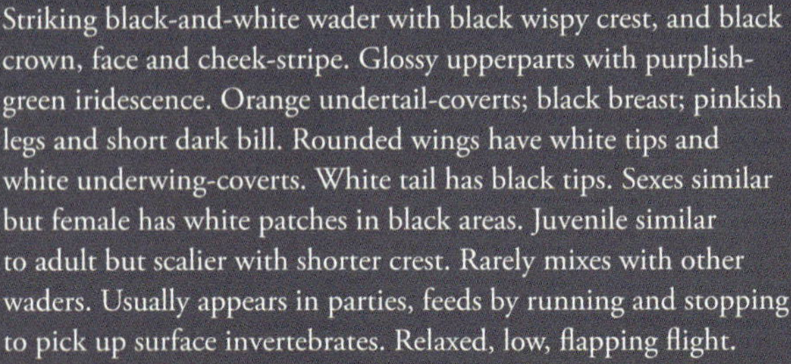

Striking black-and-white wader with black wispy crest, and black crown, face and cheek-stripe. Glossy upperparts with purplish-green iridescence. Orange undertail-coverts; black breast; pinkish legs and short dark bill. Rounded wings have white tips and white underwing-coverts. White tail has black tips. Sexes similar but female has white patches in black areas. Juvenile similar to adult but scalier with shorter crest. Rarely mixes with other waders. Usually appears in parties, feeds by running and stopping to pick up surface invertebrates. Relaxed, low, flapping flight.

GREY-HEADED LAPWING

Vanellus cinereus Charadriidae

Large, sandy-brown wader, striking in flight with extensive black wing-tips, white secondaries and black-banded white tail. Pale grey head, neck and breast; black breast-band; black-tipped yellow bill; long spindly yellow legs; red iris and bare yellow lores. Sexes alike, but male slightly larger. Juvenile has less distinct breast-band and pale fringes to wing-coverts. Feeds in shallow water on insects, worms and molluscs.

Size 37 cm

Voice Rather quiet. Call a high-pitched *chee…e…it*, similar to that of Red-wattled

Range Local winter visitor to lowland Nepal, NE India and Bangladesh. Rare elsewhere in N India

Habitat Open, usually wet grasslands, jheel and river edges and fallow. Seeks out recently burnt, damp grasslands. Feeds in typical plover fashion

RED-WATTLED LAPWING

Vanellus indicus Charadriidae

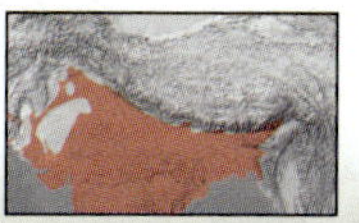

Size 35 cm

Voice Quiet. Calls include short, plaintive notes; quick-repeated notes when nest site intruded upon

Range From NW India, south through country; does not occur in extreme NE India

Habitat Dry, open country

atronuchalis

indicus

Jet-black head, neck, breast; bronze-brown upperbody; white below, continuing to broad bands up the neck-sides towards eyes; fleshy crimson facial wattles diagnostic. Solitary or pairs when breeding; often large flocks in winter; moves on open ground, feeds during mornings and evenings; vigilant species, its loud cries heraldng any new activity in an area; feeds late into evening.

juvenile

RIVER LAPWING

Vanellus duvaucelii Charadriidae

Size 30 cm

Voice Rather like that of Red-wattled, only bit softer and less shrill; also sharp *deed…did…did…*

Range Breeds in parts of E and C India, including Odisha, Andhra Pradesh and E Madhya Pradesh; may disperse in winter

Habitat Stony riverbeds, sandbanks; sometimes collects around jheels in winter

Striking bird in flight with black primaries, white underwings and upperwing secondaries, and brown upperwing-coverts. Black crest, crown, face and central throat and greyish-white nape and neck-sides. Underparts white; grey-brown breast-band; black belly-patch; brown back; white rump, black tail. Sexes alike, but male slightly larger. Juvenile has brown tips to black head feathers, sandier brown back, pale fringes to upperpart and wing-covert feathers. Usually pairs in close vicinity; may collect into small parties during winter, sometimes with other waders.

PACIFIC GOLDEN PLOVER

Pluvialis fulva Charadriidae

Size 25 cm

Voice Distinct *tu…leep* like a soft Spotted Redshank

Range Locally common winter visitor to all coasts and inland in Bangladesh and NE India. Most common in SE India and Bangaldesh. Scarce but regular passage migrant to inland and elsewhere

Habitat Coastal mudflats; salt pans and grasslands. Inland on marshes, jheels

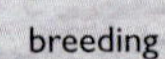

breeding

non-breeding

Medium-sized to large shorebird with short neck and fairly long, grey legs. Overall golden-brown, speckled back. Dark head and ear-coverts. Non-breeding adult has buff head, neck and breast streaked darker. Breeding adult has black face, neck, breast and belly; creamy-white forehead and supercilium. Juvenile similar to non-breeding adult, but with light barring on chest-sides, and flanks, has more distinct yellow edges and spots on feathers of crown, back and wings.

LONG-BILLED PLOVER

Charadrius placidus Charadriidae

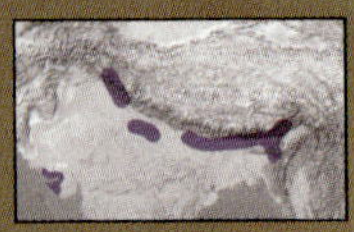

Size 22 cm

Voice Call a high *pee…wee*

Range Rare winter visitor: N rivers, Gujarat coast. Also occurs in China, N, SE and C Asia. Probably overlooked in winter

Habitat Shingle banks on rivers, muddy banks

Largest of the ringed-plovers, with long black bill, black breast-band, brown cheeks and yellowish-brown legs. Upperparts and crown muddy-brown; white forehead and rear eye-stripe; black forecrown bar and narrow breast-band, brownish cheeks. Displays thin white wing-bar and trailing edges and black subterminal tail-band in flight. Sexes alike. Solitary and unobtrusive.

LITTLE RINGED PLOVER

Charadrius dubius Charadriidae

Size 16 cm

Voice Call a *few…few…* whistle, high-pitched but somewhat plaintive, uttered mostly on wing. Warning or attention-seeking call a loud *piuu*

Range Resident and local migrant; all over India

Habitat Shingle-covered riverbanks; tidal mudflats; estuaries; edges of lakes

non-breeding

breeding

Similar to Ringed, but has yellow eye-ring and almost non-existent wing-bars. Upperparts sandy-brown; white forehead; brown cap; black eye masks and breast, white neck-ring diagnostic; white chin and throat; white belly; short, dark bill; flesh-coloured legs. Sexes alike. Walks with fast steps, stopping suddenly, then runs a small stretch again. Tramples around on sand or mud to flush prey out of hiding places. Flies rapidly, low over ground; zigzag flight.

KENTISH PLOVER

Charadrius alexandrinus Charadriidae

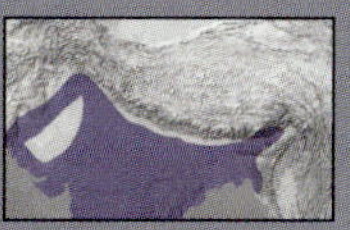

Size 17 cm

Voice Call a soft *dri…ip…*; alarm a *whi…it* on ground. In flight, an abrupt *tit…tit*

Range Fairly common winter visitor, local breeding resident to most coasts and throughout lowlands

Habitat Coastal sandflats, salt pans but inland on river sandbars, open lakeshores and drying floods

breeding

One of the smallest plovers, paler than Ringed with longer legs and thinner bill. Pale grey-brown upperparts, crown and cheeks; incomplete breast-band; white underparts. Breeding male has small white forehead, black forecrown-band, and slightly reddish hindcrown; black eye-band below slim white brow. Forages in a 'run-and-pause' rather than steady probing.

GREATER PAINTED-SNIPE

Rostratula benghalensis Rostratulidaet

Size 25 cm

Voice Common call a long-drawn, mellow note that can be likened to the noise made by blowing into a bottle mouth

Range All over India, upto about 2,000 m in the Himalayas

Habitat Wet mud; marshes; areas where there is a mix of open water and heavy low cover

Medium-sized water bird, polyandrous. Breeding female metallic-olive above, marked buff and black; buff stripe down crown centre; white patches around eyes; chestnut throat, breast and sides of neck; white below breast. Breeding male duller overall; lacks chestnut. Sexes difficult to distinguish when not in breeding plumage. Crepuscular and nocturnal. Solitary, or a few scattered birds; feeds in squelchy mud but also moves on drier ground; runs on landing.

EURASIAN WOODCOCK

Scolopax rusticola Scolopacidae

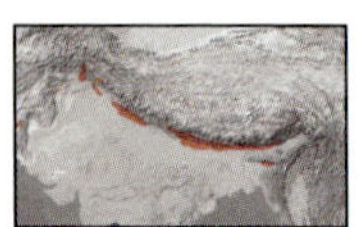

Size 33–38 cm

Voice Usually silent in winter

Range Breeds in the Himalayas

Habitat Dense forests

Medium to small wader with intricately patterned reddish-brown upperparts and buff underparts; long straight bill; head barred black; eyes set far back on head to give 360° vision; rounded wings; base of bill flesh-coloured with dark tip; legs vary from grey to pinkish. Probes ground for food with long bill. Crepuscular; rarely active during the day unless flushed.

JACK SNIPE

Lymnocryptes minimus Scolopacidae

Size 21 cm

Voice Invariably silent when flushed

Range Winter visitor: Plains of N Afghanistan, Indus Valley

Habitat Marshes; paddy fields

Extremely small, secretive bird and exceptionally well-camouflaged within habitat. Lacks central crown-stripe; two pale lateral crown-stripes separated from supercilium by dark patch; dark eye-stripe. Mottled brown upperparts and pale underparts; streaked breast; narrow, pointed wings; conspicuous long straight golden scapular and mantle-stripes; short, wedge-shaped tail; yellow back-stripes visible in flight. Forages in soft mud for insects, earthworms and plant material. Feeds in characteristic bouncing motion. Crouches in undergrowth. Low and rapid zigzag flight when flushed. Male performs an aerial display during courtship.

SOLITARY SNIPE

Gallinago solitaria Scolopacidae

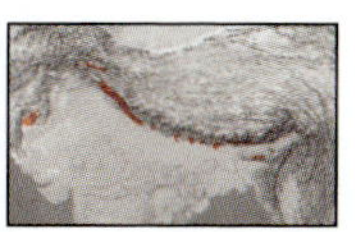

Size 30 cm

Voice Rather quiet. Loud, deep *pench* on flushing. Hoarse *kensh* call when taking off; far-carrying *chok-a-chok-a* call when displaying

Range Rare breeding resident of N mountains moving down to foothills in winter. Very rarely seen elsewhere

Habitat Alpine bogs and streams with thick cover

Small, stocky wader, with long, slender bill and pale face. Relatively short legs; heavily streaked head, neck and upperparts; fine barring on underparts; distinct warm ginger-brown wash on upper breast; white belly; olive-yellow to brownish-yellow legs; brown barring on flanks. Sexes similar, but female larger. Like other snipes, uses long bill to probe deeply in mud. Bobs up and down constantly as it feeds. Solitary and unobtrusive.

WOOD SNIPE

Gallinago nemoricola Scolopacidae

Size 28-32 cm

Voice Invariably silent when flushed

Range Breeds in the Himalayas and winters in the foothills and in S India and Sri Lanka

Habitat Marshes; paddy fields

Large, relatively short-billed snipe with broad wings. Dark-tipped pale yellow bill; distinct chestnut and black head-stripes; dark upper back with chestnut stripes running down towards tail; chestnut neck and breast; buff underparts streaked brown; creamish belly; dense barring on underwing; pale green-yellow legs. Heavy, direct flight.

PINTAIL SNIPE

Gallinago stenura Scolopacidae

Size 28 cm

Voice Call said to be *squik* or *chef*

Range Winter visitor to peninsula from about Mumbai south and to EC India and S Nepal to Arunachal Pradesh, Assam Valley

Habitat Marshes; paddyfields

Small, stocky wader with short greenish-grey legs and long, straight dark bill. Upperparts mottled brown with linear cream markings down back. Underparts pale with streaked buff breast and white belly; dark stripe through eye with lighter stripes above and below. Sexes similar. Wings less pointed than Common, lacks white trailing edge. Distinguished by shorter tail and flatter flight path when flushed.

SWINHOE'S SNIPE

Gallinago megala Scolopacidae

Size 28 cm

Voice In flight, a sudden *chrek* with abrupt ending. Pintail has more subdued *tesch;* coarse shriek

Range Probably fairly common but overlooked winter visitor mainly to E and S of the region

Habitat Marshes; wet paddy

Cryptically-patterned black, brown buff and white snipe, with extremely long bill. Very similar to *Pintail G. stenura* but distinguished by proportionately longer bill. Pale, dull upperparts. Greyish legs extend just beyond tail. Greyish flight feathers contrast with heavily barred white wing-coverts. Sexes alike. Lumbering flight. Feeds by deep, vertical probing.

COMMON SNIPE

Gallinago gallinago Scolopacidae

Size 28 cm

Voice Call a loud *scaaap* when flushed

Range Breeds in parts of W Himalayas; mostly winter visitor over the subcontinent, most common in N and C India

Habitat Marshlands; paddy cultivation; edges of jheels

Well-camouflaged bird, usually seen when flushed. Mottled-brown upperparts, with pale stripes on back and dark streaks on chest; paler underparts. Short legs; long wings; short tail and very elongated beak. Sexes alike, female may have slightly longer bill. Juvenile's wing feathers fringed with cream. Fast, zigzag flight. Probes with long beak in mud, often in shallow water; feeds mostly during mornings and evenings, often continuing through the night.

EURASIAN CURLEW

Numenius arquata Scolopacidae

Size 58 cm

Voice Famed scream; wild, rather musical *cour…leeor…cooodee…*, first note longer

Range Winter visitor: Sea coast, W to E; large inland marshes; rivers

Habitat Estuaries; creeks; large remote marshes

Breeding adult has pale buff-brown head and neck streaked darker; darkish spots on upper mantle; white lower back and rump; dark brown, barred tail; pale brown upperwing spotted dark; black-brown flight feathers. Underparts whitish, with heavily streaked belly; white underwing with variable spotting and streaking. Head finely streaked; indistinct white supercilium. Long, grey downcurved bill; bluish-grey legs and feet. Non-breeding adult duller and overall greyer. Sexes similar, but female larger with longer bill. Juvenile has more buff on breast, flanks less streaked.

non-breeding

SPOTTED REDSHANK

Tringa erythropus Scolopacidae

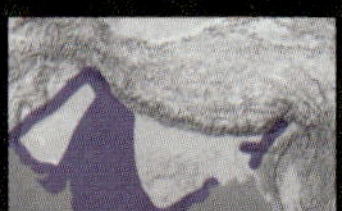

Size 33 cm

Voice Noisy. Call an explosive *chew it*

Range Fairly common winter visitor throughout lowlands. Scarce on the coast, NE India

Habitat Marshes; jheels; rivers

breeding

Slightly larger, slimmer and longer-legged than Common. No wing-bars; long cigar-shaped white patch on back between wings, extending to rump; long red legs. Non-breeding adult has light grey, speckled upperparts and whitish underparts; paler head and neck with short, white supercilium. Red lower mandible, downcurved. Breeding adult has black underparts, head and neck; dark grey upperparts, spotted white. Juvenile resembles pale Redshank.

COMMON REDSHANK

Tringa totanus Scolopacidae

Size 28 cm

Voice Quite musical, fairly loud and shrill *tleu...ewh...ewh*

Range Breeds in Kashmir, Ladakh; winter visitor all over India. Fairly common

Habitat Marshes; creeks; estuaries

breeding

Elegant-looking bird with greyish-brown upperparts, spotted dark brown and black. Whitish underparts streaked and spotted dark brown on breast, flanks and belly. White secondary flight feathers, rump, lower back and barred tail visible in flight. Breeding adult more brown above, marked black and fulvous, and more heavily streaked below. Brown head streaked and spotted darker. Orange-red legs and base of beak; long, straight bill with red base and black tip; dark brown eyes with white eyelids. Legs and feet bright red.

COMMON GREENSHANK

Tringa nebularia Scolopacidae

Size 32 cm

Voice Call a wild, ringing *tew… tew…tew…*

Range Winter visitor, fairly common over most of the region

Habitat Marshes; estuaries

Medium-sized slim wader with dark grey back and white underparts. Diagnostic long; greyish-green legs, slightly upturned, blackish-grey bill. Long neck; white rump extending into distinctive white wedge up the back, visible in flight; grey streaking on head and neck; whitish tail. Breeding adult heavily streaked, spotted darker on upperparts, head, neck and upper breast. Juvenile similar to non-breeding adult, but upperparts more brown and feathers edged buff; neck and breast more heavily streaked.

MARSH SANDPIPER

Tringa stagnatilis Scolopacidae

Size 23 cm

Voice Rather quiet. Call a briefly repeated *klew*, rather like first note of Common Redshank

Range Fairly common winter visitor throughout lowlands. Less common on coasts

Habitat Shallow freshwater jheels; village ponds; wet paddy; river shoals

breeding

Distinctive wader with long needle-like bill and very long greenish legs, often mistaken for Common Greenshank. Non-breeding adult has greyish-brown upperparts and white underparts; grey crown and hindneck; white eyebrow. Breeding adult has heavily streaked head and neck; flanks and lower breast show bars or chevrons. Juvenile has more heavily patterned upperparts than non-breeding adult; dark outer wing and slightly lighter inner wing, white wedge on lower back and rump visible in flight. Feeds upright with slow graceful movements breaking into quick dashes.

non-breeding

GREEN SANDPIPER

Tringa ochropus Scolopacidae

Size 23 cm

Voice Call a ringing *tlu...eet...weet*

Range Widespread but rather scarce winter visitor

Habitat Well-vegetated pools; streams; mangroves; village ponds

Medium-sized sandpiper, similar to Wood, but larger and stockier; shorter legs; darker and less spotted back; more uniform white flanks. Overall brown and spotted white; blackish underwings and tail with broad black lateral-stripes; white rump square. Wings dark above and below, tail white; indistinct eye-stripe; black beak with reddish base; dark brown eyes with white eye-ring.

WOOD SANDPIPER

Tringa glareola Scolopacidae

Upperparts greyish-brown, spotted white; breast and neck white and striped brown. White supercilium, extending from behind eye to back of ear-coverts; short, straight beak with deep olive-green base; long yellow to greenish-yellow legs; brownish tail contrasts with white rump-patch. Breeding adult more olive-brown, spotted white and bill has pale base. Juvenile similar to non-breeding adult, but upperparts much darker, warmer brown; more spotting and streaking on breast.

Size 21 cm

Voice Quite noisy; sharp, trilling notes on ground. Call a shrill, somewhat metallic *chiff...chiff* when flushed; sometimes loud, sharp *tluie...*

Range Winter visitor throughout the region

Habitat Wet cultivation; marshes; tidal creeks; mudflats

breeding

COMMON SANDPIPER

Actitis hypoleucos Scolopacidae

Size 20 cm

Voice Vocal in flight. Call includes a 3-note sound with distinctive 3-note, piping-like cry; often represented as *twee-wee-wee*

Range Breeds in the Himalayas, Kashmir to Uttarakhand to about 3,000 m; winter visitor all across the region

Habitat Freshwater marshes; lakes; tidal areas; creeks

breeding

Small to medium-sized bird, with relatively long legs. Upperparts olive-brown, streaked on head and neck-sides; white underparts; lightly streaked, brown breast; narrow white wing-bar, brown rump; white 'hook' at shoulder conspicuous in flight. Breeding adult has darker and more speckled upperparts. Active; feeds on ground on crustaceans, insects, worms, and other coastal creatures; makes short dashes, bobbing and wagging short tail; stiff-winged flight.

TEMMINCK'S STINT

Calidris temminckii Scolopaidae

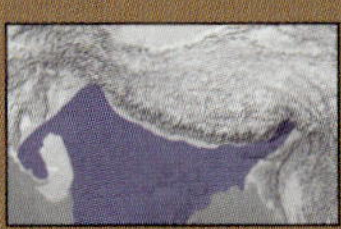

Size 14 cm

Voice Call a dry, high-pitched trilling in flight

Range Common winter visitor throughout lowlands. Scarce on the coast

Habitat Vegetated freshwater habitats favouring flooded short grass and paddy fields

Small, uniform brown sandpiper, similar in size to Little, but darker and greyer. Greyish-brown head and chest; blackish-brown bill and brown iris; thin, downcurved bill; well-defined line between breast and white belly; greenish-brown legs. Uniform chest-patch and greyish upperparts similar to Common Sandpiper. V-shaped white mark on back; extensive white edge to black-centered tail conspicuous in flight.

breeding

non-breeding

LONG-TOED STINT

Calidris subminuta Scolopacidae

Size 14 cm

Voice Call a trilling, slightly throaty *krrrt*

Range Mainly E, NE India and Bangladesh

Habitat Marshes; riverbanks; mudflats

Tiny, delicate wader with distinctive shape, small head, and long slim neck. Variegated rufous, black and buff upperparts; brown scapulars and tertials with broad rufous fringes; roundish belly, short rear-end, long legs and long toes, short, pointed bill; yellow-green legs and feet, pale-brown or yellow base to lower mandible. Brown crown and white supercilium; brown spots on cheek and brown forehead. Similar to Red-necked, but has darker and brighter upperparts.

LITTLE STINT

Calidris minuta Scolopacidae

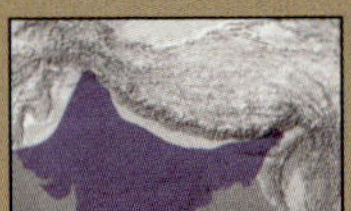

Size 14 cm

Voice Call a piercing, repeated *stit…it*

Range Abundant winter visitor throughout lowlands; all coasts

Habitat Coastal mudflats; salt pans; shallow open freshwater; muddy lakes; river margins

breeding

Tiny wader. In breeding plumage, edges of back feathers, flanks and cheeks turn rusty-red with darker mottling, and white underparts. Dark and split cap; white supercilium. Short, straight and narrow-tipped beak. Thin wing-bars and distinct white V on back, prominent in flight. White lengthwise stripes on backs and grey on tail feathers diagnostic. Black legs, beak and iris. Sexes similar. Juvenile similar to Temminck but with pale forehead and pale eyebrow-stripe split into two. Swift flight with extremely rapid wingbeats.

RUFF

Philomachus pugnax Scolopacidae

Size Male 30 cm; Female 23 cm

Voice Silent. No call recorded

Range Abundant winter visitor mainly to W and S parts of the region

Habitat Marshes; jheels; stubble; cultivation; mudflats; salt pans

Medium-sized wader with long neck, small head, rather short, slightly droopy bill and medium-long orange or reddish legs. Non-breeding adult has scalloped brown-grey upperparts. Breeding male has striking ruff ranging from black or brown to orange or white with pronounced black stripes and ear tufts. Female (known as Reeve) and male in non-breeding plumage similar, with orange bills and white feathers at bill base, but male much larger; upper flanks marked with dark spots. Shows white U on tail, separating dark rump and dark tail-tip in flight.

♀

breeding

breeding

breeding

ORIENTAL PRATINCOLE

Glareola maldivarum Glareolidae

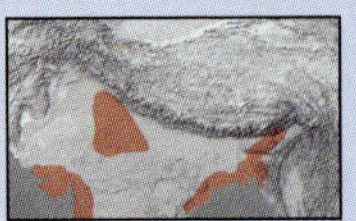

Size 25 cm

Voice Call a tern-like *krek…krek* in flight

Range Resident, local migrant; common breeding resident. Most frequent in N and extreme S, including Sri Lanka

Habitat As Collared; more tolerant of dry fallow away from water. Favours river sandbanks

Very similar to Collared, but distinguished by brown breast extending down to belly and merging into white; long, narrow wings and short, forked tail; much less contrast above and no white trailing edges seen in flight. Short bill; brown back and head; wings brown with black flight feathers. Sexes alike.

juvenile

BROWN-HEADED GULL

Chroicocephalus brunnicephalus Laridae

Size 42 cm

Voice Call a deep *kraaa*

Range Breeds in Ladakh. Common winter visitor to most coasts, sometimes inland

Habitat Coasts, rivers and lakes. Very gregarious, often with Black-headed

Slightly larger than Black-headed; summer adult has pale brown head, pearl-grey body, chocolate-brown partial hood, red bill and legs. In non-breeding adult, mask reduced to brown ear patch. Black-tipped primary wing, feathers have large, conspicuous white spots; grey underwing; black flight feathers. Juvenile has brownish tinge to wings, black tail-bars, pale iris and white eye-rings. Sexes alike. Light, easy flight. Swims buoyantly, often among ducks and coots. Breeds colonially in high-altitude bogs.

BLACK-HEADED GULL

Chroicocephalus ridibundus Laridae

Size 38 cm

Voice Noisy. Call includes querulous *kree…ah…* screams

Range Common winter visitor; most common on W seaboard; also strays inland, both on passage and for short halts

Habitat Sea coasts; harbours; sewage outflows; refuse dumps. Disciplined skeins

Greyish-white plumage; dark ear patches; white outer flight feathers, with black tips. Breeding adult has coffee-brown head and upper neck. Sexes alike. Highly gregarious; large flocks on sea coasts, scavenges in harbours; wheels over busy seaside roads or beaches; large numbers rest on rocky ground and sand; follow boats in harbours.

TIBETAN SANDGROUSE

Syrrhaptes tibetanus Pteroclidae

Size 48 cm

Voice Call a deep, musical *guk...guk*

Range Locally common breeding resident in Ladakh, Himachal Pradesh and Sikkim. Also occurs in C Asia

Habitat High altitude, stony pastures and semi-desert where it is the only sandgrouse

Large sandgrouse with pigeon-shaped body that can be identified by white belly and dark underwing. Small head and bill; feathered legs and feet; long, pointed wings. Adult male overall pale sandy-brown. Orangish face; fine black barring on breast; scapular spots. Sexes similar, but female has shorter tail and barred upperparts. Feeds on plant material. Nests on bare ground. Fast flight.

HILL PIGEON

Columba rupestris Columbidae

Size 33 cm

Voice Call a rather high-pitched *guk... guk...guk*

Range Common resident in the Himalayas from Kashmir to Nepal

Habitat High rocky country; village cultivation

High-altitude, pale grey pigeon with greenish-purple iridescence on neck and breast. White back; grey rump; dark bars on inner wing; dark tail with striking, broad, white subterminal band. Very similar to Common Pigeon but paler, with white band on tail and dark terminal band. Sexes alike. Juvenile more brown and lacks metallic sheen on body. Feeds on grains.

SNOW PIGEON

Columba leuconota Columbidae

Size 35 cm

Voice Call a high *coo...coo...coo*

Range The Himalayas, 2,800-5,000 m, may descend to about 1,000 m in winter

Habitat Open meadows; cultivation; mountain habitation; cliff-faces

Blackish-brown head separated from dull brown back by whitish collar; extensive white on lower back and three dark bands in grey wings, seen both at rest and in flight; very dark tail with white subterminal band; black beak and red feet. Sexes alike. Flocks of variable size gleaning on ground, frequently around mountain habitations, freshly-sown cultivations and vicinities of melting snow; flight very strong; breeds in large colonies on cliffs and in rock-caves.

SPECKLED WOOD PIGEON

Columba hodgsonii Columbidae

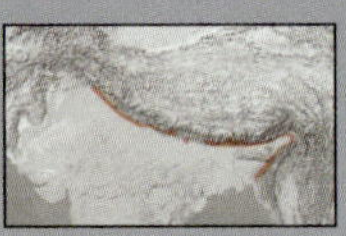

Size 38 cm

Voice Utters a deep *whock... whr...ooooo...whroo*

Range Resident: The Himalayas, hills of NE India

Habitat Oak-rhododendron forests

Overall very dark maroonish-brown with silvery-grey head. Grey neck heavily speckled with dark maroon-brown; maroon mantle and maroon underparts, (grey in female). Distinguished from Ashy Wood by lack of buff neck-patch and white spotting on wing-coverts. Juvenile similar to female, but less distinct neck patterning. In pairs or small groups, seen flying swiftly through forest. Feeds mainly in trees on fruit and sometimes in cultivation.

ASHY WOOD PIGEON

Columba pulchricollis Columbidae

Size 36 cm

Voice Call a slightly booming, repeated *whuoo…whuoo…whuoo*

Range Resident: The Himalayas, hills of NE India

Habitat Dense foliage in broadleaved forests

Creamy-buff collar, pale grey head and blackish-grey mantle diagnostic. Similar to Speckled but distinguished by slate-grey upperparts, lack of white speckles on wing-coverts and uniform dark slate-grey breast. Iridescent green-and-purple on lower neck and back. Juvenile has more brown upperparts, with less distinct patterning on neck, and rufous fringes to feathers of breast and belly. Singly, or in pairs; sits quietly in tree canopy; disappears swiftly when flushed. Nests in flimsy structures of intertwined twigs. Feeds mostly on fruit.

ROCK PIGEON

Columba livia Columbidae

Size 33 cm

Voice Call a deep *tru…troo…tru*

Range Abundant feral and wild breeding resident throughout

Habitat Urban areas; cultivation

intermedia

neglecta

Common sight in urban areas around the world; medium-sized, blue-grey pigeon with darker head and neck and black wing-bars, interbreeds with domestic pigeons, so several colour varieties possible. Blue-grey with green-purple sheen across neck. Wings darker. Some races have white lower back. Always has two long black bars across wing-coverts. Gregarious, mixing with other doves. Feeds in flocks on split grain and sprouting cereals. Also in remote rocky places with cliffs and ruins. Nests colonially in cavities and on ledges in buildings and cliffs.

ORIENTAL TURTLE DOVE

Streptopelia orientalis Columbidae

Size 32 cm

Voice Call a deep and grating *ghur...ghroo...goo...*

Range Several races, resident and migratory, distributed over much of the Indian region

Habitat Mixed forests; vicinity of cultivation; orchards

Large, stocky dove with grey-and-black spotted patch on neck-sides. Rufous-brown back and scapulars, with black markings diagnostic; slaty-grey lower back, rump; whitish border to roundish tail, best seen when tail fanned during landing. Sexes alike. In pairs or loose parties, occasionally solitary birds; feeds mostly on ground; rests during hot hours in leafy branches; perches on overhead wires.

EURASIAN COLLARED DOVE

Streptopelia decaocto Columbidae

Size 32 cm

Voice Call a characteristic *kukkoo...kook...*

Range Most of the region, except extreme NE Himalayas; resident and local migrant; most common in NW, W and C India

Habitat Cultivation; open scrub; dry forests

Similar to Red Collared female but larger with different tail pattern. Greyish-brown plumage; lilac wash about head and neck; black half-collar on hindneck distinctive; broad whitish tips to brown tail feathers, seen as terminal band when fanned during landing; dull lilac breast and ash-grey underbody. Sexes alike. Small parties, when not breeding; often associates with other doves; large gatherings glean in cultivated country; strong flier, chases intruders in territory.

RED COLLARED DOVE

Streptopelia tranquebarica Columbidae

Size 23 cm

Voice Call a quick repeated *gru... gurgoo...*, with more stress on first syllable

Range Throughout the region, south of the Himalayan foothills

Habitat Cultivation; scrubs; deciduous country

Male has deep ash-grey head; black hindneck-collar; rich wine-red back; slaty grey-brown lower back, rump and uppertail; whitish tips to all but central tail feathers. Female much like Eurasian Collared, but smaller size and more brownish colouration distinctive. Solitary, in pairs or small parties; associates with other doves but less common; feeds on ground, gleaning on harvested croplands; perches and suns on leafless branches and overhead wires.

SPOTTED DOVE

Stigmatopelia chinensis Columbidae

Size 30 cm

Voice Familiar bird sound of India, a soft, somewhat doleful *crook...cru...croo or croo...croo...*

Range Subcontinent, upto about 3,500 m in the Himalayas

Habitat Open forests; scrubs; habitation; cultivation

Slender dove with long wedged tail. Grey and pink-brown above, spotted white; white-spotted black hindneck-collar (chessboard) diagnostic; dark tail with broad white tips to outer feathers seen in flight; vinous-brown breast, merging into white on belly. Sexes alike. Juvenile barred above and lack chessboard. In pairs or small parties on ground; frequently settles on paths and roads, flying further on intrusion; quite tame and confiding in many areas; drinks often; at harvest times, seen along with other doves in immense gatherings.

LAUGHING DOVE

Stigmapelia senegalensis Columbidae

Size 27 cm

Voice Call a somewhat harsh but pleasant *cru…do…do…do…do*

Range Almost across India upto about 1,200 m in the outer Himalayas; uncommon in NE states

Habitat Open scrub; cultivation; neighbourhood of habitation

Pinkish grey-brown plumage with black-and-buff chessboard on sides of foreneck; white tips to outer-tail feathers and broad grey wing-patches best seen in flight; small size distinctive. Sexes alike. In pairs, or small flocks; associates freely with other doves in huge gatherings at harvest time; feeds mostly on ground, walking about silently.

BARRED CUCKOO DOVE

Macropygia unchall Columbidae

Size 41 cm

Voice Call a deep *croo…umm*

Range C Nepal east to entire NE Indian region

Habitat Dense broadleaved evergreen, tropical, subtropical and temperate forests; secondary growth

Large and distinctive dove with slim body and long graduated tail; reddish-brown upperparts and tail heavily barred with brown; male has paler unbarred buff head and underparts; iridescent green on nape and crown; some barring on sides of neck and upper breast; female has barring on underparts and some iridescence on nape and sides of neck. Forest-dwelling, often acrobatic in effort to reach food. Most often glimpsed flying between trees. Feeds mostly on small fruits and berries.

EMERALD DOVE

Chalcophaps indica Columbidae

Size 26 cm

Voice Call a deep, plaintive *hoo… oon…hoo…oon…*, many times at a stretch

Range Almost throughout the subcontinent upto about 2,000 m. Absent in Pakistan

Habitat Forests, bamboo clearings; foothills

Bronze emerald-green upperbody; white forehead and eyebrows; grey crown and neck; white on wing shoulder and across lower back; whitish rump diagnostic in flight; rich pinkish-brown below; coral-red beak and pink-red legs. Sexes similar with female duller. Solitary, or in pairs; moves on forest paths and clearings or darts almost blindly through trees, usually under 5 m off ground; difficult to spot on ground.

♀

ORANGE-BREASTED GREEN PIGEON

Treron bicinctus Columbidae

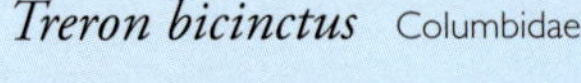

Size 33 cm

Voice Call a typical green pigeon whistle; quiet gurgle

Range Throughout the region

Habitat Subtropical moist deciduous broadleaved evergreen forests; secondary growth; well-wooded country

Smallish green pigeon with blue eyes. Male has distinctive bright orange breast with lilac border above; face and forehead yellowish green; nape and hindneck bluish-grey; unmarked plain green mantle. Female has yellower wash on underparts. Both have dark uppertail-coverts; central tail feathers grey; light grey banding on tail; yellow bordered wing-coverts. Gregarious; in small flocks; often in large groups or mixed feeding parties with other frugivores; arboreal; in fruiting trees; quiet; hard to detect; acrobatic.

ASHY-HEADED GREEN PIGEON

Treron p phayrei Columbidae

Size 28 cm

Voice Call includes fluty whistles

Range NE India

Habitat Foothills, evergreen and moist-deciduous forests

Similar to Thick-billed Green but distinguished by distinct grey crown, thin blue-grey bill; lacks red base to bill and greenish orbital skin. Male has maroon mantle; broad orangish breast-band on yellowish underparts; buffy-orange thighs; dark brown undertail-coverts. Female has dull grey mantle and white undertail-coverts. Often found in company of Orange-breasted. Mostly arboreal, descending only to drink or at salt-licks.

THICK-BILLED GREEN PIGEON

Treron curvirostra Columbidae

Size 27 cm

Voice Calls include musical whistles and throaty *kloo…kloo*

Range Scarce resident: NE India, parts of Bangladesh and Nepal

Habitat Forests; groves

Medium-sized green pigeon. Male has greyish nape and crown; maroon mantle; brown undertail-coverts; broad bluish-green orbital skin; heavy, large bill with scarlet red base. Female has greyish crown and nape while mantle and underparts green. Gregarious, and often found with other green pigeons. Primarily forest bird, but often seen in forest fringes, gardens and plantations.

YELLOW-FOOTED GREEN PIGEON

Treron phoenicopterus Columbidae

Size 33 cm

Voice Call includes rich, mellow whistling notes

Range South roughly of line from S Rajasthan to N Odisha to Sri Lanka; rarer in Pakistan

Habitat Forests; orchards; city parks; cultivated village vicinities

Male ash olive-green above; olive-yellow collar, dark, slaty tail has band; lilac-red shoulder-patch (mostly absent in female); yellow legs and underbody. Female slightly duller than male. The nominate (northern) race has grey lower breast and belly. Small flocks; mostly arboreal, rarely coming to salt-licks or cropland; remains well hidden in foliage but moves briskly; has favourite feeding trees.

PIN-TAILED GREEN PIGEON

Treron apicauda Columbidae

Size 42 cm

Voice Call a soft, winding *ko…kla…oi…oi…oi…oilli…illio…kla*

Range Uttarakhand eastwards through entire NE Indian region

Habitat Tropical, subtropical mature broadleaved, usually evergreen forests

Large, green pigeon with long, pointed central feathers in grey tail; vivid yellow-green rump; green head, back and mantle; grey cast on upper mantle, stronger in male; pale yellow edges to wing-coverts; male also has light orange wash to breast, lacking in female; both sexes have blue-grey around base of bill and eye. Strong flier. In small flocks, sometimes in mixed feeding parties.

WEDGE-TAILED GREEN PIGEON

Treron sphenurus Columbidae

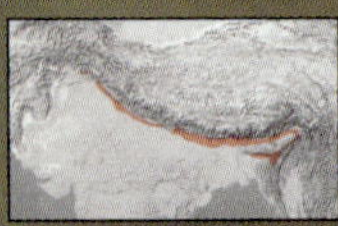

Size 33 cm

Voice Call a melodious whistling *hoo …whoo…huhuhu…*

Range Himachal Pradesh east to the entire NE Indian region

Habitat Subtropical broadleaved mixed forests; edges of forests

Largish pigeon with distinctive wedge-shaped tail; dark grey-green plumage on upperparts; maroon-patch of male restricted to shoulders and lower mantle; grey upper mantle; pale orange crown and breast; only faint, narrow yellow edges to wing-coverts; yellowish green face, throat, underparts. Often associates with other green pigeons.

GREEN IMPERIAL PIGEON

Ducula aenea Columbidae

Size 43 cm

Voice Deep chuckling notes, quite pleasant-sounding and somewhat ventriloquistic

Range Forested parts of N India, from Garhwal Terai eastwards; forested regions of C and E India, Western Ghats south of Mumbai; resident in many areas but also moves considerably

Habitat Evergreen forests

Large forest pigeon, often confused with similar Mountain Imperial, but much smaller. Greyish head, neck and underbody with distinct pinkish wash; metallic bronze-green upperbody, unbanded tail; chocolate-maroon undertail; reddish legs. Sexes alike. Juvenile overall duller. Known for aerial display, repeatedly rises to dive with half-closed wings. In pairs, or small parties on fruiting trees, not infrequently with other species; chiefly arboreal but comes to ground, at salt-licks and water; strong flight; has favourite feeding spots. Several regional variations.

MOUNTAIN IMPERIAL PIGEON

Ducula badia Columbidae

Very large pigeon with grey head and neck tinged with pink. Wings and mantle brownish-maroon, throat and chin white. Pinkish-grey underparts; dark-based tail with broad, pale terminal band. Red-based bill and red eye-rings with pale iris. Pinkish feet. Sexes alike.

Size 45 cm

Voice Call a booming *oomp…oomp*

Range Fairly common breeding resident: Western Ghats, NE India, parts of Nepal

Habitat Closed forests

RED-BREASTED PARAKEET

Psittacula alexandri Psittacidae

Size 38 cm

Voice Rather quiet. Call a sharp *quawnk*

Range Scarce breeding resident in N foothills east from Uttarakhand

Habitat Foothill forests

Adult has green upperparts; green or yellow median wing-coverts forming large patch on wing; grey head, with varying tinges of blue, and around eyes washed with green; black narrow line from forehead to eyes, black wide band across lower cheeks; salmon/pink throat to upper abdomen duller in female; green lower abdomen to undertail-coverts with blue suffusion; blue central tail feathers tipped with yellow/green. Bill coral red. Eye pale yellow. Juvenile has green crown and underparts; dark brown lower cheeks; brown/grey wash on green sides of head; green median wing-coverts margined with yellow/green. Tail short. Bill pale red. Eye grey.

VERNAL HANGING PARROT

Loriculus vernalis Psittacidae

Size 15 cm

Voice Quiet but distinctive and rapid *zzit…zzit* in flight

Range Scarce breeding resident of lower hills of SW, E India and Bangladesh, subject to local movements

Habitat Forests

Small short-tailed and primarily emerald green-plumaged bird with blue patch on throat; red rump and uppertail-coverts; red bill; white eye. Female similar to male but with little or no blue on throat. Juvenile similar to adult but has dull greyish-green on forehead and cheeks; no blue on throat; dull red rump washed green; pale orange bill; brown eye. Unique for its ability to sleep upside down. Very arboreal.

ALEXANDRINE PARAKEET

Psittacula eupatria Psittacidae

Size 53 cm

Voice Call a high-pitched *kreeak*... scream, on wing as well as on perch; popular cage bird, learning to imitate some notes and few human words

Range Almost throughout the region, south of the Himalayan foothills

Habitat Forests; orchards; cultivated areas; towns

Rich, vibrant-coloured bird. Male has rich grass-green plumage; hooked, heavy red beak; deep red shoulder-patch; rose-pink collar and black stripe from lower mandible to collar distinctive. Female smaller and lacks collar and black stripe. Yellow undertail in both sexes. Seen in small flocks and large gatherings; feeds on fruiting trees in orchards and on standing crops; strong flier; roosts along with other birds at favoured sites.

ROSE-RINGED PARAKEET

Psittacula krameri Psittacidae

Size 42 cm

Voice Call a shrill *keeak*...; screams

Range Subcontinent, south of the Himalayan foothills

Habitat Light forests; orchards; towns; villages

♀

Male has grass-green plumage; short, hooked, red beak; rosy-pink and black collar distinctive (attained only during third year). Female lacks pink-and-black collar; instead, pale emerald-green around neck. Gregarious; large flocks of this species familiar sight in India; causes extensive damage to standing crops, orchards and garden fruit trees; also raids grain depots and markets; large roosting colonies, often along with mynas and crows.

SLATY-HEADED PARAKEET

Psittacula himalayana Psittacidae

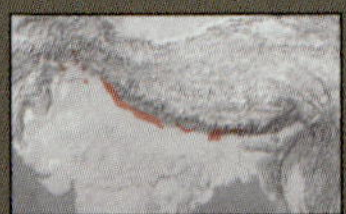

Size 40 cm

Voice Noisy. Call a distinctive high-pitched, musical *tool...tool*

Range Common breeding resident of N hills; resident in the Himalayas (600-2,500 m) from Pakistan to Arunachal Pradesh in forests, well-wooded areas

Habitat Hill forests and cultivation; descends much lower in winter

Adult of both sexes overall green, washed blue; bluish-grey head; blackish chin; wide stripe across lower cheeks; blue-green band around hindneck bordered with fine black line; base of tail green graduating to deep blue, tipped with bright yellow; red upper mandible and lower pale yellow; pale yellow eyes. Male has prominent maroon patch on inner median wing-coverts and long central tail feathers. Female lacks maroon patch, has central tail feathers. Juvenile has greyish-green face; dull green head; faint pale green stripe below cheeks to hindcrown; maroon wing-patch absent; short tail; orange bill; grey eye.

GREY-HEADED PARAKEET

Psittacula finschii Psittacidae

Size 33 cm

Voice Call includes steeply upturned, clear prolonged whistles

Range Resident of extreme NE Himalayas. S Assam Hills

Habitat Forests and open woodland; city gardens

Adult of both sexes overall yellowish-green; dark grey head; black chin; wide stripe across lower cheek narrowing to thin line around hindneck; small purplish-red patch on inner median wing-coverts; central tail feathers long (shorter in female); bluish-purple uppertail tipped with yellow or white. Female lacks maroon shoulder-patch of male. Immature has dark bill similar to Slaty-headed's; greyish-green face; faint pale green band below cheeks to hindcrown; wing-patch absent. Short tail, orange bill; orange-and-grey eye.

PLUM-HEADED PARAKEET

Psittacula cyanocephala Psittacidae

Size 36 cm

Voice Call includes loud, interrogative *tooi…tooi…* notes in fast flight; also other chattering notes

Range Subcontinent, south of the Himalayan foothills

Habitat Forests; orchards; cultivation in forest

Male has yellowish-green plumage; plum-red head washed purplish-blue on hindcrown; black chin strap; black and bluish-green collar; maroon-red wing shoulder-patch; dark red spot on inner median wing-coverts; white tips to central tail feathers distinctive. Female dull, greyer head; yellow collar; almost non-existent maroon shoulder-patch. In pairs, or small parties; arboreal, but descends into cultivation in forest clearings and outskirts; sometimes huge gatherings in cultivation; strong, darting flight over forest.

♀

BLOSSOM-HEADED PARAKEET

Psittacula roseata Psittacidae

Size 36 cm

Voice As Plum-headed's

Range Mainly hills of NE India and Bangladesh

Habitat Open forests

Male has rosy-pink cheeks, forehead and ear-coverts; pale purplish-blue nape and crown; black chin strap graduating to fine stripe around hindneck; dark reddish-brown spot on inner median wing-coverts. Central tail feathers blue-tipped with pale yellow; side tail feathers greenish-yellow, tipped pale yellow. Orangish-yellow upper mandible; dark grey lower mandible; pale yellow eye. Female has dull blue-grey head, dull yellowish-green collar and smaller shoulder spot. Juvenile has green head, shorter tail, pale yellow bill and grey eye. Gregarious and noisy.

♀

DERBYAN PARAKEET

Psittacula derbiana Psittacidae

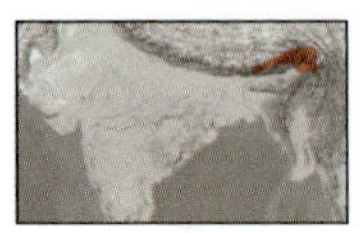

Size 46 cm

Voice Loud call, very nasal

Range Evidently common in border regions of NE Arunachal Pradesh

Habitat Little known; typically in small flocks. Seen in Mishmi Hills in September

Very large Tibetan parakeet with purple head and underparts; large bill; with black broad moustache. Male has red upper mandible; black in female. Juvenile duller, with mostly greyish head and duller, paler lore-line and moustache; some green feathers on face and some rusty-brown feathers below. In flight, blue wing-lining visible. Frequently visits nest-holes in tall trees.

♀

CHESTNUT-WINGED CUCKOO

Clamator coromandus Cuculidae

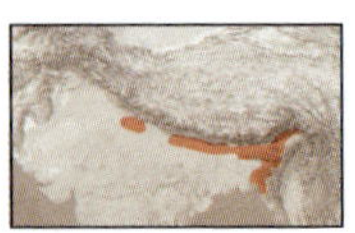

Size 45 cm

Voice Call a whistling *peep… peep* in breeding season. Also, hoarse screech

Range Scarce, local breeding summer visitor to N foothills

Habitat Forests; thick scrub

Slender, long-tailed cuckoo with chestnut wings, white collar and long, black, erect crest. Top of head and upperparts to tail of adult glossy metallic black, pale orange-brown throat to upper breast, breast and upper belly; white belly; blackish undertail-coverts; tail tipped white. Juvenile has dark brown head and upperparts, feathers edged paler, smaller crest; white underparts; rufous-edged wing-coverts and buff edge and tip of tail. Swift direct flight with rapid wingbeats.

LARGE HAWK CUCKOO

Hierococcyx sparverioides Cuculidae

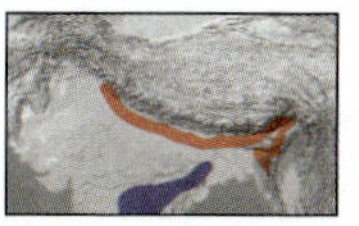

Size 38 cm

Voice Call a measured *kee… keeah…kee…keeah* usually without crescendo. Heard at night as well as day

Range Fairly common breeding summer visitor: Himalayas and hills of NE India. Winters sparsely in lowlands

Habitat Broadleaved evergreen forests

Large greyish-brown bird with rufescent subterminal bar to white-tipped tail; rufous-washed belly, barred brown-and-white; black chin; orange iris; pale yellow feet; bill black above and greenish-yellow below. Immature has chestnut-brown upperparts, barred with rufous; buff underparts with black streaks.

COMMON HAWK CUCKOO

Hierococcyx varius Cuculidae

Size 34 cm

Voice Famous call notes; interpreted as brain-fever, uttered untiringly in crescendo; also described as *pipeeha…pipeeha…*; very noisy in overcast weather

Range Subcontinent, south of the Himalayan foothills; uncommon, even during rains, in arid zones

Habitat Forests; open country; near habitation

Popularly known as the Brainfever bird; medium-sized cuckoo with ash-grey upperparts; dark bars on rufescent-tipped tail; dull white below, with pale ash-rufous on breast; barred below. Juvenile broadly-streaked dark below; pale rufous barrings on brown upperbody. Sexes alike. Solitary, rarely in pairs; strictly arboreal; noisy during May–September; silent after rains. Brood-parasite, laying eggs in nests of babblers.

juvenile

HODGSON'S HAWK CUCKOO

Hierococcyx fugax Cuculidae

Size 31 cm

Voice Call includes a series of paired, thin, sharp, high-pitched gee…*whiz*

Range Summer visitor: E Himalayas from E Nepal to Assam

Habitat Deciduous forests; winters in evergreen forests

Medium-sized slaty-grey cuckoo with barred tail and rufous breast with white streaks; black chin; white throat; yellow or red iris; black bill with yellow tip and base. Similar to Large Hawk, but smaller in size and distinguished by grey upperparts, whitish belly, grey head sides and lacks moustachial-stripe and white band on nape. Shy and difficult to locate, but may sing incessantly in breeding season.

INDIAN CUCKOO

Cuculus micropterus Cuculidae

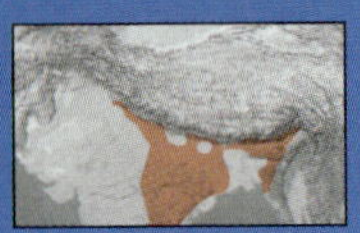

Size 33 cm

Voice Very distinct call; 4-noted mellow whistle, variously interpreted, *bo…ko…ta…ko or crossword…puzzle* best known

Range Subcontinent, south from the Himalayas to about 2,500 m, excepting drier and arid parts of NW India; absent in Pakistan

Habitat Forests; orchards

Medium-sized, solitary and shy bird. Slaty-brown above; greyer on head, throat and breast; whitish below, with broadly spaced black cross-bars; broad subterminal tail-band (characteristic of the non-hawk cuckoos of genus *Cuculus*); female often has rufous-brown wash on throat and breast; call notes most important identification clue. Sexes alike. Arboreal, not easy to see; overall appearance very hawk-like, but distinctly weaker-looking flight.

EURASIAN CUCKOO

Cuculus canorus Cuculidae

Size 33 cm

Voice Well-known, repetitive *cuc…koo.* Also, rapid bubbling, mainly by female

Range Common breeding summer visitor to N mountains. Scarce winter visitor elsewhere in lowlands

Habitat Woodlands and scrubs, where brood-parasites. Winters in wooded country and cultivation. Typically flies with wings held low and rather humped back

hepatic

Medium-sized grey bird. Adult male has bluish-grey upperparts and finely barred white belly with dark barring; bluish-grey head, throat and upper breast. Darker flight feathers and black tail bordered white; yellow iris and eye-rings. Female occurs in two morphs, one similar to male but with buff-brown breast, barred darker, buff coloured with dark barring; other more reddish-brown, intensely barred darker. Juvenile slaty-grey with hints of reddish-brown.

HIMALAYAN CUCKOO

Cuculus saturatus Cuculidae

Size 31 cm

Voice Call a distinctive, repetitive *po…po…po…po* in series of 4- to 8-notes. Often calls at night

Range Breeding summer visitor to N hills. Scarce winter visitor to lowlands

Habitat Hill forests

hepatic

Very similar to Eurasian, but smaller in size, and distinguished by darker back and more strongly barred underparts; plain vent and beige wash to undertail-coverts; yellow to brown iris and eye-rings. Female and juvenile occur as grey and rufous morphs, grey morph and rufous morph difficult to see except when calling from tree-tops. Flight and shape as Eurasian. Brood-parasites in warbler's nests.

LESSER CUCKOO

Cuculus poliocephalus Cuculidae

Size 25 cm

Voice Strong, cheerful song, rendered as pretty-*peel...lay...ka*

Range Breeds in the Himalayas from N Pakistan east to Arunachal Pradesh

Habitat Forests; well-wooded country

hepatic

Adult male has slaty-grey upperparts, pale slaty-blue head, neck, throat and upper breast; white lower breast and rest of underparts, boldly-barred black. Grey morph female similar to male, but has rufous wash on upper breast; hepatic morph has rufous upperparts with blackish barring except on rump, white underparts barred black, tail barred rufous and black with white tip. Juvenile has dark grey-brown upperparts with variable, narrow whitish to rufous barring and broadly barred underparts.

BANDED BAY CUCKOO

Cacomantis sonneratii Cuculidae

Size 24 cm

Voice Call a shrill whistle

Range From N Uttar Pradesh east to Assam and Bangladesh

Habitat Dense broadleaved forests in Nepal; lightly wooded country in India; edges of forests, patches of shifting cultivation and open forests in Sri Lanka

Small cuckoo with longish, curved bill. Upperparts rufous-brown, strongly barred, uniformly and regularly, dark brown. Adult male has broad white supercilium (cross-barred with black), which encircles brown ear-coverts; dark eye-stripe; whitish cheeks; white-tipped tail. Whitish underparts, washed pale buff from belly to flanks, finely and uniformly barred; central tail feathers barred and darker on each side of shaft. Juvenile similar to adult, but whiter on head and upper mantle; less barring on underparts.

PLAINTIVE CUCKOO

Cacomantis merulinus Cuculidae

Size 23 cm

Voice Mournful, rising 'play to *tee*' often in a trailed-off crescendo

Range Generally scarce breeding resident in NE India, most frequent in Bangladesh

Habitat Wooded country including parks and gardens

Small, palish cuckoo with grey upperparts, buff-grey chin and upper breast, rest of underparts warm orange. Pale grey head and throat; some rufous on wing-coverts and rump; black tail, tipped white. Grey morph similar to male but with whitish barring on belly. Hepatic female dark rufous, heavily barred above; throat, breast and tail uniform rufous; rest of underparts whitish, barred black. Calls actively in rapid restless flights; brood-parasites in warbler's nests.

ASIAN EMERALD CUCKOO

Chrysococcyx maculatus Cuculidae

Size 18 cm

Voice Call a loud *kee... kee...kee*; in flight, sharp *chweek*; whistle; trill

Range Uttarakhand east to Assam, Arunachal Pradesh and S Assam Hills

Habitat Primary broadleaved evergreen forests; secondary growth

♀

Tiny cuckoo with distinctive iridescent emerald green head, neck, breast and upperparts; white underparts barred prominently metallic green; orange orbital skin; black-tipped yellow bill; female similar to female Violet, but brighter rufous crown and upper mantle; glossy bronze-green wash on lower mantle and wings; rufous wash on face. Juvenile overall paler. Arboreal; mainly in canopy, venturing out occasionally to pursue insects.

VIOLET CUCKOO

Chrysococcyx xanthorhynchus Cuculidae

Size 17 cm

Voice Calls *che wick* in flight; shrill trilling

Range Assam; Arunachal Pradesh; S Assam Hills; Bangladesh

Habitat Broadleaved evergreen forests; secondary growth

Tiny, distinctive forest bird with iridescent dark purple head, upperparts and upper breast. White underparts strongly barred deep purple, bright orange bill; white-spotted dark undertail. Female similar to female Asian Emerald, but dark bronze-brown above and white underparts barred brown; rufous outer-tail feathers; dull orange-yellow bill. Female like female Asian Emerald, but dark bronze-brown above with green tinge, rufous outer tail feathers and orange-yellow bill with black tip. Juvenile is more rufous.

DRONGO CUCKOO

Surniculus lugubris Cuculidae

Size 23 cm

Voice Diagnostic; noisy during monsoon. Call a short whistled *pee…pee…pee…pee*

Range Hills of C and SW India. Summer visitor to the Himalayas, hills of NE India

Habitat Open forests; orchards; shade trees

Smallish, mainly glossy black cuckoo, similar to drongo but with smaller, slimmer, downcurved bill, long, black, square-cut tail, with only slight fork or notch; tail and vent white-barred, unlike those of true drongos; white thighs; sometimes, white nape spot; no white rictal spot of Black Drongo. Juvenile duller, white-spotted; quieter, shyer, more inconspicuous than the bolder and more active drongos; cuckoo-like flight; mostly arboreal; sometimes in lower growth or ground; sings from bare branches. The square-tailed and forked-tailed forms are sometimes considered to be separate species.

forked-tailed

square-tailed

ASIAN KOEL

Eudynamys scolopaceus Cuculidae

Size 43 cm

Voice Familiar call of Indian countryside. Very noisy between March and June, coinciding with breeding of crows; loud *kuoo…kuooo…* whistling calls in crescendo by male koel, first syllable longish; water-bubbling call of female

Range Subcontinent, upto about 1,800 m in the outer Himalayas; uncommon in drier areas

Habitat Light forests; orchards; city parks; cultivation; open areas

Large cuckoo with metallic, bluish-greenish black plumage; greenish beak and crimson eyes. Female dark brown, thickly-spotted and barred white; whitish below, dark-spotted on throat, barred below. Solitary, or in pairs; arboreal; mostly silent between July and February; fast flight.

GREEN-BILLED MALKOHA

Rhopodytes tristis Cuculidae

Size 51 cm

Voice Rather silent, sometimes croaks quietly

Range Scarce breeding resident: N foothills, NE India, Eastern Ghats

Habitat Forests; scrub undergrowth

Large, long-tailed bird with pale green, robust bill. Overall greenish-grey with paler head and underparts; grey underparts, darker on breast; glossy green, graduated tail, black with white feather-tips; red facial skin; black bristles around gape. Juvenile duller than adult with shorter retrices and narrower white tail-tip. Narrow white border surrounding red orbital skin. Holds tail straight when running through tangled vegetation.

LESSER COUCAL

Centropus bengalensis Centropodidae

Size 33 cm

Voice Call a deep, rapid *oop... oop...oop* varying in tone. Also *kutook...kutook* and variants

Range Local breeding resident and summer visitor: N foothills from Uttarakhand east to Myanmar border, throughout NE India, south to Odisha and including Bangladesh. Also SW India

Habitat Grasslands; open country

Small coucal with short decurved beak. Breeding adult glossy bluish-black. Bright buff shaft streaks on scapulars and lesser wing-coverts; wings mottled dark brown and rufous. Non-breeding adult has dark brown head and mantle, dark brown rump barred rufous; pale buff throat and breast streaked darker. Juvenile similar to non-breeding adult, but has dark and light buff streaking on head and upperparts. Usually solitary, or in pairs. Feeds mainly on grasshoppers.

juvenile

GREATER COUCAL

Centropus sinensis Centropodidae

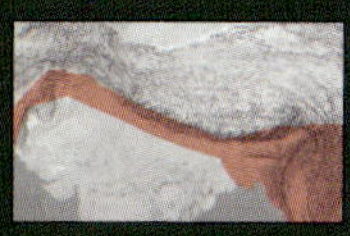

Size 50 cm

Voice Loud and resonant *coop... coop...coop...* call familiar; occasionally a squeaky call

Range Subcontinent, from outer Himalayas to about 2,000 m

Habitat Forests; scrubs; cultivation; gardens; derelict patches; vicinity of habitation

Beautiful terrestrial bird with glossy bluish-black plumage; chestnut wings; blackish, glossy dark green, long, graduated tail; strong, heavy, darkish bill; deep red eyes; dark grey feet. Female somewhat larger than male. Sexes alike. Solitary, or in pairs; moves amidst dense growth, fanning and flicking tail often; clambers up into trees, but poor flier, lazily flying short distances.

BARN OWL

Tyto alba Tytonidae

Size 35 cm

Voice Call a long-drawn, wild shriek; variety of snoring, hissing notes

Range Almost all over India, south of the Himalayan foothills

Habitat Grasslands; cultivation; human habitation; town-centres

Dull golden-buff above, finely speckled black-and-white; white below, often with fine, dark spots; heart-shaped, white facial disc with brown edge; brownish wash between lower edge of eyes and base of pale pink bill. Sexes alike. Solitary, or in pairs; nocturnal, but sometimes hunts during day; normally rests during day, mostly in tree-cavity, dense creepers or some dark loft; perches upright; flies silently, mostly under 4 m from ground; pounces on prey.

juvenile

EASTERN GRASS OWL

Tyto longimembris Tytonidae

Size 36 cm

Voice Hissing scream, similar to that of Barn, though tends to be more silent than Barn

Range Resident; NE and SW India, and S Nepal

Habitat Tall grasslands

Similar to Barn in size but distinguished by darker eyes and whitish face and underparts. Adult male has white facial disc, while female has more beige facial disc. Dark brown upperparts mottled with fine white and ochre spots; creamy-white underparts blotched darker; long wings; three dark bars on primaries; shortish tail has three or four bars. Feathered legs with blackish-brown claws and yellowish-grey toes. Female similar, but slightly larger. Mainly nocturnal, but occasionally seen during day; ground bird; hides in grass. Breeds colonially; several birds hunt in same area.

ORIENTAL BAY OWL

Phodilus badius Tytonidae

Size 29 cm

Voice Calls include a series of eerie, upward-inflected whistles

Range Resident; NE India

Habitat Dense evergreen broadleaved forests

Sri Lanka Bay Owl

Medium-sized owl with whitish-vinaceous, elongated facial disc, short, rounded wings and short tail. Pale V-shaped, brownish-grey forehead and dark brown vertical eye-patches. Long legs feathered to feet. Large dark eyes; white necklace; rich chestnut and buff upperparts spotted and barred with black. Pale yellow-brown underparts, speckled with blackish-brown and buff. Chestnut tail has few narrow bars. Nocturnal bird, roosts in holes and hollows in tree trunks. The similar Sri Lanka Bay Owl *P. b. assimilis* is found in SW India and Sri Lanka.

MOUNTAIN SCOPS OWL

Otus spilocephalus Tytonidae

juvenile

Size 27 cm

Voice Song an eerie, gliding whistle *whi...whoo...ee...yo*

Range The Himalayas, NE and Bangladesh

Habitat Dense forests; mangrove edges

Seen in many morphs and individually variable. Adult has reddish-brown facial disc with pale base and dark-tipped bristles; yellow eyes; blackish cheeks and ear-coverts; paler head sides and forehead. Dark tawny or rufous brown upperparts, darkly vermiculated. Whitish underparts, barred rufous with small triangular paired, black-and-white spots. Like other scops owls, completely nocturnal and difficult to spot.

COLLARED SCOPS OWL

Otus b lettia Strigidae

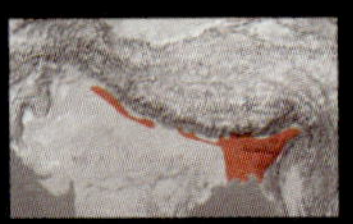

Size 23 cm

Voice Call fluty and questioning. Calls throughout the night

Range Resident of the Himalayas, NE India

Habitat Forests; cultivation; orchards; trees in vicinity of habitation

Small owl with buff and brown 'imitation face' on nape. Small ear tufts and upright posture. Greyish-brown above; buffy nuchal-collar diagnostic; buffy-white underbody, streaked and mottled dark. Sexes alike. Solitary, or in pairs; remains motionless during day in thick, leafy branches or at junctions of stems and branches; very difficult to spot; flies around dusk.

ORIENTAL SCOPS OWL

Otus sunia Strigidae

Size 19 cm

Voice Distinctive call of slowly repeated *wug-chug-chug*

Range Locally common breeding resident in plains and lower hills mainly in north from N Pakistan, east to Myanmar border, Bangladesh, Sri Lanka, Western Ghats and S peninsular India

Habitat Forests; groves; orchards

Small mottled brown owl with short ear tufts. Breast heavily streaked with black; orange-yellow iris; greyish bill and feet. Cryptic, mottled plumage in three morphs: rufous (shown), brown and grey. Latter two not readily separable from rarer Eurasian *O. Scops* and call only reliable identification factor. Well-streaked crown and underparts distinguish it from Mountain and Pallid. Prominent white scapular lines. Large vertical ear tufts often suppressed. Strictly nocturnal, roosts in day close to trunks in thickly-foliaged trees. Hunts in smaller trees on forest edge, clearings and secondary growth. Nests in holes.

rufous morph

EURASIAN EAGLE OWL

Bubo bubo Strigidae

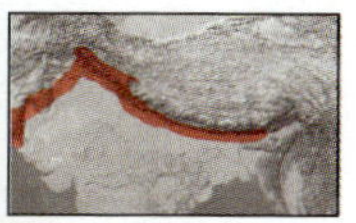

Size 60 cm

Voice Call a deep, booming *bu… boo…*; snapping calls at nest

Range Northern hills of Pakistan and Himalayas, from about 1,500 m

Habitat Ravines; cliffsides; riversides; scrubs; open country

Large owl with conspicuous ear tufts and heavily feathered, powerful talons; tawny-buff facial disc, mottled blackish-brown; blackish bill; greyish-olive cere; bright orange-red to golden-yellow eyes; white chin and throat, continuing down to centre upper breast. Brownish-black and tawny-buff upperparts; tawny-buff underparts except for chin, throat finely-barred.

SPOT-BELLIED EAGLE OWL

Bubo nipalensis Strigidae

Size 63 cm

Voice Low, blood-curdling moan and scream

Range Uttarakhand eastwards, throughout NE Indian region; also in Western Ghats and Sri Lanka

Habitat Dense broadleaved evergreen forests

Large, dramatic-looking bird of prey. Pallid, overall stark, greyish-brown with prominent horizontally-held ear tufts; characteristic dark heart or chevron-shaped markings on white underparts diagnostic; dark brown primaries striped lighter; heavily-barred secondaries; plain white facial discs; white supercilium; large, pale yellow bill, dark brown eyes. Juvenile overall whiter with distinctive crown and mantle. Nocturnal; roosts by day in thickly-forested areas; hunts deep in forests, but sometimes ventures to edges at dusk; formidable strength allows to take on large prey.

juvenile

BROWN FISH OWL

Ketupa zeylonensis Strigidae

Size 56 cm

Voice Call a deep *whom...whom*. Also, an undulating *cur...ree*

Range Scarce breeding resident throughout lowlands

Habitat Well-wooded areas with water, including village groves near fish-rich ponds

Large owl with flat-head and outward-facing ear tufts; tawny ill-defined facial disc; conspicuous white patch on throat and foreneck. Dark rufous-brown upperparts, heavily streaked darker; paler underparts with dark streaking; blackish-brown back and mantle with buff margins and pale spots near tips. Dark brown primaries and secondaries banded with white or fulvous; very short tail with white tips and three to four buff-white bands; yellow iris; greyish-black bill. Sexes alike. Mainly nocturnal, roosting in leafy trees. Hunts fish, crabs and frogs.

TAWNY FISH OWL

Ketupa flavipes Strigidae

Size 61 cm

Voice Call a low, resonant *whoo... hoo; buh...huh...woo;* cat-like mewing

Range Uttarakhand eastwards to NE India

Habitat Primary broadleaved tropical forests near water; riverbanks, streams, pools; deep, well-wooded gorges

Similar to Buffy, but more unmarked. Rufous-brown with prominent flattened ear tufts, smallish facial disc; rich tawny plumage; white patch on front of neck, black bill; short white supercilium; heavy black and tawny mottling, streaking on upperparts; broad black streaking below; generally in pairs; partly diurnal; roosts by day in dense foliage trees, earthen banks; actively hunts by dusk; will hunt and fish in daylight, in breeding season.

BUFFY FISH OWL

Ketupa ketupu Strigidae

Size 50 cm

Voice Call a monotonous *bup...bup...bup...bup... bup...bup...bup*

Range NE India; Bangladesh

Habitat Forested streams in plains and mangroves

Medium to large owl with prominent, outward-facing ear tufts. Rich brown upperparts, more blackish on back and mantle. Dark brown primaries and secondaries with whitish bands; dark brown tail feathers tipped and banded whitish. White forehead and eyebrows; yellow eyes and black-lined eyelids; blackish-grey bill; similar to Tawny, but much smaller and with finer streaking on underparts. Distinguished from Brown by white forehead, more rufous-orange upperparts with thicker and more prominent black streaking, orange-buff underparts with more clearly defined black streaking on breast, and lack of black cross-barring on feathers of underparts.

BROWN WOOD OWL

Strix leptogrammica Strigidae

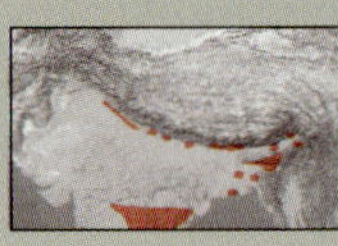

Size 47-53 cm

Voice Calls include *hoo... hoohoohoo...(hoo)* and loud eerie scream

Range The Himalayas, NE India, Eastern and Western Ghats, Bangladesh and Sri Lanka

Habitat Dense broadleaved subtropical or temperate forests

Medium-sized owl with warm-brown plumage; no ear tufts; fulvous or rufous-brown facial disc with narrow but distinct black rim. The Himalayan *S.l. newarensis* has dark brown face, with prominent white eyebrows, and striking white band across foreneck. Underparts greyish-white, heavily barred with brown.

juvenile

TAWNY OWL

Strix aluco Strigidae

Tawny Owl

Himalayan Wood Owl

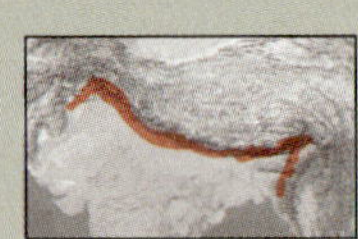

Size 46 cm

Voice Calls include wavering *tu...who...oo* and sharp *ker wik*. Sometimes, combined to sound like *tu... wit...to woo*

Range Fairly common breeding resident: N, NE mountains

Habitat Mountain broadleaved, coniferous forests

Now split into Himalayan Wood Owl by some authorities, which is similar to Tawny, but distinguished by unstreaked upperparts, white patch on throat and arrow-shaped spotting on breast. Overall colouration ranges from greyish to rufous-brown. Dark streaking on upper and underparts and well-barred wings and tail. Whitish scapular lines and V-mark on forehead. Large, pale dark-rimmed facial disc. Nocturnal, roosts high and close to tree trunk. Both forms occur in the region.

COLLARED OWLET

Glaucidium brodiei Strigidae

Size 17 cm

Voice Noisy when breeding. Call a liquid *poop...po...poop...poop*

Range Locally common breeding resident: N mountains from N Pakistan, east to Myanmar border. Moves lower down in winter

Habitat Thick forests at lower-levels

Smallest owl in Asia; short-tailed, dark, barred owlet with distinctive 'face' marks on hindneck; rufous or greyish upperparts; dark brown barring on mantle, wings, tail and on sides of upper breast; relatively large, rounded head with tiny buffy spots and bright yellow eyes; white underparts have brown bar across throat and rufous-brown 'droplet'-shaped spots along sides. Sexes alike.

ASIAN BARRED OWLET

Glaucidium cuculoides Strigidae

Size 23 cm

Voice Call a bubbling *wowowowowowo* which gets deeper and louder. Also, abrupt *kao...kuk*

Range Locally common breeding resident in N hills

Habitat Hill forests

rufescens

Smallish, heavily-barred owl with bright lemon yellow eyes; white eyebrows; white moustache; yellowish-green bill; greyish-green cere. Upperparts overall olive-brown; nape and head finely speckled pale buff; faintly barred mantle. Underparts plainer with indistinct markings; white patch on throat; whitish barring on dark brown breast. Yellow feet. Sexes alike. Eastern race more rufous. Hunts during day.

cuculoides

JUNGLE OWLET

Glaucidium radiatum Strigidae

Size 20 cm

Voice Noisy; musical *kuo…kak…kuo…kak…* call-notes, rising in crescendo for few seconds only to end abruptly, other pleasant bubbling notes

Range All over India, from about 2,000 m in the Himalayas; probably absent in extreme NE states

Habitat Forests; partial to teak and bamboo mixed forests

radiatum

malabaricum

Darkish-brown above, barred rufous and white; flight-feathers barred rufous and black; white moustachial stripe, centre of breast and abdomen; remainder of underbody barred-dark rufous-brown-and-white. Sexes alike. Solitary, or in pairs and sometimes in small groups; crepuscular, but sometimes also active and noisy by day; otherwise spends day in leafy branch; flies short distance when disturbed.

LITTLE OWL

Athene noctua Strigidae

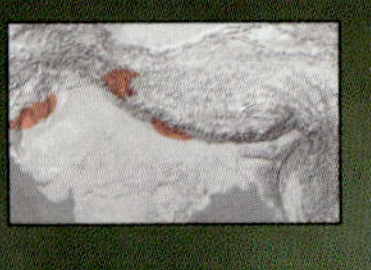

Size 23 cm

Voice Calls include repeated *kee…u* and low bark

Range Scarce and very local breeding resident in NW mountains east to Nepal

Habitat Rocky desert areas with cliffs and ruins

Diminutive, brown owl with flat crown and plump-round body. Two subspecies: western (east to Ladakh); smaller, paler Ludlow's Owl *A. n. ludlowi*. Eastern (from Ladakh eastwards); darker Hutton's Owl *A.n. bactriana*. Both have extensive white marking on head. Underparts have large white spots and blotches, breast has larger white patches. Wings and tail broadly barred. White collar and eyebrows and pale facial disc. Juvenile paler and more uniformly patterned.

SPOTTED OWLET

Athene brama Strigidae

Size 21 cm

Voice Assortment of scolding and cackling notes, screeches and chuckles

Range Throughout the region, upto about 1,800 m in outer Himalayas

Habitat Open forests; orchards; cultivation; vicinity of habitation

Small, stocky owlet with greyish-brown upperparts, spotted white; no ear tufts; yellowish eyes; broken whitish-buff nuchal-collar. Juvenile more thickly-marked white; darkish streaks below breast. Sexes alike. In pairs, or small parties; roosts during day in leafy branches, tree cavities or cavities in walls; active in some localities during daytime; when disturbed flies to nearby tree or branch and bobs and stares at intruder.

BROWN HAWK OWL

Ninox scutulata Strigidae

Size 32 cm

Voice Call includes an extended, liquid *oowup... oowup...oowup*

Range Locally common breeding resident mainly in lower hills from Uttarakhand east to Myanmar border, Bangladesh, peninsular India and Sri Lanka

Habitat Well-wooded country, usually near water

Slender, dark owl. Dark brown facial disc has white radial streaks; chocolate-brown crown and nape with ochre streaks; mantle and wing-coverts plain chocolate-brown; some white on back and wings; underparts have intense, drop-shaped streaks, becoming chevron-shaped towards flanks; long, grey-banded tail with whitish tip; no ear tufts; yellow eyes; feathered legs. Andaman and Nicobar race all dark. Sexes alike, male larger than female. Hunts singly, or in pairs, insects, birds and other animals from favoured perch. Hawk-like flight with flaps and long glides. Crepuscular or nocturnal. Roosts during day in thick canopy.

LONG-EARED OWL

Asio otus Strigidae

Size 35-37 cm

Voice Territorial call of male a long drawn, subdued *os* or *flu*

Range Winter visitor to Pakistan and NW India

Habitat On passage, in winter frequents stunted trees and poplar plantations

Medium-sized owl with distinct, erect ear tufts that sit in middle of forehead. Pale ochre-brown facial disc bordered black; short creamy-white eyebrows. Upperparts ochre-brown, finely speckled darker; crown finely mottled with dark grey; hindneck and nape have grey shaft streaks; ochre-brown tail is washed grey with seven or eight dark, narrow bands. Underparts pale ochre-brown, more streaked towards upper breast, graduating to cross-bars near belly. Noiseless, gliding flight.

HODGSON'S FROGMOUTH

Batrachostomus hodgsoni Batrachostomidae

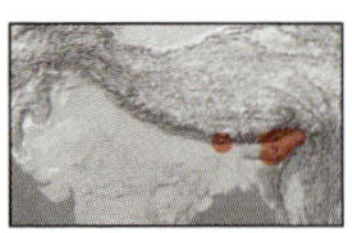

Size 26 cm

Voice Calls include slightly trilled whistles; *wheeow*; *whurree*; soft *gwaa* notes

Range Pockets in E Bhutan and Arunachal Pradesh

Habitat Primary subtropical broadleaved evergreen forests; pine

Medium-sized frogmouth with large head; wide gape; very broad, hooked bill; long facial bristles; slit-like nostrils, and forward-facing eyes. Male mottled grey-rufous with washed rufous-buff, with white collar made up of large spots; large white spots on scapulars; blackish crown. Rufous underparts roughly barred with black-and-white. Female more rufous with white-spotted collar, scapulars, breast; nocturnal. Assumes alarm posture when disturbed; head and neck stretched and bill pointing upwards and freezing.

GREAT-EARED NIGHTJAR

Eurostopodus macrotis Caprimulgidae

Size 40-41cm

Voice Call a clear, wailing *pee…wheeeu*

Range Mainly NE India, Bangladesh and Western Ghats

Habitat Tropical and subtropical broadleaved moist forests; secondary growth

Very large and vividly coloured nightjar. At rest, shows prominent ear tufts, and generally more richly-marked with golden buff and rufous than other nightjars.

JUNGLE NIGHTJAR

Caprimulgus indicus Caprimulgidae

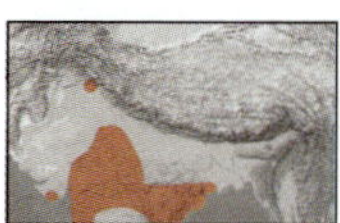

Size 30 cm

Voice Somewhat whistling *chuckoo…chuckoo*, upto seven minutes at a stretch, with pauses in-between; quick-repeated, mellow *tuck…tuck…tuck* call, eight to 50 at a stretch; occasionally pleasant *uk…kukrooo…*; vocal between dusk and dawn

Range Resident and summer visitor from E Rajasthan to Bihar and Odisha, W peninsula

Habitat Forest clearings; broken scrubby ravines

Large greyish-brown nightjar. Upperparts grey-brown streaked darker; white tip to tail in male; cream sub-moustachial stripe; large white patch on throat-sides; brownish bill, legs and feet; dark brown iris. Underparts also grey-brown, barred darker and becoming more buff towards belly and flanks; calls highly diagnostic. Flies around dusk, hawking insects in zigzag flight; settles on cart tracks and roads.

GREY NIGHTJAR

Caprimulgus i jotaka Caprimulgidae

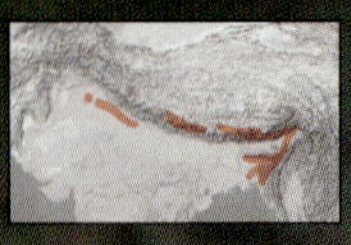

Size 32 cm

Voice Song a *kowrr…kowrr…kowrr;* guttural *tuk…tuk*

Range Himalayas and NE India

Habitat Forest clearings

Medium-sized nightjar with long pointed tail; short legs; short bill with rectal bristles larger than Sykes's, with longer wings and tail. Small dark arrowhead-shaped markings on crown, and irregular buff spotting on nape forms indistinct collar. Roosts on the tree along length of branch.

LARGE-TAILED NIGHTJAR

Caprimulgus macrurus Caprimulgidae

Size 30 cm

Voice Call a resounding, rather slow *chunk...chunk...chunk*

Range Fairly common resident along Gangetic Plains and throughout NE India, south to Andhra Pradesh

Habitat Lowland forests; woodlands

Large, long and broad-tailed nightjar. Grey-brown upperparts streaked darker; more broadly on crown; indistinct buff collar; bright buff-edged black scapular lines; white moustache and breast-patch; small bill. Male has broad white (female buff) apical tips to tail and primary patches. Roosts on ground well-camouflaged by dead leaves. Hunts flying insects at night. Erratic, stiff-winged flight.

HIMALAYAN SWIFTLET

Collocalia brevirostris Apodidae

Size 14 cm

Voice Call a low, rattling and twittering *chit...chit* at roost

Range The Himalayas; NE India

Habitat Similar to Indian's

Large swiftlet with very obvious forked-tail and looks boomerang-shaped in flight with back-swept wings. Slightly glossed upperparts. Underparts paler grey-brown; distinct pale grey rump-band; rounded wings; lightly feathered legs; small, rounded beak with bristles; short legs let the bird cling to vertical surfaces. Sexes similar. Juvenile has indistinct rump-band. Distinguished from Edible-nest by larger size, more forked-tail, less distinct rump-band. Larger than Indian. Roosts in caves; forages over forest.

WHITE-RUMPED SPINETAIL

Zoonavena sylvatica Apodidae

Size 11 cm

Voice Call a twittering *chick…chick*, uttered on wing

Range The Himalayas from N Uttar Pradesh, east to Sikkim

Habitat Broadleaved evergreen and moist deciduous forests

Small, stocky, broad-winged needletail. Has bulging secondaries, with wings pinched in at base and pointed at tip. Typically, flight action fast with rapid wingbeats, and banking from side-to-side, interspersed with short glides on slightly bowed wings. Upperparts mainly blue-black with contrasting white rump; throat and breast grey-brown, merging into whitish lower belly and undertail-coverts. From below, long white undertail-coverts contrast with black of sides and tip of undertail. 'Spines' at tip of tail visible at close range.

WHITE-THROATED NEEDLETAIL

Hirundapus caudacutus Apodidae

Size 20 cm

Voice Utters feeble, rapid metallic chittering, audible only at close range

Range Summer visitor; the Himalayas and NE India

Habitat Often seen over ridges, cliffs, forest, upland grasslands and river valleys

Like other needletails, strong flier combining very strong flapping with swooping, gliding and soaring, often at very high speeds. Like other species has pale 'saddle' on upperparts, and dramatic white 'horseshoe' crescent at rear-end. Distinguished from Silver-backed and Brown-backed by clearly demarcated white throat, and white inner webs to tertials (showing as white patch, although may be obscured). Additional differences from Brown-backed include smaller size, dark lores, and more contrasting pale 'saddle'. Also shows shorter, square-ended tail projection beyond white undertail-coverts, and tail 'spines' less distinct. Juvenile has less clear-cut white throat (more similar to Silver-backed); has black streaking and spotting on white of hind flanks, and dark fringes to white undertail-coverts. Usually occurs solitary, or in loose parties. Roosts colonially on cliffs and trees.

BROWN-BACKED NEEDLETAIL

Hirundapus giganteus Apodidae

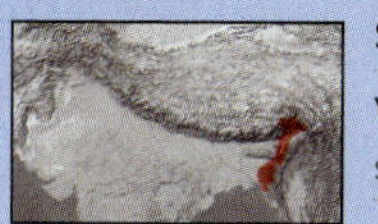

Size 23 cm

Voice Rather quiet. Calls include various soft squeaks and trills

Range Scarce breeding resident of Western Ghats, Sri Lanka and NE India

Habitat Forested areas

Large, dark, extremely fast-flying swift with white vent crescent and pointed tail. All sooty-brown with paler back, distinct white vent extending as crescent up the flanks. Needles in tail feathers visible and long enough to form pointed tail. Flapping of wings often audible in low flight. Roosts and breeds in large hollow trees. Flight exceptionally powerful and flexible; quite difficult to follow with binoculars. Hunts aerial insects low over forest in loose parties.

ASIAN PALM SWIFT

Cypsiurus balasiensis Apodidae

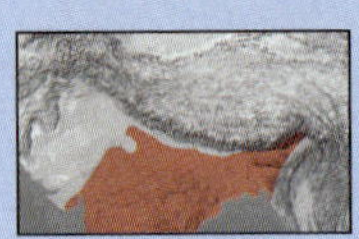

Size 13 cm

Voice Call a 3-note shrill scream, uttered very fast and always on wing

Range All over peninsular India, south of the Himalayan foothills (except NW); also in NE hill states

Habitat Open country, cultivation; this bird's life revolves around palms

Sooty-brown plumage; typical swift wings, long and sickle-like; deeply forked-tail distinctive, specially in flight. Sociable; small parties in open, palm-dotted country; strong in flight, and uttering lively screaming notes on wing; hawks insects all day, occasionally rising very high; roosts on underside of palm frond (leaf).

ALPINE SWIFT

Tachymarptis melba Apodidae

Size 23 cm

Voice Calls include shrill *chrrrr… chee…chee…* screams in fast flight; twittering notes at roost sites

Range All over India, from about 2,500 m in the Himalayas; uncommon over N Indian plains

Habitat Hill country; cliffsides

Very long, sickle-shaped, pointed wings; dark sooty-brown above; white underbody; broad, brown band across breast diagnostic in flight; dark undertail-coverts. Loose 'parties' dashing erratically at high speed in skies; extremely strong flier; seen high in skies around dusk, many birds wheeling and tumbling, their shrill screams rending the air; drinks at ponds and puddles by skimming over water surface. Sexes alike.

COMMON SWIFT

Apus apus Apodidae

Size 17 cm

Voice Call a high-pitched scream *screee...screee...screee*

Range Summer visitor to Balochistan, Pakistan, and the Himalayas from N Pakistan east to Nepal; Maldives

Habitat Chiefly in mountains, but can occur fleetingly over any habitat

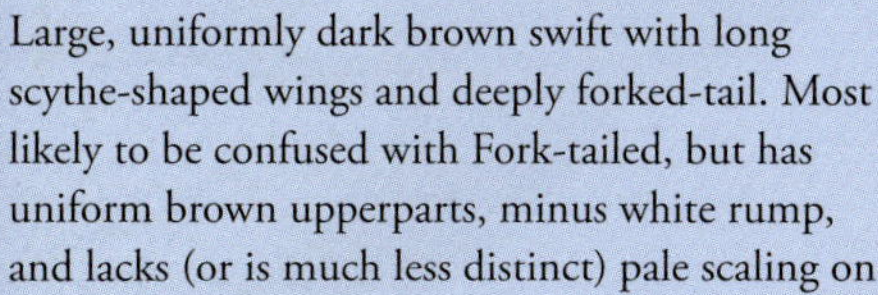

Large, uniformly dark brown swift with long scythe-shaped wings and deeply forked-tail. Most likely to be confused with Fork-tailed, but has uniform brown upperparts, minus white rump, and lacks (or is much less distinct) pale scaling on underparts. Distinguished from the very similar Pallid and Dark-rumped. Juvenile has whiter forehead and more extensive white throat, and extensive pale scaling on underparts (although not so prominent as on Fork-tailed).

PALLID SWIFT

Apus pallidus Apodidae

Size 17 cm

Voice Call a disyllabic *cheeu...eet* or *chumic*

Range Winter visitor to coastal regions; status unknown, but probably frequent in extreme W

Habitat Similar to those of Alpine

Large, uniformly grey-brown swift, very similar in shape and appearance to Common, and with similar flight, but has slower wingbeats than latter. Paler grey-brown in colouration than Common, appearing almost pale in bright light, with more extensive pale throat and forehead, which contrasts with dark eye-patch. Has dark outer primaries and leading edge to wing, contrasting on both upperside and underside with rest of wing, which is pale. Also, has pale fringes to feathers of underparts, giving scaly appearance.

SALIM ALI'S SWIFT

Apus (pacificus) salimali Apodidae

Very similar to Fork-tailed Swift, with which it is usually considered conspecific. Breeds from the eastern Tibetan plateau eastwards, but wintering range unknown; may occur in NE as breeder or migrant. Larger than Fork-tailed with a deeper tail-fork and a small white throat-patch.

FORK-TAILED SWIFT

Apus pacificus Apodidae

Size 15 cm

Voice Call a hard *shkree* in flight

Range Locally common breeding summer visitor to N mountains. Wintering areas unknown

Habitat Open skies

Medium-sized, blackish, long-winged and fork-tailed swift with narrow white rump-band, its most striking feature. Blackish-brown with small white throat-patch. Deep and obvious tail-fork; sickle-shaped wings. Best chance of seeing the bird when flying low before weather front or passing thunderstorm. Very fast, lucid flight without fluttering, distinguishes it from House Martin. High aerial feeder (often out of sight) in loose flocks or singly with other aerial feeders.

DARK-RUMPED SWIFT

Apus acuticauda Apodidae

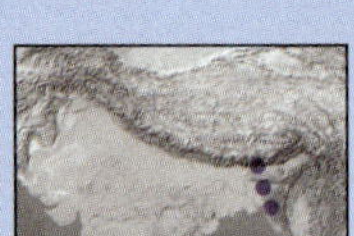

Size 17 cm

Voice Very high-pitched call uttered by flocking birds in vicinity of breeding cliffs

Range Resident, endemic to the subcontinent

Habitat Rocky cliffs, gorges

All-dark swift, similar to Fork-tailed. Distinguished from that species by all-dark rump, and lack of clearly-defined white throat. Greyish-white throat, with dark streaking, patterning merging with rest of underparts. Does not appear as slim and long-winged as Fork-tailed; sharper tail-fork, with narrower and more pointed outer-tail feathers. Very similar in shape to Common.

LITTLE SWIFT

Apus affinis Apodidae

Size 15 cm

Voice Musical squeals on wing; very vocal at sunset, but also through the day

Range Throughout the region, upto about 2,400 m in the Himalayas

Habitat Human habitation; cliffs; ruins

Overall dark swift with white rump and throat distinctive; short, square tail. Highly gregarious; on wing during day, hawking insects, flying over human habitation, cliffs and ruins; strong flier, exhibiting great mastery and control in fast-wheeling flight; frequently utters squealing notes on wing; retires to safety of nest colonies in overcast weather.

CRESTED TREESWIFT

Hemiprocne coronata Hemiprocnidae

Size 23 cm

Voice Call a parrot-like *kea*... *kea*...; double-noted faint scream

Range Subcontinent, south of the Himalayan foothills; absent in arid parts of NW India

Habitat Open, deciduous forests

Male bluish-grey above, with faint greenish wash; chestnut sides of face and throat; ash-grey breast, whiter below. Female similar to male, but lacks chestnut on head. Backward-curving crest and long, deeply forked-tail diagnostic. In pairs or small, scattered parties; flies during day, hawking insects; has favourite foraging areas; flight graceful, not as fast as other swifts, but displays typical swift mastery; calls from perch and in flight; unlike other swifts, perches on bare, higher branches; drinks in flight from surfaces of forest pools.

RED-HEADED TROGON

Harpactes erythrocephalus Trogonidae

Size 35 cm

Voice Call includes a scaled sequence of *chaup...chaup... chaup* notes

Range Scarce breeding resident in NE India including parts of Nepal and Bangladesh

Habitat Dense broadleaved forests

Brilliantly-coloured bird with long, square-ended tail. Head and neck bright crimson, white crescent-shaped breast-band; underparts more pinkish. Golden-orange back; dark grey wings and black closely barred with white. Tail edged with black with slim white outer borders; broad bill; weak legs. Female has ruddy-brown head and breast. Hawks insects. Nests in tree cavities or termite mounds. Shy but inquisitive. Habits as Malabar Trogon. Equally difficult to see.

WARD'S TROGON

Harpactes wardi Trogonidae

Size 38 cm

Voice Call includes dull, rapid rising, then dropping notes *klew... klew...klew*

Range E Bhutan and Arunachal Pradesh

Habitat Dense broadleaved evergreen montane forests; bamboos

♀

Large, vividly-coloured trogon. Male has deep pink forehead and supercilium; pale blue orbital skin; slaty-grey hindneck, maroon upper breast; rest of underparts pinkish-red; short, broad, pink beak, and long, broad pink tail; upperparts, head and upper breast maroon. Female has olive-brown head; bright yellow forehead; and pale yellow underparts. Can sit still for long periods; prefers lower or middle forest storeys. Solitary, or in pairs; agile in hawking insects.

INDIAN ROLLER

Coracias benghalensis Coraciidae

Size 31 cm

Voice Usually silent; occasionally harsh *khak...kak...kak...* notes; exuberant screeching notes and shrieks during courtship display, diving, and screaming wildly

Range Almost entire subcontinent, south of outer Himalayas, where found upto about 1,500 m

Habitat Open country; cultivation; orchards; light forests

affinis

Pale greenish-brown above; pinkish-brown breast; deep blue tail has light blue subterminal band; in flight, bright blue wings and tail, with Cambridge-blue bands distinctive. Sexes alike. Solitary, or in pairs; perches on overhead wires, bare branches, earthen mounds and small bush-tops; either glides and drops on prey or pounces suddenly; batters prey against perch. Elaborate courtship display, performs startling aerobatics including a series of 'rolls'.

DOLLARBIRD

Eurystomus orientalis Coraciidae

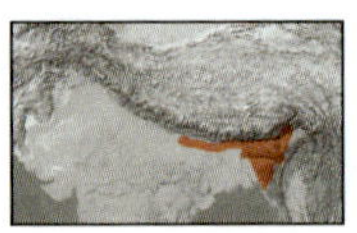

Size 31 cm

Voice Call a rasping *drak...drak*

Range Scarce breeding resident, partial migrant to NE India, Western Ghats

Habitat Forest edges and clearings, also nearby cultivation

Dark greenish-brown upperparts, washed bluish-green on back and wings. Brown breast; throat and undertail glossy blue; silvery-blue 'coin' on primaries, visible in flight; pale belly and undertail-coverts; stout red bill with black tip; red legs and eye-rings. Perches high in trees on bare branches from where it launches itself to catch large-flying insects. Crepuscular and sociable, groups often hunt after dusk. Nests in tree holes.

STORK-BILLED KINGFISHER

Pelargopsis capensis Halcyonidae

Size 38 cm

Voice Noisy. Call a *kee...kee...kee*, repeated many times

Range Subcontinent, except drier parts of NW India

Habitat Canals, streams, coastal backwaters in well-wooded country

capensis

Large kingfisher with blue-green back, blue wings and blue tail. Enormous red bill diagnostic; red legs. Dark grey-brown head with yellowish and blue collar on back of neck. Brownish-yellow underparts. Sexes alike. Solitary, more heard than seen. Does not normally hover. Laboured flight.

intermedia

RUDDY KINGFISHER

Halcyon coromanda Halcyonidae

Size 25 cm

Voice Call a descending and high-pitched *tititititititi*

Range E Himalayan foothills, NE India, Bangladesh

Habitat Pools and streams in dense broadleaved tropical and subtropical evergreen forests; also mangrove swamps

Overall orange-rufous bird with large coral-red bill; rufous-orange upperparts washed violet, and lighter rufous underparts; bluish-white rump, conspicuous in flight. Juvenile has darker and more brown upperparts, bluer rump, faint blackish barring on rufous underparts, and blackish bill. Solitary, or in pairs. Secretive; more heard than seen; perches in understorey dropping to capture prey.

WHITE-THROATED KINGFISHER

Halcyon smyrnensis Halcyonidae

Size 28 cm

Voice Noisy, loud, crackling laugh, often audible over crowded urban areas; song a longish, quivering whistle, sounding *kilililili*... characteristic feature of hot season, in breeding; fascinating courtship display

Range Subcontinent, south of outer Himalayas

Habitat Forests, cultivation, lakes, riversides; also coastal mangroves and estuaries

Chestnut-brown head, neck and underbody below breast; bright turquoise-blue above, often with greenish tinge; black flight feathers with white wing-patch visible in flight; white chin, throat and breast distinctive; coral-red beak and legs. Sexes alike. Solitary, or scattered pairs atop overhead wires, poles and tree-tops; frequently found far from water; drops on to ground to pick up prey.

ORIENTAL DWARF KINGFISHER

Ceyx erithaca Alcedinidae

Size 13 cm

Voice Call a sharp, squeaky *chicheee... or chcheee...*

Range Apparently disjunct. From E Garhwal through NE states; Western Ghats south from around Mumbai; Nilgiris. Appears in many areas only with the onset of SW monsoons

Habitat Forest streams; nullahs

Brownish-chestnut crown; iridescent purple back, rump; deep purplish-blue of closed wings often hides the back; deep blue and white spots on neck sides and short, chestnut tail; orangish-yellow underbody and large, bright coral-red beak striking. Sexes alike. Solitary, or in pairs; tiny forest bird, usually overlooked when perched on stumps or tangled roots along nullahs and mud walls, often by forest path or road.

BLUE-EARED KINGFISHER

Alcedo meninting Alcedinidae

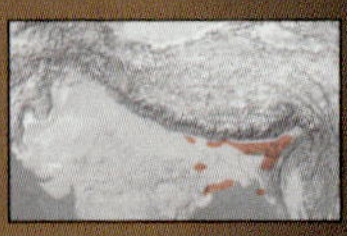

Size 17 cm

Voice Call a shrill *chichee... chichee*

Range C Nepal eastwards in lowlands

Habitat Rivers, pools, streams in dense tropical and subtropical evergreen forests, bamboo thickets, or near shady vegetation

juvenile

Small, short-tailed and vividly-coloured kingfisher. Brilliant ultramarine blue upperparts and rufous-red underparts; rufous loral spot; bright blue line down centre of back; stronger blue and black barring on crown; blue ear-coverts; creamy-white throat and neck-patch; wing-coverts spangled lighter blue. Dark wings. Solitary and very shy; sits patiently near pools, bobs head and flicks tail; dives to catch prey.

COMMON KINGFISHER

Alcedo atthis Alcedinidae

Bright blue above, greenish on wings; top of head finely-banded black-and-blue; ferruginous cheeks, ear-coverts and white patch on neck-sides; white chin and throat and deep ferruginous underbody distinctive; coral-red legs and blackish beak. Sexes alike. Solitary, or in scattered pairs; never found away from water; perches on pole or overhanging branch; flies low over water, brilliant blue streak, utters shrill notes; sometimes tame and confiding; dives for fish from perch; occasionally hovers over water before diving.

Size 18 cm

Voice Call a shrill *chichee...chichee*

Range Subcontinent, south of 2,000 m in the Himalayas; various races differ in shade of blue-green upperbody

Habitat Streams, lakes, canals; also coastal areas

BLYTH'S KINGFISHER

Alcedo hercules Alcedinidae

Larger than Common with brilliant blue upperparts and rufous underparts; long, robust bill; pale blue spangling on crown and nape; orange lores; blue ear-coverts; creamy-white chin and throat. Perches on overhanging branches near water. Shy and averse to disturbance.

Size 22 cm

Voice Call a surprisingly loud and strong *cheee*

Range E Nepal eastwards in lowland forests. S Assam Hills

Habitat Shady streams in dense broadleaved tropical forests

CRESTED KINGFISHER

Megaceryle lugubris Cerylidae

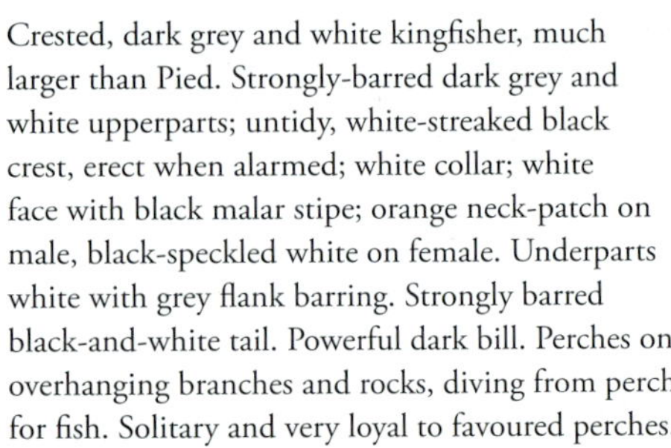

Size 41 cm

Voice Quiet; occasional *kik* note

Range Scarce breeding resident of N and NE uplands

Habitat Fast-flowing rivers

Crested, dark grey and white kingfisher, much larger than Pied. Strongly-barred dark grey and white upperparts; untidy, white-streaked black crest, erect when alarmed; white collar; white face with black malar stipe; orange neck-patch on male, black-speckled white on female. Underparts white with grey flank barring. Strongly barred black-and-white tail. Powerful dark bill. Perches on overhanging branches and rocks, diving from perch for fish. Solitary and very loyal to favoured perches.

PIED KINGFISHER

Ceryle rudis Cerylidae

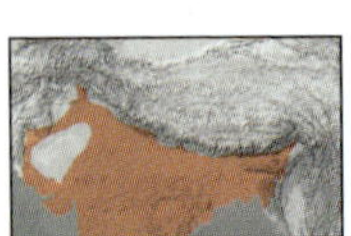

Size 25 cm

Voice Call includes piercing, twittering *chirrruk…chirruk…* cries in flight, sounding as if the bird is complaining

Range Subcontinent, upto about 2,000 m in the Himalayas

Habitat Streams, rivers, ponds; sometimes coastal areas

Kingfisher with black-and-white plumage; long dagger-like bill; untidy black crest on hindcrown; irregular black eye-band, continuing to back of head; black-and-white speckled underparts; white underwing; double black gorget across breast in male. Female has single, broken breast gorget. Solitary, in pairs or in small groups. Noisy and gregarious; hovers with flayed wings.

travancoreensis

lecucomelanura

GREEN BEE-EATER

Merops orientalis Meropidae

Size 21 cm

Voice Noisy; cheerful trilling notes, chiefly uttered on wing

Range Subcontinent, south of about 1,800 m in outer Himalayas

Habitat Open country and cultivation; light forests

Small bee-eater with bright green plumage; red-brown wash about head; pale blue on chin and throat, bordered below by black gorget; slender, curved black beak; rufous wash on black-tipped flight feathers; elongated central tail feathers distinctive. Sexes alike. Small parties; perches freely on bare branches and overhead telegraph wires; attends to grazing cattle, along with drongos, cattle egrets and mynas; also seen in city parks and garden; launches graceful sorties after winged insects; batters prey against perch before swallowing. Large flocks of upto 300 birds roost communally.

orientalis

beludschius

BLUE-BEARDED BEE-EATER

Nyctyornis athertoni Meropidae

Size 34 cm

Voice Harsh *korrr…korrr* croaking notes, often followed by softer chuckling call

Range Outer Himalayas to about 1,800 m, from Himachal to extreme E; Western Ghats and Nilgiris; forested parts of Madhya Pradesh, Eastern Ghats through Andhra Pradesh, Odisha, Bihar and West Bengal

Habitat Edges of forests, clearings

Unmarked grass-green above, bluer on forehead; elongated, blue feathers along centre of throat to breast appear beard-like, prominent when bird is calling; buffy-yellow below breast, streaked green; tail lacks long central pins; long sickle-shaped tail. Sexes alike. In pairs, or in groups; arboreal, rarely descending low; makes short aerial sallies after winged insects; batters prey on perch; usually not an easy bird to observe from close.

non-breeding

BLUE-CHEEKED BEE-EATER

Merops persicus Meropidae

Size 27 cm

Voice Noisy. Call a liquid, disyllabic *priit…priit* mainly in high flight

Range Locally common breeding summer visitor: Pakistan, NW India

Habitat Dry, open country near water

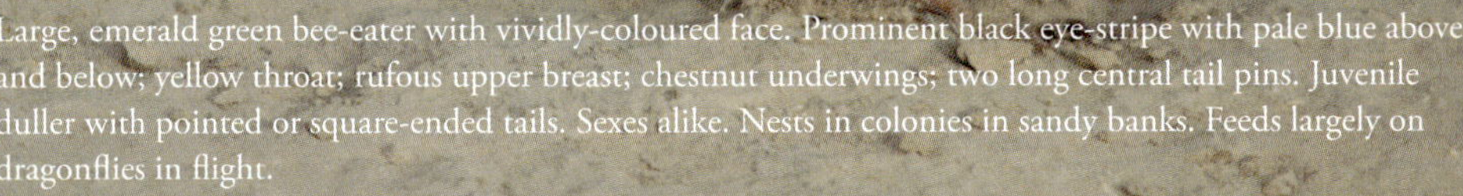

Large, emerald green bee-eater with vividly-coloured face. Prominent black eye-stripe with pale blue above and below; yellow throat; rufous upper breast; chestnut underwings; two long central tail pins. Juvenile duller with pointed or square-ended tails. Sexes alike. Nests in colonies in sandy banks. Feeds largely on dragonflies in flight.

CHESTNUT-HEADED BEE-EATER

Merops leschenaulti Meropidae

Size 21 cm

Voice Musical twittering notes, mostly uttered on wing, and sometimes from perch

Range Disjunct; the Himalayan foothills, from Uttarakhand to extreme NE; Western Ghats south of Goa; also, Sri Lanka. Occasionally may be encountered elsewhere in the peninsula, especially during monsoon

Habitat Vicinity of water in forested areas

Grass-green plumage; chestnut-cinnamon crown, hindneck and upper back; yellow chin and throat; rufous and black gorget. Sexes alike. Small gatherings on telegraph wires or bare upper branches of trees from where it launches short aerial sallies; fast, graceful flight; noisy when converging at roosting trees.

COMMON HOOPOE

Upupa epops Upupidae

Size 31 cm

Voice Call a pleasant, mellow *hoo...po...po...*

Range Subcontinent, upto about 5,500 m in the Himalayas; several races; spreads considerably in winter

Habitat Meadows, open country, garden lawns, open-light forests

Fawn-coloured plumage; black-and-white markings on wings, back and tail; black-and-white-tipped crest; longish, gently curved beak. Sexes alike. Solitary, or in scattered pairs; small, loose flocks in winter; probes ground with long beak, sometimes feeding along with other birds; flits among tree branches; crest often fanned open.

BROWN HORNBILL

Anorrhinus austeni Bucerotidae

Size 60-75 cm

Voice Noisy; normal call a shrill squealing note; also other squeals and screams

Range Almost throughout India, upto about 1,500 m in the Himalayas; absent in arid NW regions and heavy rainfall areas of S Western Ghats

Habitat Forests; orchards; tree-covered avenues; vicinity of habitation

Medium-sized hornbill with dark brown upperparts and bright rufous-brown underparts. Male white on head and neck-sides; large, pale bill; small, keel-shaped casque; pale blue orbital-patch; whitish cheeks, throat and upper breast, white tips to tail and primaries, visible in flight. Female has paler underparts, pale brown tips to wing-coverts, and pinkish orbital skin.

ORIENTAL PIED HORNBILL

Anthracoceros albirostris Bucerotidae

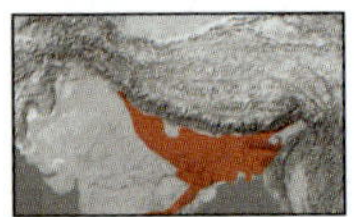

Size 60 cm

Voice Calls include loud cackles and screams; also rapid *pak...pak...pak*

Range Haryana and Uttarakhand to extreme NE; Eastern Ghats, south to Bastar and N Andhra Pradesh

Habitat Forests; orchards; groves

Similar to Malabar Pied, but tail much black; white face-patch, wing-tips (seen in flight) and tips to outer-tail feathers; black throat and breast; white below. Black and yellow beak with large casque. Sexes alike, female slightly smaller. Small parties, occasionally collecting into several dozen birds on favourite fruiting trees; associates with other birds; arboreal but often feeds on ground, hopping about.

GREAT HORNBILL

Buceros bicornis Bucerotidae

Size 100 cm

Voice Calls include loud and deep barking; loud *tokk* at feeding sites, audible from considerable distance

Range Lower Himalayas east of Uttarakhand, upto about 1,800 m; another population exists in Western Ghats

Habitat Forests

Black face, back and underbody; two white-bars on black wings; white neck, lower abdomen and tail; broad black tail-band; huge black and yellow beak with enormous concave-topped casque distinctive. Female slightly smaller. Sexes alike. In pairs, or small parties; occasionally large flocks; mostly arboreal, feeding on fruiting trees, plucking fruit with tip of bill, tossing it up, catching it in the throat and swallowing; may settle on ground to pick up fallen fruits; noisy flight; alternation of flapping and gliding, less undulating than in other hornbills.

RUFOUS-NECKED HORNBILL

Aceros nipalensis Bucerotidae

Size 100 cm

Voice Call a deep, single, far-carrying staccato *wok*

Range Globally threatened. Rare breeding resident in NE hill forests

Habitat Primary forests

Large impresive hornbill with dramatic downward curved bill. Male has rufous head and underparts; bright turquoise orbital skin; red chin pouch. Terminal half of tail white. Immature has rich rufous head, neck and most of underparts. Female has black head and underparts. Arboreal, feeding mainly on fruit. Nests as other hornbills.

WREATHED HORNBILL

Rhyticeros undulatus Bucerotidae

Size 80 cm

Voice Call a loud *kuk...kwek*; wings make whooshing sound in flight

Range Fairly common breeding resident. NE plains, foothills

Habitat Forests with fruiting trees

Black hornbill with completely white tail. Male has white face, chestnut crown and nape, red orbital-patch; yellow pouch with black stripe. Female has blue pouch and black head. Female seals itself into tree holes while male hornbill feeds female and chicks through narrow slit. Feeds mainly on fruits, travelling in, sometimes, large parties to favoured sites. Roosts communally.

GREAT BARBET

Megalaima virens Megalaimidae

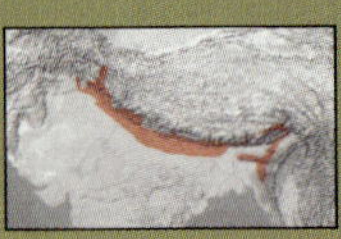

Size 33 cm

Voice Very noisy, especially between March and July; loud, somewhat mournful *pi…you* or *pi…oo*

Range The Himalayas, 800-3,200 m

Habitat Forests; orchards

Bluish-black head and throat; black bristles at base of nostrils, on front of lores and chin; black orbital skin; reddish-brown eye; brown forehead, nape, lores, chin and throat maroon-brown back; yellowish hind-collar; green on lower back; green tail; deep brown upper breast; pale yellow below, with thick, greenish-blue streaks; red undertail-coverts distinctive. Long, broad, yellowish beak; olive-grey legs and feet. Female similar to immature with duller colour, sooty-brown head and pinkish undertail-coverts. Either solitary, or in small bands; arboreal, but comes into low-fruiting bushes; difficult to spot and mostly heard.

LINEATED BARBET

Megalaima lineata Magalaimidae

Size 28 cm

Voice Call a persistent, rather subdued *kuruk… kuruk*, usually with long guttural start-up note

Range Locally common breeding resident in the NE, Bangladesh and the Himalayan foothills west to Himachal Pradesh

Habitat Foothill forests, parks and gardens

Large green and brown barbet with light brown head streaked buff; pale yellow orbital-patch; large yellowish- horn-coloured bill; bight green body with unmarked wings; heavy white streaking on head, neck, mantle and underparts to upper belly; white throat. Sexes alike. Similar to Green-eared, but lacks green rear-coverts. Strictly arboreal. Feeds on fruits. Very well camouflaged and rather secretive. Nests in tree holes. Calls from open branches.

GOLDEN-THROATED BARBET

Megalaima franklinii Megalaimida

Size 23 cm

Voice Start-up call *krrr* followed by monotonous *pukwok…pukwok*

Range Locally common breeding resident in N plains and hills from C Nepal east to Myanmar border

Habitat Forest trees, particularly fruiting figs

Plump, medium-sized, green barbet with distinct head pattern; yellow upper throat and greyish lower throat; red forehead and hindcrown and yellow crown centre; broad black stripe through eye; whitish cheeks. Mainly green upperparts and greenish-yellow underparts; bluish wing shoulders. Short tail. Sexes alike. Juvenile duller with weaker head pattern. Feeds mainly on fruits. Solitary, in pairs or small parties. Difficult to see in foliage. Nests in tree holes.

BROWN-HEADED BARBET

Megalaima zeylanica Megalaimidae

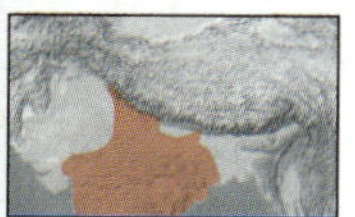

Size 28 cm

Voice Noisy; *kutroo…kutroo or pukrook…pukrook* calls one of the most familiar sounds of the Indian forests; call often begins with a guttural *kurrrr*

Range Most of India, south of the Himalayan foothills (Himachal Pradesh to Nepal)

Habitat Forests, groves; also city gardens

Overall green bird with brownish head, neck and upper back, streaked white; bare yellowish-orange patch around eye; thick reddish-pink bill; short, green tail with brown-black shafts; wing-coverts tipped whitish; uniform green underparts. Sexes alike. Solitary, or in pairs; occasionally small parties; strictly arboreal; keeps to fruiting trees, often with other frugivorous birds; difficult to spot in canopy; noisy in hot season; strong, undulating flight.

BLUE-EARED BARBET

Megalaima australis Megalaimidae

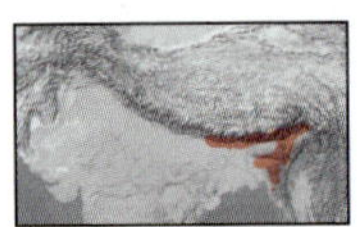

Size 17 cm

Voice Call a rapidly repeated *koo…trrk*

Range Scarce breeding resident in plains from E Nepal east to Myanmar border and Bangladesh

Habitat Forest trees, particularly fruiting figs

Small, green barbet with distinct marking on face and head; blue cheeks broadly bordered red; blue throat; blackish forecrown; black spot in centre of breast. Juvenile mainly green with hints of blue on face and neck; red-and-black absent on head. Sexes similar. Difficult to see in foliage. Nests in tree holes. Solitary, in pairs or in small parties.

BLUE-THROATED BARBET

Megalaima asiatica Megalaimidae

Size 23 cm

Voice Call similar to that of Brown-headed of plains; on careful hearing, sounds somewhat softer and there is a short note between the two longer ones; can be interpreted as *kutt…oo…ruk…*; also 4-note song when breeding

Range The Himalayas east from Pakistan and Kashmir; found upto about 2,250 m; also found in West Bengal, including Kolkata

Habitat Forests; groves

Medium-sized barbet with grass-green plumage; black, crimson, yellow-and-blue around head; blue chin and throat diagnostic; crimson spots on throat-sides. Sexes alike. Solitary, or in pairs; sometimes small parties on fruiting trees, along with other fruit-eating birds; strictly arboreal; keeps to canopy of tall trees; difficult to spot but loud, monotonous calls indicator of its presence. Secretive. Nests in tree holes.

COPPERSMITH BARBET

Megalaima haemacephala Megalaimidae

Size 17 cm

Voice Noisy between December and end of April; monotonous *tuk...tuk...* one of the best-known bird calls of India, likened to a coppersmith working on his metal

Range All over India, upto about 1,800 m in the outer Himalayas

Habitat Light forests; groves; city gardens; roadside trees

Small, vividly-coloured bird. Grass-green plumage; yellow throat; crimson breast and forehead; dumpy appearance. Sexes alike. Solitary, in pairs or small parties; strictly arboreal; feeds on fruiting trees, often with other birds; visits flowering *Erythrina* and *Bombax* trees for flower nectar; often spends early morning sunning itself on bare branches.

juvenile

YELLOW-RUMPED HONEYGUIDE

Indicator xanthonotus Indicatoridae

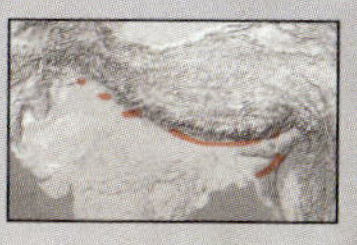

Size 15 cm

Voice Call note a sharp *cheep...*, mostly uttered on wing, and rarely on perch

Range The Himalayas, from Pakistan to Bhutan. Overlooked species

Habitat Rock faces and cliffs in forests; in some areas above treeline

Olive-brown plumage; bright orangish-yellow forehead, cheeks and rump (lower back) diagnostic, seen also when perched, with wings drooping slightly; finch-like beak; overall appearance sparrow-like. Sexes alike. Solitary, or in small scattered parties; keeps to cliffs and rock faces around honeybee colonies; no indication of guiding humans or any other mammal to honeycomb sites.

EURASIAN WRYNECK

Jynx torquilla Picidae

Size 17 cm

Voice Call a high-pitched *pee… pee… pee.* Hisses in nest

Range Breeds in Kashmir. Scarce but widespread winter visitor mainly to N areas

Habitat Breeds in edges of forests in N mountains. Elsewhere in scrubs and cultivation

Small, rather reptilian-looking woodpecker, the colour of tree bark. Basically grey-and-brown with dark eye-stripes and dark stripe running from crown to rump. Underparts barred and throat warm buff. Tail long and barred, making it look rather shrike-like in flight. Bill short and pointed. Twists neck round and often raises crown feathers. Unobtrusively feeds with long tongue on ants on ground and tree branches. Does not drill holes or use tail as support. Nests in tree holes.

SPECKLED PICULET

Picumnus innominatus Picidae

Size 10 cm

Voice Call a sharp, rapid *tsip… tsip…*; also loud drumming sound

Range The Himalayas, W to E, foothills to at least 2,500 m

Habitat Mixed forests, fondness for bamboo jungles

Sexes alike. Olive-green above (male has some orange-and-black on forecrown); two white stripes on head-sides, upper one longer; dark-olive band through eyes, moustachial stripe; creamy-white below, boldly spotted with black. Usually in pairs; moves around thin branches, or clings upside-down; taps with beak, probes crevices; exhibits typical woodpecker behaviour.

♀

WHITE-BROWED PICULET

Sasia ochracea Picidae

Size 9-10 cm

Voice Calls include a series of rapid *tseek… tseek* notes, high-pitched trills, also drumming and tapping, usually on bamboos

Range Restricted to NE regions of the subcontinent

Habitat Dense broadleaved forests, secondary growth with bamboos

Very tiny, almost sparrow-like bird with almost negligible tail, giving tail-less appearance. Olive-brown upperparts, rufous underparts; characteristic gold-yellow forehead and short white supercilium behind eye distinguishing features; red orbital-patch. Solitary, in pairs, or small groups, also in mixed hunting parties, exhibits typical woodpecker behaviour while moving along branches.

GREY-CAPPED PYGMY WOODPECKER

Dendrocopos canicapillus Picidae

Size 14 cm

Voice Call a high rattling *trill* and weak *pik*

Range Fairly common breeding resident in N foothills including parts of Bangladesh

Habitat Unobtrusive inhabitant of forests and open woodlands in N plains

Small, dark woodpecker with dark iris. Barred black-and-white above with, usually, unbarred central tail feathers. Dark buff below with very bold dark streaking. Grey crown (red nape on male) and black eye-stripes contrasting with broad white supercilium and cheeks. Slight malar stripe. Often in pairs with mixed-species flocks feeding acrobatically high in canopy on smallest branches but also low on small trees. Feeds on insects and grubs in bark. Uses tail as prop. Nests in self-made holes.

FULVOUS-BREASTED WOODPECKER

Dendrocopos macei Picidae

Size 18 cm

Voice Call a hard *tik*, sometimes extended into chatter

Range Common breeding resident in N hills, NE India, Bangladesh and Eastern Ghats

Habitat Open, broadleaved and coniferous forests; edges of forests

♀

Medium-sized, pied woodpecker with heavily barred black-and-white underparts. Male has distinct red crown, orange forehead, while black in female. Buff belly with light barring and streaking on flank; red undertail; whitish cheeks partially bordered black. Feeds on invertebrates. Often props itself on tail. Can be seen with other species in mixed flocks. Locally common. Nests in self-made tree holes.

STRIPE-BREASTED WOODPECKER

Dendrocopos atratus Picidae

Size 21-22 cm

Voice Calls include explosive *tchick* and whinnying rattle

Range Hills of NE India and Bangladesh

Habitat Open forests, also edges of evergreen and broadleaved forests

Medium-sized woodpecker with heavily streaked underparts; narrow white barring on black mantle; white head and neck-sides. Underparts, dull olive-yellow; red head extending to nape. Easily confused with Fulvous-breasted. Male has white nasal tufts beneath dark lower forehead. Female has all-black crown. Juvenile male has dull red tinge on upper crown. Nests in holes excavated high in trees. Status uncertain and unknown, but certainly uncommon.

BROWN-FRONTED WOODPECKER

Dendrocopos auriceps Picidae

Size 20 cm

Voice Calls include fast chattering *chik...chik chik...rrr* and short *chik*

Range Locally common endemic breeding resident in N hills from Balochistan, east to Nepal. Moves lower down in winter

Habitat Deciduous, coniferous hill forests

Medium-sized Himalayan woodpecker. Overall pied; yellow crown; black upperparts barred white; black moustache extends to breast; black-streaked white underparts; deep pink vent. Male has brown forecrown with yellow centre; red rear crown; red vent. Female has entirely yellow crown. Often with mixed hunting groups. Uses tail as prop. Feeds on invertebrates and seeds in trees and bushes. Nests in self-made holes.

YELLOW-CROWNED WOODPECKER

Dendrocopos mahrattensis Picidae

Size 17 cm

Voice Call a soft but sharp *clic...click... clickrrr...*; drums when breeding

Range Common and widespread; subcontinent, from the Himalayan foothills south; uncommon in NE regions

Habitat Open forests; scrubs; cultivation; vicinity of habitation; gardens

Male brownish-black above, spotted all over with white golden-brown forehead and crown; small scarlet crest; pale fulvous below throat, streaked brown; scarlet patch in centre of abdomen distinctive. Female lacks scarlet crest. Solitary or in pairs; sometimes small bands of upto six birds; occasionally seen with mixed hunting parties; moves in jerks along tree stems and branches; hunts in typical woodpecker manner; rather confiding in some areas; birds keep in touch with faint, creaking sounds.

DARJEELING WOODPECKER

Dendrocopos darjellensis Picidae

♀

Size 25 cm

Voice Call a short *tsik*, rattling *di...di...di...di...dttttt...dit*

Range Locally common breeding resident in N mountains from C Nepal east

Habitat High forests

Medium-sized woodpecker with creamy-white lower forehead, black upper forehead; black crown, broad red band on nape, black hindneck; white lores, white head-sides washed-buff; white cheeks and long black moustache extending to upper breast. Upperparts mostly black, with large white, scapular patches and white-barred flight feathers and tail sides; red vent. Red nape-band absent in female. Feeds on invertebrates on and in upper branches and mossy trunks. Solitary, or in pairs.

HIMALAYAN WOODPECKER

Dendrocopos himalayensis Picidae

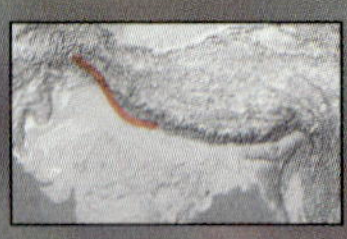

Size 24 cm

Voice Fairly loud calls, uttered in night

Range The Himalayas, from Kashmir to W Nepal; 1,500–3,200m

Habitat The Himalayan forests

Male has black back and upperbody; white shoulder-patch; white spots and barring on wings; crimson crown and crest; white lores, cheeks and ear-coverts; broad, black moustachial stripe; yellowish-brown underbody, darker on breast; crimson under tail. Female has black crown and crest. Mostly in pairs, moves about in forest; jerkily moves up and around tree stems or clings on under sides of branches; like other woodpeckers, often moves few steps back, as if to re-examine; sometimes seen in mixed hunting parties of Himalayan birds.

♀

CRIMSON-BREASTED WOODPECKER

Dendrocopos cathpharius Picidae

Male has white forehead, chin and throat; black crown; buffy-white ear-coverts; black malar stripe extends to hindneck. Plain black back, mantle and scapulars; black wing with white patch on coverts; primaries spotted or barred whitish; buff-washed white underparts streaked black; pinkish-red vent. Male has variable red patch on nape, absent in female. Juvenile has less streaked underparts and less crimson on breast.

Size 18 cm

Voice Call a loud, monotonous *tchick*, higher-pitched and less sharp than Darjeeling's; shrill *kee…kee*

Range The Himalayas, NE India

Habitat Broadleaved forests

RUFOUS-BELLIED WOODPECKER

Dendrocopus hyperythrus Picidae

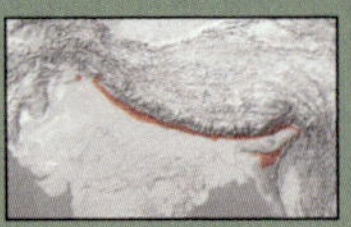

Size 24 cm

Voice Call a short *kit*, sometimes extended excitedly

Range Common breeding; endemic resident in NW mountains

Habitat Montane forests with preference for coniferous trees

♀

Distinct woodpecker with rufous underparts and strongly barred black-and-white upper mantle; white face and chin; black rump and central tail. Male has red crown while female has black crown spotted white. Juvenile black above, boldly spotted white. The west Himalayan race is larger than the nominate east Himalayan. Singly, or in pairs; probes bark for sap. Nests in self-made tree holes. Confiding and approachable.

GREAT SPOTTED WOODPECKER

Dendrocopos major Picidae

Size 24 cm

Voice Call a resonant creaking

Range Scarce breeding resident in NE India only

Habitat Oak and pine forests

♀

Medium-sized pied woodpecker with white neck and face-sides. Diagnostic black band forms Z from base of beak to neck and back to breast. Male has distinct crimson patch on back of head. Glossy black upperparts with broad white patches from shoulder to lower back and white barring on flight feathers and tail edgings. Underparts buff with extensive bright red vent. Juvenile male has red crown and black nape. Distinct bouncing flight.

BAY WOODPECKER

Blythipicus pyrrhotis Picidae

Size 27 cm

Voice Call a loud, cackling laugh *keek…kik…kik…kik…kik*; chattering *kerere…kerere…kerere*

Range E Nepal to Myanmar; S Assam Hills

Habitat Thick primary broadleaved and montane forests, dense secondary undergrowth, bamboos

Rare and seldom seen woodpecker, often confused with Rufous. Conspicuous, long, yellow bill. Tufted hindcrown; pale cinnamon face and nape; chestnut above with bold black and red-brown barring; faint barring on rusty-brown flanks; lightly barred rufous tail; brown iris with blue orbital-ring; greyish-olive legs. Sexes similar, but female lacks crimson patch on lower neck-sides. Juvenile overall duller with heavier barring on mantle. Secretive; most often seen in flight.

RUFOUS WOODPECKER

Micropternus brachyurus Picidae

Size 25 cm

Voice Rather vocal between January and April; call a loud, high-pitched 3- or 4-noted *ke…ke…kr…ke…*; drums when breeding

Range Subcontinent, south of outer Himalayas, found upto 1,500 m

Habitat Mixed forests

Plumage mixture of different shades of brown; fine black cross-bars on upperbody, including wings and tail; paler edges to throat feathers; crimson patch under eye in male, absent in female. Sexes alike. Usually in pairs; sometimes four or five scattered birds close by; mostly seen around ball-shaped nests of tree ants; clings to outside of nests and digs for ants; plumage often smeared with gummy substance.

LESSER YELLOWNAPE

Picus chlorolophus Picidae

chlorolophus

chlorigaster

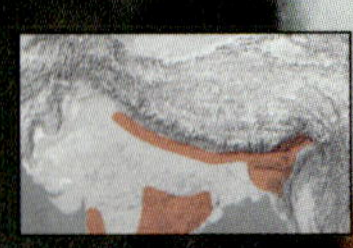

Size 27 cm

Voice Noisy. Call a loud, sad *pee...oo* and descending *ke... ke...ke...ke*

Range Locally common breeding resident in N foothills from Himachal Pradesh to Myanmar border and peninsular hills, Sri Lanka and Bangladesh

Habitat All types of open forests and plantations

Medium-sized woodpecker with green upperparts; bright yellow, tufted nape. Olive-green neck and breast; whitish belly, finely barred green; black rump and tail. Adult male has green head and white throat; red markings above eye and nape; red moustachial stripe. Female has red patch above ear-coverts. Juvenile similar to female, but duller. Feeds on invertebrates at lower levels, including ground, and often in mixed hunting groups.

GREATER YELLOWNAPE

Picus flavinucha Picidae

Similar to Lesser, but larger. Lesser has smaller, dark bill, red markings on head, red stripe on whitish chin, smaller crest and barred underparts; prominent yellow-crested nape and throat. Underparts dark olive-green and grey. Brownish crown; flight feathers chestnut-barred black. Feeds on invertebrates from ground to canopy often with mixed-species parties. Shy, flushes readily if disturbed. Uses tail as prop. Nests in tree holes.

Size 33 cm

Voice Calls include loud, plaintive *keeyu* and hard *chep* note. Also, an accelerating trill *quee… quee…quee*

Range Fairly common breeding resident of N foothills, NE India, Bangladesh and Eastern Ghats

Habitat Upland broadleaved forests

STREAK-THROATED WOODPECKER

Picus xanthopygaeus Picidae

Size 30 cm

Voice Call an occasional faint *pick*… mostly silent; also drums on branches

Range Subcontinent; found upto 1,500 m in outer Himalayas

Habitat Mixed forests; plantations

Male grass-green above; crimson crown and crest; orange and black on nape; white supercilium and malar stripe; yellow rump; bold, black scaly streaks on whitish underbody, with tawny-green wash on breast; throat greyer, also streaked. Female has black crown and crest. Solitary, or in pairs; works up along tree stems; moves either straight up or in spirals; taps with beak for insects hiding in bark; also settles on ground.

SCALY-BELLIED WOODPECKER

Picus squamatus Picidae

Size 35 cm

Voice Contact call a hard, repeated *quik*. Also musical, repeated *peeko…peeko*

Range Fairly common breeding resident in N mountain forests east to E Nepal

Habitat Upland coniferous and broadleaved forests; also open, dry and cultivated country with scattered trees

Similar to Streak-throated, but larger with unstreaked throat and upper breast. Strong, black moustachial stripe; white supercilium speckled black; large pale bill; distinct scaling from breast to vent; strongly barred tail. Male has red forehead, crown and nape, while female has dark slaty-grey crown. Feeds on ants and termites and also berries. Forages solitary, or in pairs. Nests in self-made tree holes.

GREY-HEADED WOODPECKER

Picus canus Picidae

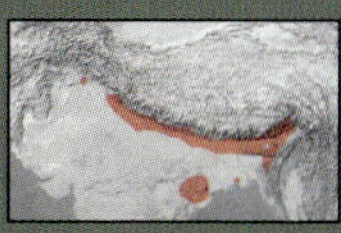

Size 32 cm

Voice Loud, chattering alarm; common call a high-pitched *keek...keek...* of 4- or 5-notes; drums often between March and early June

Range The Himalayas, from the lower foothills country to about 2,700 m

Habitat Deciduous and temperate forests

Male darkish-green above; crimson forehead; black hindcrown, faint crest and nape; dark sides of head and black malar stripe; yellow rump, white-barred dark wings and blackish tail; unmarked, dull greyish-olive underbody diagnostic. Female black from forehead to nape; no crimson. Solitary, or in pairs; typical woodpecker, moving on tree stems and larger branches, hunting out insects from under bark; descends to ground, hopping awkwardly; also digs into termite mounds.

♂

♀

HIMALAYAN GOLDENBACK

Dinopium shorii Picidae

Size 30-32cm

Voice Call a rapid repeated *klok…klok…klak…klok…klak*

Range The Himalayas; locally in hills of peninsula and Bangladesh

Habitat Mature forests

♀

Largish woodpecker with golden upperparts. Male has black hindneck; brownish-buff throat centre with irregular border of black spots; indistinctly divided moustachial stripe; brownish-buff centre, with small red patch; reddish or brown eyes; blackish bill; greenish-brown feet. Underparts boldly streaked and scalloped black, and on some, almost unmarked. Three-toed. Female has black crest, streaked white. Confiding. Often seen in mixed feeding flocks. Locally common.

LESSER GOLDENBACK

Dinopium benghalense Picidae

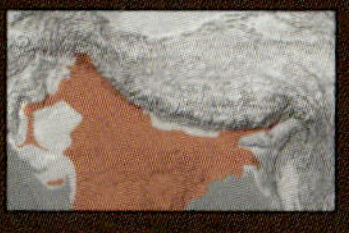

Size 30 cm

Voice Noisy. Call a loud, high-pitched cackle, like laughter; drums often

Range Subcontinent, upto about 1,800 m in outer Himalayas; also found in drier areas of NW India

Habitat Forests, both dry and mixed deciduous; orchards; gardens; also neighbourhood of villages and other habitation

Male has shining golden-yellow and black above; crimson crown and crest; black throat and sides of head, with fine white streaks; white underbody, streaked black, boldly on breast. Female has black crown spotted with white; crimson crest. In pairs, sometimes half a dozen together; widespread and common; moves jerkily up and around tree stems or clings on undersides of branches; taps out insects; often associates in mixed hunting parties; may descend to ground, picking off ants and other insects.

♀

psarodes

GREATER GOLDENBACK

Chrysocolaptes lucidus Picidae

Size 33 cm

Voice Noisy. Loud, grating scream; calls mostly in flight

Range Uttarakhand to NE India; parts of Eastern Ghats, SE Madhya Pradesh; Western Ghats, Kerala to Tapti River; plains to about 1,500 m

Habitat Forests

Male has crimson crown and crest; golden-olive above; white and black sides of face and throat; whitish-buff below, profusely spotted with black on foreneck, and speckled over rest of underbody; extensive crimson rump and black tail and flight feathers distinctive. Female has white-spotted black crown and crest.

PALE-HEADED WOODPECKER

Gecinulus grantia Picidae

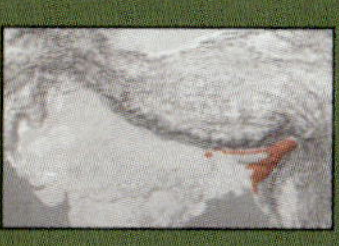

Size 25 cm

Voice Drumming loud, full, fairly short in duration and evenly pitched

Range Local resident in the Himalayas from E Nepal and E Arunachal Pradesh

Habitat Chiefly in bamboo jungles; also moist broadleaved secondary forests

Arguably India's rarest woodpecker. Golden-brown or green head; unmarked face; maroon-brown mantle and back; mainly brownish wings with pink barring on primaries; dusky-olive underparts; red iris; pale bill with greenish base; olive-green legs with three toes. Female lacks reddish-pink central crown. Juvenile resembles female, but head duller and upperparts more brown. Numbers rapidly declining due to loss of bamboo forests. Wary and difficult to circumvent. Feeds lower down, though seldom descending to ground.

♀

GREAT SLATY WOODPECKER

Mulleripicus pulverulentus Picidae

Size 51 cm

Voice Call a loud bleating, like a goat; very loud cackle in flight

Range The Himalayas

Habitat Mature trees in tropical forests and forest clearings

Probably the largest living woodpecker, with reptilian look, due to its thin serpent-like neck, rounded head and long tail. Overall grey with bluish wash; ear-coverts and neck speckled white; paler underparts; breast faintly speckled white; cream to golden throat and upper neck; darker tail and wings. Brown iris and grey orbital-ring. Male has pinkish-red patch on malar region and pink on lower throat. Long, robust bill with grey-yellow lower mandible and grey upper mandible; bluish-grey legs. Juvenile overall duller with brown cast to upperparts. Forages chiefly on trunks and major branches in large trees. Often seen in large flocks.

LONG-TAILED BROADBILL

Psarisomus dalhousiae Eurylaimidae

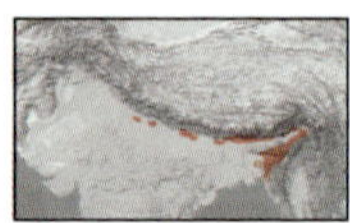

Size 28 cm

Voice Calls include loud, repeated whistles; *tseeay…pseeuw*

Range Uttarakhand eastwards to the entire NE Indian region

Habitat Tropical, subtropical semi-evergreen, evergreen forests; bamboos, *sal*

Gregarious, noisy forest-dwelling bird with vivid plumage. Long, thin, blue tail; black head; yellow face and throat-sides; blue patch on crown; yellowish blue ear-covert patch; yellow-green bill; large eyes; bright green upperparts; blue-green underparts. Diagnostic white patch on blue underwing visible in flight. Juvenile duller, mostly green. Arboreal and crepuscular; feeds on insects. Perches upright.

SILVER-BREASTED BROADBILL

Serilophus lunatus Eurylaimidae

Size 19 cm

Voice Call a mostly squeaky *pee…ou*

Range Scarce breeding resident, now restricted to extreme NE India along Myanmar border

Habitat Lowlands; foothill forests

Adult male has red lores; rusty head-sides and ear-coverts; greyish forehead; broad black eyebrow continuing through to neck; yellow eye-ring. Black wings with blue-and-white wing-patches; ash-brown mantle; chestnut lower back; brown rump; black tail with white border. Silvery-grey throat and chest graduating to white belly; black thighs. Iris varies from emerald-green to sapphire blue. Female identified by thin silver band running through upper chest.

♀

BLUE-NAPED PITTA

Pitta nipalensis Pittidae

Size 25 cm

Voice Powerful double whistle

Range Rather local resident

Habitat Tropical and subtropical moist broadleaved evergreen forests; bamboo-dominated secondary growth in deserted forest clearings

Olive-green pitta with striking blue hindcrown and nape. Fulvous head-sides, forehead and ear-coverts; black patch behind eye. Plain, uniform fulvous underparts; brownish-green wings; brown tail washed green. Brown iris and bill. Female has rufous-brown crown and smaller, greenish-blue patch on nape. Forages on forest floor amidst fallen leaves.

BLUE PITTA

Pitta cyanea Pittidae

Size 23 cm

Voice Song a liquid *pleoow…whit*

Range Rare resident; NE India and Bangladesh

Habitat Broadleaved evergreen forests; moist ravines

Medium-sized, distinctly azure blue pitta. Pinkish-red hindcrown; broad, black eye-stripe and moustachial stripe. Bright blue tail. Pale underparts tinted blue, with bold black spotting and barring. Small white patch in wing visible in flight. Female has dark olive upperparts with variable blue tinge; buffish breast. Juvenile overall dark brown, streaked and spotted rufous-buff; prominent buff supercilium and dark eye-stripe.

HOODED PITTA

Pitta sordida Pittidae

Size 19 cm

Voice Calls include explosive, double whistle *whee…whee* and harsh *skyew*

Range Rare and very local breeding; summer visitor to N foothills from Himachal Pradesh to Myanmar border including Nepal and Bangladesh

Habitat Forest undergrowth and thick scrub. Favours dark, damp, leaf-strewn areas

Unmistakable bright emerald-green pitta with black face and rusty-brown forehead, crown and nape; blue rump and shoulders; bright red rump; brown iris; black bill; strong, longish, flesh-coloured legs. Paler green underparts; short tail. Large white patches on dark wings prominent in flight. Feeds on wet forest floor on invertebrates with bounding hops. Calls and roosts in trees. Solitary and secretive. Nests low down.

LARGE WOODSHRIKE

Tephrodornis virgatus Tephrodornithidae

Size 23 cm

Voice Call a tuneful *kew…kew…kew*

Range Lowlands; E Nepal

Habitat Moist evergreen, broadleaved forests; glades

Plain, thickset, shrike-like bird with drab plumage; heavy, black bill; distinct nasal tufts. The Himalayan and eastern race *pelvicus* have grey crown and nape; brown mantle, upperparts; fairly broad, dark mask; black bill; usually, yellow eyes; breast, flanks have pale pink-grey wash. Female duller, with brown upperparts and ill-defined mask; paler bill. Juvenile has spotted, scaly crown. Fairly confiding, but quiet and inconspicuous.

COMMON WOODSHRIKE

Tephrodornis pondicerianus Tephrodornithidae

Size 16 cm

Voice Calls include whistling *wheet…wheet…* and interrogative, quick-repeated *whi…whi…whi…whee* afterwards; other trilling, pleasant notes when breeding

Range Across the country, S Himalayan foothills; most common in low country

Habitat Light forests; edges of forests; cultivation; gardens in and around habitation

Sri Lanka Woodshrike

Greyish-brown plumage; broad whitish supercilium and dark stripe below eye distinctive; grey-brown lores; white outer-tail feathers seen when bird flies. Dark stripe may be slightly paler in female. Sexes alike. In pairs, or small parties; quiet for greater part of year, vocal when breeding (February–May); keeps to middle levels of trees, hopping about, sometimes coming to ground. Nest is a small cup of moss and lichen.

ASHY WOODSWALLOW

Artamus fuscus Artamidae

Size 19 cm

Voice Call a harsh *chey…chey…* or *chaek…chaek…*, often uttered in flight; short song occasionally when breeding, mix of harsh and melodious notes

Range Roughly towards east and south from W Gujarat to Shimla; widespread but not continuously distributed; upto about 1,800 m in outer Himalayas

Habitat Open country; edges of forests

Slaty-grey plumage, greyer on head; paler on rump, underbody; short square tail, tipped white; white undertail-coverts; somewhat heavy-looking bird, rather swallow-like in appearance, but wings much shorter and broader. Sexes alike. Small numbers in open country; perches on leaf stalks, overhead wires or flies characteristically, few wingbeats and glide; hunts flying insects; quiet during hot hours, feeds mostly in mornings and evenings.

COMMON IORA

Aegithina tiphia Aegithinidae

Male greenish above (rich black above, with yellowish rump, in some races); black wings and tail; two white wing-bars; bright yellow underbody. Female has yellow-green plumage; white wing-bars; greenish-brown wings. Pairs keep to leafy branches, often with other small birds; moves energetically amidst branches in hunt for insects, caterpillars; rich call notes often a giveaway of its presence in an area.

Size 14 cm

Voice Renowned vocalist; wide range of rich, whistling notes; common call a single or 2-note long-drawn *wheeeeeee* or *wheeeeeee…chu*; another common call a 3-note whistle

Range Subcontinent, upto about 1,800 m in the Himalayas; absent in arid NW India, desert regions of Rajasthan, Kutch

Habitat Forests; gardens; orchards; tree-dotted cultivation; habitation

tiphia

multicolor

humei

LARGE CUCKOOSHRIKE

Coracina macei Campephagidae

Size 28 cm

Voice Noisy. Call a 2-noted ringing whistle, *ti…treee…* second note long-drawn and higher; somewhat like Blossom-headed Parakeet's call

Range Most of India, from about 2,200 m in the Himalayas; absent in the drier, semi-desert regions of Kutch, C and N Rajasthan and much of NW India

Habitat Forests; gardens; tree-dotted cultivation

nipalensis

♀

macei

Male grey above; broad, dark stripe through eyes to ear-coverts; black wings, tail; greyish breast, whitish below. Female barred grey-and-white below; paler stripe through eyes. In pairs, or small bands of four to six birds; characteristic flight over forest, few wingbeats and glide, often calls in flight; flicks wings on perching; keeps to upper branches, but may descend into bushes; very active and noisy when breeding (March–June).

BLACK-WINGED CUCKOOSHRIKE

Coracina melaschistos Campephagidae

Size 22 cm

Voice Calls include loud, descending *twit…twit to…we* and *peeo…peeo…peeo*

Range Local breeding resident in N mountains from N Pakistan, east to Myanmar border. Winters lower down in foothills and plains mainly in Bangladesh and NE India south to Odisha. Scattered winter records throughout peninsular India

Habitat Open forests; edges of forests, groves

Medium-sized, dark cuckooshrike with unbarred, grey underparts. Male dark grey above with contrasting black wings and tail. Underside of tail shows broad white feather-tips. Female paler with very faint barring on underparts. Feeds on invertebrates in canopy and undergrowth; singly or in pairs. Joins mixed hunting groups. Undulating flight. Nests in trees.

ROSY MINIVET

Pericrocotus roseus Campephagidae

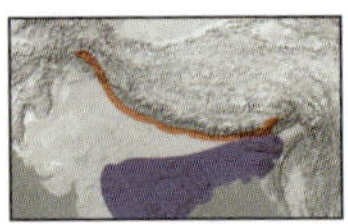

Size 18 cm

Voice Not well-known. Squeaky, trilling note recorded

Range Scarce and very local breeding resident, summer visitor: N mountains from N Pakistan, east to Myanmar border. Winter in Bangladesh and India south to Kerala but records very sporadic. Most frequently, recorded in NE India and Eastern Ghats

Habitat Poorly known species. Forests; woodlands; gardens

♀

Has grey-brown upperparts. Male has pinkish-red patch on wings and tail; reddish rump; silvery-white face; pale grey crown and nape; blackish-brown wings and long tail. Pale buffy-pink underparts. Female has yellow underparts with yellow-olive rump. Behaviour similar to other minivets. Feeds in canopy on invertebrates. In small parties and less active than other minivets. Nests in trees in open broadleaved forests.

SMALL MINIVET

Pericrocotus cinnamomeus Campephagidae

Size 15 cm

Voice Call a soft, low *swee… swee…* notes uttered as birds hunt in foliage

Range Most of India, upto about 900 m in outer Himalayas; absent in arid parts of Rajasthan

Habitat Forests; groves; gardens; tree-dotted cultivation

cinnamomeus

♀

pallidus

Male has dark grey head, back and throat; orange-yellow patch on black wings; black tail; flame-orange breast, graduating to yellow on belly and undertail; strong dark beak; long tail. Female paler above and overall duller; orange rump; dusky-white throat, breast tinged with yellow; yellowish belly and undertail. Juvenile has more brown upperparts than female with faint barring and scaling; faintly speckled underparts. In pairs, or small flocks; keeps to tree-tops, actively moving amidst foliage; flutters and flits about in untiring hunts for small insects, often in association with other small birds; also hunts flycatcher-style.

LONG-TAILED MINIVET

Pericrocotus ethologus Campephagidae

Size 18 cm

Voice Call a distinctive descending whistle *pee...ru*

Range Common breeding resident and summer visitor to N hills from W Pakistan, east to Myanmar border and Bangladesh. Winters widely in plains south to Maharashtra

Habitat Broadleaved and coniferous hill forests when breeding. Winters in open woodlands and groves. Nomadic in winter

♀

Male has glossy blue-black upperparts, hood, chin and throat; scarlet rump; scarlet underparts; black wings with bright scarlet patches on secondaries and inner greater coverts forming U shape; long tail with red outer-tail feathers. Female has yellow on forehead and supercilium; grey cheeks; greenish-yellow-grey, mantle, back and rump; pale yellow throat graduating to orange-yellow on breast and flanks.

GREY-CHINNED MINIVET

Pericrocotus solaris Campephagidae

Size 17 cm

Voice Call a thin *tsee...sip*

Range Local breeding resident in the mountains east from C Nepal to Arunachal Pradesh and Myanmar border hills. Also occurs in China and SE Asia

Habitat Hill forests

♀

Small, brightly-plumaged minivet with dark grey face, head and mantle; pale grey chin; orange-yellow throat, washed grey; short, black bill. Male has bright to dull orange underparts; orange lower back and rump; orange tips on greater coverts. Female duller grey with bright yellow underparts, and in wings and tail. Dark mid-wing-bar visible in flight. Feeds actively, mainly in tree canopy in small, calling parties. Sometimes briefly descends to eye level.

SHORT-BILLED MINIVET

Pericrocotus brevirostris Campephagidae

Size 19 cm

Voice Call a high whistled *tsee…tup*

Range C Nepal eastwards. S Assam Hills

Habitat Open broadleaved forests; edges of forests; secondary growth

Adult male has black hood, throat, mantle, wings; deep red underparts; similar to Long-tailed; shorter tail, like Scarlet, but smaller, more slender; wings lack red spots or 'drops' on tips of tertials, secondaries. Female brighter yellow below, including on throat; no wing spots; more yellow on forehead, including forecrown; yellower cheeks.

SCARLET MINIVET

Pericrocrotus (flammeus) speciosus Campephagidae

Size 20 cm

Voice Call a pleasant, 2-note whistle; also longer, whistling warble

Range Disjunct; several isolated races

Habitat Forests; gardens; groves

Male has glossy bluish-black head and upper back; deep scarlet lower back and rump; black-and-scarlet wings and tail; black throat, scarlet below. Female has rich yellow forehead, supercilium; grey-yellow above; yellow-and-black wings and tail; bright yellow underbody. In pairs, or small parties; sometimes several dozens together; keeps to canopy of tall trees; actively flits about to hunt for insects; also launches aerial sallies after winged insects; often seen in mixed hunting parties of birds; spectacular sight of black, scarlet and yellow as flock flies over forests.

BAR-WINGED FLYCATCHER-SHRIKE

Hemipus picatus Tephrodornithidae

Size 14 cm

Voice Noisy. Calls include persistent *tsit…it…it…tsit…it…it…,si…* and short *chip*

Range Fairly common breeding resident in foothills from E Himachal Pradesh to Myanmar border, Eastern and Western Ghats and Sri Lanka. Makes attitudinal and other local movements

Habitat Open forests, edges of forests including adjoining scrubs

picatus

capitalis

Pied shrike with distinct black cap and hindneck. Brown mantle in the Himalayan race. Black in southern races. Long white patches on black wings showing V in rear views. Tail black with white borders. Throat white, contrasting with pinkish-grey underparts. Female more brown. Feeds on insects in noisy, active flocks, often in mixed hunting groups in canopy and lower down. Often flycatches. Nests high in trees.

BROWN SHRIKE

Lanius cristatus Laniidae

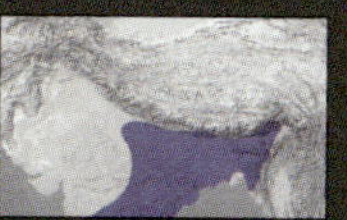

Size 19 cm

Voice Calls include harsh chattering, grating; sometimes sings in low chirruping tone with bill closed

Range Winter visitor to peninsular India

Habitat Open country; cultivation; edges of forests; scrubs; gardens

juvenile

Adult male has uniform rufous-brown upperparts and darkish-brown crown; Broad, black 'bandit-mask' through eye; white brow over. Pale creamy underparts, washed buff; rufous flanks; rufous tail; brown wings; Female has less contrast and faint scalloping on underside. Immature has stronger scalloping on underparts. Solitary; perches in open or tree stumps and returns to same perch repeatedly; territorial.

BAY-BACKED SHRIKE

Lanius vittatus Laniidae

Size 18 cm

Voice Call a harsh, *churr;* lively warble of breeding male; sometimes imitates other bird calls

Range Subcontinent, upto about 1,800 m in the Himalayas; absent in the NE

Habitat Open country; light forests; scrubs

Deep chestnut-maroon back; broad black forehead-band, continuing through eyes to ear-coverts; grey crown and neck, separated from black by small white patch; white rump distinctive; black wings with white in outer flight feathers; white underbody, fulvous on breast and flanks. Sexes alike. Solitary, or in scattered pairs in open terrain; keeps lookout from perch on some tree stumps, overhead wire or bush-tops, usually under 4 m off ground; pounces once potential prey sighted; usually devours prey on ground, tearing it; sometimes carries it to perch; keeps to fixed territories, defends aggressively.

juvenile

BURMESE SHRIKE

Lanius collurioides Laniidae

Size 20 cm

Voice Alarm call a loud, rapid, harsh chattering, *chikachikachitchit, chekoochekoochitititititit, chetetetetet*

Range Locally common passage migrant, mainly in Assam and Manipur

Habitat Subtropical or tropical moist lowland forests; subtropical or tropical moist montane forests

Medium-sized shrike with long slender tail. Adult male has black forehead and ill-defined face mask; slaty-grey hindneck; dark grey crown; chestnut mantle, rump and uppertail-coverts; white wing-patch; white sides to tail. Adult female has whitish forehead and paler chestnut mantle.

LONG-TAILED SHRIKE

Lanius schach Laniidae

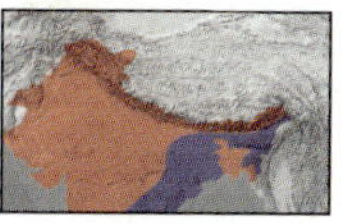

Size 25 cm

Voice Noisy. Calls include a harsh mix of scolding notes, shrieks and yelps; excellent mimic. Rather musical song of breeding male

Range Three races; undergo considerable seasonal movement; subcontinent, from about 2,700 m in the Himalayas

Habitat Open country, cultivation, edges of forests, vicinity of habitation, gardens; prefers neighbourhood of water

Pale grey from crown to middle of back; then bright rufous till rump; black forehead, band through eye; white 'mirror' in black wings; whitish underbody, tinged pale rufous on lower breast and flanks. Sexes alike. Mostly solitary; boldly defends feeding territory; keeps lookout from conspicuous perch; pounces onto ground on sighting prey; said to store surplus in 'larder', impaling prey on thorns; nicknamed Butcher-bird.

erythronotus

tricolor

caniceps

GREY-BACKED SHRIKE

Lanius tephronotus Laniidae

Size 25 cm

Voice Call a grating shrek; mimics other birds

Range Locally common breeding summer visitor to the Himalayas from Ladakh, eastwards to hills of NE India. Winters lower down to plains including Bangladesh

Habitat Open areas, usually with trees, but also in open high altitude steppe

Large shrike with dark grey upperparts; black mask; yellowish flanks; long tail; rufous uppertail-coverts and belly. Similar to Long-tailed but has darker grey, no rufous on upperparts and grey forehead; larger head and bill. Usually lacks white primary patch on blackish wings. Breeds at high altitudes.

juvenile

INDIAN GOLDEN ORIOLE

Oriolus (oriolus) kundoo Oriolidae

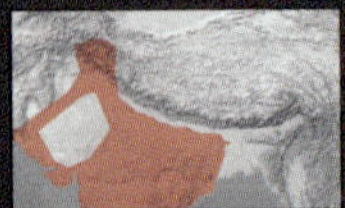

Size 25 cm

Voice Call includes a fluty whistle of 2- or 3-notes, interpreted *pee...lo...lo*

Range Summer visitor to the Himalayan foothills, spreads in winter to plains; breeds in many parts of peninsula

Habitat Forests; orchards; gardens around habitation

Male has bright golden-yellow plumage; black stripe through eye; black wings and centre of tail. Female yellow-green above; has brownish-green wings; dirty-white below, streaked brown. Juvenile similar to female. Solitary, or in pairs; arboreal, sometimes moving with other birds in upper branches; regularly visits fruiting and flowering trees; hunts insects in leafy branches; usually heard, surprisingly not often seen, despite bright colour; seen only when emerges on bare branch or flies across.

juvenile

SLENDER-BILLED ORIOLE

Oriolus tenuirostris Oriolidae

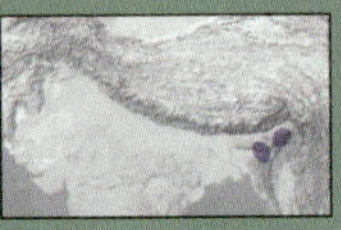

Size 27 cm

Voice Utters mellow fluty notes, *wheeow* or *chuck...tarry...you*

Range Breeds in the Himalayas from E Bhutan to Arunachal Pradesh

Habitat Well-wooded areas, groves, large trees in open country. Winters lower in broadleaved forests

Adult male has golden-yellow head; broad black band extending from lores around eye and across back of head. Very similar to Black-naped, but distinguished by longer and more downcurved bill and call and narrower nape-band. Olive-yellow wing-coverts and panel across tertials/secondaries. Female has more olive tinge to yellow in plumage and some indistinct barring in underparts. Juvenile hard to distinguish from Black-naped except by longer bill.

BLACK-NAPED ORIOLE

Oriolus chinensis Oriolidae

Size 25 cm

Voice Call similar to Indian's but less musical

Range Breeds on Andaman and Nicobar Islands. Scarce winter visitor to Kerala and SE Bangladesh. Scattered records elsewhere in peninsula

Habitat Rubber plantations

Easily differentiated from Golden by broad black eye-stripe continuing to join on nape (and much stouter bill). Female more greenish or olive on mantle. Overall yellow with black in-flight feathers and black tail with yellow patches. Female more greenish-yellow. Juvenile has some streaking on underparts and more diffused eye-stripe. Indulges in high-speed aerial chases. Raids nests of other birds, taking their eggs and chicks.

BLACK-HOODED ORIOLE

Oriolus xanthornus Oriolidae

Size 25 cm

Voice Assortment of melodious and harsh calls; fluty 2- or 3-noted *tu...hee or tll...yow...yow...*more common; also single, mellow note

Range Subcontinent, upto about 1,000 m in the Himalayan foothills

Habitat Forests, orchards, gardens, often amidst habitation

Golden-yellow plumage; black head diagnostic; black-and-yellow wings and tail; deep pink-red beak seen at close quarters. Sexes alike. In pairs, or small parties; strictly arboreal, only rarely descending into lower bushes or to ground; active and lively; moves a lot in forests and birds chase one another, rich colours striking against green or brown of forests; very vocal; associates with other birds in mixed parties, frequently joins mixed hunting groups; visits fruiting and flowering trees.

MAROON ORIOLE

Oriolus traillii Oriolidae

Size 28 cm

Voice Most commonly a cat-like squawking *meow*. Also, fluty *pi... lio...ilo*

Range Locally common breeding resident in N hills from E Himachal Pradesh to Myanmar border. Moves lower down to foothills and nearby plains, including Bangladesh, in winter

Habitat Subtropical or tropical moist lowland forests

Adult male has maroon body and black head and wings. Deep scarlet-red tail; strong, decurved grey-blue bill; startling white iris. Female has blackish upperparts, dull maroon back; white underparts heavily streaked maroonish-brown. In pairs, or singly, often in mixed hunting groups. Well-hidden in canopy; feeds on invertebrates, nectar and fruits.

♀

BLACK DRONGO

Dicrurus macrocercus Dicruridae

Size 31 cm

Voice Call a harsh *tiu...tiu*; also *cheece...cheece*

Range Subcontinent, upto about 1,800 m in the outer Himalayas

Habitat Open country; orchards; cultivation

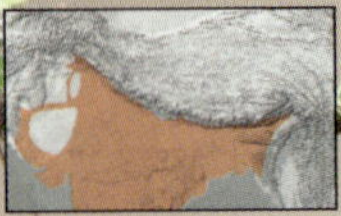

Glossy black plumage; long, deeply forked-tail. Diagnostic white spot at base of bill. Sexes alike. Usually solitary, sometimes in small parties; keeps lookout from exposed perch; most common bird seen on rail and road travel in India; drops to ground to capture prey; launches short aerial sallies; rides atop grazing cattle; follows cattle, tractors, grass cutters, fires; consumes vast numbers of insects; bold and aggressive species, with several birds nesting in same tree.

ASHY DRONGO

Dicrurus leucophaeus Dicruridae

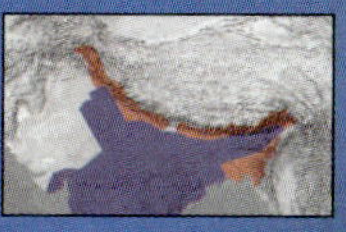

Size 30 cm

Voice Noisy and varied. Calls include *cha…ke wip…kit…whew* and *cheece…cheece…chichuk…*

Range Fairly common breeding summer visitor to N foothills from Pakistan, east to Myanmar border. Winters in plains and peninsula, including Sri Lanka

Habitat Forests and more open woodlands in winter

Adult has ash-grey upperparts; slightly lighter underparts, paler towards belly; red or reddish-brown iris; black legs and bill; black chin. Juvenile more brown than adult, with white edge on underside of tail and brown iris. Sexes similar, but male slightly larger. Agile flier, executing remarkable twists and turns in air with skill and speed. Mimics calls of other birds. Forages near edges of forests; perches on high, open branch to detect prey; swoops down to catch insects on ground or in mid-flight.

CROW-BILLED DRONGO

Dicrurus annectans Dicruridae

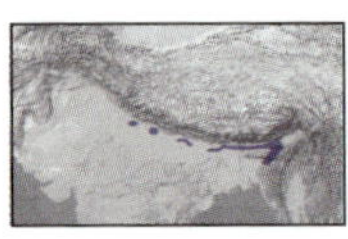

Size 28 cm

Voice Calls include loud, musical whistle and *churr*, characteristic descending series of harp-like notes

Range Winters in NE India and Bangladesh. Seen east of Almora upto 800 m

Habitat Dense broadleaved evergreen and moist deciduous forests

Stout drongo with thick, squat bill, covered at base by dense rictal feathers. Black plumage glossed bluish-green. Easily confused with Black, but distinguished by habitat. Short, broad tail with shallow fork but widely splayed and upcurved at tip. Immature has white speckled breast, belly and flanks, and undertail-coverts. Hawks from perch. Locally common.

LESSER RACKET-TAILED DRONGO

Dicrurus remifer Dicruridae

Size 25 cm

Voice Noisy like Greater. Musical whistle and screech. Mimics other birds

Range Locally common breeding resident in N foothills from Uttarakhand east to Myanmar border. Winters lower down and in Bangladesh

Habitat Shady understoreys of forests often near streams

Medium-sized, glossy black drongo with short crest and long streamers that end in feather-shaped rackets; square-ended rather than forked-tail. Juvenile duller, with flat-ended tail and no extensions. Sexes alike. Usually in pairs, or in mixed hunting groups or bird waves, feeding on invertebrates. Sits on perch waiting to swoop on prey, but often flycatches. Nests in trees.

immature

BRONZED DRONGO

Dicrurus aeneus Dicruridae

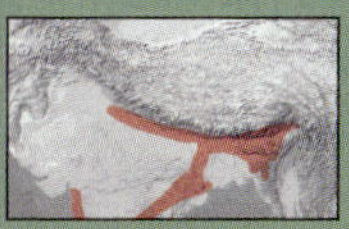

Size 24 cm

Voice Noisy. Varied whistles and grating calls. Also *cheet… chi… chew*

Range Fairly common breeding resident in foothills from E Punjab to NE India, including Bangladesh, then south through Eastern Ghats and throughout the length of Western Ghats. Makes some local movements

Habitat Clearings in thick forests, usually near streams

Smallish drongo with glossy, black plumage, and bluish-green/purple iridescence. Relatively short, spade-shaped tail with shallow fork, splayed at tips; short and heavy black bill; spiky rictal feathers give whisker-like appearance. Dark underparts, with more gloss over breast. Sexes alike. Perches high on exposed branch, hawking for insects. Very vocal and conspicuous; territorial. Pairs perform noisy displays.

SPANGLED DRONGO

Dicrurus hottentottus Dicruridae

Size 32 cm

Voice Noisy; mix of whistling, metallic calls and harsh screams

Range Lower Himalayan foothills, east of Uttarakhand; down through NE India, along Eastern Ghats, Odisha, Bastar through to Western Ghats, up north to Mumbai, occasionally even further north

Habitat Forests

Glistening blue-black plumage, fine hair-like feathers on forehead; longish, downcurved, pointed beak; diagnostic tail, square-cut and inwardly bent (curling) towards outer ends. Sexes alike. Solitary, or scattered pairs, strictly arboreal forest bird; small numbers may gather on favourite flowering trees; rather aggressive; often seen in mixed hunting parties of birds. Selects exposed branch and flies out to prey.

GREATER RACKET-TAILED DRONGO

Dicrurus paradiseus Dicruridae

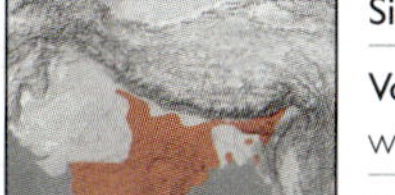

Size 32 cm (plus 30 cm streamers)

Voice Noisiest forest bird; amazing mimic; calls include wide variety of whistles and screams, perfect imitations

Range Forested parts of India, roughly east and south of line from S Gujarat to Uttarakhand; upto about 1,400 m

Habitat Forests; edges of forests; orchards

Glossy blue-black plumage; prominent crest of longish feathers, curving backwards; elongated, wire-like outer-tail feathers, ending in 'rackets' diagnostic. Distinguished from Lesser by larger size and wider rackets. Sexes alike. Solitary, or in pairs, sometimes small gatherings; arboreal, but often descends into low bushes; moves a lot in forests; confirmed exhibitionist, both by sight and sound; extremely noisy, often vocal long before sunrise; bold and aggressive, seen mobbing bigger birds 100 m over forests.

nicobarensis

YELLOW-BELLIED FANTAIL

Chelidorhynx hypoxantha Rhipiduridae

Size 13 cm

Voice Call a persistent *sip…sip…sip.* Also, musical *wee…too…wee too…wee*

Range Common breeding resident of foothills from extreme NE Pakistan to Myanmar border

Habitat Mainly broadleaved forests, often near water

Small, olive-green bird with broad, black tail, tipped white. Upperparts mostly olive with fine, white wing-bar; yellow head; olive rear crown; dark mask and eye-stripes. Underparts yellow. Very active; forages for insects in foliage; frequently flycatches, returning to perch.

WHITE-THROATED FANTAIL

Rhipidura albicollis Rhipiduridae

Size 17 cm

Voice Call a harsh *chukrrr…* note

Range Fairly common breeding resident of foothills from extreme NE Pakistan to Myanmar border, throughout NE India

Habitat Shaded forests, scrubs and gardens, favouring well-wooded ravines

Distinguished by dark fan-shaped tail edged with white. Overall brown-and-white bird with broad, white tip to tail (except to two central tail feathers); white throat and supercilium. Himalayan *R. a. canescans* has slaty-grey upperparts and underparts, and black eye mask, while *R. a. albogularis,* found in peninsular India, has dark grey upperparts, whitish underparts, and grey breast-band. Sexes alike.

WHITE-BROWED FANTAIL

Rhipidura aureola Rhipiduridae

Size 17 cm

Voice Call a lively whistle of 6- to 8-notes; grating *chuck… chuck …chuckrrr* note, usually when disturbed and agitated

Range Most of the country, south of the Himalayan foothills; absent in arid parts of NW India

Habitat Forests; orchards; gardens; tree-dotted cultivation

Characteristic habit of fanning black-and-white tail and flicking wings. Dark brown upperparts; black crown and face-sides; white forehead, broad stripe on nape; wing bars are two rows of white spots; black centre of throat and breast-sides; white throat sides; white underparts. Sexes alike, but female slightly duller. Solitary, or in pairs. Flits about constantly in lower and middle storey, makes short hunting dashes; tame and confiding.

BLACK-NAPED MONARCH

Hypothymis azurea Monarchidae

Size 16 cm

Voice Common call a sharp, grating, high-pitched *chwich... chweech* or *chwae...chweech*, slightly interrogative in tone, two notes quickly uttered; has short, rambling notes when breeding

Range India, south of outer Himalayas, to about 1,200 m, east of W Uttarakhand; absent in arid NW and N India

Habitat Forests; bamboos; gardens

Male has lilac-blue plumage; black patch on nape, gorget on breast; slight black scaly markings on crown; sooty on wings and tail; white below breast. Female ash-blue, duller; lacks black on nape and breast. Solitary, or in pairs in forests, often amidst mixed hunting parties; extremely active and fidgety, flits and flutters about, often fans tail slightly; calls often as it moves about, calls are often first indication of its presence.

♀

INDIAN PARADISE-FLYCATCHER

Terpsiphone paradisi Monarchidae

intermediate phase

Size 20 cm (male's tail 30 cm more)

Voice Call a sharp, grating *chwae* or *chchwae*…; melodious warbling song and display of breeding male

Range The Himalayas, foothills to about 1,800 m, rarely 2,500 m; N India, south to Bharatpur; absent in broad belt across Gangetic Plains widespread in peninsular India

Habitat Light forests; gardens; open country

Glossy blue-black head, crest and throat; black in wings; silvery-white body, long tail-streamers. Male occurs in two morphs: rufous phase has white parts replaced by rufous-chestnut with white underparts. White phase more variable, but has predominantly white plumage. Female and juvenile have no tail-streamers; shorter crest; rufous above; ash-grey throat and nuchal-collar; whitish below. Short legs; tends to sit upright on perch. Solitary, or in pairs; makes short sallies; flits through trees, tail-streamers floating; strictly arboreal, sometimes descending into taller bushes; cheerful disposition.

rufous phase

white phase

BLACK-HEADED JAY

Garrulus lanceolatus Corvidae

Size 33 cm

Voice Usually, single harsh *kraaa*

Range Locally common endemic breeding resident in N mountains from W Pakistan, east to Nepal. Some move lower in winter

Habitat Mixed temperate forests, particularly oaks, but often in more open areas than Eurasian

Similar to Eurasian, but range restricted to W Himalayas. Adult has black head with crest; pinkish-buff body, washed grey on rump and mantle. Wings regularly patterned black, blue-and-white; tail black-barred blue. White-streaked throat contrasting with black head; yellow bill. Sexes alike. Less shy than Eurasian, and often around human habitation.

EURASIAN JAY

Garrulus glandarius Corvidae

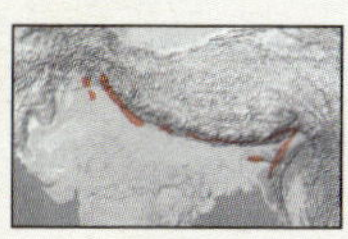

Size 33 cm

Voice Noisy; guttural chuckles, screeching notes and whistles; good mimic

Range Across the Himalayas, 1,500-2,800 m, somewhat higher in the east; may descend low in winter

Habitat Mixed temperate forests

Pinkish-brown plumage; velvety-black malar stripe; closely black-barred, blue wings; whitish crown streaked black; rufous lesser and median coverts; pinkish-brown underparts; white rump contrasts with jet-black tail. Sexes alike. Juvenile similar to adult, but darker body, greyer bill, bluish eyes, brighter legs. In small, noisy groups, often along with other Himalayan birds; inquisitive and aggressive; mostly keeps to trees, but also descends into bushes and onto ground; laboured flight.

YELLOW-BILLED BLUE MAGPIE

Urocissa flavirostris Corvidae

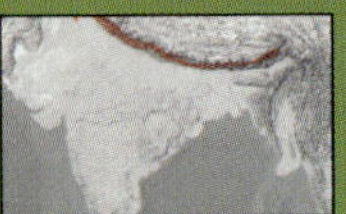

Size 66 cm

Voice Noisy. Calls include a great mix of metallic screams, loud whistles and raucous notes, often imitating other birds

Range The Himalayas, west to east; 1,500-3,600 m; may descend low in winter

Habitat Forests; gardens; clearings

Purple-blue plumage; black head and breast; white nape-patch and underbody; very long, white-tipped tail; yellow beak and orange legs. Sexes alike. In pairs or small bands, often associating with jays, laughing thrushes and treepies; wanders a lot in forests, flying across clearings, entering hill station gardens, one bird following another; arboreal, but also hunts low in bushes; even descends to ground, long tail cocked as bird hops about.

RED-BILLED BLUE MAGPIE

Urocissa erythrorhyncha Corvidae

Size 70 cm

Voice Calls include loud *pit* and sharp *kwerer…pig…pig*. Other calls similar to Yellow-billed's

Range Locally common breeding resident in foothills of N mountains from Himachal Pradesh

Habitat Mixed forests; cultivation and gardens at lower altitude than Yellow-billed

Slaty-blue bird with very long-tail and robust, red bill, black head, neck and breast with bluish spotting on crown. Creamy-grey underparts. Larger than Yellow-billed and bluer above (purplish in eastern race). White nape-patch larger. Black subterminal band to white-tipped tail. Red legs. Sexes alike. Juvenile has greyish bill, brownish head and back, very similar to Yellow-billed's.

COMMON GREEN MAGPIE

Cissa chinensis Corvidae

Size 47 cm

Voice Very variable. Call a loud *kik...wee* note. Complex mixture of whistles, squeals and wails. Also mimics

Range Locally common breeding resident in N mountains from Uttarakhand to Myanmar border, and also Bangladesh

Habitat Dense broadleaved forests, particularly ravine sides

Large green magpie with vivid red bill. Brilliant emerald-green upperparts; paler green underparts. Bold, broad black stripe extending from bill through eyes to short crest onto rear crown. Red legs. Wings black and white-tipped chestnut. Long, graduated, white-tipped tail. Sexes alike. Feeds low down in foliage or ground in pairs or small groups. Joins mixed hunting groups.

RUFOUS TREEPIE

Dendrocitta vagabunda Corvidae

Size 50 cm

Voice Common call a fluty 3-note *goo... ge...lay* or *ko...ki... la*; harsh, guttural notes often uttered

Range Almost all over India, upto about 1,500 m in outer Himalayas

Habitat Forests; gardens; cultivation; habitation

pallida

Sexes alike. Rufous above; sooty grey-brown head and neck; black, white and grey on wings, best seen in flight; black-tipped, grey tail, long and graduated. In pairs, or small parties; feeds up in trees, but also descends low into bushes and onto ground to pick up termites.

vagabunda

GREY TREEPIE

Dendrocitta formosae Corvidae

Size 40 cm

Voice Noisy and variable. Call a loud, clanking *klok…ti…klok…ti…ti*

Range Locally common breeding resident in N hills from extreme NE Pakistan to Myanmar border; Eastern Ghats

Habitat Forests; secondary growth

Duller and less rufous than the Rufous; long tail; grey-and-brown plumage; dusky grey face and grey head, neck and underparts; rufous vent; radiated grey tail black-edged and tipped; brownish back; black wings with small white patch. Sexes alike. Less often near human habitation than Rufous. Behaviour and food as Rufous but shyer. Arboreal, often in groups or mixed hunting groups. Seems to seek company of drongos.

COLLARED TREEPIE

Dendrocitta frontalis Corvidae

Size 38 cm

Voice Various loud calls, similar to other treepies'

Range Patchy distribution in extreme E Nepal, Bhutan and Arunachal Pradesh

Habitat Thick tropical, subtropical, temperate moist evergreen, semi-evergreen forests; bamboos

Smaller treepie with compact body and long tail. Similar to Grey, Rufous, but distinctly separated by black forecrown, face, throat contrasting with pale grey hindcrown, nape, breast, upper belly; rufous mantle, lower belly, rump, vent; long black, not grey, tail; black wings have grey panels on coverts, no white patch. In flight, black tail, rufous vent, rump, distinguish it from Rufous. Singly, or in small groups; like all treepies, joins mixed feeding parties with other forest species; mainly arboreal; not as noisy as Rufous, Grey.

EURASIAN MAGPIE

Pica pica Corvidae

Pied bird with glossy black head, neck, upper back, wings; tail glossed bronze-green and purple-blue; white scapulars, lower back (rump), belly; black undertail. Sexes alike. Tibetan race *bottanensis* can be identified by black rump. Usually, several in vicinity; moves on ground, perches on fence-posts, trees, house-tops; frequents high-mountain villages; typical crow, bold and aggressive, but also extremely alert; flicks tail often.

Size 52 cm

Voice Call a loud, grating *chak...chak*; also other piping notes

Range High NW, the Himalayas, Chitral, N Kashmir, Ladakh, Himachal Pradesh; Tibetan race found in Bhutan and Arunachal Pradesh, 1,500-4,700 m

Habitat Open valleys; cultivation; habitation

SPOTTED NUTCRACKER

Nucifraga caryocatactes Corvidae

Size 32-35 cm

Voice Noisy. Call a guttural *kharr…kharr*

Range The Himalayas, 1,800-4,000 m, sometimes descending to about 1,200 m in winter

Habitat Coniferous, oak, rhododendron forests

Chocolate-brown plumage, thickly-speckled with white; dark central tail feathers, tipped white; white outer-tail and undertail-coverts; heavy, pointed beak distinctive. Sexes alike. The race *hemispila*, found between Kangra and CE Nepal, has smaller white spots; rump lacks white spots. Small parties in temperate forests; keeps to tree-tops but readily descends onto ground; rather wary; flies short distances across glades; rather noisy, usually attracting attention by its calling.

Large-spotted Nutcracker

ALPINE CHOUGH

Pyrrhocorax graculus Corvidae

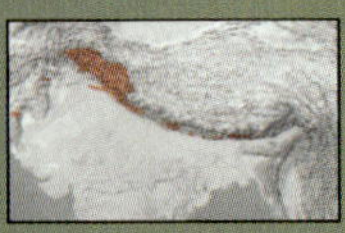

Size 38 cm

Voice Less noisy than Red-billed. Calls include high rolling *krerrr*, high *kee…u* and deep *kruu*

Range Common breeding resident of N mountains from W Pakistan, east to Arunachal Pradesh. Many move lower in winter

Habitat As Red-billed's, with which it sometimes mixes, but usually at higher altitudes

Glossy black crow with diagnostic short, yellow, decurved bill. Similar to Red-billed, but shorter wings with bulging trailing edges and longer tail with rounded edges. Overall black plumage with bluish-green gloss on wings; short and inconspicuous nasal tuft; orangish-yellow bill, more greenish at base. Confiding. Large flocks often seen performing aerial displays, sweeping down mountainsides.

RED-BILLED CHOUGH

Pyrrhocorax pyrrhocorax Corvidae

Size 45 cm

Voice Call a melodious, high-pitched *cheeao… cheeau…*

Range High in the Himalayas

Habitat Cliffsides; alpine pastures; cultivation; vicinity of mountain habitation

Velvety black crow with characteristic coral-red decurved beak and red legs; upper mandible slightly overlaps lower; inconspicuous nasal tuft; square-ended tail. Sexes alike. Highly gregarious; feeds in cultivation; probes ground and dung for insects; does not hesitate to rob corn stored in attics of upland houses; flocks often fly high into skies, rising on thermals, playing and dancing in air currents in wild splendour; tame and confiding in some areas.

EURASIAN JACKDAW

Corvus monedula Corvidae

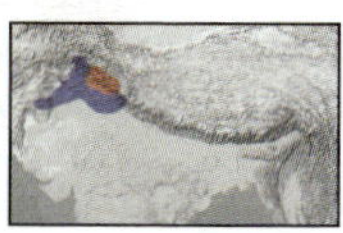

Size 33 cm

Voice Noisy. Commonest calls include abrupt *jack* and repeated *kyaa*

Range Locally common breeding summer visitor to N Pakistan, Kashmir. Winters in Pakistan plains in variable numbers, individuals sometimes occurring as far south and east as Uttar Pradesh

Habitat Mountain cultivation and pastures usually near cliffs. Also cultivation in winter in plains

Smallish black and grey crow; black crown and face; white iris; small, short beak; black legs. Distinguished from House Crow by smaller size and smaller bill. In flight, looks short-headed and stocky. Juvenile has dark eye, darker grey parts and lacks pale silvery-grey ear-coverts. Very gregarious; large flocks often wheel around cliffs. Runs on ground. Nests in holes.

HOUSE CROW

Corvus splendens Corvidae

Size 43 cm

Voice Call a familiar *caw*; occasionally pleasant *kurrrrr* note; several other notes

Range Subcontinent, reaching about 2,500 m in the Himalayas

Habitat Rural and urban habitation; cultivation, edges of forests; wide range of habitats

splendens

zugmayeri

Sleek-looking crow with glossy black plumage; grey collar, upper back and breast; glossy black on forehead, crown and throat; long, prominent, arched bill; black feet; brown eyes. Sexes alike. Mobs other birds, even large raptors; performs important scavenging services; occasionally flies very high into skies, either when flying long distance, or simply for fun; roosts communally.

protegatus

ROOK

Corvus frugilegus Corvidae

Size 48 cm

Voice Call a hoarse *karrh…karrh*

Range Locally common winter visitor to W and N Pakistan, Kashmir. No recent substantiated records from elsewhere in India

Habitat Cultivation; pastures

Large crow with long, pointed bill and whitish face and peaked crown. Long, slim unfeathered bill also has whitish base. Often has small throat pouch. Fingered, straight-edged, narrow-based wings and slightly wedge-shaped tail give different flight shape. Very gregarious, feeding and roosting in flocks, often with Eurasian Jackdaws. Walks rather cockily about fields feeding on invertebrates, for which it probes deeply. Also eats young shoots and seeds.

CARRION CROW

Corvus corone Corvidae

Size 48 cm

Voice Call a deep harsh *karr…karr*

Range Scarce breeding resident: N Pakistan, Kashmir. Hooded Crow is scarce winter visitor to same area but common in Ladakh

Habitat Open country and cultivation, often near human habitation

Similar to Rook and Large-billed, but distinguished by much stouter bill, feathered at base and slightly decurved; flatter head; shorter, more rounded tail; Hooded Crow *C. c. cornix* grey with black head and breast-patch, wings and tail. Broad, even-edged wings and square-ended tail. Sexes alike. Lazy flight with steady wingbeats; soars and glides. Shy and wary. Solitary, or in pairs but roosts communally; feeds with other species, especially on carrion; eats almost anything. Inquisitive feeder, searching methodically.

NORTHERN RAVEN

Corvus corax Corvidae

Size 58-69 cm

Voice Call a deep, resounding *kraa…kraa; gonk…gonk…; wock…wock*

Range Kashmir to Bhutan (Northern) and in NW (Punjab Raven)

Habitat High-altitude Trans-Himalayan stony desert; alpine meadows (Northern), deserts and semi-deserts (Punjab)

Northern Raven

Impressively-sized, glossy black crow. Long, decurved bill with distal culmen; prominent nasal bristles. Similar to Large-billed, but has larger, less domed head; beard-like throat feathers, pale brownish-grey, less curved bill; distinct wedge-shaped tail conspicuous in flight. Flight feathers and tail more brown. Juvenile duller and less glossy with bluish-white iris. Powerful flight; soars on thermals; pairs indulge in aerial rolling displays. Singly, in pairs or small groups; sometimes larger flocks; roosts communally.

Punjab Raven

LARGE-BILLED CROW

Corvus macrorhynchos Corvidae

Size 48 cm

Voice Call a harsh *khaa…khaa*; several variations among various races

Range The Himalayas

Habitat Forests, rural habitations; small numbers in towns and cities

Glossy black plumage; heavy beak, with noticeable culmen-curve. Relatively broad wings, particularly primaries; long tail, slightly wedged, obvious only in flight; nasal tufts; black bill and legs; dark iris. Sexes alike. Solitary, or in groups of two to six; most common around villages and only small numbers in urban areas; overall not as 'enterprising' as familiar House; in forested areas, behaviour often indicates presence of carnivore kills. Large nest, untidy assembly of twigs.

EASTERN JUNGLE CROW

Corvus (m.) levaillantii Corvidae

Size 42 cm

Voice Identical to Indian Jungle's

Range NE India, from Nepal eastwards and Andaman Islands

Similar to Large-billed, but shorter, more pointed, slender bill; flatter forehead profile and shorter, square-ended tail.

INDIAN JUNGLE CROW

Corvus (m.) culminatus Corvidae

Size 42 cm

Voice Similar to House's

Range South of the Himalayas; peninsular (except NW) India and Sri Lanka

Difficult to tell apart from Indian Jungle and Large-billed. Recently split.

BOHEMIAN WAXWING

Bombycilla garrulus Bombycillidae

Size 25 cm

Voice Call a high, dry, metallic, rapid clattery even-tempo *trill*

Range Winter vagrant: Hills of Balochistan, to Karachi (once), the Himalayas of N Afghanistan-Pakistan frontier to C Nepal

Habitat Mixed coniferous, deciduous forests

Grey, rust, black, yellow, red, white bird with narrow, sharply-defined black face mask finely bordered with white; black chin; rusty wash to forehead and cheeks; wings slightly darker grey; whitish lower abdomen; dull orange undertail-coverts; grey wings marked white, bordered red-and-yellow with dark tips; tail grey to black with broad bright yellow terminal band. Sexes similar. Juvenile similar but lacks red-and-yellow tips on wing feathers; facial markings less defined. Highly gregarious; dense, nervous flocks gather in trees.

CINEREOUS TIT

Parus major Paridae

Size 13 cm

Voice Call a loud, clear whistling *whee…chi… chee…*; other whistling and harsh notes

Range Widespread in the Himalayas, foothills to about 3,500 m; peninsular India

Habitat Open forests; gardens; habitation

Adult has grey back; black crown continuing along neck-sides to broad black band from chin along centre of underbody; white cheeks, nape-patch, wing-bar and outer feathers of black tail; ashy-white sides. Sexes alike. In pairs or small bands, often with other small birds; restless, clings upside down, and indulges in acrobatic displays while hunting among leaves and branches; holds food fast between feet and pecks at it noisily; tame and confiding.

GREEN-BACKED TIT

Parus monticolus Paridae

Size 13 cm

Voice Similar to Great's. Calls include loud *teacher… teacher*-note and repeated *whitee… whittee*

Range Locally common breeding resident to N mountains from N Pakistan east to Myanmar border. May move lower down in foothills during winter

Habitat Deciduous, coniferous mixed forests and tropical moist lowland forests

Yellow-green, and black tit distinguished by two white wing-bars, bright green upperparts and blue leading edges on wing feathers. White cheeks. Similar to Great but has brighter green mantle and back-and-yellow underparts. Sexes similar. Feeds mainly near ground on invertebrates and fruits.

BLACK-LORED TIT

Parus xanthogenys Paridae

Size 14 cm

Voice Cheerful, musical notes. Call a loud tailorbird-like *towit… towit* near nest; other 2- to 4-noted whistling calls; whistling song. Also, harsh *charrr* and some chattering notes

Range The Himalayas to E Nepal; 1,200-2,500 m, widespread in parts of C, E and W India

Habitat Forests; gardens

Large tit with diagnostic bushy, black crest. Olive-green back; black crest, faintly-tipped yellow; stripe behind eye, broad central band from chin to vent; bright yellow nape-patch, supercilium and sides of underbody. Sexes alike. In pairs or small flocks, often with other small birds; arboreal, active; feeds in foliage; sometimes enters gardens. Female and juvenile like male, but may have black replaced by olive.

YELLOW-CHEEKED TIT

Parus spilonotus Paridae

Size 14 cm

Voice Calls include *sit, si…si… si* and *chrrrr*. Great Tit-like song *chee…o…chee…pui*

Range Locally common breeding resident in N mountains from E Nepal east to Myanmar border. Moves lower down in winter

Habitat Open forests

Black-and-yellow tit with unmistakably erect and pointed black crest, tipped yellow, yellow forehead. Regional variations: yellow and green in the Himalayan region; greyer and black with yellow cheeks in rest of the region. Short, black lines behind eye; heavily streaked greenish mantle; grey rump; white wing-bars. Sexes similar, but female duller. Forages low down.

RUFOUS-VENTED TIT

Periparus rubidiventris Paridae

Size 10 cm

Voice Noisy. Calls include thin *seet* and *psst*. Rattling song

Range Common breeding resident in N mountains from Himachal Pradesh east to Nagaland. Moves lower down in foothills during winter

Habitat Open, coniferous and broadleaved forests, particularly rhododendron

Black-crowned bird with spiky crest and black bib. *Western Himalayan* race has olive-washed, dark grey upperparts, reddish-rufous underparts, pinkish-rufous belly, pale rufous-washed nuchal patch, white cheek-patch, greyish flanks. *Eastern Himalayan* race *R. beavani* has whitish nuchal spot, blue-washed, dark grey underparts, buff-grey bib, and only rump has hint of cinnamon. Sexes similar, male darker. Juvenile duller with smaller crest.

COAL TIT

Periparus ater Paridae

Size 11 cm

Voice Call includes thin *tsi... tsi.* Song a low-pitched, slow *wee...tsee...wee...tsee... wee...tsee*

Range Common breeding resident in the Himalayas western race *melanolophus* (Spot-winged Tit) from NW Pakistan to W Nepal, and *aemodius* in C and E Himalayas

Habitat Coniferous forests

Slender-billed small tit with largish head and floppy crest. Black crown and upper mantle; large, white nuchal and cheek-patches; extensive black bib continuing to black nape. Underparts mainly buffy-white (*aemodius*) or grey with rufous breast-sides (*melanolophus*). Slaty-bluish grey upperparts graduating to buffy olive-brown towards rump; two distinct white-spotted wing-bars and white-tipped tertials. Sexes alike. Very active; sometimes shy. Solitary, or in pairs; in flocks outside breeding.

aemodius

melanolophus

RUFOUS-NAPED TIT

Periparus rufonuchalis Paridae

Size 13 cm

Voice Noisy. Calls include *tsee… tsee… peeou…, peep* and *seep*

Range Fairly common breeding resident in N mountains from E Balochistan to W Nepal. Moves lower down in foothills during winter

Habitat Open, coniferous forests

Dark tit with upright crest and large creamy-white cheek-patch. White nuchal-patch finely bordered rufous; extensive black bib, covering entire breast; dark grey upperparts and belly; rufous nape, sides of breast and vent. Sexes similar, but female has less extensive bib. Juvenile has much paler bib, less demarcated from lower breast and belly. Gregarious; appears often with other tit species or mixed hunting groups.

GREY-CRESTED TIT

Lophophanes dichrous Paridae

Size 12 cm

Voice Calls include thin *zai* and *ti…ti…ti…ti* and *chea…chea* alarm. Song *wee…wee tz…tz…tz*

Range Locally common breeding resident in N mountains from E Kashmir to Bhutan. Commonest in E. Moves lower down in foothills during winter

Habitat Hill forests

Adult has dull brownish-grey upperparts; similarly coloured upright crest; dirty whitish sub-moustachial stripe extending around neck to form collar; decurved eye-stripe; mottled-grey cheeks; lighter grey-brown throat. Underparts washed pale cinnamon. Sexes alike. Juvenile similar to adult with shorter crest and less uniform underparts. Often in mixed hunting groups. Rather quiet and inconspicuous; acrobatic behaviour.

SULTAN TIT

Melanochlora sultanea Paridae

Size 20 cm

Voice Noisy. Call a loud, whistling *cheerie…cheerie;* other shrill whistling notes, often mixed with harsh *churr* or *chrrchuk;* varied chattering notes

Range The Himalayan foothills, east from C Nepal; NE; foothills to about 1,200 m, sometimes ascending to 2,000 m

Habitat Mixed forests; edges of forests

Male black above; yellow crown and crest; black throat and upper breast; yellow below. Female has deep olivish wash to black upperbody and throat; crest similar to male; some yellow also visible on throat. Small bands, seen often along with other birds in mixed hunting flocks; active and inquisitive; clings sideways and upside down; checks foliage and bark crevices; feeds in canopy but also descends to tall bushes.

FIRE-CAPPED TIT

Cephalopyrus flammiceps Paridae

Size 9 cm

Voice Call a soft *tsit* and *tsee… tsee… tsee*. Song a quiet *we… two…we two…we…two*

Range Local breeding summer visitor to N mountains from E Pakistan to Arunachal Pradesh. Winters in foothills, rarely in plains south to Maharashtra and Madhya Pradesh

Habitat Alpine forests

Small, rounded, yellow and green tit. Sharp-tipped, small, conical bill. Breeding male has bright scarlet-red crown and throat, golden-yellow lores and short, yellow supercilium. Green upperparts; two thin, white wing-bars. Deep yellow underparts. Non-breeding male has olive-yellow upperparts and yellow rump. Female has paler underparts while almost white in juvenile. Beady black eyes and very short pointed bill. Forest feeding on invertebrates, nectar and pollen, usually high in canopy but will descend to low growth.

GROUNDPECKER

Pseudopodoces humilis Paridae

Size 20 cm

Voice Call a weak repeated *cheep*

Range Locally common breeding resident in N Nepal, Sikkim and Ladakh. Usually above 4,000 m

Habitat Grassy, stony habitats high in altitude steppe with low scattered bushes

Small, plain-coloured bird with fluffy, sandy-brown upperparts and whitish underparts. Dusky lores; whitish nape; creamy-white throat and head-sides; white tips to darker wing shoulder; white outer-tail feathers; short, thin, curved bill; black legs. Sexes similar. Juvenile has faint barring on throat and breast. In pairs, or family parties. Long bounding hop, frequently flicking tail, flying rarely. Digs actively for insects within turf, soil, and yak dung; nests in holes.

BLACK-THROATED TIT

Aegithalos concinnus Aegithalidae

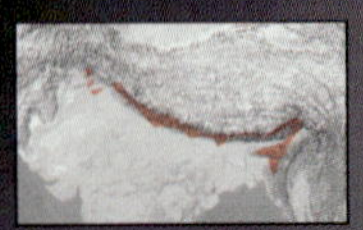

Size 10 cm

Voice Calls include soft but insistent *trrr… trrr* and *chek…chek*

Range Common breeding resident in N mountains from N Pakistan east to Myanmar border. Moves lower down to foothills during winter

Habitat Open forests; gardens; edges of forests

Small black and grey tit with bright chestnut crown. Bluish-grey upperparts; darker tail, bordered and tipped white; white chin and sub-moustachial stripe; white-bordered black throat, broad, black band through eye; prominent white supercilium. Pale rufous-buff underparts. Juvenile has paler crown and lacks black throat. Sexes alike. Very active and gregarious; confiding and inquisitive. Small parties, sometimes in bird waves; feeds on invertebrates and fruits. Communal rooster. Nests in low bushes.

WHITE-CHEEKED TIT

Aegithalos leucogenys Aegithalidae

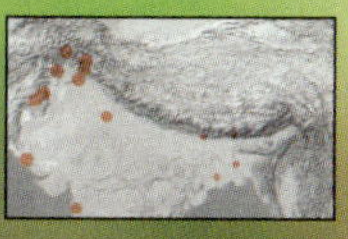

Size 11 cm

Voice Hyphenate high-pitched call

Range Scares resident Baluchistan and Kashmir

Habitat Open scrub forest

Adult has both a black bib and throat. Long and narrow dark mask. Cheek white and prominent; cinnamon crown, iris yellow; brown mantle. Juvenile told apart by its brownish-white throat and light streaking on breast. Often seen along water.

WHITE-THROATED TIT

Aegithalos niveogularis Aegithalidae

Size 11 cm

Voice Call a frequently uttered *t…r…r…r…r…t*. Song longer and more elaborate than that of other *Aegithalos* tits; has rapid chattering *tweet…tweet* interspersed with high-pitched *tsi…tsi* notes and short warbling phrases

Range The Himalayas from E Pakistan to NW Nepal

Habitat Bushes in mixed birch and coniferous forests

Small tit with distinct white forehead and forecrown and whitish throat. Black lores, head sides and cheeks; pure white sub-moustachial patch and neck-sides; blackish mask merges with cinnamon-brown hindcrown and ear-coverts. Greyish-brown upperparts; pinkish-rufous patch on rump; greyish-brown tail, edged and tipped white. Underparts cinnamon, darker cinnamon band between throat and breast; pale grey chin and throat. Juvenile similar to adult, has dull pinkish throat, darker and more prominent breast-band (with paler lower breast and belly), and brown upperparts.

RUFOUS-FRONTED TIT

Aegithalos iouschistos Aegithalidae

Size 11 cm

Voice Calls include *trrr…trrr; trrup; si…si…si*

Range Nepal to Arunachal Pradesh

Habitat Broadleaved and coniferous forests; rhododendron; scrubs

Black-browed Tit

Distinguished by extensive black head-sides and lores. Cinnamon forehead, centre of nape, crown-stripe and cheeks; narrow rufous sub-moustachial stripe extends to breast-sides; black chin and malar border; prominent white throat; silver-grey breast and rich rufous-buff on rest of underparts. Grey upperparts washed buff on upper mantle; pale cinnamon patch on rump. Appears in groups of upto 40 outside breeding. Forages in canopy as well as in shrubs. There have been several recent sightings of the Black-browed Tit in Arunachal Pradesh.

PLAIN MARTIN

Riparia paludicola Hirundinidae

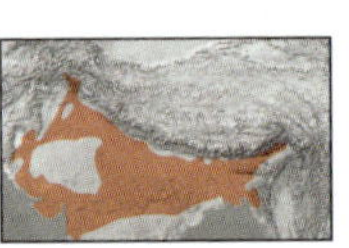

Size 12 cm

Voice Calls *brret…*, rather harsh in tone, usually on the wing around nest colony. Twittering song

Range NW and N India, from the outer Himalayas, south at least to line from vicinity of Mumbai-Nasik to C Odisha; moves considerably locally

Habitat Vicinity of water, sandbanks, sandy cliffsides

Long wings and slightly forked-tail. Grey-brown above, slightly darker on crown; dark brown wings and tail; dull grey below, whiter towards abdomen. Sexes alike. Gregarious species, always in flocks, flying around sandbanks along water courses; individual birds occasionally stray far and high; hawks small insects in flight; flocks perch on telegraph wires.

SAND MARTIN

Riparia riparia Hirundinidae

Size 13 cm

Voice Call a dry, quiet *trass*

Range Scarce breeding resident in Assam. Local winter visitor to Bangladesh. Scarce and irregular passage migrant, perhaps winter visitor in NW India

Habitat Vicinity of water

Adult has greyish-brown upperparts; darker tail and wings; long wings; slightly notched tail; dark underwings, white throat and underparts; contrasting brown chest-band sometimes extending to centre of belly; small, black beak; blackish or dark brown legs and feet. Sexes similar. Juvenile has buff or cream wash on belly, pale rust wash on face, neck, chin and breast. Gliding swallow-like flight. Northwestern Pale, similar in flight but much paler. Feeds on aerial insects close to surface of water. Sociable. Nests in tunnels in sandbanks.

PALE MARTIN

Riparia diluta Hirundinidae

Size 13 cm

Voice Undocumented

Range Breeds in the Himalayas; winters in Pakistan and probably farther E

Habitat Large waterbodies

Treated as conspecific with Pale Sand. However, smaller and slimmer with shallower tail-fork; paler upperparts; greyish-brown; breast-band paler, more greyish-brown and less distinct with diffuse lower border. In some, the breast-band only slightly darker than rest of underparts, gives impression of broken breast-band with paler centre merging to darker sides; paler head, particularly crown and ear-coverts, contrasting with dark eye and darker lores; pale (often almost pure white, or buffish) throat.

BARN SWALLOW

Hirundo rustica Hirundinidae

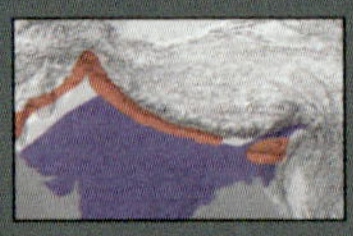

Size 18 cm

Voice Calls vary with object of alarm. Hard *vit* in flight and twittering rambling song

Range Common breeding resident to N mountains from W Pakistan east to Myanmar border. Common winter visitor throughout rest of the region

Habitat Cultivation, towns and villages usually near or over water

Slender bird with long, narrow, pointed wings, and deeply forked-tail with long streamers; spends most of its life on wing. Steel bluish-black upperparts; black wings and tail; pale underparts; red throat; steel-blue breast-band. Sexes alike, but male may have longer streamers. Juvenile has paler underparts and less deeply forked-tail. Agile flier; low, fast, powerful in flight. Constructs nest under eaves of buildings. Gregarious.

PACIFIC SWALLOW

Hirundo tahitica Hirundinidae

Size 13 cm

Voice Call a hard *qwik...qwik*

Range Resident in Andaman Islands

Habitat Open country and along coasts and rivers

Distinguished from Barn by lack of blue breast-band and streamers. Blue-black upperparts; short, forked-tail. Rufous from forehead to breast; greyish-white belly; dark grey vent with white scalloping; grey underwing-coverts. Hunts alongside Barn, but does not associate with them otherwise. Feeds socially on aerial insects. Flight less sweeping than Barn. Often perches on wires and bare branches. Nests against wall in building or against bank or culvert.

WIRE-TAILED SWALLOW

Hirundo smithii Hirundinidae

Size 14 cm

Voice Call a soft twittering note; pleasant song of breeding male

Range Common breeding (summer) visitor to N India, to about 1,800 m in the Himalayas; breeds in many other parts of India; widespread over the area, excepting arid zones

Habitat Open areas; cultivation; habitation, mostly in vicinity of canals, lakes, rivers

Glistening steel-blue above; chestnut cap; unmarked, pure white underbody distinctive; two long, wire-like projections (tail-wires) from outer-tail feathers diagnostic. Sexes alike. In solitary, or small parties; almost always seen around water, either perched on overhead wires or hawking insects in graceful, acrobatic flight, swooping and banking; often flies very low, drinks from surface; roosts in reed beds and other vegetation, often with warblers and wagtails.

EURASIAN CRAG MARTIN

Ptyonoprogne rupestris Hirundinidae

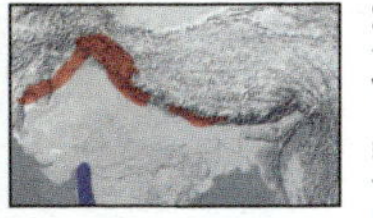

Size 15 cm

Voice Calls include short *plee*, musical *weeeh* and harsh *tshrr*

Range Fairly common but local breeding resident and summer visitor in W Pakistan and N mountains from N Pakistan to Bhutan. Winter visitor to Western Ghats

Habitat Rocky gorges; cliffs; old hill forts

Dusky-brown upperparts and crown; dark brown wings; dark, wedge-shaped tail spotted white on underside; pale chin and throat speckled darker graduating to pale buff-brown on breast and greyish-brown on belly. Pale chevron-shaped scalloping on sides of vent. Sexes similar. Juvenile has lighter throat and indistinct mottling on underparts. Less slender than other species in this family. Feeds close to cliff faces; seen in pairs, or small groups.

RED-RUMPED SWALLOW

Cecropis daurica Hirundinidae

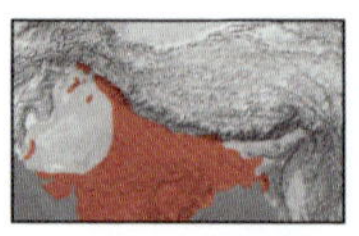

Size 18 cm

Voice Call a mournful chirping note. Pleasant twittering song of breeding male

Range Six races over the subcontinent, including Sri Lanka; resident, migratory

Habitat Cultivation; vicinity of human habitation; town centres; rocky hilly areas

Glossy steel-blue above; chestnut supercilium, head-sides, neck-collar and rump; dull rufous-white below, streaked brown; deeply forked-tail diagnostic. Sexes alike. Small parties spend much of day on wing; migrant, winter-visiting race *nipalensis* highly gregarious; hawks insects along with other birds; freely perches on overhead wires, thin branches of bushes and trees; hunts insects amongst most-crowded areas of towns, over markets and refuse heaps, flying with amazing agility, wheeling, banking and stooping with remarkable mastery.

STRIATED SWALLOW

Cecropis striolata Hirundinidae

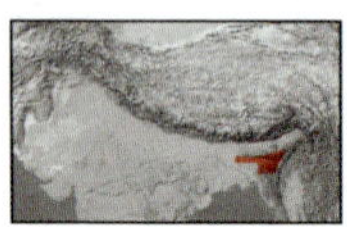

Size 19 cm

Voice Call a *pin* or long drawn-out *quitsch*, and *chi…chi… chi* when alarmed. Song a soft twittering

Range Hills of NE India and Bangladesh

Habitat Little information from the region; around steep cliffs in hills

Glossy steel-blue crown and back; indistinct, rufous hind-collar; narrowly streaked chestnut rump; deeply forked-tail; dark chestnut face and underwing-coverts. Similar to Red-rumped, but distinguished by larger size, stronger streaking on underparts and broader, blacker streaking on rump. Juvenile less glossy with paler rump. Feeds singly, or in small groups. Nest enclosed, with long tunnel, made of mud.

STREAK-THROATED SWALLOW

Petrochelidon fluvicola Hirundinidae

Size 12 cm

Voice Calls include *chrrp* and *trr…trr*

Range Locally common breeding resident in Indo-Gangetic Plains from E Pakistan to Uttar Pradesh and south through W peninsula to Karnataka. Mainly summer visitor to N areas

Habitat Open country, cultivation near water

Glossy black upperparts; some whitish edges to dorsal feathers; dark-rufous crown; brownish rump; white underparts with black mesial streaks to feathers from throat to breast; pale brown underwing; tail slightly furcate, small whitish spot towards tip of inner web of each feather. Upto 200 birds nest communally on cliff faces.

juvenile

COMMON HOUSE MARTIN

Delichon urbicum Hirundinidae

Size 14 cm

Voice Noisy. Calls include soft twittering chirps and short *prrit…prrit*

Range Local breeding summer visitor to N mountains from N Pakistan east to Himachal Pradesh. Scarce passage migrant throughout India, but perhaps overlooked because it flies so high. Some winter in Western Ghats

Habitat Mountain valleys with cultivation, cliffs and gorges

Adult has steel-blue upperparts and white underparts. Glossy bluish-black head; white rump and underwings conspicuous in flight; short legs with downy feathers; brown eyes; small black bill; deeply forked-tail. Sexes alike. Juvenile sooty-black, and wing-coverts, quills edged and tipped white. Sociable. In groups of several hundreds or even thousands of individuals. Spends time in open country. Cup-shaped nest made of mud and grass.

ASIAN HOUSE MARTIN

Delichon dasypus Hirundinidae

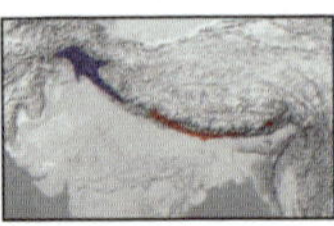

Size 12 cm

Voice Calls *jeep…jeep*. Twittering, trilling song

Range Pakistan to Myanmar, S Assam Hills

Habitat Mountain cliffs, gorges; steep, grassy hillsides; forest; cultivation; near watercourses; mountain settlements

Distinguished from Nepal by shallow fork to tail, blackish underwing-coverts, dirty-white rump and vent. Adult has blue cap, dark eye-patch, dusky wash on whitish underparts; throat and vent whiter than breast and belly; duskier underparts; white vent; unmarked whiter throat; whiter, less marked rump. Feeds gregariously on aerial insects, often high in sky. Mixes with swifts and other swallows.

NEPAL HOUSE MARTIN

Delichon nipalense Hirundinidae

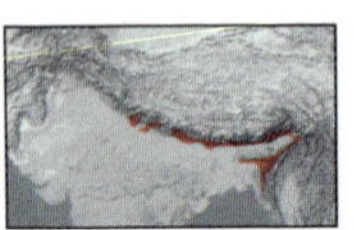

Size 12 cm

Voice Call a shrill *chee…ee*. Short song

Range Uttarakhand to Myanmar. S Assam Hills

Habitat Mountain cliffs, gorges, valleys, ridges; forest; hillside cultivation; along mountain rivers; villages

Smallish martin with square tail, dark underwings, black throat and vent. Blue cap; cheeks, chin and throat, upper breast streaked dark; dark underwing-coverts; white belly and breast. Similar to Asian House, but distinguished by no fork in tail, whiter underparts, darker chin, vent, undertail-coverts, underwing-coverts, and smaller white rump with black markings.

WHITE-BROWED TIT WARBLER

Leptopoecile sophiae Sylviidae

Size 10 cm

Voice Call a soft *teet* and hard *tzrit*. Loud chirping song

Range Locally common breeding resident in high mountains from N Pakistan east to W Nepal. Moves lower down in winter

Habitat Montane scrub, bushes by streams

One of the most difficult birds to see in the region. Very small, but distinctive, with obvious white supercilium. Rufous crown; greyish underparts, washed pinkish-blue; white outer-tail feathers; grey-brown mantle and wings; rump and flanks bluish; Female paler overall with greyish-brown head-sides. Eastern race *sophiae* different from that of the west Himalayan *obscura*. Feeds on invertebrates in small parties or mixed hunting groups. Very active; rather shy. Cocks tail. Nests low down in bushes.

♀

BENGAL BUSH LARK

Mirafra assamica Alaudidae

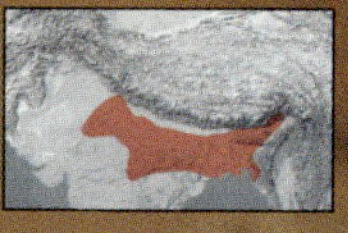

Size 15 cm

Voice Call a thin, high *p…zeee* or *tzee…tzee* delivered in high, circling song flight

Range Locally common breeding resident in N Indian plains from E Punjab to NE India and Bangladesh

Habitat Open grasslands, irrigated cultivation

Adult has weakly streaked, grey-brown crown and nape; pale indistinct supercilium; brownish ear-coverts; rufous-buff underparts, with diffused streaking on breast. Similar to Jerdon's Bush which is more brown and paler on belly. Nests on ground. Feeds on invertebrates and seeds on ground. Solitary, or in pairs.

TIBETAN LARK

Melanocorypha maxima Alaudidae

Large brown lark, with small head, long neck and long, pale decurved bill. Upperparts mottled and streaked dark brown with dark-centred median coverts and variable blackish-patches on breast sides. Greyish-buff below with breast streaking. White trailing edges to secondaries and white tail-tip. Sexes alike. Feeds on invertebrates and seeds on ground. Twitches wings when singing. Confiding.

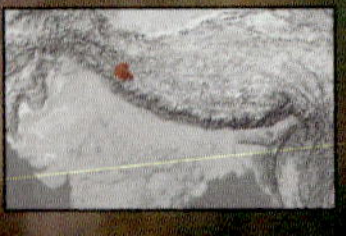

Size 21 cm

Voice Calls *tchu lip*. Song slow and hesitant

Range Local breeding resident on high plateaux of Ladakh and Sikkim

Habitat Montane grassy marshes

HORNED LARK

Eremophila alpestris Alaudidae

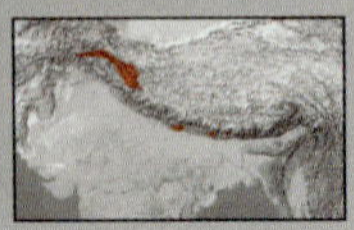

Size 19 cm

Voice Call a somewhat plaintive, soft *tsee...n...* . High-pitched, squeaky song of breeding male (May-August)

Range High mountain bird; from Chitral, Gilgit east through Ladakh, Lahaul, Spiti to Bhutan and E India

Habitat Open barren areas; scrub; meadows

Adult male has pinkish-brown upperparts and white underparts; black crown-band with conspicuous black 'horns' on either side; dull yellow-white face, throat; black cheeks and breast-band (gorget) separated by narrow white band distinctive; western race *albigula* of Gilgit and Chitral has black cheeks continuous with black gorget. Female has crown streaked black; overall less black, duller-black cheeks, gorget; tiny 'horns'. Juvenile duller and has spotted plumage.

juvenile

♀

longirostris

ZITTING CISTICOLA

Cisticola juncidis Cisticolidae

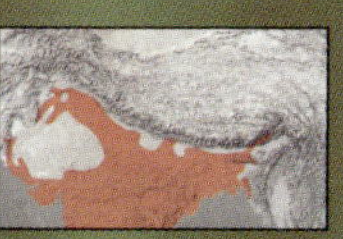

Size 10 cm

Voice Call a sharp, clicking *zit...zit*, continuous during display in air

Range Subcontinent, south of the Himalayan foothills; absent in extreme NW Rajasthan

Habitat Open country; grass; cultivation; reed beds; also coastal lagoons

non-breeding

Rufous-brown upperparts, prominently streaked darker; rufous-buff, unstreaked rump; white tips to fan-shaped tail diagnostic; buffy-white underbody, more rufous on flanks. Diagnostic calls. Sexes alike. Seen in pairs, or several birds over open expanse; great skulker, lurking in low growth; usually seen during short, jerky flights, low over ground; soon dives into cover; most active when breeding, during rains; striking display of male, soaring erratically, falling and rising, incessantly uttering sharp, creaking note; adult arrives on nest in similar fashion.

BRIGHT-HEADED CISTICOLA

Cisticola exilis Cisticolidae

Size 10 cm

Voice Calls *nyaae*. Sings from perch or in rapid display flight, *bzzeee...joo...ee*

Range Scarce and local breeding resident in N Terai from Uttarakhand east to Arunachal Pradesh, NE plains and hills including parts of Bangladesh and SW hills

Habitat Tall, dry grasslands and scrubs, usually on hillsides. Drier habitat than Zitting's

Small cisticola with short, rounded tail in breeding and slightly longer in non-breeding. Similar to Zitting, in non-breeding plumage, but unstreaked, chestnut hindneck, supercilium and rump and indistinct brownish tips to tail diagnostic. Breeding male has bright golden-orange head, throat and breast (unstreaked, creamy crown in the NE, chestnut in Western Ghats). Sexes alike. Behaviour and food as Zitting's but display flight less bouncy and ends with steep dive. Low flight more direct. Nests in grass. Uses spiders' threads to stitch together nest.

SWAMP PRINIA

Prinia b cinerascens Cisticolidae

Size 15 cm

Voice Song an elaborate warble, resembling Rufous-vented's, but longer, more varied and faster

Range Brahmaputra plains in NE India and Bangladesh

Habitat Elephant grass in swamps and by large rivers

Recently separated from Rufous-vented. Olive-grey streaked upperparts; bold streaking on forehead; narrow, whitish eye-ring and dirty-white lores. Less distinct collar than Rufous-vented. Greyish-white underparts, largely unstreaked; grey flanks, and undertail-coverts; greyish-brown flight feathers. Larger than similar Graceful, but has broader tail with no white tips or dark subterminal spots.

BLACK-THROATED PRINIA

Prinia atrogularis Cisticolidae

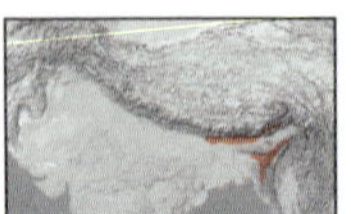

Size 17 cm

Voice Call includes buzzing, scraping notes

Range E Nepal, Bhutan, Arunachal Pradesh and S Assam Hills

Habitat Forest edges; clearings; grassy hillsides; scrubs; hillside cultivation

khasiana

Large, plain prinia, with very long tail. Breeding adult has black throat and upper breast; black-and-white spotting on breast; prominent, long, white moustachial stripe; greyish face; grey-brown upperparts; fulvous-buff flanks; whitish centre of belly. Non-breeding adult has unstreaked upperparts; white supercilium; paler buff below, with varying degrees of dark streaking and mottling. Typical prinia-like skulking behaviour; very active ascending, than descending. In bushes, and undergrowth; breeding male sings from exposed perches.

STRIATED PRINIA

Prinia crinigera Cisticolidae

Size 16 cm

Voice Calls include grating *chitzweet… chitzweet* and hard *chak*

Range Common breeding resident in N hills from Pakistan east to Myanmar border. Moves lower down to foothills in winter

Habitat Grassy and scrub-covered hillsides and terraced cultivation

Fairly large, drab-looking hill warbler with long, graduated, pointed tail. Breeding male greyish-brown with dark streaking; darker lores. Underparts dirty-white, speckled dark. Non-breeding male more rufous-brown with light streaking on head, breast and upperparts; buffish lores and eye-ring. Indistinct dark tips to tail, dark strong bill and flesh-coloured legs. Sexes alike, but female slightly smaller. Juvenile overall more olive-brown above and yellowish wash to underparts. Usually solitary, or in pairs; feeds low down on insects and quite skulking. Male sings openly from bush-tops and wires. Nests low down in cover.

GREY-CROWNED PRINIA

Prinia cinereocapilla Cisticolidae

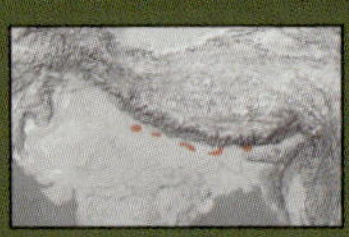

Size 11 cm

Voice Song a squeezed-out *cheeeeeeeesum... zip...zip...zip*

Range The Himalayan foothills and Assam

Habitat Bushes at forest edges and secondary growth. Globally threatened

Medium to small grass prinia with short, rounded wings. Ashy-grey crown; rufous wash to forehead; thin, rufous supercilium (absent in breeding); dark grey lores; ashy-grey ear-coverts. Warm rufous upperparts; fulvous underparts. Long, thin, slightly decurved bill; pale yellowish-brown legs; graduated tail with subterminal bands. Considered rare, numbers in rapid decline due to habitat loss. No longer found in many earlier breeding areas.

RUFESCENT PRINIA

Prinia rufescens Cisticolidae

Size 11 cm

Voice Call a buzzing *peez... eez...eez...eez.* Song a rhythmic *chewp...chewp...chewp*

Range The Himalayas in Nepal and from Sikkim east to Arunachal Pradesh; hills of NE India and Bangladesh; Simlipal hills, Odisha and Andhra Pradesh

Habitat Tall grasslands; grass under deciduous forests; bushes around terraced cultivation; open wooded areas; secondary growth and edges of forests

Rather plain-looking, dull-coloured prinia. Short, rounded wings; white lores and supercilium; medium-sized, graduated tail with buffish-white tips and subterminal band on outer feathers; uppertail more chestnut brown. Breeding adult has rufous brown upperparts; greyish-brown nape and ear-coverts. Underparts dirty-white with yellowish-beige wash on belly, undertail-coverts and flanks. Thin, longish, decurved bill. Non-breeding adult has rufous-brown crown and ear-coverts and longer tail.

GREY-BREASTED PRINIA

Prinia hodgsonii Cisticolidae

Size 11 cm

Voice Noisy when breeding. Longish, squeaky song; contact calls, almost continuous squeaking

Range All over India, S Himalayan foothills upto about 1,800 m; absent in arid W Rajasthan

Habitat Edges of forests; cultivation; gardens; scrub, often in and around habitation

Grey-brown, with some rufous above; long grey tail, tipped black-and-white; white underbody; when breeding, soft grey breast-band diagnostic. Sexes alike. Small bands always on the move; keeps to low growth but often clambers into middle levels; singing male may climb to tops of trees; few nearly always present in mixed hunting parties. Confiding.

GRACEFUL PRINIA

Prinia gracilis Cisticolidae

Size 13 cm

Voice *Szeep...szip...* call note. Longish warble when breeding; wing-snapping and jumping display of male

Range NW Himalayan foothills, Terai, south to Gujarat, across Gangetic Plains

Habitat Scrub; grass; canal banks; semi-desert

Dull grey-brown above, streaked darker; very pale around eyes; long, graduated tail, faintly cross-barred, tipped white; whitish underbody, buffy on belly. Plumage more rufous in winter. Sexes alike. Small parties move in low growth; usually does not associate with other birds; restless, flicks wings and tail often; occasionally hunts like flycatcher.

ASHY PRINIA

Prinia socialis Cisticolidae

Size 13 cm

Voice Nasal *pee...pee...pee...* song. Loud and lively *jivee... jivee...jivee...* or *jimmy...jimmy...*, rather like Common Tailorbird's in quality, but easily identifiable once heard

Range Subcontinent south of the Himalayan foothills, upto about 1,400 m; absent in W Rajasthan

Habitat Cultivation; edges of forests; scrubs; parks; vicinity of habitation

Adult has rich, ashy-grey upperparts and rufous wings. Long, graduated, white-tipped tail with black subterminal spots; short, black bill; whitish lores; grey crown. Underparts dull rufous. In winter, less ashy, more rufous-brown; longer tail; whitish chin and throat. Sexes alike. Solitary, or in pairs. Common and familiar as Common Tailorbird in some areas; actively moves in undergrowth; hops on ground foraging for insects. Often flicks and erects tail; typical jerky flight when flying from bush to bush; noisy and excited when breeding. Delivers song from perch on bush. Nests close to ground, on shrubs or tall grass.

YELLOW-BELLIED PRINIA

Prinia flaviventris Cisticolidae

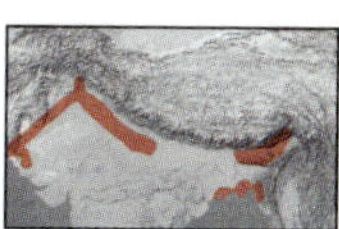

Size 13 cm

Voice Calls include *tzee* and *chink… chink.* Song a musical *twee…dulu…lu…lee*, often from high reed. Snaps wings

Range Locally common breeding resident in N river valleys in Indo-Gangetic Plains and the NE including Bangladesh coast

Habitat Reed beds; tall grass and tamarisk scrub near water

Small to medium-sized warbler with short, rounded wings and long, graduated tail (shorter in breeding). Upperparts olive-grey; grey crown; distinct white supercilium and eye-ring; creamy white chin and breast; yellow belly and vent. Sexes alike. Active, inquisitive and confiding, often appearing high on reed stem to look around and call. Feeds on insects low in cover; usually solitary, or in pairs. Nests low down.

MOUNTAIN TAILORBIRD

Phyllergates cuculatus Cettiidae

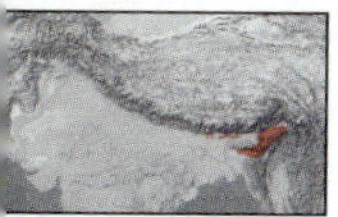

Size 13 cm

Voice Alarm call a *kiz…kiz…kiz.* Song a high, musical whistle

Range E Nepal, Bhutan, Arunachal Pradesh, Assam and S Assam Hills

Habitat Forest undergrowth; bamboo, grass thickets; secondary growth

Bright-coloured tailorbird, with distinct markings. Rich rufous crown and forehead; dark grey nape and hindcrown; thin white supercilium and eye-ring; yellow above eye; dark grey eye-stripe and lores. Upperparts olive green; yellow belly, flanks and undertail-coverts; grey sides of throat and breast with some mottling; paler grey centre of throat; dark brown tail, edged olive. Solitary, in pairs or small parties. Active in lower forest storeys; occasional aerial sallies. Skulks. Strong, direct, short flights.

COMMON TAILORBIRD

Orthotomus sutorius Cisticolidae

Size 13 cm

Voice Very vocal. Call a loud, familiar *towit…towit*. Song a rapid version of call, with slight change, loud *chuvee…chuvee…chuvee*, uttered for upto seven minutes at a stretch; male sings on exposed perch

Range Subcontinent to about 2,000 m in outer Himalayas

Habitat Forests; cultivation; habitation

Olive-green above; rust-red forecrown; buffy-white underbody; dark spot on throat sides, best seen in calling male; long, pointed tail, often held erect; central tail feathers about 5 cm longer and pointed in breeding male. Sexes alike. One of India's best-known birds; found usually in pairs; rather common amidst habitation, but keeps to bushes in gardens; remains unseen even when at arm's length, but very vocal; tail often cocked, carried almost to back; clambers up into trees more than other related warblers.

DARK-NECKED TAILORBIRD

Orthotomus atrogularis Cisticolidae

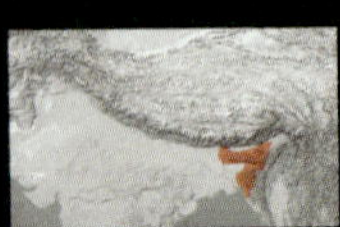

Size 13 cm

Voice Calls include loud, nasal *krrri…krrri… krrri* and *tew*

Range Scarce and local breeding resident in plains and lower hills of NE India and Bangladesh

Habitat Dense scrub; forest undergrowth, edges of forests

Small, greenish warbler with long-tail. Breeding male has dark throat-patch and longer tail. Non-breeding male similar to female, but with stronger streaking on throat and breast. Very similar to Common but more extensive chestnut crown and lores; yellow vent and bend of wings. Behaves and nests as Common but much less confiding. Call attracts attention.

CRESTED FINCHBILL

Spizixos canifrons Pycnonotidae

Size 22 cm

Voice Call a long, dry bubbling trill *purr...purr...prruitprruit...prruit.* Long, dry warble

Range Hills of NE India upto 3,000 m

Habitat Secondary growth, thickets; glades

Medium to large bulbul with short, pale, conical bill. Dark grey head, pale grey forehead, chin, throat, mask and hindcrown; dark brown iris; pinkish feet; broad, black terminal band on tail. Yellowish-green underparts. Juvenile has more green tinge to head and shorter greenish crest and brownish breast-band. Noisy, conspicuous. In flocks, in non-breeding season. Forages high in trees, also bushes and undergrowth.

BLACK-HEADED BULBUL

Pycnonotus atriceps Pycnonotidae

Size 18 cm

Voice Calls include plaintive whistle *whiwhi...tyee* and metallic *chirp*

Range Locally common breeding resident in Bangladesh. Status uncertain in neighbouring parts of NE India and in Andaman Islands

Habitat Open forests; scrubs; gardens

Medium-sized bird, more heard than seen. No crest; glossy, black head and throat; broad, yellow tip to tail with dark subterminal band, diagnostic. Dark olive-green upperparts with bright yellowish-green wing-patches and uniform yellow underparts. More greyish-yellow in some birds. Pale blue iris. Sexes alike. In pairs, or small flocks of six to eight. Nests low down in thick cover. Feeds on fruits and insects at all levels.

BLACK-CRESTED BULBUL

Pycnonotus (melanicterus) flaviventris Pycnonotidae

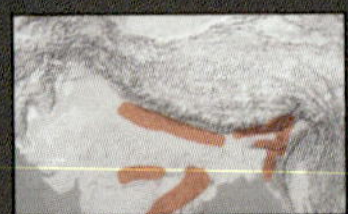

Size 18 cm

Voice Cheerful whistles; also harsh *cburrr* call; 4- to 8-note song

Range The Himalayas, from Himachal Pradesh eastwards; NE India; foothills to about 2,000 m

Habitat Forests; bamboos; clearings; orchards; forest and dense scrub

Distinctive-looking bird with glossy black head, tall, erect crest and black throat; olive-yellow nape and back, graduating to brown on tail; yellow below throat. Sexes alike. In pairs or small parties, sometimes with other birds; arboreal. Sits conspicuously on open perch and calls. Feeds on fruit and insects.

RED-WHISKERED BULBUL

Pycnonotus jocosus Pycnonotidae

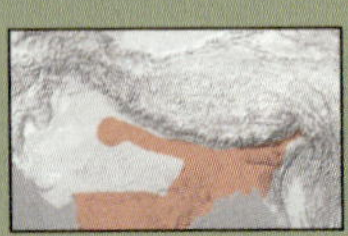

Size 20 cm

Voice Calls include cheerful whistling notes; also harsh, grating alarm notes

Range From Uttarakhand east along the Himalayan foothills to about 1,500 m; most common in south of Satpura mountains in peninsular India; disjunct population in hilly areas of S, SE Rajasthan and N Gujarat

Habitat Forests, clearings, gardens and orchards; vicinity of human habitation

emeria

fuscicaudatus

Slim bulbul with prominent, black crest; black crown and nape; black moustachial stripe; prominent white cheeks with red patch behind eye. Mostly dark brown above. Whitish underparts; buff flanks with white tail-tips and underparts; sometimes broken dark, chest-band; long, brown tail, tipped white; red vent. Sexes alike.

HIMALAYAN BULBUL

Pycnonotus leucogenys Pycnonotidae

Size 20 cm

Voice Calls include pleasant whistling notes

Range Found in the Himalayas, from the foothills to about 3,400 m

Habitat Open scrub, vicinity of habitation, edges of forests. Breeds in wooded valleys, also bushy hillsides

Medium-sized bulbul with conspicuous curved crest. Brown head; short, white superciliary-stripe; black around eyes, chin and throat; white cheeks with black crescent-shaped patch below; white blaze on neck-sides; reddish iris with narrow yellow eye-ring. Upperparts mostly greyish-brown; darker flight feathers; brownish-black tail with some whitish subterminal markings. White underparts with grey-buff wash on breast and belly; bright sulphur yellow undertail-coverts. Black bill and legs. Sexes alike. Juvenile has duller brown head than adult. In pairs or small parties; active birds on the move, attracts attention by their pleasant calls; hawks insects; perches on tops of bushes, shakes tail and calls frequently. Agile flier. Common in the hills, where quite confiding and noisy.

FLAVESCENT BULBUL

Pycnonotus flavescens Pycnonotidae

Size 22 cm

Voice Harsh alarm call. Song a jolly phrase of usually 3-6 notes

Range Hills of NE India

Habitat Open country with scattered bushes and trees; thick bushes in deserted cultivation and secondary growth

Medium to large-sized, dull-looking bulbul. Stout, black bill; short white supercilium and/or white eye-crescents; black lores; short crest. Olive-brown upperparts tinged greenish; brownish-grey underparts with yellow cast; yellow undertail-coverts; olive-yellow in wings and tail. Juvenile has less prominent supercilium, browner upperparts, rufous edges to flight feathers and paler bill. Rather quiet. Forages inside bushes and trees, rather than perching conspicuously on top. Arboreal. Keeps in flocks of six to 30 birds.

RED-VENTED BULBUL

Pycnonotus cafer Pycnonotidae

Size 20 cm

Voice Cheerful whistling calls; alarm calls on sighting snake, owl or some other intrusion, serving to alert other birds

Range Subcontinent, to about 1,800 m in the Himalayas

Habitat Light forests; gardens; haunts of man

Dark sooty-brown upperparts; pale edges of feathers on back and breast give scaly appearance; glossy, black head, with slight crest; almost black throat; white rump and bright red vent distinctive; dark tail tipped white; brown breast graduated to white belly. Sexes alike. In pairs or small flocks, but large numbers gather to feed; arboreal, keeps to middle levels of trees and bushes; well-known Indian bird, rather attached to human habitation; pleasantly noisy and cheerful, aggressive and quarrelsome; indulges in dust-bathing; also hunts flycatcher-style.

bengalensis

humayuni

WHITE-THROATED BULBUL

Alophoixus flaveolus Pycnonotidae

Size 22 cm

Voice Variety of nasal calls, variously described as *chi…chack, chi…chack; kake… kake*; etc.

Range Nepal to Myanmar; S Assam Hills

Habitat Dense primary, secondary evergreen hill forests, with heavy undergrowth; open lowland forests

Olive-green, brown-and-yellow bulbul with diagnostic long, untidy, brown crest. Greyish white lores, ear-coverts; brown eye-ring; prominent white throat; olive-green mantle; darker, rufous brown on wings, tail; bright yellow underparts. Seen in small parties when not breeding; arboreal; moves in middle, lower forest storeys, usually in thick undergrowth; sometimes in canopy.

OLIVE BULBUL

Iole virescens Pycnonotidae

Size 19 cm

Voice Call a disyllabic, musical *whe...ic*

Range NE India (Assam, Manipur, Meghalaya, Mizoram) and Bangladesh

Habitat Dense, moist, broadleaved evergreen forests; secondary growth in deserted cultivation in forests

Small, nondescript bulbul. Yellowish-olive head-sides; paler ear-coverts; crown and upperparts strongly tinged olive; pale rufous vent; rufous-brown tail. Brownish horn bill with paler lower mandible. Similar to Flavescent, but smaller, with shorter tail and longer bill. Legs and feet brownish-pink (black on Flavescent).

MOUNTAIN BULBUL

Ixos mcclellandii Pycnonotidae

Size 23 cm

Voice Noisy, with a variety of calls. Most commonly, metallic *tsyi... tsyi* and *cheep...har...lee*

Range Fairly common breeding resident in N mountains from Uttarakhand east to Myanmar border and perhaps Bangladesh. Moves lower down to foothills and even adjacent plains in winter

Habitat Forests and secondary growth with scattered trees

Large, but slim, olive-and-rufous bulbul with shaggy brown crown. Cheeks and breast pale rufous, streaked with buff. Olive-green upperparts. Streaked white throat, often puffed out; buff belly and vent. Long powerful bill. Sexes alike. Usually in pairs, or small groups. Nests high in trees. Feeds mainly on fruits, mostly in canopy.

STRIATED BULBUL

Pycnonotus striatus Pycnonotidae

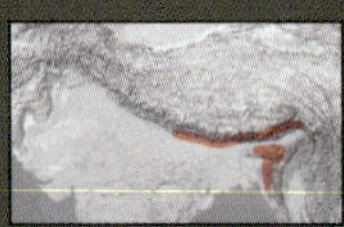

Size 20 cm

Voice Chatters. Calls include *tee… wut, pik…pik* and *chee…tu*

Range Locally common breeding resident in N mountains from C Nepal to Myanmar border. Moves lower down in winter

Habitat Forests

Large, heavily-streaked, long-tailed bulbul. Long, pointed crest; greenish-brown cheeks and crown; yellow lores and eye-ring, chin and vent; heavily streaked whitish on head and mantle; grey and yellow underparts, also heavily streaked. Sexes alike. Often in small parties. Strong flight. Nests in bushes. Feeds mainly on fruits in canopy; also flycatches.

ASHY BULBUL

Hemixos flavala Pycnonotidae

Size 20 cm

Voice Noisy. Calls include liquid, descending *tew…de…de…do…it* and variants

Range Common breeding resident in N foothills from Uttarakhand east to Myanmar border. Also Bangladesh. Winters lower down, sometimes in plains

Habitat Sub-montane forests; plantations

Grey bulbul with large, pale green patch on wing. Brownish-grey head, face and crown; black, tringle-shaped patch on lores; brown cheeks; white throat. Dark grey outer wings and tail. Whitish underparts, washed grey. Sexes alike. Nests low down. Feeds on fruits, nectar and insects in canopy and middle storey, often in flocks. Flycatches.

BLACK BULBUL

Hypsipetes leucocephalus Pycnonotidae

Ashy-grey plumage; black, loose-looking crest; coral-red beak and legs diagnostic; whitish below abdomen. Sexes alike. Flocks in forest, often dozens together; strictly arboreal, keeps to topmost branches of tall forest trees, rarely comes down into undergrowth; noisy and restless, hardly staying on trees for few minutes; feeds on berries, fruits, but also hunts insects in flycatcher manner.

white-headed

Size 23 cm

Voice Very noisy. Calls include an assortment of whistles and screeches

Range Several races; resident in the Himalayas and NE India. Southern race *H.l. ganeesa* darker with square tail and is found in Western Ghats and Sri Lanka. White-headed races are vagrants to the NE of the region

Habitat Tall forests; hill-station gardens

'forked-tailed'

'squared-tailed'

CHESTNUT-HEADED TESIA

Oligura castaneocoronata Cettiidae

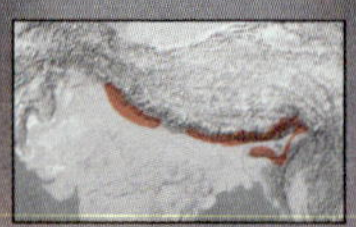

Size 8 cm

Voice Call a high-pitched *si-si-si-si* or loud, piercing *tzit*, repeated when alarmed

Range Resident in the Himalayas, Nepal; hills of NE India, upto 3,900 m. Winters in foothills; lower in non-breeding

Habitat Thick undergrowth in moist forests; dark ravines near streams; moss-covered boulders or logs

Tiny bird with a dumpy, rounded body. Dark olive-green back; bright chestnut-red hood; lemon-yellow chin and throat and breast-sides and flanks; rest of upperparts, dull green; underparts olive-washed yellow; small white crescent behind eye; long legs; stubby, short tail, barely extending beyond wings. Pale bill shorter than other tesias. Juvenile has drab olive upperparts and faded yellow underparts with rufous cheeks, flanks and breast-band; chestnut head absent. Singly or in pairs. Shy and elusive, jerks body when calling; keeps to forest floor, hopping around in bushy undergrowth.

GREY-BELLIED TESIA

Tesia cyaniventer Cettiidae

Size 9 cm

Voice Call similar to Slaty-bellied's. Song preceded by soft twitter before 3 trilling notes

Range Resident, altitudinal migrant in the Himalayas from Uttarakhand east to Arunachal Pradesh; hills of NE India and Bangladesh

Habitat Summers in thick undergrowth near small streams or moist ravines in broadleaved forest; winters in shady, broadleaved forests and secondary growth

Plain-looking tesia. Upperparts uniformly olive-green; crown and mantle olive-green; bright green supercilium; pale grey chin, throat and middle of belly; lighter green underwing-coverts; short, square-ended tail; dark bill with white tip. Similar to Slaty-bellied, but has paler grey underparts and stronger black stripe behind eye.

SLATY-BELLIED TESIA

Tesia olivea Cettiidae

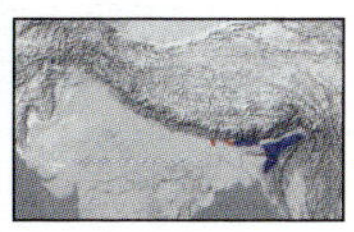

Size 8 cm

Voice Calls *chirik*. Song includes pleasant but tuneless jumbled whistles

Range Himachal Pradesh to Arunachal Pradesh; S Assam Hills

Habitat Dense damp waterside undergrowth, with ferns and nettles in moist subtropical and tropical evergreen forests

Similar to Grey-bellied, but has brighter yellow crown and no prominent supercilium. Upperparts dark olive-green; crown and nape vivid greenish-gold; face and underparts uniform dark slaty grey; long legs; bright orange lower mandible; slender, pointed bill; red inside of mouth; almost tail-less. Juvenile similar to Grey-bellied, but has darker underparts, duller crown and paler bill. Singly, or in pairs. Skulks in undergrowth, hopping around; active; inconspicuous; curious, but shy; rarely emerges from cover.

CHESTNUT-CROWNED BUSH WARBLER

Cettia major Cettiidae

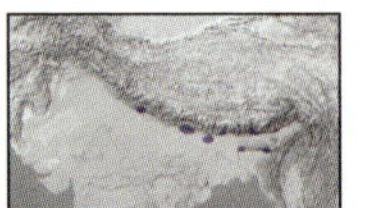

Size 13 cm

Voice Call an explosive bunting-like *pseek*. Song a 6-noted, ascending *wi…wi*

Range Resident: the Himalayas from Uttarakhand east to Arunachal Pradesh; hills of NE India

Habitat Summers in rhododendron, fir and oak forests; winters in lowland reed beds

Dark brown upperparts; whitish underparts; greyish-olive sides of breast; chestnut forehead, crown and nape; brownish-olive flanks; distinct white eye-ring. Distinguished from Grey-sided by larger size, bigger bill, longer supercilium and whiter underparts. Juvenile lacks chestnut on crown and even olive-brown above. The sub-species *C m vafra* is found in Assam and S Assam Hills.

BROWN-FLANKED BUSH WARBLER

Cettia fortipes Cettiidae

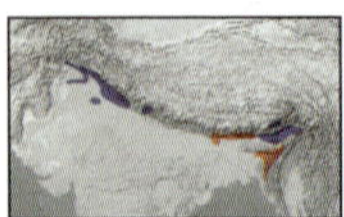

Size 11 cm

Voice Loud 3-note call; single note *chak…*or *suck…*

Range Locally common breeding resident: the Himalayas; S Assam Hills; winters lower down to foothills and adjacent plains

Habitat Undergrowth on hillsides; edges of forests; bamboos; tea plantations; grasslands

Small, dark, nondescript warbler. Rounded crown; rufescent olive-brown above; buff eyebrow; dark through eyes; dull whitish below, tinged ashy-brown on throat; buff-brown flanks and undertail; relatively long tail; dark grey bill; pinkish-yellow lower mandible; pale pinkish-brown legs. Sexes alike. Feeds singly, on invertebrates close to the ground. Loner, shy and secretive, sneaking in undergrowth; rarely seen; located by loud distinctive call. Nests low in thick cover.

PALE-FOOTED BUSH WARBLER

Cettia pallidipes Cettiidae

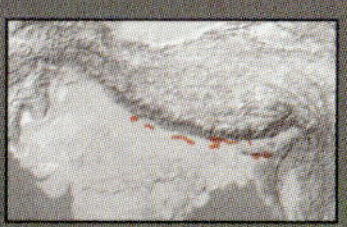

Size 11 cm

Voice Call a series of sharp chirps. Song a loud, explosive *zip…zip… tschuk…o…tschuk*

Range Resident, altitudinal migrant in the lower Himalayas, NE India and S Andaman Islands

Habitat Tall grass and bushes on forest edges

Small, plain-looking bush warbler with short tail; large, rounded head; olivish-brown forehead, crown and nape; whitish supercilium; white chin, throat and middle belly and undertail-coverts; brown tail with indistinct greenish-brown fringe. Distinguished from Brown-flanked by smaller size, paler underparts; brownish-olive breast-sides and flanks; more rufescent upperparts; shorter, square-ended tail; pale pinkish legs and feet. The Andaman race *osmastoni* has a bigger bill, with richer brown upperparts.

ABERRANT BUSH WARBLER

Cettia flavolivacea Cettiidae

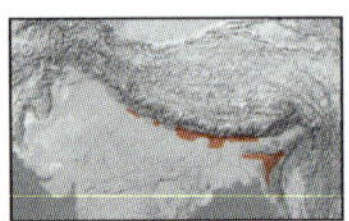

Size 12 cm

Voice Calls *thrit*. Song a loud, tuneful, wavering whistle

Range Altitudinal migrant: S Himalayas from Uttarakhand east to Arunachal Pradesh; S Assam Hills

Habitat Forest edges and clearings; scrubs and long grass; bushes in pine forests

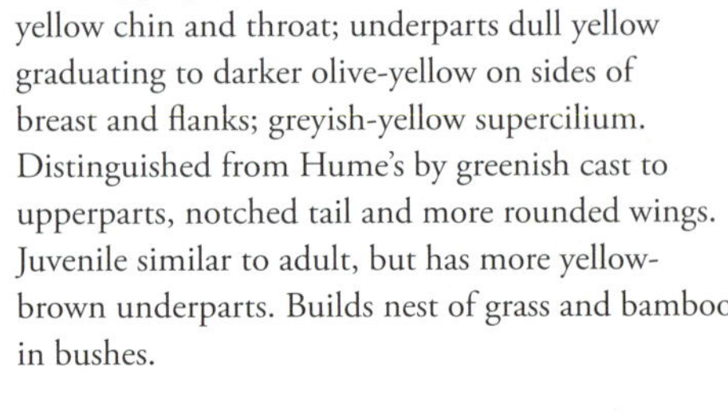

Olive upperparts with yellowish tint; sulphur yellow chin and throat; underparts dull yellow graduating to darker olive-yellow on sides of breast and flanks; greyish-yellow supercilium. Distinguished from Hume's by greenish cast to upperparts, notched tail and more rounded wings. Juvenile similar to adult, but has more yellow-brown underparts. Builds nest of grass and bamboo in bushes.

HUME'S BUSH WARBLER

Cettia brunnescens Cettiidae

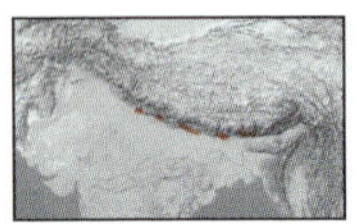

Size 11 cm

Voice Calls *trrrt*. Song comprises ascending 3-4 short whistles

Range Resident: high Himalayas from Uttarakhand east to Arunachal Pradesh; S Assam Hills

Habitat Open forest upto treeline; bamboo thickets

Recently split from Yellowish-bellied. Small bush warbler with thin, long bill. Overall warm brown with greyish-brown wings; creamish supercilium, above a narrow, dark eye-stripe; rufous wash on crown. Warm brown upperparts; cinnamon tips to flight feathers; square-tipped tail; breast and throat creamy-white; rump, belly and flanks have a yellowish wash. Pinkish-grey bill dark-tipped. Juvenile greenish-grey above and pale yellow below.

GREY-SIDED BUSH WARBLER

Cettia brunnifrons Cettiidae

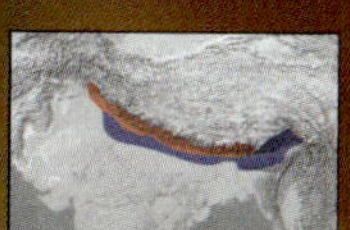

Size 11 cm

Voice Call a soft *tsik…tsik*. Song a repetitive, an extended *whooeeu…whooweeou*

Range Locally common breeding resident in the Himalayas; altitudinal migrant; breeds upto 4,000 m; winters below 2,200 m

Habitat Rhododendrons; shrubberies and bushes on forest edges; open forests; winters in tea gardens

Small warbler with a distinct head pattern. Bright rufous cap; long pale supercilium (well-defined in front of the eye) with bold dark eye-stripe. Uniform rufous-brown upperparts; whitish chin, throat and belly; conspicuous grey breast -sides and flanks; vent, olive-brown. Dark grey bill, with pale yellow lower mandible; pinkish wash to grey-brown feet. Juvenile has less distinct head pattern; overall duller, thereby mistaken for other species. Usually remains close to the ground, feeding in the undergrowth. Breeding male flicks and cocks tail. Secretive in breeding. Nests low, in thick cover.

SPOTTED BUSH WARBLER

Bradypterus thoracicus Locustellidae

Size 13 cm

Voice Call a rhythmic *trick…i…di, tric…i…di* or *tri…tri…tri…tree*. Song a low buzzing drone

Range Altitudinal migrant; breeds locally in the Himalayas from Kashmir to Arunachal Pradesh; winters in foothills, NE Indian plains

Habitat Open, grassy pastures; rhododendron upto treeline; scrubs upto 4,000 m

Small bush warbler, with a distinct song that rings through the Himalayas. Dark olive-brown (with a rufescent cast), unstreaked upperparts; pure white chin and abdomen; ash-brown throat; long, boldly-patterned undertail-coverts with darker brown centres and white tips; unpronounced ashy-brown supercilium; greyish ear-coverts and sides of neck; olive-brown flanks; short, graduated tail. Could be confused with Long-billed, Chinese, Baikal and Russet Bush Warblers, but distinguished by a gorget of numerous spots on breast and throat; shorter tail and ash-brown on the sides of head. Juvenile has more yellowish-green underparts, with darker mottling on breast and flanks.

WEST HIMALAYAN BUSH WARBLER

Bradypterus kashmirensis Locustellidae

Size 13 cm

Voice Call a rhythmic *trick…i…di, tric…i…di* or *tri…tri…tri…tree*

Range Breeds locally in the Himalayas in Kashmir

Habitat Same as Spotted's

Similar to Spotted Bush but has paler throat. Recently split from Spotted. Has two morphs: one paler and duller than the other, which has an obvious supercilium. Yet to be studied closely.

BAIKAL BUSH WARBLER

Locustella davidi Locustellidae

Similar to Spotted Bush, but smaller in size. Recently discovered in the Tinsukia area of Northern Assam, normally breeds in northeast China. Habitat said to be boreal forests. Little is known about its breeding status in India.

BROWN BUSH WARBLER

Bradypterus luteoventris Locustellidae

Size 13 cm

Voice Calls include rapid, reeling *tic tic tic tic tic* and *teck teck*

Range E Himalayas upto Arunachal Pradesh; S Assam Hills

Habitat Grassy hillsides; undergrowth in coniferous forests

Rather nondescript bird, narrow whitish eye-ring being the only distinguishing feature. Upperparts reddish-brown; white underparts, with pale brown wash on breast; rufous-buff ear-coverts, sides of neck, breast and flanks; throat, centre of breast and belly whitish; faint rufous-buff supercilium to eye; throat, plain breast and undertail-coverts. Juvenile has yellowish wash to underparts.

RUSSET BUSH WARBLER

Bradypterus mandelli Locustellidae

Size 14 cm

Voice Call a hard *shtuk*. Song a 2-note series followed by a sharp *tic*

Range E Himalayas; S Assam Hills

Habitat Edges of forests; secondary growth; shrubby thickets; bamboos

Warm-brown slender-bodied warbler with russet upperparts. Similar to Spotted, but identified by longer and broader tail and plainer undertail-coverts edged with pale buff. Also lacks grey on cheeks. Underparts slightly lighter brown; hint of whitish supercilium (which does not extend beyond the eye); blackish bill and brown ear-coverts; short, rounder wings; long, graduated tail. Some birds have brown spots on lower throat and upper breast, but not as prominent as on Spotted.

BLACK-BROWED REED WARBLER

Acrocephalus bistrigiceps Acrocephalidae

Size 13 cm

Voice Call a soft, repeated *chuc*; churring *currr*. Song prolonged and jumbled, interspersed with mimicry

Range Winter visitor; mainly NE India and Bangladesh

Habitat Reed beds; paddy fields

Medium-sized, dull-coloured, unstreaked warbler. Creamy underparts tinged yellow; short, rounded wings; rounded tail; long undertail-coverts; faint streaking on crown, nape and mantle; pale rump with rufous tinge; prominent buffish-white supercilium extends beyond eye; black eyebrow above and fine eye-stripe below supercilium; black lateral crown-stripe; brown ear-coverts; dark legs and feet. Similar to Paddyfield but has broader supercilium. Perches on tall reeds when singing.

MOUSTACHED WARBLER

Acrocephalus melanopogon Acrocephalidae

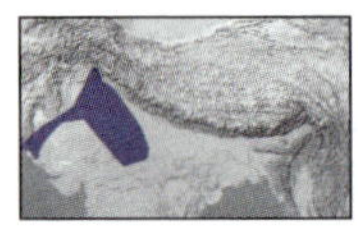

Size 13 cm

Voice Calls include deep *truk* and a short *trik*. Song an ascending rattling trill

Range Scarce but probably overlooked winter visitor to Pakistan and NW India

Habitat Reed beds, particularly typha; waterside bushes. Feeds low down in reeds and also on floating vegetation

Medium-sized, perky warbler with streaked crown. Overall dark, with whitish underparts with rufous-buff wash; short wings; bold, square-ended, creamy supercilium; streaked crown has black border; dark eye-stripe and ear-coverts; greyish cheeks and white throat; unstreaked rusty rump. Sexes alike. Juvenile more heavily streaked. Remains hidden for long periods. Singly, or in pairs. Cocks tail when alarmed. Feeds on invertebrates low down in reed litter and on floating vegetation. Secretive and unobtrusive but will climb to top of reeds to call.

BLUNT-WINGED WARBLER

Acrocephalus concinens Acrocephalidae

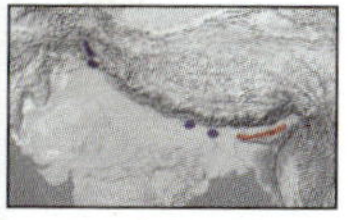

Size 13 cm

Voice Calls include *check* and soft drawn-out *churr*

Range Breeds in W Himalayas; N Pakistan, east to Kashmir; resident in Assam

Habitat Breeds in tall marshes and grass close to water and rivers; in Kashmir

Smallish dull-coloured warbler. Upperparts dark grey-brown; rump and uppertail-coverts marginally darker brown; pale bill has dark tip; breast and flanks pale buff; short, rounded wings; long, rounded tail; pale buff-white underparts; bluish grey soles of feet. Similar to Paddyfield, but distinguished by shorter and less distinct supercilium, which does not extend beyond eye, lack of stripe behind eye and dark border above supercilium. Confiding, except in breeding season.

BLYTH'S REED WARBLER

Acrocephalus dumetorum Acrocephalidae

Medium-sized warbler with olive, brown-and-grey upperparts and whitish underparts with greyish flanks; long sloping forehead; longish bill; grey legs. Sexes alike. Juvenile more rust above. Feeds on invertebrates at all levels, including canopies, bushes and ground. Rarely in reed beds. Flicks wings and fans tail. Usually singly or in loose groups.

Size 13 cm

Voice Call a loud quick *tchik..* or *tchi..*. Rarely, a warbling song

Range Common winter visitor to plains of S India, Bangladesh, NE India. Common passage migrant in N India

Habitat Well-wooded, often quite dry country

MOUNTAIN CHIFFCHAFF

Phylloscopus sindianus Phylloscopidae

Size 11 cm

Voice Noisier than Common. Call a *tiss…yip* or *swe…eet*

Range Common breeding visitor to N mountains

Habitat Scrubs and open woodlands. Often near water. Usually spends winters close to water. Similar to Common's

Small, roundish warbler, almost identical to Common, but does not show any olive-green or yellow. Upperparts plain greyish-brown; distinct supercilium; deep grey lores; grey-brown ear-coverts; darker flanks; cream underparts washed pale buff. Sexes alike. Similar but smaller; northwestern Plain Warbler *P neglectus* more brown with shorter tail and wings and a tiny bill. Behaviour same as Common.

DUSKY WARBLER

Phylloscopus fuscatus Phylloscopidae

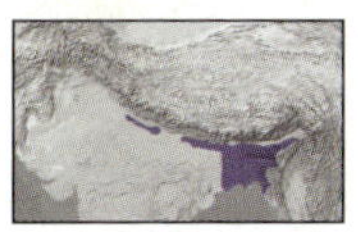

Size 11 cm

Voice Call a strong *chock…chock*

Range Winter visitor; Himalayan foothills; NE India and Bangladesh

Habitat Bushes; long grass

Upperparts, wings and tail vary between dark and pale brownish-grey; whitish underparts with touches of buff on breast-sides and flanks; slender, dark legs; broad, dark eye-stripe; whitish-grey eye-ring; greyish lores. Sexes alike. Northeast wintering *P. f weigoldi* darker above, and duskier below, and with touch of yellow on underparts in fresh plumage. Skulking; keeps low in undergrowth, often on ground.

SMOKY WARBLER

Phylloscopus fuligiventer Phylloscopidae

Size 10 cm

Voice Calls include low *tsrrk* and *chup*

Range Rare breeding summer visitor to the Himalayas. Sometimes, spends winters in plains

Habitat Montane scrub and boulder fields in summer

Upperparts, wings and tail dark grey-brown; underparts from dusky-yellow to olive-green; dark eye-stripe; dull yellow lores; short, yellowish or whitish (in eastern race) supercilium; thin, dark legs; dark brown tail; pale base to lower mandible. Similar to Dusky; paler above and whiter below, with bolder supercilium and eye-stripe, pale legs. Confiding; feeds on ground. Spends winters near water. Feeds on invertebrates, close to water. Sometimes, flycatches over water.

TICKELL'S LEAF WARBLER

Phylloscopus affinis Phylloscopidae

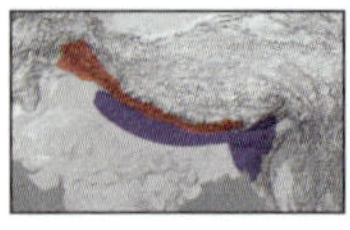

Size 11 cm

Voice Call a strong *chip* or *tsip*

Range Not uncommon breeding summer visitor to N mountains. Winters mainly in Bangladesh, hills of NE and SW India

Habitat Summers in montane scrub. Winters in edges of forests, scrubs and gardens

Small roundish warbler with dark olive-green upperparts; underparts yellow, graduating to buff on sides; no wing-bar; distinct yellow supercilium extends behind crown; pale yellow eye-ring; chin, throat and belly paler buff-yellow; prominent dark eye-stripe; pale legs and lower mandible; long wings; slightly forked tail. Sexes alike. Feeds on invertebrates, close to the ground; flits through the foliage singly or in small parties. Confiding and conspicuous. Nests close to ground.

ASHY-THROATED WARBLER

Phylloscopus maculipennis Phylloscopidae

Size 9 cm

Voice Call a loud *zit*, repeated often. Song a rhythmic *sweechu… sweechu*

Range Common breeding resident in N mountains from Himachal to Arunachal Pradesh. Also, hills of NE India. Moves lower down in winter

Habitat Forests and secondary growth

Small, bright yellow and green warbler. Upperparts bright olive-green; distinctive grey face and throat; whitish grey median crown-stripe and supercilium; dark grey crown sides and eye-stripe. Underparts pale yellow; short, rounded wings with a double wing-bar; forked tail; white outer-tail feathers noticeable in flight. Similar to Lemon-rumped and Buff-barred, but has grey head and throat diagnostic. Sexes alike. Feeds on invertebrates, singly or in pairs and in mixed hunting groups in non-breeding season. Often hovers. Nests high in trees.

BUFF-BARRED WARBLER

Phylloscopus pulcher Phylloscopidae

Size 10 cm

Voice Call a strong *swit*

Range Common breeding resident in the Himalayas. Moves lower down in winter

Habitat High-altitude shrubberies and forests in summer. Broadleaved forests in winter

Small, brightly-coloured roundish warbler with diagnostic orangish-buff wing-bars. Upperparts olive-brown; faint grey crown-stripe; indistinct, greyish median crown-stripe; forehead and crown blackish-grey; yellow supercilium; dark eye-stripe; greyish-olive cheeks and ear-coverts. Underparts yellowish; short, rounded wings; touches of white on outer tail; yellow rump; short, spiky, pale bill and pale, slender legs. Sexes alike. Feeds high in canopy on invertebrates, often in mixed hunting groups. Arboreal. Frequently flicks tail open. Rarely hovers. Nests low down.

HUME'S LEAF WARBLER

Phylloscopus humei Phylloscopidae

Size 10-11 cm

Voice Calls include disyllabic *whit-hoot* and sparrow-like *chwee*. Song a repeated *wesoo*, often followed by descending high-pitched *zweeeeeeeoooo*

Range Breeds in the Himalayas. Winters in plains

Habitat Breeds in subalpine forests. Winters in forest and secondary growth

Small, fairly bright warbler. Overall greyish-olive upperparts; yellowish-green mantle and back; brownish crown; indistinct beige supercilium, beige ear-coverts; greyish-green lores and eye-stripe; creamish underparts; short, rounded wings; dark brown tail with greenish edges; poorly-defined median-covert bar but two wing-bars much more obvious; greater-covert wing-bars buffish-white; dark bill and legs. Colours brighter when fresh, duller when worn. Very similar to Yellow-browed, but paler grey above. Singly, or in pairs but often found in mixed feeding parties outside breeding season. Very shy. Arboreal. Feeds in canopy at all levels.

YELLOW-BROWED WARBLER

Phylloscopus inornatus Phylloscopidae

Size 10-11 cm

Voice Call a loud *cheweest*, with a distinct rising inflection, and typically quite different from that of Hume's

Range Winters from C Nepal east to NE India and Bangladesh, and in Kerala, Tamil Nadu, and Andaman and Nicobar Islands

Habitat Gardens, groves and open forests

Small warbler, with well-marked plumage pattern. Overall olive-green above and creamy-white with pale yellow streaking below; yellowish-white supercilium, ear-coverts and wing-bars. Similar to Lemon-rumped, but no yellow rump and has well-defined yellowish-white crown-stripe. In fresh plumage, brighter green above compared with Hume's, in worn plumage, greyer above with whiter supercilium, wing-bars and underparts.

LEMON-RUMPED WARBLER

Phylloscopus chloronotus Phylloscopidae

Size 9 cm

Voice Call a high *tsip*. Loud trilling song

Range Breeding resident in N hills of the Himalayas. Winters lower down in NE hills; S Assam Hills

Habitat Hill forests; secondary growth

Small, brightly-coloured warbler. Upperparts olive-green; strong patterning on head; dark lateral crown-stripe; distinct long pale yellow supercilium; broad grey-green eye-stripe and lores; underside whitish, sometimes with a pale yellow wash; pale yellow rump and a dark bill; two yellow wing-bars; short tail; pale legs. Sexes alike. Seen in mixed groups year round. Nests in trees. Feeds on invertebrates at all levels.

LARGE-BILLED LEAF WARBLER

Phylloscopus magnirostris Phylloscopidae

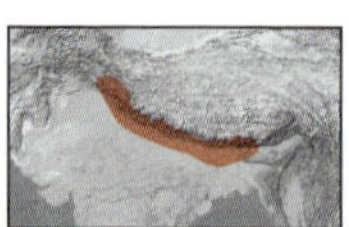

Size 13 cm

Voice Call a distinctive *dir…tee*, the first note slightly lower. Loud, ringing song

Range Breeds in the Himalayas. Spends winters over most of the peninsula, though exact range uncertain

Habitat Forests; groves

Medium-sized, brightly-coloured leaf warbler. Upperparts brown-olive; greenish-grey wash on breast-sides and flanks; yellowish supercilium, dark eye-stripe distinctive; one or two faint wing-bars, not always easily seen. Underparts dull-yellow below. Sexes alike. Usually solitary, sometimes in mixed parties of small birds; quite active; spends most time in leafy upper branches of medium-sized trees; not easy to sight, but characteristic call notes help in confirming presence.

TYTLER'S LEAF WARBLER

Phylloscopus tytleri Phylloscopidae

Size 10 cm

Voice Call a long *sooeeet*; also a harsh *huweest*

Range Rare endemic breeding summer visitor restricted to N Pakistan and Kashmir. Winters mainly in Western Ghats; passage records elsewhere

Habitat Forest undergrowth; coniferous forests

Slim, small warbler with plain, unmarked upperparts; a long, thin black bill. Underparts whitish, sometimes with pale yellow wash; long, whitish supercilium; dusky cheeks; short tail; flanks olive-tinged; dark lores and eye-stripe; mottled cheeks and ear-coverts; dark legs. Sexes alike. Arboreal. Feeds very actively on invertebrates on leaves and stems and sometimes flycatches. Not confiding, but difficult to see. Nests in trees. Winter habits little known.

WESTERN CROWNED WARBLER

Phylloscopus occipitalis Phylloscopidae

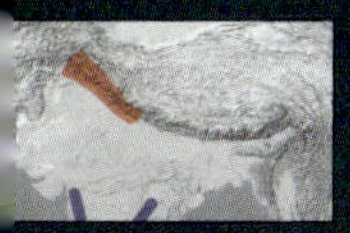

Size 11 cm

Voice Mostly silent. Though sometimes *chit…weei*

Range Summer breeding visitor to N hills upto E Uttarakhand. Winters mainly in Eastern and Western Ghats. Scattered records elsewhere and more widespread in India on passage

Habitat Forests

Stocky warbler with pale central crown-stripe, pale lower mandibles and dark legs. Upperparts greyish-green, with more green on wings and tail; two yellowish wing-bars on each wing; striking yellowish supercilium; underparts white. Sexes alike. Feeds on invertebrates actively in canopy and also in shrub layers. Seen in small parties and mixed hunting groups. Alternately flicks wings half-open. Confiding. Nests low down.

GREENISH WARBLER

Phylloscopus trochiloides Phylloscopidae

Size 11 cm

Voice Call a loud *tis...lee*

Range Breeding resident in the Himalayas. Winters widely in penisular lowlands and Sri Lanka. Common passage migrant elsewhere

Habitat All types of wooded country, including gardens

Dull greenish-brown bird with cream underparts. Medium-sized; slim; prominent, long, sweeping supercilium; whitish eye-ring; broad eye-stripe; mottled ear-coverts; strong patterning on head; one wing usually visible; brown legs. Sexes alike. Arboreal. Feeds on invertebrates, mainly in the canopy but also lower down. Active and restless. Frequently flycatches. Usually in scattered parties or mixed hunting groups. Nests low down.

YELLOW-VENTED WARBLER

Phylloscopus cantator Phylloscopidae

Size 10 cm

Voice Calls *pio...pio*. Long, loud, sweet song

Range E Nepal to rest of region

Habitat Dense, moist broadleaved evergreen forests; light forests

Overall yellowish-green bird, distinguished by bright yellow median crown-stripe and supercilium; dark lateral crown; olive-grey eye-stripe and lores; cheeks and ear-coverts mottled; underparts bright yellow-green; bright yellow chin, upper breast and undertail-coverts; lower breast and belly white; distinct yellow wing-bar on edge of greater covert; thin, pale bill and pale orange legs. Arboreal. Prefers vegetation close to water. Seen singly, or in pairs when breeding; gregarious; joins mixed foraging flocks with other insectivorous species in winter; usually active in lower forest storeys; flicks and fans tail when calling.

BLYTH'S LEAF WARBLER

Phylloscopus reguloides Phylloscopidae

Size 11 cm

Voice Call a *kee…kew…i*, see… *pit*. Long, trilling song

Range Summer visitor to NW Himalayas. Resident in E Uttarakhand to S Assam hills

Habitat Oak, rhododendron, coniferous; wet evergreen forests; edges of forests; shrubberies

Medium-sized, brightly-coloured leaf warbler. Upperparts almost uniform green; dusky olive crown; whitish-yellow median crown-stripe; yellowish supercilium extends to nape; dark lores and eye-stripe; dark sides to crown; two broad, yellowish wing-bars; underparts range from white to pale yellow, with a grey tint; white edges to outer-tail feathers; racial variations. Habit of alternate flicking of wings distinguishes it from other leaf warblers. Singly, in pairs, sometimes in mixed foraging flocks with other insectivorous species.

CHESTNUT-CROWNED WARBLER

Seicercus castaniceps Phylloscopidae

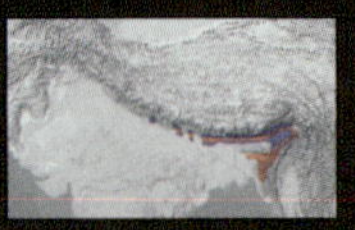

Size 9.5 cm

Voice Call a *tsik; chi…chi; sitsitsit*

Range Nepal to Myanmar; S Assam Hills

Habitat Dense oak, or mixed oak-rhododendron forests

Very colourful warbler with a distinct chestnut crown edged white on hindneck; prominent white eye-ring; face and mantle grey; whitish throat and breast; centre of belly white; rump and flanks bright yellow; mantle and back olive-green; two broad, yellow wing-bars; long, blunt bill and flesh-coloured legs and feet. Similar to Broad-billed but distinguished by dark lateral crown-stripe, absence of white supercilium and dark eye-stripe. Arboreal, seen mostly in mid to upper canopy; highly active. Usually found in pairs, small groups or mixed hunting parties; hovering and making short aerial sallies.

WHITE-SPECTACLED WARBLER

Seicercus affinis Phylloscopidae

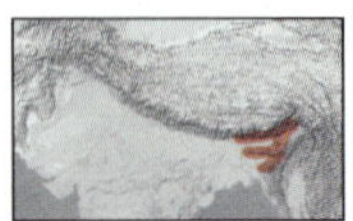

Size 10 cm

Voice Call a strong *che weet*

Range Common breeding resident in NE and S Assam Hills. Winters lower down in foothills and nearby plains

Habitat Undergrowth in dense, damp, broadleaved forests

Small, rounded warbler, with a domed head. Upperparts green and yellow; prominent white eye-ring; dark grey crown, nape and sides of head; darkish lateral crown-stripe; olive-green wings have single yellow wing-bar; broad, blunt bill and pale lower mandible. Very similar to Golden-spectacled, but grey extends down to nape and cheeks greenish. Sexes alike. Similar Grey-cheeked; *S. pologenys* has grey head and lores; white chin with only indistinct crown-stripe. Active in middle storey. Singly, in pairs or small groups.

GREY-CROWNED WARBLER

Seicercus tephrocephalus Phylloscopidae

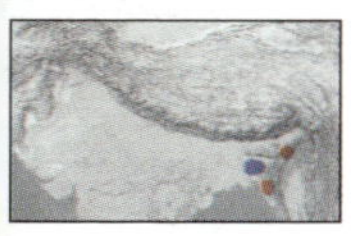

Size 11-12 cm

Voice Song sweet and clear with many trills, rather similar to Green-crowned's but without the slurring, warbling quality of Whistler's

Range Summer visitor; hills of NE India

Habitat Forest understorey

Largish warbler, with obvious grey crown with dark crown-stripe. Underparts bright yellow. Similar to Green-crowned, but crown and supercilium greyer than olive-green. Sides of crown darker than Whistler's; lacks prominent wing-bar; narrower yellow eye-ring. Skulks low in vegetation.

GREY-HOODED WARBLER

Phylloscopus xanthoschistos Phylloscopidae

Size 10 cm

Voice Call a double-note *psit, psit…tyee, tyee*; quite vocal; familiar calls in the Himalayan forests. Loud, high-pitched, pleasant, trilling song

Range The Himalayas (900-3,000 m); altitudinal movement in winter

Habitat Himalayan forests; gardens

Plump, rounded warbler. Grey upperparts; crown, nape and back grey; prominent, long pale eyebrow; distinct white eye-rings; dark eye-stripe; dark grey lateral crown-stripe extends up to nape; yellowish rump and wings; bright yellow throat; yellow underparts, merging into olive-green flanks; white in outer-tail seen in flight; long, blunt bill; paler lower mandible. Sexes alike. Juvenile has a paler grey crown, tinted greenish. Arboreal, mainly in middle storey. In pairs or small bands, often along with mixed hunting parties; actively hunts and flits in canopy foliage and tall bushes; highly energetic, making frequent sallies to catch insects.

GREEN-CROWNED WARBLER

Seicercus burkii Phylloscopidae

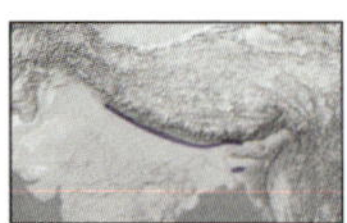

Size 11 cm

Voice Fairly noisy. Calls include sharp *chip...chip* or *cheup... cheup* notes

Range Breeds in the Himalayas. Winters in foothills, parts of C and E peninsula, N Maharashtra, S Madhya Pradesh, NE Andhra Pradesh

Habitat Forest undergrowth

Brightly-coloured warbler with a distinctive yellow eye-ring. Olive-green upperparts; greenish or grey-green eyebrow bordered above with prominent black coronal bands; greyish-green nape and crown; greenish sides of face; completely yellow below; greyish-brown wing-coverts edged with green; orange lower mandible; brownish-yellow legs. Sexes alike. Small, restless flocks, often in association with other small birds; keeps to low bushes and lower branches of trees.

WHISTLER'S WARBLER

Seicercus whistleri Phylloscopidae

Size 10 cm

Voice Calls *tiu*. Rich, warbling song

Range Resident: the Himalayas; Pakistan to Myanmar. Moves down in winter

Habitat Undergrowth in coniferous, deciduous or evergreen forests

Colourful warbler with green upperparts, bright yellow underparts; domed head, deep olive crown; prominent pale yellow eye-ring; diffused crown-stripe. Similar to Green-crowned but has broad, dark lateral crown-stripe, pale yellow lores and broader eye-ring; upperparts duller, front less distinct, lower mandible pale; breast-sides and flanks have touches of green or brown; usually more distinct wing-bar; more white in tail. Usually found in pairs, or in mixed foraging flocks; active in undergrowth. Skulking and secretive. Northwestern race paler plumaged than Eastern.

GREY-CHEEKED WARBLER

Seicercus poliogenys Phylloscopidae

Size 10 cm

Voice Calls *tweest.* Sings *sweetu… sweetu; chewchi…chewchi*

Range C Nepal to Myanmar; S Assam Hills; altitudinal migrant

Habitat Evergreen forests; secondary growth with bamboo

Small, vividly-coloured warbler. Underparts bright yellow; green upperparts; dark grey hood, nape and sides of head; greyish-black lateral crown-stripe; paler cheeks and ear-coverts; pale grey lores and white eye-ring. Underparts bright yellow; whitish chin, throat and tail have olive-green tint; single yellow wing-bar; pale brown legs. Similar to Green-crowned but distinguished by white, not yellow, eye-ring and broader wing-bar. Juvenile has overall less colour intensity than adult. Singly or in pairs; outside breeding season in flocks with other small birds; active, unobtrusive, hovering, fluttering, making short aerial sallies to catch invertebrates.

BLACK-FACED WARBLER

Abroscopus schisticeps Cettiidae

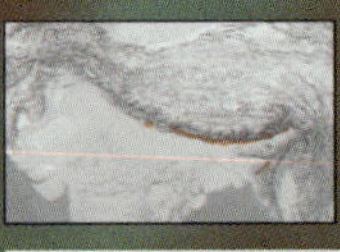

Size 9 cm

Voice Call a buzzing alarm. Trilling song

Range Breeding resident; W Uttarakhand to Arunachal Pradesh; S Assam Hills

Habitat Glades; thick undergrowth in moist broadleaved oak forest with mossy trees

Small, brightly-coloured warbler with distinct broad black mask; prominent broad, yellow brow; yellow supercilium, throat and vent; yellow-green lower mantle and wings; crown, nape, rear ear-coverts, upper mantle grey; underparts mostly white; pinkish bill and pale legs. Similar to Yellow-bellied Fantail, but has white, not yellow belly, short tail and no wing-bar. Eastern race, *flavimentalis*, lacks yellow breast and flanks of the Central Himalayan nominate; yellow only on breast. In small, itinerant bird waves, active in middle storeys or bush-tops.

YELLOW-BELLIED WARBLER

Abroscopus superciliaris Cettiidae

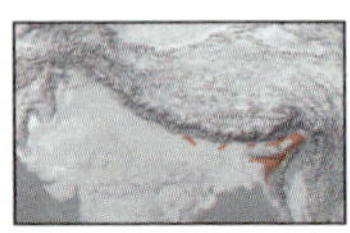

Size 9 cm

Voice Calls *chrrt...chrrt...chrrt.* Song 6-noted, ascending at the end

Range The Himalayas; hills of NE India

Habitat Bamboo forests

Very small warbler with yellowish-olive upperparts and white throat; long, white supercilium; dark crown and eye-stripe; yellowish-olive mantle. Underparts yellow; tail looks pale brownish-buff from below. Similar to Grey-hooded but lacks white in tail. Unlike Phylloscopus, distinguished by long bill, brownish-grey on crown, white throat and yellow underparts, and by narrower tail. Arboreal, keeping to middle and upper storey. Often seen near water. Singly or in pairs, but with other small birds, in non-breeding season.

RUFOUS-FACED WARBLER

Abroscopus albogularis Cettiidae

Size 8 cm

Voice Call a high-pitched tittering. Song includes high-pitched whistles and trills

Range E Nepal, Arunachal Pradesh and S Assam Hills

Habitat Edges of moist deciduous and broadleaved forests; bamboos; secondary growth

Tiny warbler with unmistakable rufous face. Buff median crown-stripe; black lateral crown-stripe; upperparts olive-green; throat white with black spotting; yellow breast-patch and vent; white belly; pale buff patch on rump; indistinct eye-ring; broad, blunt bill. Arboreal; usually in pairs when breeding; in small groups or mixed hunting parties; hyperactive; hovers, flutters, makes short aerial sallies. Joins mixed flocks. Calls frequently.

BROAD-BILLED WARBLER

Tickellia hodgsoni Cettiidae

Roundish warbler with rusty crown and forehead. Face grey; whitish supercilium and dark eye-stripe; grey ear-coverts, throat, sides of neck and breast; partial white eye-ring and crown-stripe not so prominent; nape and mantle olive-green; brown wing-coverts edged olive-green. Similar to Chestnut-crowned but belly and vent yellow, no wing-bars or yellow rump. Shorter tail and bill than Mountain Tailorbird. Singly or in pairs. Seen in forest undergrowth; rarely in canopy. Confiding.

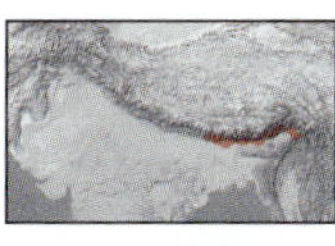

Size 10 cm

Voice Call a high-pitched twittering. Song a series of high-pitched whistled notes

Range Patchily in E Nepal, Bhutan and Arunachal Pradesh; possibly S Assam Hills

Habitat Dense undergrowth with bamboo in broadleaved evergreen forests; forest edge; dense scrub

LESSER WHITETHROAT

Sylvia curruca Sylviidac

Size 13 cm

Voice Noisy. Call a clicking *tek*; also churrs. Song a flourished rattle

Range Common winter visitor to Pakistan, W peninsula and N India; south to N Tamil Nadu and N Sri Lanka. Absent or rare from most of E and NE India, Bangladesh

Habitat Open woodlands; scrubs

Dull ash-brown warbler with dark cheek-patches; grey head; brown mantle and wings; short brown tail with white outer-tail feathers; underparts creamy-white; throat white; grey breast and belly; brownish flanks. Recently split Desert Whitethroat is smaller and paler. Often in loose groups. Horizontal carriage. Confident direct flight. Rather shy. Feeds on insects and nectar, usually high in trees but also in bushes.

HUME'S WHITETHROAT

Sylvia althaea Sylviidae

Size 13 cm

Voice Noisy. Similar to Lesser's. Song more bubbling and cheerful

Range Uncommon breeding summer visitor to N hills from W Pakistan east to Kashmir

Habitat Open woodlands and scrubs. Behaviour as Lesser's

Medium-sized, rather dark greyish warbler with even darker cheeks; large head; dark ashy-grey crown; greyish-brown back. Similar to Lesser, but distinguished by slightly larger size, stouter bill, darker top of the head and darker grey-brown back. Underparts white with grey wash on flanks. Sexes alike.

SPOT-THROATED BABBLER

Pellorneum albiventre Timaliidae

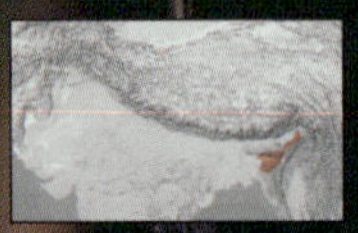

Size 14 cm

Voice Calls include harsh *chrrr-chrrrchrrr…chrrrit* and slightly explosive *tip…tip…tip*

Range The Himalayan foothills in E Bhutan, and hills of NE India and Bangladesh

Habitat Scrubs and thickets of secondary growth or bamboos; avoids dense forests

Dull, almost uniform deep olive-brown babbler. White throat with faint grey mottling; olive-brown breast and flanks; short, rounded tail; rufescent vent. Similar to Abbott, but has smaller head and bill and no rufous on tail. Similar to Buff-breasted in size and shape, but with shorter tail that has more rounded tip. Unlike Abbot's, has no rufous on tail. Skulks in undergrowth, usually in pairs.

MARSH BABBLER

Pellorneum palustre Timaliidae

Size 15 cm

Voice Calls include loud, double chirp, *chi…chew;* series of undistinguished, unobtrusive *churrs*

Range Endemic: Subcontinent, NE India and Bangladesh

Habitat Extensive reed beds and tall grasslands at edges of marshes and rivers, bushes in swampy ground

Smallish babbler with rufous-brown crown and uniform olive-brown upperparts. White throat and centre of belly; grey supercilium; blackish streaking on throat, breast and flanks. Thin bill; dark flanks; rufescent vent. Similar to Puff-throated, but less prominent supercilium, lacks rufous crown and smaller in size. Confused with Spot-throated, but distinguished by much bolder streaking and longer, rounded tail. Skulks in undergrowth. Nests in low vegetation.

PUFF-THROATED BABBLER

Pellorneum ruficeps Timaliidae

Size 15 cm

Voice Best-known call a 4-note whistle, interpreted as *he…will…beat…you.* Noisy when breeding; mellow whistle, 2, 3, or 4-noted

Range Hilly-forest areas; the Himalayas, to about 1,500 m, east of SE Himachal Pradesh; NE states; S Bihar, Odisha, Satpura range across C India, Eastern and Western Ghats

Habitat Forest undergrowth; bamboos; overgrown ravines; nullahs

Small bird with olive-brown upperparts; dark rufous cap; whitish-buff stripe over eye; white throat; dull fulvous-white underbody, boldly streaked blackish-brown on breast and sides. Sexes alike. Solitary, or in pairs; shy, secretive bird of undergrowth; mostly heard, extremely difficult to see; rummages on ground, amidst leaf litter; hops about, rarely ascends into upper branches.

mandellii

ruficeps

ABBOTT'S BABBLER

Malacocincla abbotti Timaliidae

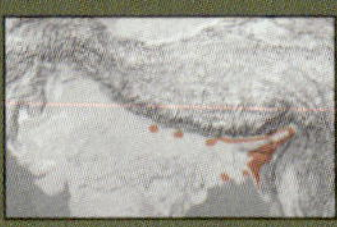

Size 17 cm

Voice Calls include trills, churrs, mews. Whistled song *tchwee…tchu…tchwee*; occasionally, duets

Range Nepal, Bhutan, Assam and Arunachal Pradesh

Habitat Thick undergrowth in moist broadleaved evergreen forests; thickets; streams; tree ferns

Plain, drab, brownish babbler with short tail, thick bill, stocky appearance; light-grey supercilium and lores; greyish or greyish-white throat and breast; olive-brown above; unmarked throat and breast; rufous breast-sides; olive-brown flanks; rufous tail, uppertail-coverts; brighter rufous vent and undertail-coverts. Solitary, or in pairs; territorial and site-loyal; terrestrial; forages on or near ground; shy and secretive; stays close to dense cover; rarely flies. Juvenile has dark rufescent-brown crown and upperparts.

BUFF-BREASTED BABBLER

Pellomeum tickelli Timaliidae

Resident in NE Indian hills. Plain-looking, has dark brown underparts; whitish belly. Often confused with Abbott's as well as Spot-throated. Skulks in undergrowth in damp moist forest floors as well as in bamboo thickets. Sharp and loud call often attracts attention.

LARGE SCIMITAR BABBLER

Pomatorhinus hypoleucos Timaliidae

Upperparts overall olive-brown; grey ear-coverts; mottling on sides of neck and supercilium. Lacks strong white supercilium. Underparts grey with rufous wash; white throat; breast streaked white; grey legs and feet; less curved and stouter bill. Juvenile has shorter, dull-coloured bill; more rufous on underparts and less rufous on vent. Usually in pairs or small flocks. Feeds on insects on ground. Usually located by call.

Size 28 cm

Voice Sings with loud, hollow, variable piping notes; with pairs, often calling antiphonally, *i…e… wiu…pu…pu…wup…up*

Range Hills of NE India (Arunachal Pradesh, Assam, Manipur, Meghalaya, Nagaland, Tripura) and Bangladesh

Habitat Canebrakes, bamboo thickets, reeds, elephant grass; dense undergrowth in broadleaved evergreen forests

SPOT-BREASTED SCIMITAR BABBLER

Pomatorhinus erythrocnemis Timaliidae

Size 12 cm

Voice Song and call quite low-pitched and persistent, fluty *tfuu…tuu*, first note stressed, followed by higher-pitched *tfuuk*

Range Hills of NE India; Bangladesh

Habitat Undergrowth in forests; scrub jungles; thickets in forest clearings and abandoned cultivation

Medium-sized babbler. Only scimitar babbler with both brown spotting on underparts and no white supercilium. Likely to be confused only with Large Scimitar. Distinguished from that species by smaller size, finer bill, rufous lores and ear-coverts, uniform olive-brown breast-sides and flanks, paler olive-brown upperparts, brownish rather than lead-grey legs and feet.

RUSTY-CHEEKED SCIMITAR BABBLER

Pomatorhinus erythrogenys Timaliidae

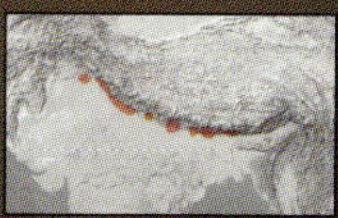

Size 25 cm

Voice Noisy. Call a mellow, fluty whistle, 2-noted *cue…pe…cue…pe*, followed by single (sometimes double) note reply by mate. Also, guttural alarm call and liquid contact note

Range The Himalayan foothills to at least 2,200 m and possibly to 2,600 m

Habitat Forest undergrowth; ravines; bamboos

Olive-brown above; orangish-rufous (rusty) forehead, sides of face, head, thighs and flanks; long, curved 'scimitar' beak; pale eye surrounded by bare, greyish mottled skin. Underparts mostly pure white. Sexes alike. Seen in small bands in forests; hops on jungle floors; turns over leaves or digs with beak; sometimes hops into leafy branches, but more at ease on ground. Juvenile overall paler and duller rufous.

WHITE-BROWED SCIMITAR BABBLER

Pomatorhinus schisticeps Timaliidae

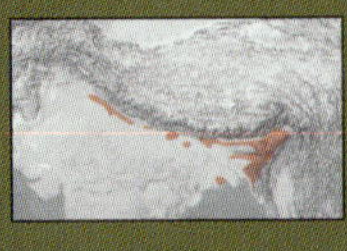

Size 22 cm

Voice Often duets, hoots, whistles

Range Punjab east throughout the region

Habitat Dense forest undergrowth; secondary growth

Largish scimitar babbler, with long, broad white supercilium; variable crown—from grey to rufous-brown, even blackish; dark lores, ear-coverts. Long, sturdy, decurved yellow bill; pale eyes; pure white throat, breast, belly. Chestnut neck-sides below, breast, flanks; olive-brown upperparts, tail. Similar to Streak-breasted, smaller with shorter bill, streaked breast. Rusty-cheeked lacks supercilium, black mask; has grey throat. In mixed foraging flocks, with other babblers; bird of mid-storey; hunts in thickets, undergrowth, small trees.

STREAK-BREASTED SCIMITAR BABBLER

Pomatorhinus ruficollis Timaliidae

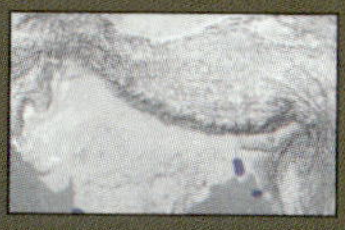

Size 19 cm

Voice Off-and-on duets between males and females *kwee…kwee*

Range Hills of E Uttarakhand to Myanmar

Habitat Forest undergrowth; hillside scrub; secondary growth

Fairly small scimitar babbler. Long, broad white supercilium merging above bill; black mask; decurved yellow bill; dark crown and olive-brown upperparts. Similar to White-browed, but smaller, with shorter bill; chestnut only around nape; olive-brown streaks on breast and belly, and plain olive-brown flanks; white only around chin, throat. In pairs when breeding, otherwise, in small groups. Skulking, secretive; more often heard than seen; forages on ground, moving quickly through dense cover, bounding along in long hops, or flies from bush to bush.

RED-BILLED SCIMITAR BABBLER

Pomatorhinus ochraceiceps Timaliidae

Size 23 cm

Voice Typically, gives hurried, hollow piping, e.g. *wu…wu…wu…* or *wu…wu…whip* or *pu…pu*

Range Uncommon resident in hills of NE India (Arunachal Pradesh, Assam, Manipur, Meghalaya, Mizoram, Nagaland); 1,500-2,400 m, moves lower down to foothills in winter

Habitat Dense undergrowth in broadleaved evergreen forests and bamboo thickets

Medium-sized scimitar babbler. Upperparts ash-brown; orange-red bill curved down; striking white supercilium; sides of neck, flanks and vent dark grey. Underparts pale buff; deep buff lower throat and breast. Similar to Coral-billed which has shorter, thicker bill and broader black mask. In pairs, or small flocks. Feeds on ground, foraging in vegetation for insects. Very secretive.

CORAL-BILLED SCIMITAR BABBLER

Pomatorhinus ferruginosus Timaliidae

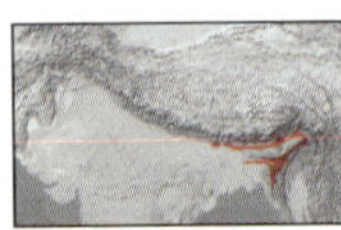

Size 22 cm

Voice Calls include soft, fluty oriole-like whistles; *churrs*

Range E Nepal to Arunachal Pradesh, S Assam Hills

Habitat Dense forest undergrowth; secondary growth; bamboos

Distinctive scimitar babbler with bright coral-red bill; long, white supercilium; long, black mask from bill to mantle; white upper throat. E Himalayan nominate race has black crown, nape; bright chestnut-rufous throat, breast, belly; bristly rufous feathers on forehead, lores. Races south, east of Brahmaputra have brown crown, thin black lateral crown-stripe, buff underparts; confused only with Red-billed, which has longer, more curved bill, white breast, belly. In pairs when breeding, or in small parties; forages on ground, bushes, small trees.

SLENDER-BILLED SCIMITAR BABBLER

Xiphirhynchus superciliaris Timaliidae

Size 20 cm

Voice Varied calls include series of repeated powerful mellow hoots, uttered rapidly

Range E Himalayas; NE India

Habitat Moist broadleaved forests, bamboo thickets

Medium-sized scimitar babbler with very long, slender, sharply downcurved black bill; small, dark slaty-grey head with long, white, feathery supercilium; grey ear-coverts. Upperparts brown; brighter rufous-brown underparts; whitish throat streaked with grey. Sexes alike. Skulking and secretive; forages in bamboos or in low undergrowth; often in small flocks.

LONG-BILLED WREN BABBLER

Rimator malacoptilus Timaliidae

Size 12 cm

Voice Only vocalisation recorded from the subcontinent a sweet chirping whistle. Alarm call includes churring...*prurr*...*prurr*...*prrit* etc, or quickly repeated *ker*...*wickit*...*ker*...*wickit*

Range The Himalayas; from Sikkim and West Bengal east to Arunachal Pradesh; NE India

Habitat Forest undergrowth on rocky ground, steep ravines, and overgrown, abandoned clearings

Largish wren babbler with diagnostic narrow, long, dark grey, downcurved bill. Upperparts brown, streaked with paler buff-brown; narrow, dark moustachial stripe; indistinct malar stripe. Underparts buffish-white; throat buff-streaked; brown breast and flanks; and rufous-brown vent and undertail-coverts. Short tail. Secretive. Forages on ground; solitary, or in pairs.

STREAKED WREN BABBLER

Napothera brevicaudata Timaliidae

Size 12 cm

Voice Sings with variable, clear, ringing whistled notes *peee*...*oo*, *pu*...*ee*, *chiu*...*ree*, *chewee*...*ee*...,*pee*...*wi* etc, sometimes single *pweeee*

Range Fairly common resident in hills of NE India (Arunachal Pradesh, Assam, Manipur, Meghalaya, Mizoram, Nagaland), subject to some altitudinal movements

Habitat Moist, thick forests on rocky ground on steep slopes and in ravines

Large, untidy-looking wren babbler. Upperparts olive-brown, streaked paler from crown to mantle. Large, heavy bill; grey lores, supercilium and ear-coverts; rufescent patch below rear ear-coverts; whitish throat streaked grey, olive-brown breast; whitish centre of belly streaked with long shafts of medium-brown. Uppertail, rump and wings uniform brown; prominent tail. Secretive. Feeds on ground.

EYEBROWED WREN BABBLER

Napothera epilepidota Timaliidae

Size 10 cm

Voice Call a plaintive, falling whistle, *cheeeeeu* or *piiiiiu*, repeated at 2-5 second intervals

Range The Himalayas; from E Bhutan eastwards; hills of NE India

Habitat Moss- and fern-covered boulders, fallen logs and stumps in dense, moist shady forest

Smallish wren babbler with strongly marked, ash-brown upperparts. Diagnostic long, pale supercilium; dark eye-stripe; dark ear-coverts; thin bill; wing-coverts spotted white; darkish spotting on breast and throat. Short tail. Sexes alike. *N. e. guttaticollis* of the E Himalayas has whiter supercilium and darker spots on breast and throat. while *N. e. roberti*, south of the Brahmaputra has paler supercilium, sides of throat and breast.

SCALY-BREASTED WREN BABBLER

Pnoepyga albiventer Timaliidae

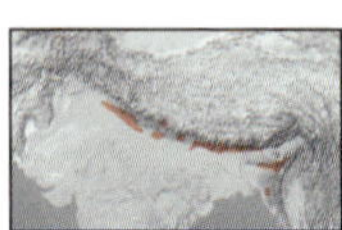

Size 10 cm

Voice Song a fine, strong warble, *tzee…tze…zit…tzu…stu…tzit*, rising and then ending abruptly

Range The Himalayas from W Himachal Pradesh east to Arunachal Pradesh; NE India

Habitat Moist, shady broadleaved forests among ferns and other tall herbage and moss-covered boulders and logs; favours ravines and edges of streams

fulvous morph

white morph

Small wren babbler. Underparts boldly scaled; paler buff mottling on lores, sides of neck and ear-coverts. Very short tail and bill. Underparts more boldly scaled in definite scallop pattern. Sexes alike. Juvenile plainer and less distinct above and more marked below. Similar to Pygmy Wren but larger and rounder in shape. Feeds on insects and seeds, skulking amidst stones and tangled vegetation.

NEPAL WREN BABBLER

Pnoepyga immaculata Timaliidae

Size 10 cm

Voice Eight high-pitched piercing notes, fairly quickly delivered, sometimes speeding up slightly towards the end, *tsi…tsu…tsitsi… si…tsu…tsi…tsi* or *si…su…si…si…swi*

Range Recently described species, east from Uttarakhand

Habitat Dense scrub

fulvous morph

white morph

Slightly larger than Pygmy Wren. Similar to Scaly-breasted, but longer bill; feathers on less scaly underparts longer, with dark centres and pale fringes; streaked breast. Lacks spotting on crown, mantle and wing-coverts. Longish pale legs; dark bill. Creeps in undergrowth in rodent-like manner.

PYGMY WREN BABBLER

Pnoepyga pusilla Timaliidae

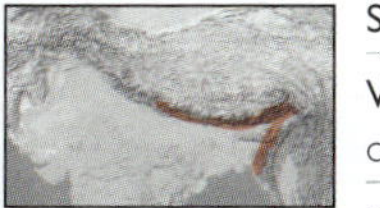

Size 9 cm

Voice Calls *tzook*. Song a repeated drawn-out *tsee…tsu*

Range Fairly common breeding resident in N mountains from W Nepal east to Burmese border and perhaps Bangladesh. Moves lower down in winter. Also occurs in China and SE Asia

Habitat Camp, ferny undergrowth of forests often among mossy boulders and fallen logs near streams

fulvous morph

white morph

Very small and overall brown babbler; extremely short tail. Upperparts dark brown with few paler spots. Underparts beige-white with dark scaling. Unmarked throat; long legs; large, grey bill. Sexes alike. Feeds on invertebrates on ground. Solitary, or in pairs. Secretive, hops away when alarmed. Flicks wings. Nests on mossy ground amidst rocks.

RUFOUS-THROATED WREN BABBLER

Spelaeornis caudatus Timaliidae

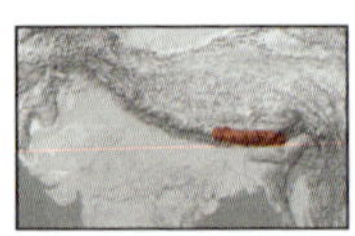

Size 9 cm

Voice Calls include chittering, churring, warbling and chirruping; *dzit…*; *whichoo… whichoo…whichoo*

Range E Nepal, Bhutan; W Arunachal Pradesh

Habitat Undergrowth in moist broadleaved evergreen forests

Small rotund wren babbler. Grey face and whitish chin; unmarked, bright orange-rufous throat, breast and flanks streaked and barred; black-and-white mottled belly; plain brown (with rufous tint) back and wings; almost tail-less. Juvenile has more rufous upperparts and more diffused scaling. Difficult to see in dense ferns, undergrowth and mossy rocks. Territorial. Forages on ground in leaf litter.

RUSTY-THROATED WREN BABBLER

Spelaeornis badeigularis Timaliidae

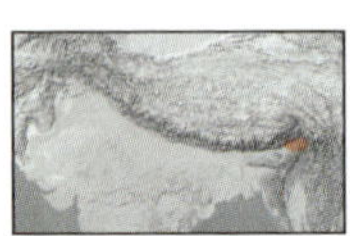

Size 8.5 cm

Voice Evidently, rather like Rufous-throated's

Range Resident in Mishmi Hills, E Arunachal Pradesh

Habitat Moist subtropical forest

Sometimes referred as the Mishmi Wren Babbler. Small, deep brown warbler with distinct rufous patch on throat. Grey ear-coverts; darkly streaked lower throat; small, whitish patch on chin. Black-and-white barred lower breast, and belly; flanks and vent dark brown. Small, short tail. Similar to Rufous-throated, except much darker and rufous restricted to throat. Largely terrestrial, foraging in thick undergrowth.

BAR-WINGED WREN BABBLER

Spelaeornis troglodytoides Timaliidae

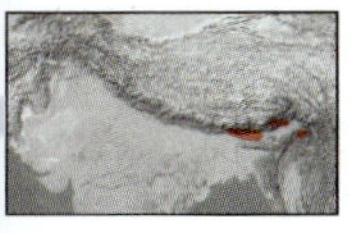

Size 10 cm

Voice Call a soft *churr…cheep.* Mellow warbling song

Range Bhutan; Arunachal Pradesh

Habitat Moist temperate evergreen forests; dense undergrowth

Rufous-brown wren babbler with distinctive markings. Chestnut-rufous crown, with paler spotting; wings and tail finely barred grey; blue-grey lores and around eyes; pale brown ear-coverts; unmarked, white chin, throat and upper breast; flanks and vent rufous-brown. Female has rufous streaking on chin, throat and breast; long tail. Feeds on ground.

LONG-TAILED WREN BABBLER

Spelaeornis chocolatinus Timaliidae

Size 10 cm

Voice Song is a clear *wee-itchy wee-oo*

Range Nagaland

Habitat Not yet distinguished from other Spelaeornis wren-babblers

Sometimes referred to as Naga Wren Babbler. Small, dark brown wren-babbler similar to Tawny-breasted and Grey-bellied (both with grey cheek and blackish stripe), but slightly longer-tailed than either with abundant, prominent white shaft-streaks on flanks. Darker upperparts than Tawny-breasted and browner underparts with fine black flecks below throat; with fine black marks on more fulvous underparts. Said to breed in May, concealing its domed or semi-domed nest on ground amongst leaf litter.

SPOTTED WREN BABBLER

Elachura formosa Timaliidae

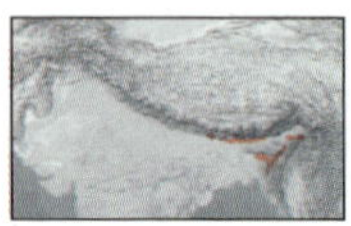

Size 10 cm

Voice Calls *sik*; *put…put*. Song includes high-pitched, stuttering whistles *dit…dit…dit*, etc.

Range Bhutan, Arunachal Pradesh and S Assam Hills

Habitat Moist broadleaved evergreen forests; mossy rocks, dense undergrowth

Very small wren babbler, with mid-length tail; broad dark barring on wings and tail, unlike finer grey-blue barring in Bar-winged; no white throat and breast, or heavy white mottling on crown and nape. Lightly spotted hindcrown, nape and mantle. Heavy speckling and vermiculation on paler underparts; sooty cast to head, mantle, breast; more rufescent on rest of underparts, wings and tail. Habits not well known; shy and skulking; close to ground in low vegetation.

CHIN HILLS WREN BABBLER

Spelaeornis oatesi Timaliidae

Size 10.5 cm

Voice Song powerful, rather shrill

Range Southern S Assam Hills (Lushai Hills, Mizoram)

Habitat Concealing domed to oval-shaped nest on damp, sloping bank or amongst very low herbage

Small ash-brown wren babbler with plainish brown face; moustachial stripe absent; comparatively longer tail; white throat and breast with dense, extensively flecked black; dull brown flanks also heavily mottled black-and-white. Distinguished from Naga by denser scaling on upperparts. Female has whiter underparts. Behaves as Naga. Breeds in Mar-Jun (Myanmar).

TAWNY-BREASTED WREN BABBLER

Spelaeornis longicaudatus Timaliidae

Warm cinnamon-brown wren babbler. Upperparts scaled in almost same colour; pale grey lores and ear-coverts; pale indistinct streak above eye; unmarked white chin; dark moustachial patch; long tail. Slimmer than other wren babblers. Similar to Long-tailed but has more plain buff underparts without spotting. Juvenile has rufous-brown upperparts, lacking dark scaling. Female has more orange-buff breast. Nests on ground amidst boulders and undergrowth.

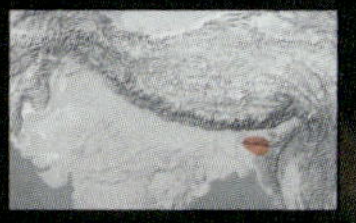

Size 10 cm

Voice Loud, clear whistle; soft churring alarm call

Range Endemic to the subcontinent. Globally threatened. Hills of NE India (Assam, Manipur, Meghalaya, Nagaland), 1,000-2,000 m; current status uncertain

Habitat Deep, moist broadleaved evergreen forests with thick undergrowth, keeping to rocky ravines; steep hillsides with rock outcrops densely-covered with moss, ferns and orchids

HIMALAYAN WEDGE-BILLED WREN BABBLER

Sphenocichla humei Timaliidae

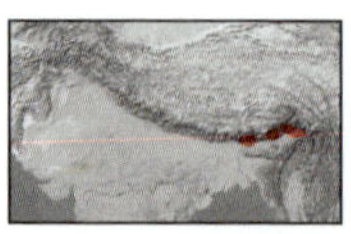

Size 18 cm

Voice Loud melodious whistles

Range The Himalayas of Sikkim, West Bengal and Arunachal Pradesh

Habitat Broadleaved evergreen forests; bamboos

Distinctly-marked babbler. Upperparts dark brown; dark, pointed bill; blackish face mask; indistinct grey supercilium; dense spotting on neck-sides. Underparts dark; barred wings and tail; pale buff scales on belly; blackish legs and feet. Forages in undergrowth and along lower parts of tree trunks.

MANIPUR WEDGE-BILLED WREN BABBLER

Sphenocichla roberti Timaliidae

Size 18 cm

Voice Alarm call a subdued, low *hrrrh...hrrrh...hrrrhhrrrit...hrrrh... hrrrh.* Song unknown

Range SE Arunachal Pradesh (Namdapha) and eastern S Assam hills (N Cachar, Nagaland and Manipur)

Habitat Often found in parties of upto 15, working through low vegetation

Large wren babbler with broad dark barring on wings distinct; large white scaling on throat and chest; plain brown cheeks; no visible supercilium; lightly spotted hindcrown, nape and mantle; greyish-brown head, mantle and breast; mid-length tail. Female overall more rufous. Juvenile more rufous with less distinct scaling. Usually seen on tree trunks or rocks in small flocks, in search of insects. Nests on lower parts of tree trunks.

RUFOUS-CAPPED BABBLER

Stachyridopsis ruficeps Timaliidae

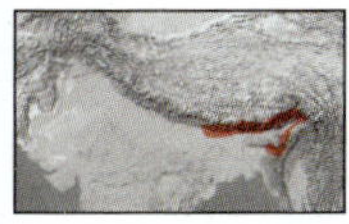

Size 12 cm

Voice Calls *wee...wee...wee... wee*. Song a high-pitched *pi...pi... pi...pi...pi...pi...pi*

Range E Nepal to Myanmar

Habitat Undergrowth in moist broadleaved evergreen forests; secondary growth; bamboo clumps

Small, buffy-brown and yellowish babbler, with bright rufous cap; very similar to Rufous-fronted, but rufous crown brighter, better defined, and extending to nape. Mantle, wings and tail richer olive; yellowish-buff face, sides of neck and underparts, with faintly streaked yellowish chin and throat. Sharp, pointed bill; pale, diffused eye-ring; in pairs when breeding; rest of the year, usually in bird waves; active in undergrowth or mid-storey trees.

RUFOUS-FRONTED BABBLER

Stachyridopsis rufifrons Timaliidae

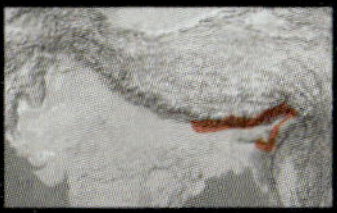

Size 12 cm

Voice Same as Rufous-capped's

Range E Nepal to Myanmar

Habitat Undergrowth in moist broadleaved evergreen forests; secondary growth; bamboos

Often confused with the very similar Rufous-capped. Has white throat, streaked faintly with black. Grey supercilium a good distinguishing feature.

TAWNY-BELLIED BABBLER

Dumetia hyperythra Timaliidae

Size 13 cm

Voice Calls include faint *cheep… cheep* contact notes; also, mix of other whistling and chattering notes

Range From SE Himachal Pradesh, east along foothills into peninsular India; absent in arid NW, Punjab plains, extreme NE states

Habitat Scrubs and bamboos, in and around forests

Olivish-brown above; front part of crown reddish-brown; white throat in western and southern races; nominate race has underbody entirely fulvous. Sexes alike. Small, noisy parties in undergrowth; rummages on floor, hopping about, always wary; hardly associates with other birds; great skulkers, difficult to see; any sign of danger and flock disperses amidst noisy chorus of alarm notes but soon reunites.

BLACK-CHINNED BABBLER

Stachyridopsis pyrrhops Timaliidae

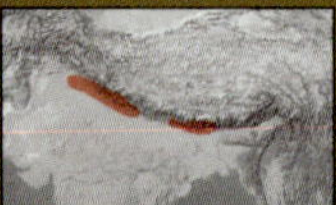

Size 10 cm

Voice Calls include mellow *wit… wit…wit…wit*; soft variable *chirrr*

Range Fairly common endemic breeding resident in N mountains from N Pakistan east to E Nepal. Moves lower down in winter

Habitat Edges of forests and secondary undergrowth, often near streams. Favours bamboos

Tiny, fulvous-brown babbler. Back of crown more olive. Diagnostic black lores and chin. Underparts orange-buff; sides of head more fulvous. Red iris; upper mandible brown; legs, feet and claws pale flesh-brown. Sexes alike. Similar to Dark-fronted *Rhopocichla atriceps* but no black head and mask. Feeds in pairs or small parties on invertebrates, often in mixed hunting groups. Active and not shy. Nests low down.

GREY-THROATED BABBLER

Stachyris nigriceps Timaliidae

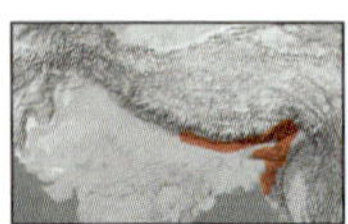

Size 12 cm

Voice Call a distinctive but variable jingling trill

Range Locally common breeding resident from C Nepal east to Burmese border. Also occurs in China and SE Asia

Habitat Undergrowth of forests, particularly with bamboos and near water

Small, plainish-brown babbler. Head marked with black-and-white; pale grey eye-stripe; grey throat; black lateral crown-stripe; underparts more rusty-buff. Sexes alike. Juvenile has less streaked head and underparts have more rufous-buff tint. Similar to Black-chinned but with less distinct black lores and chin. Skulks in undergrowth, feeds on invertebrates, often in mixed hunting groups. Very secretive. Nests low down.

GOLDEN BABBLER

Stachyridopsis chrysaea Timaliidae

Size 10 cm

Voice Similar to Rufous-capped's, but more paced

Range C Nepal, Bhutan, Arunachal Pradesh, S Assam Hills

Habitat Undergrowth in moist broadleaved evergreen forests; secondary growth

Small babbler with short, sharply pointed bill; gold head, with prominent black streaks from hindcrown to nape; partial black mask; black lores, thin brow line, and black moustachial stripe; olive green-gold upperparts; more golden underparts; dark red eye; nominate race from E Himalayas to Manipur described; *binghami* in southern parts of NE subcontinent has greyer cheeks, duller upper and underparts; in pairs when breeding; otherwise, in mixed hunting parties. Moves constantly.

PIN-STRIPED TIT BABBLER

Macronous gularis Timaliidae

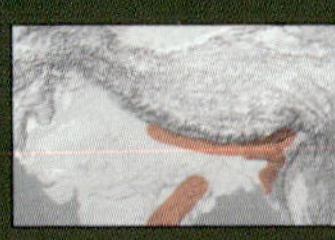

Size 11 cm

Voice Very noisy. Call a loud, regular and repeated barbet-like *chunk… chunk…chunk*. Also, *chrrr*

Range Common breeding resident in N foothills from Uttarakhand east through Nepal to Arunachal Pradesh, NE India and Eastern Ghats

Habitat Forest undergrowth and bamboos, often feeding fairly high but also on ground

Small, brownish babbler; underparts yellow-brown, streaked finely with black; rusty-brown crown; pale yellow lores; plain, rufous-brown wings and tail; mantle more olive; yellowish supercilium; pale iris; dark eye-stripe. Sexes alike. Feeds on invertebrates; in pairs or small parties, often in mixed flocks. Active but furtive, creeping on ground. Nests in undergrowth.

CHESTNUT-CAPPED BABBLER

Timalia pileata Timaliidae

Size 17 cm

Voice Calls *tik…,tik…; chit, chit…*

Range E Uttarakhand to Myanmar; Assam

Habitat Wetlands with tall grass; reed beds; scrub; secondary growth

Rather distinctive babbler, with bright chestnut cap, contrasting with sturdy black bill; black mask, extending only upto eye; white supercilium, forehead, cheeks, chin, throat and breast; finely-streaked lower throat and breast; grey neck-sides; drab olive-brown upperparts; mostly olive-buff below; relatively long, scruffy typical babbler tail. In pairs when breeding; otherwise, in small groups. Secretive; skulks in dense vegetation, remaining well hidden; may emerge briefly when singing; forages in low scrub or clambers up tall grass and reeds.

JERDON'S BABBLER

Chrysomma altirostre Timaliidae

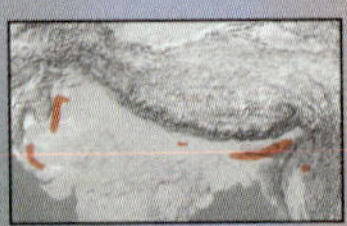

Size 17 cm

Voice Call a piercing *tew...tew...tew...tew...tew*, starting slowly but ending more rapidly and slightly falling in tone

Range Sedentary resident in Indus Plains, Pakistan, C Nepal, Brahmaputra Plains in N West Bengal, Assam, Nagaland and Bangladesh

Habitat Reed beds and extensive tracts of elephant grass

scindicum

griseigulare

Distinguished from Yellow-eyed by paler yellowish-brown bill, brown iris and dull yellowish-green orbital ring, no white lores and supercilium, and fleshy-brown legs and feet. Racial variations. *C. a. altirostre* (Indus plains) olive-brown above with pale grey throat and breast; *C. a. griseigulare* (NE subcontinent) has darker grey throat and breast, richer brown underparts, belly, flanks and vent.

SPINY BABBLER

Turdoides nipalensis Timaliidae

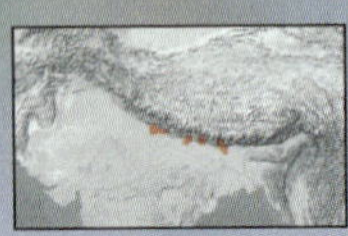

Size 25 cm

Voice Song a distinctive, harsh, ringing whistling *ter...ter...ter...ter...ter...ter*

Range Endemic resident in Nepal

Habitat Dense scrub on hillsides; favours thicker areas, away from cultivation

Upperparts dark rufescent-brown; diagnostic downcurved black bill; white face; pale iris, and strong, fine black streaking on throat and breast; tail has narrow, faint cross-bars. Usually in pairs, feeding on ground. Shy and difficult to observe.

YELLOW-EYED BABBLER

Chrysomma sinense Timaliidae

Sexes alike. Rufous-brown above; whitish lores, short supercilium; yellow iris and orange-yellow eye-rim distinctive at close range; cinnamon wings; long, graduated tail; white below, tinged pale-fulvous on flanks and abdomen. In pairs, or small bands in tall grass and undergrowth; noisy but skulking, suddenly clambers into view for few seconds, before vanishing once again; works its way along stems and leaves, hunts insects; short, jerky flight.

Size 18 cm

Voice Call a mournful *cheep… cheep*. Noisy when breeding (mostly rains); melodious, whistling notes

Range Subcontinent, from the Himalayan foothills south; absent in arid parts of Rajasthan

Habitat Scrub; tall grass; cultivation; edges of forests

STRIATED BABBLER

Turdoides earlei Timaliidae

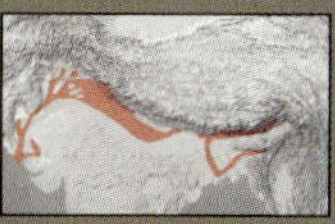

Size 25 cm

Voice Calls include loud, 3-note whistle; also quick-repeated, single whistling note

Range Floodplains of N and NE river systems, especially larger rivers

Habitat Tall grass, reed beds and scrubs

Dull brownish above, streaked darker; long, cross-barred tail; dark streaks on crown; pale supercilium; yellow eye; pale yellow bill has dark tip. Underparts buffy-brown below, with fine dark streaks on throat and breast. Long tail. Sexes alike. Juvenile more orange-brown, with plainer rufous underparts. Sociable; parties of upto 10 birds; keeps to tall grass and reed beds; flies low, rarely drops down to ground.

SLENDER-BILLED BABBLER

Turdoides longirostris Timaliidae

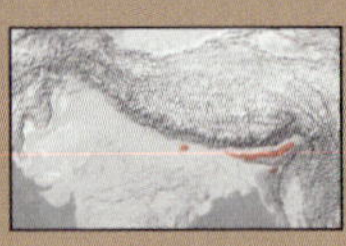

Size 23 cm

Voice Calls include shrill, rather high-pitched, quite strident series of notes, and a rather clear, high-pitched *wiii...wii...jiu...di*

Range C Nepal, NW Bihar, NE India and Bangladesh. In Nepal, recorded only at Chitwan, where locally fairly common

Habitat Tall grass and reeds, especially near water

Rufous-brown babbler with unstreaked upperparts and comparatively long tail. Diagnostic downcurved blackish bill; whitish lores and buff ear-coverts; short eyebrow; whitish throat; unstreaked deep buff underparts; indistinct cross-bars on tail. In pairs, or small flocks. Secretive, staying under cover of tall grass. Feeds on ground. Nests in low bushes.

JUNGLE BABBLER

Turdoides striata Timaliidae

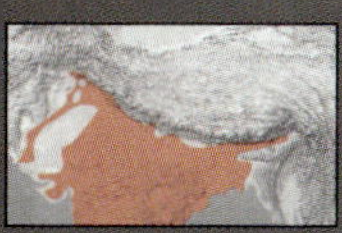

Size 25 cm

Voice Very noisy. Calls include harsh *ke…ke…ke* and hysterical chattering and squeaking in chorus

Range Common endemic breeding resident throughout lowlands and foothills except parts of NE India and Sri Lanka

Habitat Open woodlands; scrub; cultivation; gardens; villages

sindiana

Overall grey-brown babbler. Light-brown head; whitish iris; stout, yellow bill; short, dark eyebrow; pale lores; dark brown tail. Underparts paler with some greyish streaking on breast. Western race *somervillei* may be separate species, with chestnut tail and dark brown primaries. Extremely noisy. Feeds in groups on insects and seeds, mainly on ground. Confiding and inquisitive. Breeds throughout the year. Nests in bushes.

CHINESE BABAX

Babax lanceolatus woodi Timaliidae

Size 20 cm

Voice Call a short, clear, musical slurred whistle

Range Lushai Hills, Mizoram above 1,200 m. Locally common

Habitat Open broadleaved evergreen forests; edges of forests; secondary growth; scrubs and grass; bamboos

Medium-sized, rather pale and heavily streaked bird. Decurved bill; pale face, pale yellow eyes and black moustache; brown tail. Juvenile has overall more buff with less streaking. Quite shy, occurring in pairs or small parties, mainly on ground and roads, but freely ascends trees.

GIANT BABAX

Babax waddelli Timaliidae

Ash-brown babbler with heavily streaked upperparts; strong downcurved bill; head and mantle darkly streaked. Underparts have less dense streaking. Blackish-brown wings tipped grey similar to Chinese but large in size, darker grey head, and darker streaking. Chinese has sub-moustachial stripe, more downcurved bill, and dark grey tail.

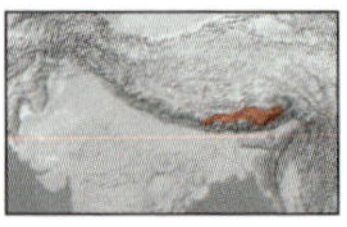

Size 31 cm

Voice Harsh grating call; rapid series of quavering whistles. Pleasant thrush-like song

Range Extreme NE Sikkim

Habitat Dry scrub; favours *Hippophae rhamnoides*

WHITE-THROATED LAUGHINGTHRUSH

Garrulax albogularis Timaliidae

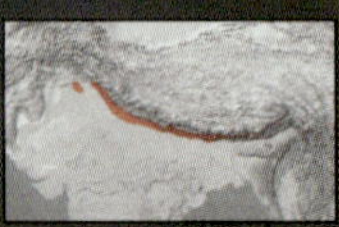

Size 28 cm

Voice Noisy. Alarm call a strident *twitz…tzee*. Lot of squealing, hissing and chattering

Range Locally common breeding resident in N hills from N Pakistan east to Assam. Rarer in E India. Moves lower down in winter

Habitat Undergrowth of forest and scrubs

Large laughingthrush, with uniform sepia-brown upperparts; slight rufous on forehead; distinct white throat and upper breast; graduated tail with white tips; flight feathers more ash-brown; pale rufous vent and belly; white iris and black lores. Sexes alike. Feeds on invertebrates and fruits. Confiding. Usually seen in large groups, often with other species. Nests in shrubs or trees.

WHITE-CRESTED LAUGHINGTHRUSH

Garrulax leucolophus Timaliidae

Size 28 cm

Voice Very noisy. Sudden explosive chatter or laughter; also pleasant 2- or 3-note whistling calls

Range The Himalayas, east of N Himachal Pradesh; foothills to height of 2,400 m, most common between 600-1,200 m

Habitat Dense forest undergrowth; bamboos; wooded nullahs

Large, olive-brown laughingthrush. Diagnostic white head, crest, throat, breast and sides of head; black eye mask extending to ear-coverts; pale grey nape; rusty-orange nuchal-collar encircling breast. Juvenile has smaller crest and mask. Moves rapidly in forest undergrowth but also tree foliage branches; makes short sallies between trees; extremely noisy; often seen along with other laughingthrushes, treepies and drongos; hops on ground, rummages in leaf litter.

LESSER NECKLACED LAUGHINGTHRUSH

Garrulax monileger Timaliidae

Size 27 cm

Voice Noisy. Calls include subdued *turrrr* and *kaaaaaa*. Song a loud, mellow *tee…too…ka…kew…kew…kew*

Range The Himalayas from WC Nepal east to Arunachal Pradesh; NE India and Bangladesh

Habitat Dense broadleaved evergreen and moist deciduous forests with thick undergrowth, dense secondary growth and bamboo thickets

Large, brown laughingthrush, with black necklace. Centre of breast and belly white; strong, black moustachial stripe, rufous flanks, whitish-grey wing panel; brown-black outer-tail feathers tipped white; white throat, edged rusty-orange; orangish cast above necklace where throat adjoins necklace. Similar to Greater but smaller and slimmer with finer bill and narrower tail. Feeds on ground, foraging for invertebrates.

GREATER NECKLACED LAUGHINGTHRUSH

Garrulax pectoralis Timaliidae

Size 29 cm

Voice Whistles; *week...week...week.* Melodic song

Range W Nepal to Myanmar. Bangladesh and S Assam Hills

Habitat Broadleaved forest undergrowth; secondary scrub; bamboo forests

Large, stocky laughingthrush, with striking black 'necklace'; olive-brown above; rufous flanks, sides of breast, neck; whitish centre of belly; long, graduated white-tipped tail. Similar to Lesser, but has bigger bill, necklace enclosing larger area on whitish breast; throat buff-washed; variable ear-coverts (white, black-and-white or black) completely enclosed by black moustachial stripe joining bill to necklace; black base to primaries; grey legs. In pairs when breeding; otherwise in larger flocks, often with Lesser and White-crested. Wary.

STRIATED LAUGHINGTHRUSH

Grammatoptila striatus Timaliidae

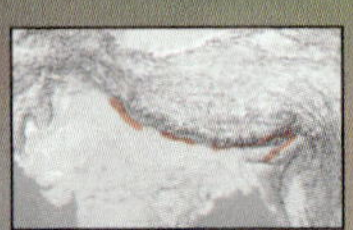

Size 28 cm

Voice Calls include cackling, whistling, chattering

Range Hills from Himachal to Myanmar. Moves lower in winter

Habitat Dense forests; undergrowth

Brown laughingthrush, with bushy, rounded crest; plumage varies from pale to dark rufous-chestnut, darker wings, heavy or fine streaking depending on race; completely streaked from crown, both underparts and upperparts, with buff-white; relatively short stout, black bill; eastern races generally darker than W Himalayan nominate race; intermediate *G. s. cranbrooki* of Arunachal Pradesh has broad, dark supercilium from eye to nape; barely streaked crown; habits similar to other laughingthrushes; more arboreal; upper to lower storeys.

cranbrooki

vibex

CHESTNUT-BACKED LAUGHINGTHRUSH

Garrulax nuchalis Timaliidae

Size 23 cm

Voice Call a soft *chip*. Rich whistled song of 4- or 5-notes; unmistakable *churr* when alarmed

Range Hills of NE India (Assam, Manipur, Nagaland, Arunachal Pradesh)

Habitat Chiefly dense bushes on stony scrub-covered ravines and hills, also tall grass

Medium-sized laughingthrush, with distinctive white ear-coverts and throat-sides; white spot on grey forecrown; black face, lores, chin; bright rufous mantle; grey breast; black throat-stripe.

YELLOW-THROATED LAUGHINGTHRUSH

Garrulax galbanus Timaliidae

Size 22 cm

Voice Call a frequently uttered feeble

Range Hills of NE India

Habitat Tall grass interspersed with trees and shrubs, open scrub jungles; and margins of dense evergreen broadleaved forests

Small laughingthrush with yellow underparts, black mask, and grey crown and nape. Distinguished from Rufous-vented by greyish-olive flanks and yellowish lower belly and vent, pale olive-brown upperparts. Greyish tail becoming blacker towards tip and with broad, white tips to outer feathers. Noticeable black chin, greyish outer webs of primaries forming indistinct panel on wing, and greyish legs and feet.

RUFOUS-VENTED LAUGHINGTHRUSH

Garrrulax gularis Timaliidae

Size 23 cm

Voice Call a loud whistle, in addition to cackling laughter

Range Endemic to the subcontinent. The Himalayan foothills from E Bhutan east to E Arunachal Pradesh

Habitat Mainly dense evergreen undergrowth, dense scrub and secondary growth; also bamboos and scrub

Upperparts rufous-brown with grey crown and nape. Prominent black mask; red eye; bare patch of visible grey skin behind eye; long, black bill; rump and uppertail-coverts brighter rufous. Bright yellow throat and chin; chestnut-brown belly; grey sides to breast; orange legs. Juvenile similar to adult, but has blackish crown and rufous markings on grey breast. Shy. Forages in flocks on forest floor. Feeds on insects.

VARIEGATED LAUGHINGTHRUSH

Garrrulax variegatus Timaliidae

Size 25 cm

Voice Noisy. Calls include various whistling and squeaking notes comprising *weet, weer* and *peet weer*

Range Locally common endemic breeding resident in N mountains from N Pakistan east to E Nepal. Moves lower down in winter

Habitat Thick forest-edge, undergrowth and secondary growth

Overall grey-brown laughingthrush. Rufous forehead; dark mask; dark throat-stripe; grey crown; white iris; black chin; grey wings with black-and-white markings and grey, rufous to yellowish-green edgings. Tail dark grey, with paler grey subterminal band; rufous vent. Sexes alike. Juvenile has more rufous cast and less strong markings. Feeds on invertebrates and fruits close to ground but sometimes seen on lower level of trees. Usually in pairs, or small parties.

MOUSTACHED LAUGHINGTHRUSH

Garrulax cineraceus Timaliidae

Olive-grey laughingthrush. Black forehead and crown; whitish lores; greyish-buff supercilium; black eye-stripe; broad moustachial stripe; streaking on throat-sides, white tips to tertials and secondaries, grey panel on wing. Tail olive-grey with white-tipped black subterminal band. Sexes alike. In pairs, or small flocks. Feeds on ground.

Size 22 cm

Voice Musical call

Range Hills of NE India (Assam, Manipur, Meghalaya, Mizoram, Nagaland), subject to some altitudinal movements. Moves lower in winter

Habitat Dense undergrowth and bushes in moist forests, secondary growth and dense scrub at edges of cultivation

RUFOUS-CHINNED LAUGHINGTHRUSH

Garrulax rufogularis Timaliidae

Size 22 cm

Voice Varied calls; squeals and chuckles

Range Hills of Kashmir to Myanmar. Moves lower in winter

Habitat Thick forest undergrowth; scrub; edges of forests; secondary growth

Medium-sized, intricately-patterned laughingthrush; variable rufous on chin, upper throat, ear-coverts; black crown; buff lores; black sub-moustachial area; black, scaly barring on mantle; black bands on wings; black spotting on variable grey or buff-white underparts; bright rufous-chestnut vent and tail edges; black subterminal band on tail. Much racial variation; solitary, in pairs or small flocks; more quiet, shy and wary; near dense cover in lower forest storeys, bushes and undergrowth; forages mostly on ground.

rufogularis

occidentalis

SPOTTED LAUGHINGTHRUSH

Garrrulax ocellatus Timaliidae

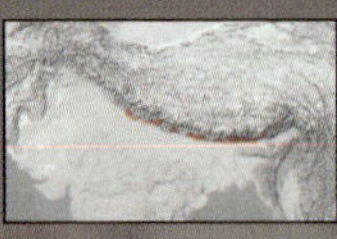

Size 32 cm

Voice Call an arresting *tchu...wee, tchu...wee, tchu...witty...*

Range E Uttarakhand to Arunachal Pradesh

Habitat Undergrowth in mixed broadleaved, coniferous forests; rhododendron

Very large and distinctive laughingthrush, with rufous face, chin, supercilium; dusky throat, ear-coverts; blackish cap; stark white iris; bold black-and-white spotting on rufous-chestnut upperparts. Dense, bold mottling, barring, spotting on buff breast, upper belly; grey-and-black edges to flight feathers; long, chestnut-grey, graduated tail, with black-and-white edges. Can be seen solitary, in pairs or small groups, often with other laughingthrushes; wary but curious. Generally in bushes, undergrowth; forages mostly on ground in leaf litter for insects, berries and seeds.

GREY-SIDED LAUGHINGTHRUSH

Garrrulax caerulatus Timaliidae

Size 25 cm

Voice Varied calls and songs; mellow whistles; squeals

Range E Nepal, Bhutan and Arunachal Pradesh

Habitat Undergrowth in dense moist evergreen forests; edges of forests; secondary growth; bamboo jungles

Dark rufous-brown, white-and-grey laughingthrush, with variable white cheek-patch and slaty-blue orbital-patch; rufous-brown cap, with black scaling; black forehead, lores, sub-moustachial stripe and bill. Deep brown upperparts, with rufous cast to wings and tail; white throat, breast and belly; grey flanks and breast-sides. Racial variations; solitary, in pairs or small groups; mostly terrestrial; forages on ground in leaf litter.

RUFOUS-NECKED LAUGHINGTHRUSH

Garrrulax ruficollis Timaliidae

Size 23 cm

Voice Varied calls; vast range of trills and whistles, squeals and babbles

Range Nepal, Bhutan, Assam and Arunachal Pradesh

Habitat Open broadleaved forests; edges of forests; undergrowth; bushes; bamboos; tea gardens

Smaller, darker laughingthrush; forecrown, face, throat black; hindcrown, nape grey; red iris; striking rufous-patch down neck, behind ear-coverts; rufous vent and lower belly; rest of plumage olive suffused with rufous; black bill and legs. Like other laughingthrushes; usually in pairs when breeding; larger flocks the rest of the year. Shy and wary; generally near dense cover in lower forest storeys, bushes and undergrowth, or forages on ground in leaf litter.

WHITE-BROWED LAUGHINGTHRUSH

Garrrulax sannio Timaliidae

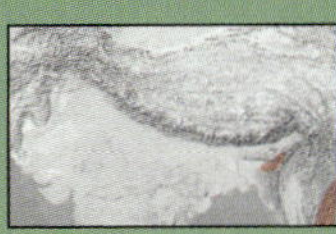

Size 23 cm

Voice Noisy. Calls include harsh, shrill, explosive *tcheu* or *tchow* notes; *tcheu…tcheu…tcheu…* etc. Pairs may call antiphonally

Range Hills of NE India

Habitat Undergrowth in dense forests; secondary growth; bamboo thickets and scrub-covered hillsides

Almost uniform, olive-brown laughingthrush. Crown has brown post-ocular line; nape chestnut-brown, broad supercilium; paler lores and patch on cheek, cinnamon-brown ear-coverts, sides of neck and throat, buff; brown tail. Sexes alike. Underparts more buff-brown; rufous undertail-coverts. Confiding. In small flocks or solitary, or in pairs. Nests in low vegetation.

STREAKED LAUGHINGTHRUSH

Garrrulax lineatus Timaliidae

Size 20 cm

Voice Noisy. Constant whistling and squeaking notes including *pitt...wee...err*

Range Common breeding resident in N mountains from W Pakistan east to Arunachal Pradesh. Moves down to foothills in winter

Habitat Low scrub; edges of forests; gardens and roadside grass patches. Often around habitation

Medium-sized, grey-brown babbler. Upperparts almost entirely streaked, except rump and vent. Distinct rufous ear-coverts; wings and tail more chestnut-brown; grey-tipped tail. Unstreaked underparts. Sexes alike. Feeds on invertebrates and fruits. In pairs, or small flocks. Short, weak flight, diving for cover. Not shy, but rather furtive. Nests in low cover.

BHUTAN LAUGHINGTHRUSH

Garrulax imbricatus Timaliidae

Size 20 cm

Voice Calls *krreerrr; tchu...wee...yuh*

Range Bhutan, straying into W Arunachal Pradesh

Habitat Undergrowth in open forests; secondary growth; hillsides, roadside scrub; gardens

Small, dark russet-brown laughingthrush, once classified as a race of Streaked; distinguished from that species by darker plumage, little or no dark streaking on crown, nape; paler greyish-brown lores, ear-coverts; finer white streaking overall; longer tail. Usually in pairs, or small parties; terrestrial; mostly forages on ground on grassy banks, low bushes, creeping through herbage; will also climb onto mossy walls. Fairly tame; easily seen around habitation, though generally stays near cover.

STRIPED LAUGHINGTHRUSH

Garrulax virgatus Timaliidae

Size 25 cm

Voice Call a plaintive, hurried *chwi...pieu* or *wiwiweu*

Range Hills of NE India

Habitat Dense undergrowth in moist broadleaved evergreen forests; thick secondary growth

Medium-sized laughingthrush with white streaking on upperparts and underparts. Confused with Streaked; easily distinguished by broad, greenish-white supercilium, broad buff-patch on ear-coverts, rufous lores, deep chestnut throat contrasting with rufous-buff breast and belly, chestnut-brown crown and nape, fine but considerably more distinct white shaft streaking on upperparts and underparts, uniform, olive-brown tail.

BROWN-CAPPED LAUGHINGTHRUSH

Garrulax austeni Timaliidae

Size 22 cm

Voice Sings with loud, plaintive, jolly phrases, *whit... wee...wiweeoo, whit...wi...chooee, whichi...wi...chooee whiwiwi...weeee...weeoo* etc

Range Hills of NE India

Habitat Undergrowth in oak and rhododendron forests; bushes and bamboo thickets at edges and clearings of forests; ravines

Medium-sized, maroon-brown laughingthrush. Whitish streaks on rufous-brown crown and nape; white, scaled underparts; rufous olive-brown mantle; rufous-brown wings and tail. Greater coverts, tertials and secondaries white-tipped. Tail has narrow white tips to blackish outer feathers, with rufous-brown central feathers. Similar to Chestnut-crowned but has plain brownish face and throat without any grey. In pairs, or small parties. Feeds on ground.

BLUE-WINGED LAUGHINGTHRUSH

Garrulax squamatus Timaliidae

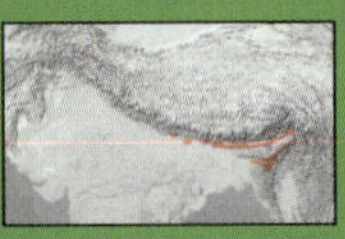

Size 25 cm

Voice Alarm call a scratchy seek. Song a *cur...white...to...go*

Range The Himalayas; NE India

Habitat Dense undergrowth in moist evergreen forests

Overall dark brown, finely-scaled laughingthrush. Black supercilium; rusty-orange and sooty-grey wings; distinct wing panel created by blue-grey outer webs on primaries; rufous wings with darker outer edges; chestnut-brown flanks and vent; chestnut undertail-coverts; black tail with rufous tip. Striking white iris. Female more rufous overall with less scaling. Juvenile even more rufous-red and even less scaling. Similar to Scaly which has yellow rather than rufous on wings. Very shy, hiding in dense undergrowth.

SCALY LAUGHINGTHRUSH

Garrulax subunicolor Timaliidae

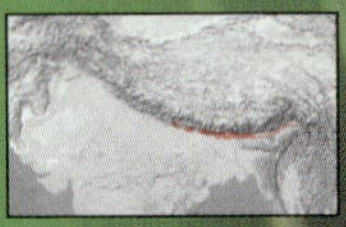

Size 23 cm

Voice Normal song a 2- or 3-part wolf-whistle that is buzzy and more slurred than several similar laughingthrush songs

Range The Himalayas from WC Nepal east to Arunachal Pradesh

Habitat Thick undergrowth in moist broadleaved and mixed broadleaved-coniferous forests

Olive-brown laughingthrush with dense black scaling all over. Greyish crown; dark, short bill. Diagnostic yellow in wings and tail feathers, tipped white; primaries show little blue-grey. Underparts and vent olive-brown. Secretive. Keeps to dense vegetation. In pairs, or small flocks, feeds on berries and invertebrates.

SPOT-BREASTED LAUGHINGTHRUSH

Garrulax merulinus Timaliidae

Size 25 cm

Voice Song consists of repetition at intervals of 4-10 seconds, of plaintive phrase, e.g. *wichi...pi...choo* or *whi...pi...choo* or *whi...choo...it*

Range Rare resident in NE Indian hills

Habitat Degraded broadleaved forests

Uniform, dark chestnut-brown laughingthrush with longish bill and short tail. Breast and throat strongly marked with brown spots; very abbreviated supercilium behind eye; wings, flanks, tail olive-brown. Juvenile has paler rufous upperparts, and less prominent streaking on breast and throat. Very shy. In pairs, or small flocks; feeds under dense vegetation.

ASSAM LAUGHINGTHRUSH

Garrrulax chrysopterum Timaliidae

Size 26 cm

Voice Songs differ from Chestnut-crowned's in their lower pitch, mellower quality, and greater complexity and length

Range Hills of NE India

Habitat Forests; bamboos

Largish laughingthrush with bright rufous patch on crown. Grey supercilium; grey forehead; ear-coverts streaked; rufous breast; mantle shows faintly diffused streaking. Juvenile has lighter brown crown rather than rufous and lighter markings.

BLACK-FACED LAUGHINGTHRUSH

Garrrulax affinis Timaliidae

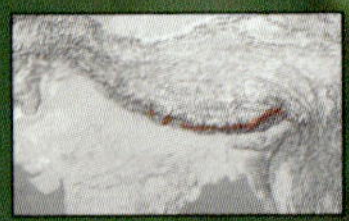

Size 25 cm

Voice Alarm call a rolling *whirrr*. Various high-pitched notes, chuckles. A 4-noted, somewhat plaintive song

Range The Himalayas, from W Nepal eastwards; descends to 1,500 m in winter

Habitat Undergrowth in forests; dwarf vegetation in higher regions

Diagnostic blackish face, throat and part of head and contrasting white malar-patches, neck-sides and part of eye-ring; rufous-brown above, finely scalloped on back; olive-golden flight feathers tipped grey; rufous-brown below throat, marked grey. Sexes alike. In pairs or small bands, sometimes with other babblers; moves on ground, in low growth; also ascends into middle levels of trees; noisy when disturbed or when snakes or other creatures arouse its curiosity.

BUGUN LIOCICHLA

Liocichla bugunorum Timaliidae

Size 22 cm

Voice Fluty calls on a descending scale, slightly slurred and inflected at the end *weee…keew, yu…weee…keew, wieuu…weei…tuui…tuuuw…tuoow*

Range Globally threatened. Eaglenest Wildlife Sanctuary, Arunachal Pradesh

Habitat Disturbed hillsides with dense shrubberies, small trees and bushes

Olive-brown laughingthrush with black crown. Diagnostic orange-yellow lores; yellow post-ocular spot; grey cheeks; yellow, red and white patches in wings; black tail with reddish tip, and scarlet red undertail-coverts.

CHESTNUT-CROWNED LAUGHINGTHRUSH

Garrrulax erythrocephalus Timaliidae

Size 28 cm

Voice Songs quite variable in form, quick, sweet, clear, wiry and emphatic

Range The Himalayas from W Himachal to NE Arunachal Pradesh

Habitat Dense vegetation in broadleaved forests

nigrimentus

erythrocephalus

Variable laughingthrush with brilliant green-gold panel on wings and sides of tail, heavy black spots on upper mantle and scales on breast, chestnut forehead scales and fine black centres on ear-coverts (looking frosted); usually pale eyes. Juvenile has duller crown, more chestnut-tinged upperparts, no spotting or scaling. Nominate racial group has entirely rufous crown, and rufous cheek. In W Himalayas, nominate pale with bright rufous crown, greyish-olive mantle (greyer on scapulars) and pale, dull buff underparts.

RED-FACED LIOCICHLA

Liocichla phoenicea Timaliidae

Distinctive, mainly brown-and-crimson babbler; dark brown upper and underparts; streaked crown; black supercilium; bright red face, ear-coverts, neck sides; large, crimson and orange patch on primaries; silver and black on secondaries; red undertail-coverts; extensive orange on wing-tips, underside and tips to black tail. Solitary, in pairs when breeding; in small parties or mixed hunting flocks with other species. Shy and secretive; not easily seen; usually forages on ground, or lurks in forest undergrowth; sometimes in mid-storey.

Size 23 cm

Voice Calls include churrs, rattles, mews. Melodious whistled song

Range Bhutan to Myanmar; S Assam Hills; possibly E Nepal

Habitat Thick undergrowth in moist deciduous or evergreen forests; secondary growth

SILVER-EARED MESIA

Mesia argentauris Timaliidae

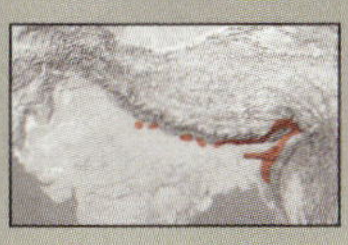

Size 15 cm

Voice Call a chattering *tiweet…cheweet…cheweet*

Range Hills of Uttarakhand to Myanmar

Habitat Bushes in evergreen forests; edges of forests; secondary growth

Striking, unmistakable babbler, with bright yellow bill, forehead, chin, upper throat; orange-yellow lower throat, breast, upper mantle; black face, crown, partially encircling large, silver-grey ear-covert patch. Crimson wing panel on greenish orange-yellow wings; grey on rest of mantle, back; greenish-yellow on rest of underparts; yellow-edged dark tail. Male has crimson uppertail, undertail-coverts; female duller, paler, with olive-gold uppertail, orange-yellow undertail-coverts. In pairs, or fairly large parties, often in mixed flocks, moving through foliage in lower, middle, sometimes canopy, levels.

RED-BILLED LEIOTHRIX

Leiothrix lutea Timaliidae

Size 13 cm

Voice Quite vocal; often utters a wistful, piping *tee…tee…tee*; mix of sudden explosive notes. Song a musical warble. Noisy

Range The Himalayas, from Kashmir to extreme NE India; 600-2,700 m

Habitat Forest undergrowth; bushy hillsides; plantations

Upperparts olive-grey; dull, buffy-yellow lores and eye-ring; yellow, orange, crimson-and-black in wings; forked-tail, with black tip and edges; yellow throat, orange-yellow breast diagnostic; scarlet beak. Red on wing considerably reduced or absent in the western race *kumaiensis*. Female has yellow, instead of crimson in wings. Small parties or often in mixed hunting parties in forests; rummages in undergrowth, but frequently moves up into leafy branches; lively bird.

HIMALAYAN CUTIA

Cutia nipalensis Timaliidae

Size 20 cm

Voice Calls include toots; squawks; *cheet...cheet*

Range C Nepal to Myanmar; S Assam Hills

Habitat Dense moist broadleaved evergreen, oak and pine forests

Round and unmistakable babbler, with slaty-blue head; male has broad, bluish-black mask, short, sturdy, slightly decurved bill; white underparts, with diagnostic bold, dark barring on buff-washed sides of breast and flanks; blue panels on bluish-black wings; rufous-chestnut mantle, back and long uppertail-coverts; long, buff undertail-coverts, with just tip of black tail visible; orange legs. Female has paler crown, brown mask, mantle streaked brown. Seen in pairs, small groups, or in mixed flocks; arboreal; active on mossy trees.

♀

WHITE-BROWED SHRIKE BABBLER

Pteruthius flaviscapis Timaliidae

Size 16 cm

Voice Churrs in alarm. Song *chyip...chyip...chyip*

Range Pakistan to Myanmar

Habitat Broadleaved evergreen forests; coniferous or mixed forests

♀

Strikingly-patterned, with short, shrike-like bill, hooked at end; male has broad, white supercilium over and behind eye; bluish-black crown, nape, ear-coverts; grey mantle, back and rump; rufous-chestnut panel on black wings; white-tipped primaries and secondaries; white underparts, with pinkish wash on flanks. Female has pale or no supercilium; grey crown; brownish mantle; rufous wing panel; greenish-yellow wings; buff underparts. Solitary, in pairs, or small parties; arboreal; canopy-feeder.

GREEN SHRIKE BABBLER

Pteruthius xanthochlorus Timaliidae

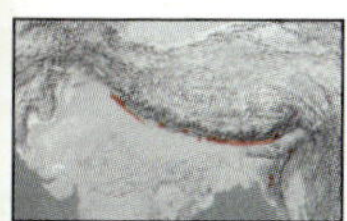

Size 13 cm

Voice Call a harsh *cha; whee...tee, whee...tee*

Range Uttarakhand to Myanmar

Habitat Broadleaved evergreen forests; oak and rhododendron, coniferous and mixed forests

zanthochlorus

occidentalis

Small, plain and rather drab-looking shrike babbler; warbler-like, but stocky, and with tiny, stubby bill; grey crown and ear-coverts; olive-green mantle, wings, tail; thin, but clear, wing-bar; black patch on primary coverts; greyish-white underparts; pale yellow belly, and yellowish wash on sides of breast and flanks; white-tipped tail, tertials and secondaries. Female has paler crown. Singly, in pairs, or in mixed hunting parties with other species. Arboreal; forages in most forest storeys; quiet, unobtrusive and not very active. *Occidentalis* is found in the W Himalayas, *zanthochlorus* is resident of E Himalaya while *hybrida* is found south of the River Brahmaputra.

hybrida

BLACK-EARED SHRIKE BABBLER

Pteruthius melanotis Timaliidae

Size 11 cm

Voice Calls *tchew...whee, tchew...whee*

Range W Nepal to Myanmar

Habitat Moist broadleaved evergreen forests

♀

Very small, brightly-coloured shrike babbler; prominent white eye-ring, bordered with black; small, hooked bill; Male has yellow forehead, black lores and eye-stripe curving behind yellow ear-coverts; broad, grey supercilium from behind eye to nape; yellowish-green crown, mantle; two broad, white wing-bars on black wing-coverts; bluish-grey panel on primaries and secondaries; chestnut throat, breast; yellow undersides. Female has chestnut only on malar stripe; duller, with buff wing-bars. Solitary, in pairs, or mixed hunting parties; arboreal; mostly in upper forest storeys; quiet, unobtrusive, slow-moving.

BLACK-HEADED SHRIKE BABBLER

Pteruthius rufiventer Timaliidae

Size 17 cm

Voice Song a bright *pew…pew…peee…ti*, repeated without much variation

Range The Himalayas from WC Nepal east to Arunachal Pradesh; NE India

Habitat Broadleaved forests

Sexes dissimilar. Male has rufous-brown upperparts; black crown and nape; pale grey throat; yellowish patches on breast-sides; rufous-pink belly and vent; rufous-brown rump; grey eyes. Female larger than male; diffused streaking on olive-brown mantle; wings and tail olive-brown; sides of head grey; steel-grey cheeks; black-scaled crown. Juvenile male similar to adult male, but more olive-brown upperparts. Male similar to White-browed but larger and slimmer, and no supercilium. Female distinguished from female White-browed by steely-black crown and nape, olive-brown mantle, sometimes with black markings.

CHESTNUT-FRONTED SHRIKE BABBLER

Pteruthius aenobarbus Timaliidae

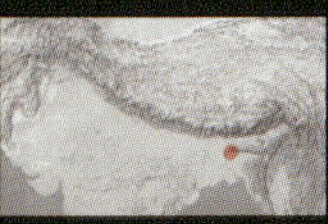

Size 11 cm

Voice Song a monotonous *chip... chip...chip*

Range Meghalaya

Habitat Evergreen forests

Small shrike babbler with distinctive chestnut forehead and bright yellow forecrown. Chestnut throat and upper breast. Similar to Black-eared but both sexes have no black border to ear-coverts; no grey on nape, and silvery-white wing panel. Female not known, but probably similar to female *P a: intermedius* (Burma), which differs from female Black-eared by being duller and with whitish underparts. Nests high in trees.

WHITE-HOODED BABBLER

Gampsorhynchus rufulus Timaliidae

Size 23 cm

Voice Calls include harsh *kaw...ka...yawk*; hard rattling

Range Rather scarce breeding resident in N foothills from extreme eastern Nepal to Burmese border

Habitat Forest undergrowth; bamboo thickets

Large babbler with white head and long tail. Warm brown above and pale rufous-buff below; tail-tip and vent buff; pale iris, bill and legs. Sexes alike. Juvenile has orange crown and nape and buff underparts. Feeds on invertebrates in small parties or mixed hunting groups. Nests in bushes.

STREAK-THROATED BARWING

Actinodura waldeni Timaliidae

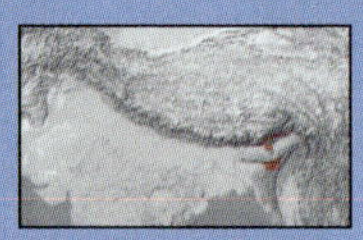

Size 22 cm

Voice Contact calls rather nasal, grumbling *grrr...ut...grrr...ut* and *grr...grr...grr...grr...gr* etc.

Range Fairly common resident in hills of NE India (Arunachal Pradesh, Assam, Manipur, Nagaland)

Habitat Mossy, broadleaved evergreen and mixed forests

Two races. *A. w. daflaensis* (E Himalayas) has greyish-white throat, breast and belly diffusely streaked with brownish-grey, and looks like Hoary-throated (although there is no known overlap in ranges). Best distinguished by streaked underparts, lack of bold shaft streaking on crown and nape; no moustachial stripe, and even rufous-brown mantle. *A. w. waldeni* (hills south of the Brahmaputra) has same tawny-brown colouration like Rusty-fronted; best distinguished by lack of rusty 'front' to head.

HOARY-THROATED BARWING

Actinodura nipalensis Timaliidae

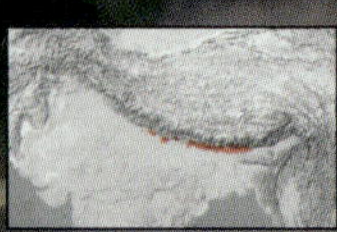

Size 20 cm

Voice Calls *jay...jay...jay; dewit...dewit...dewit*

Range C Nepal to Myanmar; S Assam Hills

Habitat Moist oak, broadleaved evergreen forests; mixed coniferous forests

Mainly grey, buff and brown barwing; feathery grey-brown crest on crown, nape, with pale buff or white shaft streaks; pale grey throat, upper breast, generally unstreaked; grey ear-coverts; diffused dark moustachial stripe; buff or white streaking on mantle, scapulars; grey wing-bar on greater coverts; greyish-buff underparts; more distinctly barred tail than in Rusty-fronted. In pairs, or small parties; often in mixed hunting flocks; arboreal; forages on mossy, epiphytic-covered branches of trees in middle to canopy levels.

RUSTY-FRONTED BARWING

Actinodura egertoni Timaliidae

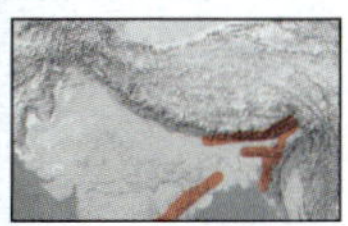

Size 23 cm

Voice Calls include *cheep*; rattles. Song a sweet, whistled *tee… tee…ta*

Range Nepal to Bhutan and W Arunachal Pradesh

Habitat Thick undergrowth, broadleaved evergreen forests; bamboo thickets

Larger, slender barwing, with dark rufous-chestnut forehead, lores and chin; relatively long tail; feathery, unstreaked blue-grey crest, nape, upper mantle and sides of neck; unmarked, rufous-brown lower mantle; unbarred rufous-chestnut on greater coverts and base of primaries; buff-barred primaries and secondaries; blue-grey edge to flight feathers; plain olive-brown below; marked racial variations. In pairs, or small parties. Arboreal; usually in dense bushes and vegetation of lower and mid-storey.

lewisi

egertoni

BLUE-WINGED SIVA

Siva cyanouroptera Timaliidae

Size 15 cm

Voice Calls *chip…; chik*. Song a loud, high-pitched, whistled *pee… peeoo…; si…seeow*

Range Hills of Uttarakhand to Myanmar. Moves lower in winter

Habitat Broadleaved evergreen forests; mixed broadleaved-coniferous forest; edges of forests; secondary growth

Fairly small, slender, distinctive babbler, with blue crown, wings, tail; deep blue streaks and lateral stripes on blue-grey crown and nape; long, white supercilium; pale, greyish-white face, dark, beady eye and pale, flesh-coloured bill; mauve underparts; brown mantle; blue wings, with grey-blue panel; blue-sided, square-ended tail; usually in small groups.

RED-TAILED MINLA

Minla ignotincta Timaliidae

Size 14 cm

Voice Calls include *wi…wi…wi; chik…chik…chik…chik; tsi; chitititit; twiyitwiyuwi*

Range Hills of C Nepal to Myanmar. Moves lower in winter

Habitat Moist, broadleaved evergreen forests; mixed broadleaved, coniferous forests; secondary growth

Small babbler, with black crown, prominent broad, white supercilium and black mask extending to nape; brown mantle and back; pale yellowish underparts; light grey streaks sometimes visible on breast and flanks; white-edged black wing-coverts, secondaries and tertials. Male has red panel on flight feathers; female yellowish-orange; male has chestnut cast to brown mantle; black tail, with red outer-tail and undertail feathers, tip. Arboreal; seen in small mixed flocks.

BAR-THROATED SIVA

Siva strigula Timaliidae

Size 14 cm

Voice Calls include whistling *tsee...tsi...tsay...tsse* and *pseep*

Range Locally common breeding resident in N mountains from Himachal Pradesh east to Burmese border. Moves lower down in winter. Also occurs in China and SE Asia

Habitat Lower canopy; high undergrowth of forests

Small, brightly-coloured babbler with high-domed chestnut crown. Olive-brown above with black, white-and-chestnut-patterned wings and chestnut-centred black tail with yellow edgings. Dusky cheeks and finely black-barred white throat. Feeds actively on invertebrates and fruits in small parties or in mixed hunting groups. Nests low down in cover.

YELLOW-THROATED FULVETTA

Pseudominla cinerea Timaliidae

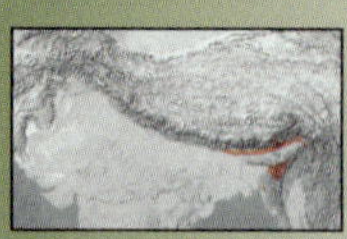

Size 10 cm

Voice Calls include *si…si…si… si…si…si; chrrp…prrp*

Range Hills of NE India

Habitat Understorey in dense, subtropical broadleaved evergreen forests; bamboo thickets; secondary scrub

Small, mainly brown-and-yellow fulvetta; long, broad, yellow supercilium, bordered by dark eye-stripe below and dark lateral crown-stripe above; greyish scaling and mottling on brownish crown; yellowish-brown upperparts. Brown wings; grey streaking on yellowish face; yellow throat and yellowish underparts; dusky flanks and breast-sides. Usually in small flocks, often in mixed hunting parties with other insectivorous species; confiding; active in forest understorey; feeding behaviour like leaf warblers.

WHITE-BROWED FULVETTA

Fulvetta vinipectus Timaliidae

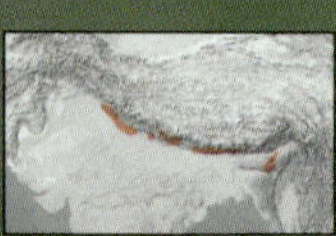

Size 11 cm

Voice Call a fairly sharp *tsuip* or *tship*; also some harsh churring notes, when agitated

Range The Himalayas from W Himachal Pradesh; E Himalayas; NE regions; 1,500-3,500 m, over 4,000 m in some parts; descends to 1,200 m in severe winters

Habitat Scrubs in forest, *ringal* bamboo

austeni

chumbiensis

Brown crown and nape; prominent white eyebrow with black or dark brown line above; blackish sides of face; olive-brown above, washed rufous on wings, rump and tail; some grey in wings; whitish throat and breast; olive-brown below. Sexes alike. Upto 20 birds in low growth or lower branches; energetic, acrobatic; often seen in mixed hunting parties.

RUFOUS-WINGED FULVETTA

Pseudominla castaneceps Timaliidae

Small, rather drab, buff-and-brown fulvetta; dark chestnut-brown crown and nape with pale streaks; long, buff-white supercilium; black eye-stripe, streaked ear-coverts, moustachial stripe; olive-brown mantle; rufous-chestnut edges to primaries forming wing panel; black greater and primary covert panel; dark brown tail; dusty-white underparts, with buff sides of breast and flanks. In fairly large, fast-moving foraging flocks in under- and mid-forest storeys. Characteristic Nuthatch-like behaviour of climbing mossy tree trunks.

Size 10 cm

Voice Calls include *cheep; tew... twi...twi*

Range Hills of C Nepal to Myanmar. Moves lower in winter

Habitat Undergrowth in broadleaved evergreen forests; secondary growth

RUFOUS-THROATED FULVETTA

Schoeniparus rufogularis Timaliidae

Size 12 cm

Voice Calls include churring, buzzing, cheeping, chattering; *whee...chu whee...chu whee...chu*

Range Patchily in Bhutan and Arunachal Pradesh

Habitat Dense undergrowth in broadleaved forests; secondary growth; bamboo thickets

Slightly larger, mainly brown-and-rufous fulvetta; long, white supercilium; long, black lateral crown-stripe; rufous crown and nape; white throat and upper breast, with distinctive broad rufous gorget; white eye-ring; dark brown ear-coverts; brown wings; whitish centre of underparts; greyish-brown-washed flanks. In pairs, especially when breeding; otherwise, in small flocks; skulks in dense low shrubberies and undergrowth, close to ground, or on ground.

GOLDEN-BREASTED FULVETTA

Lioparus chrysotis Timaliidae

Size 11 cm

Voice Call a twittering *quititit*. High-pitched whistled song

Range Hills of C Nepal to Myanmar, S Assam Hills

Habitat Bamboo growth; understorey in temperate broadleaved evergreen forests; hillside scrub

Very small, striking, golden-yellow, silver grey-and-black babbler. Black face, greyish-black chin and throat; silver-grey cheeks; blackish-grey nape and mantle; golden to orangish-yellow breast and underparts; yellow-and-orange linear panels on black wings; yellow-sided black tail; *albilineata* (of hills south of River Brahmaputra) has prominent white crown-stripe. In pairs, or in large mixed flocks; confiding; active in lower or mid-level forest storeys; acrobatic feeder.

BROWN-THROATED FULVETTA

Fulvetta ludlowi Timaliidae

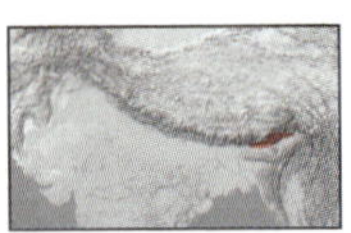

Size 11 cm

Voice Not very well-known. Calls *trrrrt* in alarm, with some see notes

Range Patchily in E Bhutan and Arunachal Pradesh

Habitat Undergrowth in broadleaved, rhododendron and coniferous forests; bamboos

Small, brown and rufous-chestnut fulvetta; lacks supercilium; brown crown, ear-coverts, with rufous hue giving a hooded appearance; brown streaks on whitish throat, breast; grey-brown mantle, upper belly, with pinkish-rufous hue; rufous-orange back, lower belly, vent. Silver grey-and-black wing panels. In pairs, when breeding; otherwise, in small flocks, often with other babblers, warblers, tits; skulks in bushes and undergrowth; occasionally in trees; not often seen.

MANIPUR FULVETTA

Fulvetta manipurensis Timaliidae

Size 11 cm

Voice Song a repeated, high-pitched *si...swu* or *see...si...wu*

Range Hills of NE India

Habitat Broadleaved evergreen forests, bamboos and bushes

Grey-brown fulvetta with prominent brown lateral crown-stripe and diffused pinkish-brown streaking on throat; grey cheeks; pale upperparts. Similar to White-browed, but lacks supercilium. Distinguished from Brown-throated by greyish ear-coverts, more buff-brown crown, mantle and breast.

RUSTY-CAPPED FULVETTA

Schoeniparus dubius Timaliidae

Size 12 cm

Voice Calls include *chu…chi…chiu; chu…witee…wee; chu…witchichu; chu…witchu…chiu; wi…chi…chiu; wi…witu…chu*

Range Hills of NE India

Habitat Bushes and dense undergrowth; especially ferns and brambles; in both thick and open forests; also at edges of forests

Large, rather long-tailed, skulking fulvetta. Has noticeably bright rufous forehead, rufous crown and nape with dark brown scaling; broad, white supercilium contrasting with black lateral crown-stripes, and dark brown ear-coverts and neck-sides, latter having prominent buff streaking. Uniform, olive-brown wings help quickly to separate this species from Rufous-winged.

NEPAL FULVETTA

Alcippe nipalensis Timaliidae

Size 12 cm

Voice Calls include buzzes; trills. Short song *shoo...shoo*

Range W Nepal to Myanmar. S Assam hills

Habitat Forest undergrowth and middle storeys

Medium-sized, largely grey-and-brown fulvetta; grey crown, nape and ear-coverts; black lateral crown-stripe; prominent white eye-ring; pale lower mandible; olive-brown upperparts and tail; whitish throat and centre of breast and belly; buffy-brown flanks, breast and undertail-coverts. In small, restless, vocal parties in mixed foraging flocks; active mainly in understorey, sometimes in trees in mid-storey, occasionally descends to ground; shy, and mostly remains hidden from view.

RUFOUS SIBIA

Malacias capistratus Timaliidae

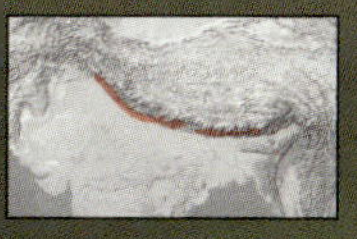

Size 21 cm

Voice Calls include a wide range of whistling and sharp notes. Rich song of 6- to 8-syllables during the Himalayan summer

Range The Himalayas, 1,500-3,000 m. Sometimes upto about 3,500 m; descends to 600 m in some winters

Habitat Temperate and broadleaved forests

Sexes alike. Rich rufous plumage; grey-brown centre of back (between wings); black crown; slightly bushy crest and sides of head; bluish-grey wings and black shoulder-patch; grey-tipped long tail; black subterminal tail-band. Small flocks, sometimes with other birds; active gymnasts, ever on the move; cheerful calls; hunts in canopy and middle-forest storeys, moves amidst moss-covered branches; springs into air after winged insects; sometimes hunts like treecreepers on stems, probing bark crevices.

RUFOUS-BACKED SIBIA

Leioptila annectans Timaliidae

Size 18 cm

Voice Chirrups. Song a loud, cheerful *chew…chew…ee, wheewhee…chee…chewee*

Range E Nepal, Bhutan and Arunachal Pradesh

Habitat Dense, moist subtropical or temperate, broadleaved evergreen forests

Smallest sibia, with relatively shorter tail; black cap, mask and upper mantle; white streaks on black nape; rufous back, rump and uppertail-coverts; mainly black wings with white-edged tertials, silvery panel formed by grey-edged primaries and secondaries, rufous bar on greater coverts; white throat, breast and belly; paler rufous flanks, lower belly and vent; yellow base to bill; yellow legs. Usually in small groups; arboreal; partial to mossy branches.

BEAUTIFUL SIBIA

Malacias pulchellus Timaliidae

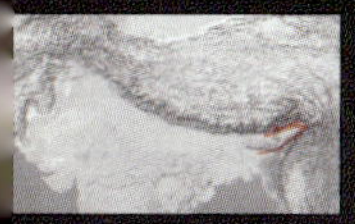

Size 22 cm

Voice Not always vocal. Rattling calls. Loud, whistled song

Range Mostly Arunachal Pradesh

Habitat Moist, broadleaved evergreen forests

Medium-sized blue sibia; pale indigo-blue crown; black lores and variable black on ear-coverts and face; grey-blue upperparts; paler, smoky grey-blue underparts; black greater and primary covert wing-patch; silver-grey edges to primaries; grey-blue secondaries; brown tertials; blue, brown-and-grey tail; dark subterminal band. In pairs, during breeding season; otherwise, small parties, larger in winter; arboreal; usually forages on mossy branches at canopy level; moves by hopping upwards on branches.

LONG-TAILED SIBIA

Heterophasia picaoides Timaliidae

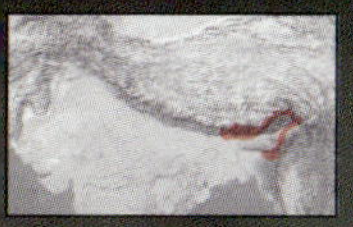

Size 30 cm

Voice Call a ringing *tsip tsip tsip*

Range Locally common breeding resident from E Nepal to Burmese border. Moves lower down in winter

Habitat Upper and middle levels of evergreen forests; edges of forests

Large, brown-grey babbler with long, white-tipped, graduated tail and distinct white wing-patch, graduated. Grey head and breast; red iris; slender, slightly downcurved bill; darkish lores. Brownish back, wings and tail. Underparts pale grey. Sexes alike. Juvenile has grey eyes. Arboreal. Feeds on nectar, invertebrates and seeds in pairs or single-species flocks. Confiding, but very active. Nests in tree-tops. Extremely noisy.

GREY SIBIA

Malacias gracilis Timaliidae

Size 21 cm

Voice Harsh, grating, slightly metallic calls typical of the genus, e.g. *trrit-trrit.* Song loud, strident, far-carrying series of well-spaced high-pitched, shrill whistled notes; *tu…tu…ti…ti…ti…tu; ti…ti…ti…ti… tiu…tu; tiutiu…tiu…tiu…tiu* etc.

Range Hills of NE India

Habitat Deciduous and evergreen broadleaved forests; mainly pine forests in Khasi Hills

Brownish-grey bird, similar to Rufous, but without any rufous. Black crown; no crest; black ear-coverts; brown-grey nape, mantle and back. Underparts white; buff rear flanks and undertail-coverts, black wings, with black edges to grey tertials; grey greater coverts; grey tail with broad, black subterminal band. Arboreal. Feeds in flocks, in trees, outside breeding season. Nests high in trees.

WHISKERED YUHINA

Yuhina flavicollis Timaliidae

Olive-brown above; chocolate-brown crown and crest; white eye-ring and black moustache seen from up close; rufous-yellow nuchal-collar (less distinct in western race *albicollis*); white underbody, streaked rufous-olive on sides of breast and flanks. Sexes alike. Flocks, almost always in association with other small birds; active and restless, flitting about or hunting flycatcher-style; moves between undergrowth and middle-levels of forests; sometimes ascending into canopy; keeps up a constant twitter.

flavicollis

Size 13 cm

Voice Quite vocal. Mix of soft twittering notes and fairly loud titmice-like 2- or 3-note call, *chee…chi…chew*

Range The Himalayas; W Himachal Pradesh to extreme NE India; 800-3,400 m

Habitat Forests

STRIATED YUHINA

Staphida castaniceps Timaliidae

Size 11 cm

Voice Call a loud cheeping or twittering *chir…chit…chir…chit*

Range NE India

Habitat Open and dense broadleaved forests with thick, bushy understorey; secondary growth in tropical and subtropical zones

Not so crested as other yuhinas, and the only one to show white on tail. Main plumage features include very short white supercilium; rufous ear-coverts with fine white streaking, white streaking on greyish-olive mantle, uniform greyish-white underparts, and white tips to graduated tail. Racial variation; three races occur in the subcontinent.

WHITE-NAPED YUHINA

Yuhina bakeri Timaliidae

Size 13 cm

Voice Calls *tsit…tsit; zhueh…zhueh*

Range Hills of E Nepal to Myanmar

Habitat Subtropical moist broadleaved evergreen forests; secondary growth

Distinctive rufous-crested yuhina; prominent white nape, better seen when crest raised; short, dark, sturdy bill; rufous crest, face, upper mantle; dark lores, eye-ring; white streaks on ear-coverts; white throat, with no moustachial stripe, as in other yuhinas; olive-brown lower mantle, with white shaft streaks; buff-brown below, with pinkish cast and fine, faint dark streaks. In pairs, when breeding; joins mixed feeding flocks with other babblers and small insectivores; very active in mid-storey trees or bushes in understorey.

STRIPE-THROATED YUHINA

Yuhina gularis Timaliidae

Size 14 cm

Voice Calls *kwee*

Range Hills of Uttarakhand to Myanmar

Habitat Temperate broadleaved, especially oak, rhododendron, forests; coniferous forests; secondary growth

Larger yuhina, with longer, upright, and slightly forward-drooping, grey crest; grey face, mantle; pale pink throat, with black streaks; narrow white eye-ring; patchy rufous-and-buff underparts; more rufous on centre of belly, vent; bright rufous wing-patch on secondaries; white-edged black primaries; pale basal two-thirds of lower mandible. As with other yuhinas, in pairs when breeding; otherwise, in small parties, especially with other babblers and small insectivores; usually in taller shrubs or lower branches of trees; partial to flowering trees.

RUFOUS-VENTED YUHINA

Yuhina occipitalis Timaliidae

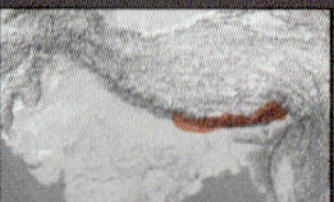

Size 13 cm

Voice Calls include rattling *trr... trr...trr* and *zee...zit*

Range Locally common breeding resident in N mountains from C Nepal to Arunachal Pradesh. Moves lower down in winter. Also occurs in Tibet, Myanmar and China

Habitat Forests, usually quite high in canopy

Upperparts brown with rufous nape and lores. Tall, grey crest; grey neck; forehead has whitish streaks; pale buff sides of head; white eye-ring; black malar stripe. Underparts paler, pink-brown; belly buff; rufous vent; reddish-brown bill and yellow-brown legs. Sexes alike. Juvenile has shorter crest and paler rufous nape and lores. Feeds on invertebrates and nectar in small active parties, often in mixed hunting groups. Nests in small trees in moss or lichen.

BLACK-CHINNED YUHINA

Yuhina nigrimenta Timaliidae

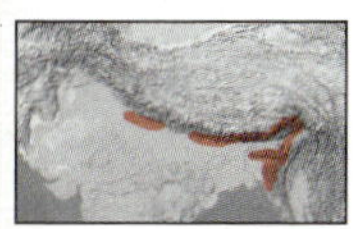

Size 11 cm

Voice Calls include chattering, twittering, buzzing. Whistled song *zeet...zut...zeet...zeet*

Range Hills of Uttarakhand to Myanmar

Habitat Subtropical broadleaved evergreen forests; secondary growth

Small, distinctive, mainly grey, brown-and-black yuhina, with relatively short tail; grey head, ear-coverts, hindneck, upper mantle; black-streaked front to upright grey crest; black lores and chin; slightly curved dark bill, with red-based lower mandible; mostly greyish-brown upperparts; pale, whitish throat, upper breast; mostly buff belly, vent. In pairs, when breeding; in small, noisy, same-species flocks or mixed hunting parties; active from understorey to canopy; acrobatic, tit-like behaviour.

WHITE-BELLIED ERPORNIS

Erpornis zantholeuca Timaliidae

Olive-yellow above and white underparts. Shortish, spiky, olive-yellow crest; light grey lores; black eyes; pale flesh-pink bill and legs. Yellow undertail-coverts and vent. Juvenile duller, with brownish cast to upperparts and shorter crest.

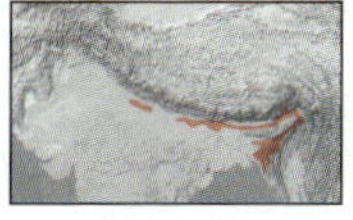

Size 11 cm

Voice Alarm calls include high, subdued, metallic *chit* and *cheaan*; nasal tit-like *na-na*. Sings with a short, high-pitched, descending trill, *si...i...i...i...i...i*

Range The Himalayas from Nepal east to Arunachal Pradesh; NE India and Bangladesh

Habitat Broadleaved forests, especially clearings and edges; secondary growth

GREAT PARROTBILL

Conostoma aemodium Paradoxornithidae

Large parrotbill, with long, rounded, orange-yellow bill; uniform brown, or grey-brown in colour; whitish forecrown; bushy-black lores and brow; no dark lateral crown-stripe; grey primary panel and sides of tail; richer rufous-brown on secondaries, wing-coverts; singly, in pairs, or small flocks; normally concealed in undergrowth, sometimes in foliage of tall trees, occasionally on ground, though not very secretive.

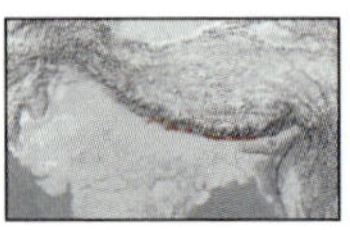

Size 28 cm

Voice Calls include *krarnk; krarnch; wheeoo...whee...wheeoo*

Range Hills of Nepal to Arunachal Pradesh

Habitat Bamboo clumps in or near forests; oak, rhododendron, open or dense broadleaved evergreen, or mixed coniferous, broadleaved forests

BROWN PARROTBILL

Cholornis unicolor Paradoxornithidae

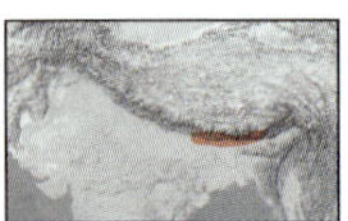

Size 21 cm

Voice Calls include *chrrt...chrrt; wheeoo...wheeoo*

Range Hills of E Nepal to Arunachal Pradesh

Habitat Bamboo stands; dwarf rhododendron shrubberies

Medium-sized parrotbill with small, bulbous, yellow or greyish bill; speckled, greyish-brown crown, sometimes raised in a crest; long, dark lateral crown-stripes; greyish supercilium, extending from behind eye to around ear-coverts; brown ear-coverts speckled with grey; pale eye-ring, broken into two crescents, above and below eye; more brown upperparts, with rich brown wing panel on primaries; greyish throat and breast; brownish belly and flanks; brown tail. Usually in small parties; acrobatic feeder; shy, secretive.

BLACK-BREASTED PARROTBILL

Paradoxornis flavirostris Paradoxornithidae

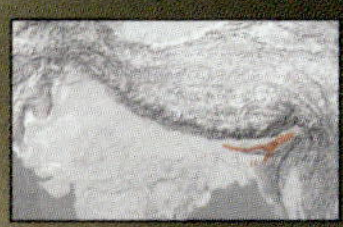

Size 19 cm

Voice Call a striking, whistling *phew… phew… phew… phuit,* ascending in pitch and volume. Also, bleating or mewing cry, and mellow 3-noted warble

Range NE India

Habitat Mixed grass and bamboos in hills, dense reed beds, elephant grass and grasses along riverbanks in lowlands

Medium-sized, stocky parrotbill with rufous-brown head and olive-brown upperparts, black patch on ear-coverts, and huge orange bill. Likely to be confused only with Spot-breasted, although different distribution. Best distinguished by black breast and solid black chin (with black barring on white throat and malar area), rufous-buff (rather than pale buff) underparts, darker rufous-brown crown and nape, even stouter bill and different call.

SPOT-BREASTED PARROTBILL

Paradoxornis guttaticollis Paradoxornithidae

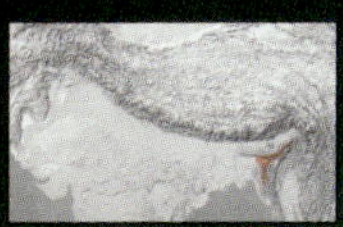

Size 21 cm

Voice Calls include *whit-whit-whit-whit-whit;* or more plaintive series, e.g. *wui… wui… wui… wui* or *whi… whi… whiwhi… whi… whi… whi* or *dri… dri… dri… dri,* etc.

Range Nagaland; Mizoram

Habitat Grass and scrub, bushes and bamboo stands, mainly in subtropical zone

Medium-sized, stocky parrotbill with rufous head and upperparts, black patch on ear-coverts, and large, orange bill. Likely to be confused only with Black-breasted, although distribution is different. Best distinguished by black arrowhead-shaped spotting on buffish-white throat and breast (lacking bold, black patch on breast), pale buff (rather than rufous-buff) underparts, brighter rufous crown and nape, less stout bill and different call.

FULVOUS PARROTBILL

Suthora fulvifrons Paradoxornithidae

Small, mainly brown parrotbill, with large head and tiny bill; fulvous crown, olive-brown lateral crown-stripes; feathery, fulvous supercilium, head, neck, throat, lower breast, upper mantle, giving a bushy, large-headed appearance; paler lower belly, vent; buff-white gorget on upper breast; buff-brown lower mantle, rufous wings; silver, black, buff wing panel on flight feathers.

Size 12 cm

Voice Calls include twitters, buzzes

Range Nepal through to Arunachal Pradesh

Habitat Montane bamboo forests

BLACK-THROATED PARROTBILL

Suthora nipalensis Paradoxornithidae

Size 10 cm

Voice Calls include twitters, trills

Range E Uttarakhand to Myanmar

Habitat Bamboos; undergrowth in oak-rhododendron forests

humii

poliotis

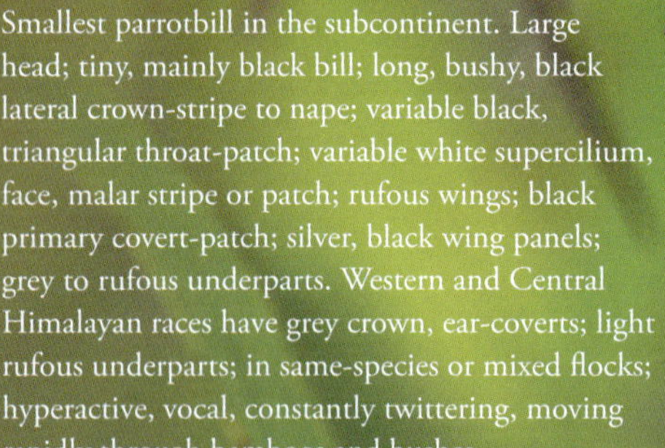

Smallest parrotbill in the subcontinent. Large head; tiny, mainly black bill; long, bushy, black lateral crown-stripe to nape; variable black, triangular throat-patch; variable white supercilium, face, malar stripe or patch; rufous wings; black primary covert-patch; silver, black wing panels; grey to rufous underparts. Western and Central Himalayan races have grey crown, ear-coverts; light rufous underparts; in same-species or mixed flocks; hyperactive, vocal, constantly twittering, moving rapidly through bamboos and bushes.

crocotius

LESSER RUFOUS-HEADED PARROTBILL

Chleuasicus atrosuperciliaris Paradoxornithidae

Size 15 cm

Voice Possible song consists of sharp, rapidly repeated chipping *tit...tit...tit...tit...tit...tit...tit*

Range The Himalayas from Nepal and West Bengal east to Arunachal Pradesh; NE India

Habitat Bamboo stands, tall reeds and grass, scrub jungles, mainly in tropical and subtropical zones

Stocky parrotbill with rufous-orange crown and nape and buffish-white underparts, stout pale bill. Distinguished from the similar Greater Rufous-headed by smaller size, smaller and stouter bill, whitish lores and paler buffish-orange ear-coverts. *P. a. oatesi* (E Himalayas) lacks black eyebrow and whiter underparts. Prominent black eyebrow and underparts buff in *P. a. atrosuperciliaris*, which occurs south and east of the Brahmaputra river.

GREATER RUFOUS-HEADED PARROTBILL

Psittiparus ruficeps Paradoxornithidae

Medium-sized, sturdy-looking parrotbill, with large, rounded bill; distinctive, bright rufous-orange crown, nape, face, ear-coverts, sharply contrasting with paler underparts; white, with buff flanks in E Himalayan *ruficeps*; buff in *bakeri* of regions S and E of Brahmaputra; bill has dark upper mandible, pale lower mandible; blue lores, orbital-ring; brown upperparts, tail. In pairs, or small groups; often joins mixed feeding flocks; shy and skulking; prefers to forage in under and lower forest storeys.

Size 18 cm

Voice Calls include chitters, churrs

Range Extreme E Nepal, Bhutan and Arunachal Pradesh; S Assam Hills

Habitat Bamboos; undergrowth in moist broadleaved evergreen forests; reeds; tall grass

GREY-HEADED PARROTBILL

Paradoxornis gularis Paradoxornithidae

Size 21 cm

Voice Call *jhiew…jhiew*; rattle. Soft, whistled song

Range Bhutan, Arunachal Pradesh and S Assam Hills

Habitat Bamboo stands; dense and open broadleaved evergreen forests; bushes

Medium-sized parrotbill, with grey crown, nape, ear-coverts and sides of neck; bright orange, bulbous and slightly hooked bill; black lateral crown-stripe, extending from around forehead to nape; white lores, eye-ring and broad malar-patch; triangular black throat-patch; rufous-brown mantle and upperparts; pinkish-white to pinkish-buff underparts, depending on race. In pairs, or small, same-species flocks; active in bushes in understorey, bamboos, trees in middle storey.

FIRE-TAILED MYZORNIS

Myzornis pyrrhoura Timaliidae

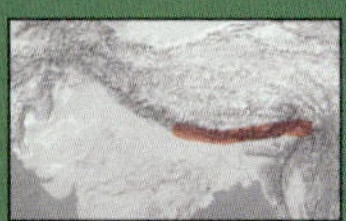

Size 12 cm

Voice Calls include high *tsi…tsi*; rattling *trr…trr*

Range W Nepal to Arunachal Pradesh

Habitat Dwarf juniper, rhododendron shrubberies; mossy oak, rhododendron forests; bamboos

Unmistakable bird; bright, rich, leaf-green above, sometimes washed with gold; slightly paler gold-green below; distinctive black spots on crown; black eye mask; diffused greenish-gold outline around eye mask, on bend of wing; thin, black, slightly downcurved bill; bright red throat and breast; orange-red to centre of underparts below, vent, undertail-coverts; orange-red, white, black wing panels; large white tips to primaries, secondaries; bright red sides to black-tipped tail. Can be spotted solitary, or in small flocks.

ORIENTAL WHITE-EYE

Zosterops palpebrosus Zosteropidae

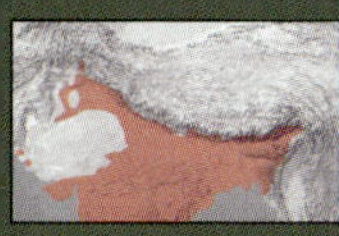

Size 10 cm

Voice Calls include soft, plaintive *tsee* and *tseer* notes. Short jingling song

Range All over India, from the Himalayan foothills to 2,000 m; absent in arid parts of W Rajasthan

Habitat Forests; gardens; groves; secondary growth

Sexes alike. Olive-yellow above; short, blackish stripe through eye; white eye-ring distinctive; bright yellow throat and undertail; whitish breast and belly. Small parties, occasionally upto 40 birds, either by themselves or in association with other small birds; keeps to foliage and bushes; actively moves amongst leafy branches, clinging sideways and upside-down; checks through leaves and sprigs for insects and also spends considerable time at flowers; calls often, both when in branches and when flying in small bands from tree to tree.

ASIAN FAIRY BLUEBIRD

Irena puella Irenidae

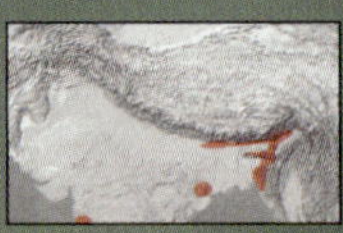

Size 25 cm

Voice Common call a 2-note *wit…weet…*; also a *whi…chu*; besides, some harsh notes, occasionally heard

Range Disjunct distribution; one population in Western Ghats and associated hills south of Ratnagiri; another in E Himalayas, east of extreme SE Nepal; Uttarakhand foothills; Andaman and Nicobar Islands

Habitat Dense, evergreen forests; *sholas*

Male glistening blue above; deep velvet-black sides of face, underbody and wings; blue undertail-coverts. Female has verditer-blue plumage; dull black lores and flight feathers. In pairs, or small, loose bands; spends day in leafy tall branches; often descends into undergrowth to feed on berries or hunt insects; utters 2-noted calls while flitting amongst trees; seen along with other birds.

GOLDCREST

Regulus regulus Regulidae

Size 9 cm

Voice Call a trisyllabic see…see…see. Song a similarly high-pitched see…*seesisyu…seesisyu…seesisyu…sweet*

Range The Himalayas

Habitat Mainly coniferous forests

Small and plump, with greenish upperparts, similar to Phylloscopus Warbler. Best distinguished by very plain face, which lacks supercilium and eye-stripe, pale ring around large dark eye, and by brilliant yellow to orange crown bordered by black. Juvenile lacks striking crown pattern of adult.

EURASIAN WREN

Troglodytes troglodytes Troglodytidae

Size 9 cm

Voice Noisy. Calls include angry *zirrr* and *tzit*. Loud, rapid song

Range Locally common breeding resident in N mountains from W Pakistan east to Arunachal Pradesh. Moves lower in winter. Also occurs in Europe, N Africa, W, N, C and E Asia, Myanmar and N America

Habitat Rocky areas with scrubs and low growth in open forests, often near water and habitation

Small, rounded wren with short tail. Upperparts dark; pale supercilium; long, pointed bill; pale, long legs. Dark brown-and-grey barring on wings, tail and underparts. Eastern race very dark. Sexes alike. Juvenile less barred. Feeds secretively and very actively, often creeps like a mouse. Male sometimes seen singing from perch. Usually solitary but may roost communally in a hole. Makes short, swift sallies. Nests in low crevices.

nipalensis

neglectus

YUNNAN NUTHATCH

Sitta yunnanensis Sittidae

Size 12 cm

Voice Call a nasal *nit*

Range Recently found in Arunachal Pradesh; the first record from India

Habitat Open forests of deciduous, broadleaved evergreen and coniferous trees

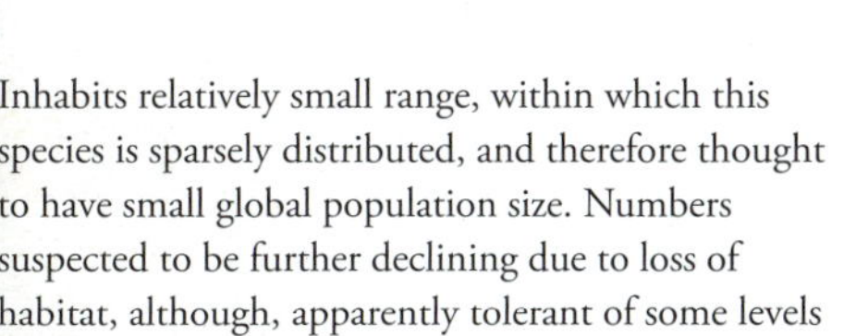

Inhabits relatively small range, within which this species is sparsely distributed, and therefore thought to have small global population size. Numbers suspected to be further declining due to loss of habitat, although, apparently tolerant of some levels of habitat degradation; considered Near Threatened.

CHESTNUT-VENTED NUTHATCH

Sitta nagaensis Sittidae

Size 12 cm

Voice Call a distinctive nasal *djeeeep* or *chuueep*. Song a level and vibrating trill, *duiduiduiduiduidui*

Range Common resident in the hills of NE India

Habitat Open forests of deciduous, broadleaved evergreen and coniferous trees

Small to medium-sized bird. Upperparts greyish-blue. Strong, black eye-stripe. Underparts paler grey (variable). Rufous undertail-coverts, with white scallop pattern on side. Female similar to male, but flanks and undertail-coverts paler rufous. Solitary, or in pairs. Appears in mixed hunting parties outside breeding season. Feeds on ground, forages around tree roots and stones for insects.

KASHMIR NUTHATCH

Sitta cashmirensis Sittidae

Size 12 cm

Voice Calls *tsip...tsip*

Range Endemic to the subcontinent, N Balochistan and NW Pakistan; the Himalayas from N Pakistan east to Kashmir, NW Nepal

Habitat Deciduous and mixed broadleaved coniferous forests and well-wooded country; more likely at slightly lower altitudes and in deciduous trees than White-cheeked

Medium-sized, bluish-grey bird. Distinct black eye-stripe extends to nape, curving around ear-coverts. Creamy-white chin, cheeks and ear-coverts; buff throat; cinnamon-buff breast; rufous flanks, undertail-coverts and vent. Female similar, but has more buff on cheeks and paler underparts with pinkish tinge on breast. Solitary, or in pairs. Confiding. Forages in lower levels.

CHESTNUT-BELLIED NUTHATCH

Sitta castanea Sittidac

Size 12 cm

Voice Calls include loud *tzsib…*; faint twitter; loud whistle during breeding season

Range Lower Himalayas east of Uttarakhand; to about 1,800 m. Also in hills of peninsular India (race *cinnamoventris*).

Habitat Forests; groves; roadside trees; habitation

Male blue-grey above; black stripe from lores to nape; whitish cheeks and upper throat; all but central tail feathers black, with white markings; chestnut below. Female duller chestnut below. In pairs or several, often with other small birds; restless climber; clings to bark and usually works up the tree stem, hammering with beak; also moves upside-down and sideways; may visit the ground.

♀

WHITE-TAILED NUTHATCH

Sitta himalayensis Sittidae

Size 12 cm

Voice Calls *tchip…tchip*. Song a musical *djuwee…djuwee…djuwee*

Range Hills of Himachal Pradesh to Myanmar. Moves lower in winter

Habitat Mixed broadleaved and coniferous forests

Smallish nuthatch, with relatively short bill; bluish-grey upperparts, darker along edges of wing-coverts and tail; diagnostic white central patch at base of tail not always easy to see; pale chin, throat becomes increasingly deeper rufous-buff on breast, belly, flanks and undertail-coverts; bold, black eye-stripe broadens and curves behind ear-coverts; lacks contrasting white throat, scalloping on undertail-coverts of Chestnut-bellied; gregarious; often in pairs; joins mixed-species foraging flocks; arboreal; usually in upper forest storey.

VELVET-FRONTED NUTHATCH

Sitta frontalis Sittidae

Small nuthatch. Male has violet-blue upperparts; jet-black forehead; stripe through eye; white chin and throat, merging into vinous-grey below; coral-red beak. Underparts variable from beige to pinkish-buff. Female lacks black stripe through eye. In pairs, or several in mixed hunting parties; creeps about on stems and branches; fond of moss-covered trees; also clings upside-down; active and agile, quickly moving from tree to tree; calls often, till long after sunset; also checks fallen logs and felled branches.

Size 10 cm

Voice Calls include fairly loud, rapidly repeated, sharp, trilling *chweet...chwit...chwit* whistles

Range From around W Uttarakhand east along lower Himalayas; widespread over hilly, forested areas of C, S and E India; absent in flat and arid regions

Habitat Forests; also tea and coffee plantations

WHITE-CHEEKED NUTHATCH

Sitta leucopsis Sittidae

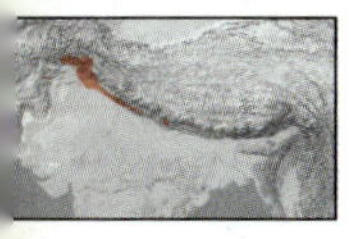

Size 12 cm

Voice Call likened to that of a young goat bleating

Range W Himalayas

Habitat Coniferous and mixed forests

Distinctive nuthatch, with black crown and nape. Upperparts dark blue-grey; large, white cheek-patches surrounding eye; white face and throat with beady eyes. Whitish underparts with buffish-wash becoming rufous on rear flanks and undertail-coverts. Juvenile has faint barring on underparts. Forages under tall trees or branches with lichen; solitary, in pairs or mixed flocks.

BEAUTIFUL NUTHATCH

Sitta formosa Sittidae

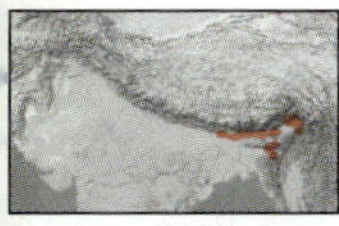

Size 15 cm

Voice Calls include chitters

Range Patchily in E Nepal, Bhutan and Arunachal Pradesh

Habitat Dense primary broadleaved evergreen forests

Unmistakable, but uncommon, large nuthatch with striking, bright blue-and-black pattern on upperparts; blue-and-white streaks down black crown and nape; broad, blue scapular-band across black mantle; prominent bluish-white fringed edging on coverts and tertials; buff-white throat and long, straight supercilium; bright rufous below, paler on breast, vent and undertail-coverts; habits not well-known; gregarious; lives in pairs or small parties; upto 20 reported, often in mixed-species feeding flocks; arboreal; movement heavier, slower; not as agile as other nuthatches.

RUSTY-FLANKED TREECREEPER

Certhia nipalensis Certhiidae

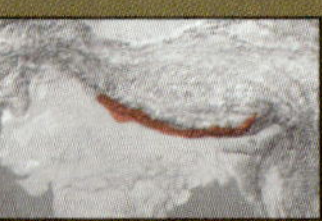

Size 12 cm

Voice Call a thin *sit…sit;…zip*. Song *si…si… ss…srrt…st…ttt*

Range Uttarakhand to Arunachal Pradesh. Moves lower in winter

Habitat Oak, rhododendron, mixed coniferous forests in summer; spends winter in mixed broadleaved forests

More warmly-coloured and distinguished from others by overall darker plumage. Rusty-brown flanks, rump, lower back; warm brown-and-black upperparts streaked with buff; pale buff supercilium encircling dark ear-coverts; shorter bill; tail unbarred; cream breast and belly, rather than whitish of Hodgson's, brownish of Brown-throated; usually solitary; may join other insectivores in mixed hunting parties; quiet and unobtrusive; likely to be missed; climbs vertically around tree trunks; flies to base of next tree; flicks wings constantly.

WALLCREEPER

Tichodroma muraria Tichodromidae

Striking bird, with black, grey-and-crimson plumage; very long, thin, pointed, slightly downcurved bill; breeding male has slaty-grey crown and mantle; bright crimson patches on black wings; black throat, upper breast; smoky-grey underparts; non-breeding adult has white throat, upper breast; inconspicuous on rock-face till it flies; shows broad, rounded, crimson-and-black wings with two rows of white spots; short, broad black tail with white tips, corners; solitary, in pairs when breeding; shy; uses long toes, strong claws to climb vertical rock-faces, walls.

Size 17 cm

Voice Calls *tu…wee*. Whistled song

Range Mountains of Pakistan to Myanmar. Moves lower in winter

Habitat Cliffs; gorges; boulders; earthen banks; ruins; old buildings; quarries

HODGSON'S TREECREEPER

Certhia hodgsoni Certhiidae

Size 12 cm

Voice Calls *tseep…tseep*

Range Mountains of Pakistan to Myanmar. Moves lower in winter

Habitat Mixed coniferous, birch, oak and rhododendron montane forests

Small, slender, warm brown treecreeper with black-and-white streaked upperparts. White supercilium; plain, long, brown, unbarred, stiff tail; relatively short, decurved bill. Creamy-white (tinged with buff) belly, flanks and vent. Distinguished from Rusty-flanked by pale buff, rather than rusty-brown flanks; paler buff ear-coverts; shorter, less-marked supercilium; distinguished from Brown-throated by whitish rather than brownish throat, breast, belly; more distinct supercilium; usually solitary; joins mixed hunting parties of insectivores in non-breeding season; quiet and inconspicuous; unlike nuthatches, uses tail to support movement on undersides of branches. Not shy. Nests behind loose barks or in tree crevices.

BROWN-THROATED TREECREEPER

Certhia discolor Certhiidae

Size 12 cm

Voice Call a high-pitched *chit…; tsit.* Song a rapid *tchitititit*

Range Nepal to Arunachal Pradesh. S Assam Hills

Habitat Mixed broadleaved oak, oak-coniferous forests

Upperparts mottled brown-and-black, streaked with lighter buff. Distinguished from other treecreepers by brownish rather than whitish throat and breast; paler below; tail unbarred; thin, buff supercilium, extending only to dark ear-coverts, but not around; duller brown on rump, lower flanks than Rusty-flanked; Race *manipurensis* of S Manipur (sometimes separated as Hume's Treecreeper) has brighter rufous on throat and breast, rather than brown of nominate race of the Himalayas; normally solitary; may join mixed hunting parties; quiet and inconspicuous; climbs vertically around lichen-covered tree trunks, uses tail as prop; also undersides of branches, probes barks for insects.

BAR-TAILED TREECREEPER

Certhia himalayana Certhiidae

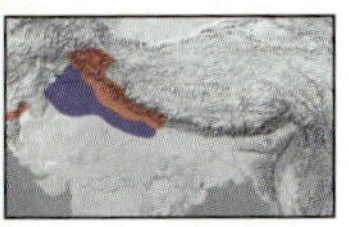

Size 12 cm

Voice Call a long-drawn squeak, somewhat ventriloquial. Loud but short, monotonous song; one of the earliest bird songs, heard much before other birds have begun to sing

Range The Himalayas, east to W Nepal; from about 1,600 m to treeline; descends in winter

Habitat The Himalayan temperate forests

Streaked blackish-brown treecreeper, with fulvous-and-grey upperparts. Pale supercilium; broad fulvous wing-band; white chin and throat; dull ash-brown below; best recognised by dark brown barring on pointed tail. Sexes alike. Solitary, or several in mixed parties of small birds; spends almost entire life on tree trunks; starts climbing from near the base; sometimes creeps on moss-covered rocks and walls.

SPOTTED CREEPER

Salpornis spilonotus Certhiidae

Size 13 cm

Voice Calls include thin *see…ee* and deep *kek…kek…kek*. Whistling song

Range Strangely rare and very local breeding resident in N peninsula from Haryana, Uttar Pradesh and Bihar south to Maharashtra and Andhra Pradesh. Also occurs in Africa, where very local

Habitat Open woodlands and groves, favouring trees with deep-fissured bark such as mangoes and babul

Plump, brown and buff bird with long, curved bill. Broad, white supercilium; dark wings; short, squarish tail, broadly-barred white. Upperparts streaked black-and-white; white throat, fulvous breast, barred and mottled brown. Sexes alike. Feeds usually singly, on invertebrates in bark at all levels in trees. Climbs rapidly up and under tree trunks and branches, often fluttering down to change position. Does not spiral. Nest made of leaves, bark and lichen, usually in branch fork.

SPOT-WINGED STARLING

Saroglossa spiloptera Sturnidae

Size 19 cm

Voice Song similar to that of Rosy, continuous harsh, unmusical jumble of dry, discordant notes and few melodious warbles

Range The Himalayan foothills from W Himachal Pradesh east to Arunachal Pradesh; NE India and Bangladesh

Habitat Open broadleaved forests, edges of forests and clearings; cultivation with groves or scattered trees of Bombax, Erythrina and Salmalia trees, which it favours

Slender, greyish-brown bird. Male has blackish face mask, rufous-brown throat; grey crown and nape; dark patterning on crown and mantle, rufous uppertail-coverts. Underparts whitish with hints of light rusty-orange on breast and flanks. Female overall more brown above and has similar markings. Juvenile like female but more even above. Seen in large flocks. Stays in canopy, rarely descending.

♀

GOLDEN-CRESTED MYNA

Ampeliceps coronatus Sturnidae

Size 22 cm

Voice Call higher-pitched, more metallic whistle than that of Hill; bell-like note

Range Assam, Manipur and West Bengal

Habitat Open, moist, broadleaved deciduous and evergreen forests; tall trees in cultivated forest clearings

Diagnostic golden throat, crown and forehead. Crown feathers extend to long crest. Overall glossy bluish-black. Sides of face, mantle and breast have more purplish gloss. Wings have yellow-and-white-patches. Naked patch around eye orange-yellow. Pale orange bill and orangish legs. Female similar, but less yellow on crown and throat. Juvenile dark brown with paler underparts; pale yellow lores and throat, and pale yellow patch on wing.

COMMON HILL MYNA

Gracula religiosa Sturnidae

Size 25-29 cm

Voice Amazing vocalist. Calls include a great assortment of whistling, warbling, shrieking notes. Excellent mimic; much sought-after cage bird

Range Lower Himalayas and the Terai, Uttarakhand eastwards; Western Ghats, from N Kanara to extreme South India, and Sri Lanka; ssp. *peninsular* is restricted to Odisha, E Madhya Pradesh and N Andhra Pradesh

Habitat Forests; clearings

Glossy black plumage, with purple-green gloss on crown, nape, mantle and breast; rest of body has greenish gloss; white in flight feathers; orange-red beak; orange-yellow legs, yellow facial skin and fleshy wattles on nape and sides of face. Sexes alike. Small flocks in forests; extremely noisy; mostly arboreal, only occasionally descending into bushes or onto ground; hops amongst branches, and on ground; large numbers gather on fruiting trees, along with barbets, hornbills and green pigeons. Such sights are one of the birdwatching spectacles of the Himalayan foothills.

GREAT MYNA

Acridotheres cinereus Sturnidae

Size 25 cm

Voice Screeches like Common, but harsher

Range Assam, S Assam Hills and lower Arunachal Pradesh

Habitat Marshes; tall grasslands; wet cultivation; settlements

Glossy, black myna, with frontal crest. Underparts dark grey; white wing-patches; white-tipped tail; lemon-yellow bill, legs and feet. Adult could be confused with Jungle, but longer tuft, darker plumage; orange-yellow bill, without dark base; reddish iris; prominent white vent. Female has shorter crest than male. Juvenile browner overall, sometimes lacking tuft and whitish underparts; distinguished in flight by large white vent; in pairs, or small groups; less bold than Common; more wary; follows cattle.

JUNGLE MYNA

Acridotheres fuscus Sturnidae

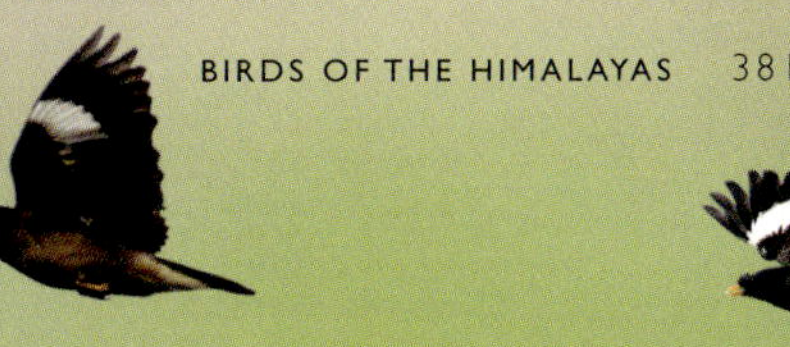

Ash-brown myna with small crest at base of bill. Black head; no orbital-patch; chin, throat and breast slaty-grey graduating to buffish-white belly; dark blue base to yellow-orange bill; yellow legs and bill; white wing-patch and white-tipped tail. Superficially similar to Common and Bank, but distinguished by greyer colour, darker cap not as defined; pale yellow eye, rather than red of Bank; also, white wing-patch and tail-tip; gregarious; in pairs, or small groups; larger flocks when not breeding; shyer, less confiding than Common, and less associated with humans; more arboreal. *Mahrattensis* is found in peninsular India while the nominate *fuscus* is found in N and NE India.

Size 23 cm

Voice Similar to Common's, but higher, more liquid

Range Hills of Pakistan to Arunachal Pradesh

Habitat Edges of forests; wooded areas near cultivation and settlements; plantations; scrubs

fuscus

COMMON MYNA

Acridotheres tristis Sturnidae

Size 23 cm

Voice Noisy. Calls include a great mix of chattering notes. One of India's most familiar bird sounds

Range Subcontinent, upto about 3,500 m in the Himalayas

Habitat Human habitation; cultivation; light forests

Medium-sized bird with rich vinous-brown plumage; black head, neck and upper breast; yellow beak, legs and naked wattle around eyes distinctive; large white spot in dark brown flight feathers, best visible in flight; blackish tail, with broad, white tips to all but central feathers; whitish abdomen. Sexes alike. Seen in solitary, or in scattered pairs or small, loose bands. India's most common and familiar bird; hardly ever strays far from human habitation; rather haughty and confident in looks; aggressive, curious and noisy; struts about on ground, picks out worms; attends to grazing cattle and refuse dumps; enters verandahs and kitchens, sometimes even helping itself on dining tables.

BANK MYNA

Acridotheres ginginianus Sturnidae

Size 21 cm

Voice Similar to Common's but softer

Range Widespread resident in N and C India

Habitat Human habitation; cultivation; grasslands

Similar to Common but smaller; has bluish-grey neck, mantle and underparts; black head with orange-red wattle around eye; orange-yellow bill, legs and feet yellow; black wings; buff-orange tail-tips and wing-patch; grey flanks have cinnamon-brown tinge. Sexes alike. Usually observed in small, scattered groups around human habitation; bold and confiding; often seen along roadside restaurants picking out scraps.

CHESTNUT-TAILED STARLING

Sturnia malabarica Sturnidae

Size 21 cm

Voice Noisy. Metallic, whistling call, becoming a chatter when in flock. Warbling song when breeding

Range India, roughly east and south from S Rajasthan to around W Uttarakhand; upto about 1,800 m in the Himalayan foothills

Habitat Light forests; open country; gardens

Slim bird with silvery-grey upperparts, with faint brownish wash. Dull rufous till breast; brighter below; black-and-grey in wings. Sexes alike. Juvenile more greyish-brown. Sociable; noisy parties in upper branches of trees, frequently along with other birds; incessantly squabbles and moves about, indulging in all manners of acrobatic positions to obtain nectar or reach out to fruits; descends to ground to pick up insects.

ASIAN PIED STARLING

Gracupica contra Sturnidae

Size 23 cm

Voice Noisy. Calls include a mix of pleasant whistling and screaming notes

Range NC, C and E India, south and east of line roughly from E Punjab, through E Rajasthan, W Madhya Pradesh to Krishna Delta; escaped cage birds have established themselves in several areas out of original range in and around Mumbai

Habitat Open cultivation; orchards; vicinity of habitation

Sexes alike. Black-and-white (pied) plumage distinctive; orange-red beak and orbital skin in front of eyes confirm identity. Sociable; small parties either move on their own or associate with other birds, notably other mynas and drongos; rather common and familiar over its range but keeps distance from human; may make its ungainly nest in garden trees, but never inside houses, nor does it enter houses; bird of open, cultivated areas, preferably where water; attends to grazing cattle; occasionally raids standing crops.

juvenile

BRAHMINY STARLING

Sturnia pagodarum Sturnidae

Size 20 cm

Voice Quite noisy. Calls include a pleasant mix of chirping notes and whistles, sounds as conversational chatter. Good mimic. Pleasant warbling song of breeding male

Range Subcontinent, to about 2,000 m in W and C Himalayas

Habitat Light forests; gardens; cultivation; vicinity of habitation

Grey, black-and-rufous myna; black crown, nape and forehead, extending to long, black crest; grey back; rich buff sides of head, neck and underbody; black wings and brown tail with white sides and tip distinctive in flight. Sexes similar. Female has slightly smaller crest. Seen in small parties, occasionally collecting into flocks of 20 birds; associates with other birds on flowering trees or on open lands; walks typical myna-style, head held straight up, confident in looks; roosts communally, with other birds.

juvenile

PIED THRUSH

Zoothera wardii Turdidae

Size 22 cm

Voice Alarm call a spitting *ptz…ptz…ptz…ptz*

Range Breeds in the Himalayas, from E Himachal Pradesh to Arunachal Pradesh, and NE India. Migrates through India to winter in Sri Lanka and Tamil Nadu

Habitat Open broadleaved forests; edges of forests; secondary scrub with scattered trees; thickly-vegetated ravines; undergrowth alongside streams; well-wooded gardens

Adult male mainly black-and-white above, with white supercilium, white wing-bars and white tips to tertials and secondaries; rump has white barring; white belly and flanks, barred with black. Female olive-brown above with buff supercilium, buff wing-bars and tail-tips; spotted olive-brown breast, white belly and flanks, darkly scaled. Juvenile like female, but has streaked mantle and breast.

BLUE WHISTLING THRUSH

Myophonus caeruleus Turdidae

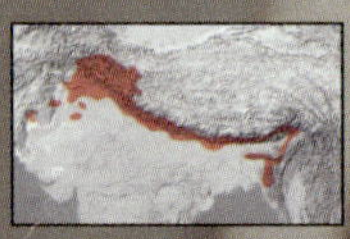

Size 33 cm

Voice Calls include piercing *tzeet* and *zee…zeee*. Rambling, whistling song

Range Common breeding resident in N mountains from E Pakistan to Myanmar border. Moves lower down in winter

Habitat Damp forests and wooded areas, near water

Large, bulky, purple-blue ground thrush with mainly yellow bill. Whole body spotted with spangles of brighter blue. Forehead, shoulders, wing and tail edges bright blue. Sexes alike. Juvenile duller with dusky bill. Noisy, bold, usually approachable. Often close to habitation, even enters buildings. Usually solitary, or in pairs; feeds on insects, crustaceans and amphibians on ground. Nests in rocks, stream-side roots or buildings. Perches on stream boulders and low branches.

ORANGE-HEADED THRUSH

Zoothera citrina Turdidae

Size 21 cm

Voice Call a shrill, screechy *kreeee*. Loud, rich song, often with mix of other birds' calls thrown in. Noisy in early mornings and late evenings

Range *Cyanotus* peninsular India south of line from S Gujarat across to Odisha; the nominate race *Citrina* breeds in the Himalayas, NE India; winters in foothills, the Terai, parts of E India, Gangetic plains and south along Eastern Ghats. *Albogularis* restricted to Andamans and Nicobar

Habitat Shaded forests; bamboo groves; gardens

citrina

Blue-grey above; orangish-rufous head, nape and underparts; white ear-coverts with two dark brown vertical stripes; white throat and shoulder-patch; vent and undertail-coverts white. Orange-headed nominate race has entire head rufous-orange. Usually in pairs; feeds on ground, rummages in leaf litter and under thick growth; flies into leafy branches if disturbed; occasionally associates with laughingthrushes and babblers; vocal and restless when breeding. Feeds on invertebrates in leaf litter. Crepuscular.

cyanotus

SIBERIAN THRUSH

Zoothera sibirica Turdidae

Size 22 cm

Voice Call a soft *stit*

Range Current status uncertain, and no recent published records; recorded in W Maharashtra, Manipur hills upto at least 1,800 m; Andaman Islands

Habitat Broadleaved, evergreen and coniferous forests

Overall slaty-grey thrush with prominent white supercilium, broad white-tipped tail; white-fringed undertail-coverts; white band on underwing tail-coverts visible in flight. Dark bill. Female dark brown with beige supercilium, dark malar stripe, dark olive-brown upperparts, whitish-spotted and scaled underparts. Juvenile similar to adult male, but overall colour paler, supercilium has buff wash.

ALPINE THRUSH

Zoothera mollissima Turdidae

Size 27 cm

Voice Usually silent. Alarm call a rattling *churr.* Song has short mellow, descending phrases

Range Local breeding resident to N mountains from N Pakistan to NE India. Above treeline

Habitat Open woodlands; grassy, fallow, bushy country

Largish, warm brown thrush with prominent black patch on cheek. Dark face and lores. Heavy barring and streaks on creamish underparts; larger spots on upper throat. Broad, white bands on underwings visible in flight. Sexes alike. Feeds in pairs or small groups on invertebrates on ground. Largely terrestrial. Shy. Flies into trees when disturbed. Sings high, but hidden, in trees. Nests on or near ground.

LONG-TAILED THRUSH

Zoothera dixoni Turdidae

Size 27 cm

Voice Mostly silent; *mollissima* has loud, rattling alarm note

Range The Himalayas, east of C Himachal Pradesh; breeds between 2,000-4,000 m; descends to about 1,000 m in winter

Habitat Treeline forests; scrubs in summer; heavy forests in winter

Plain, olive-brown above; large black patch around ear; two dull buffy wing-bars and larger wing-patch visible in flight; buffy throat, breast and flanks, rest white, boldly spotted dark brown. In pairs, or small groups in winter; feeds on ground; usually difficult to spot till it takes off from somewhere close by; flies up into tree branches if disturbed.

SCALY THRUSH

Zoothera dauma Turdidae

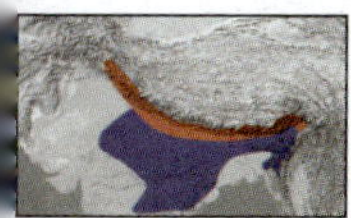

Size 26 cm

Voice Normally silent. Harsh *tchik*; varied, thrush-like song

Range Breeds Kashmir to Myanmar. Winters south to Odisha

Habitat Mixed broadleaved and coniferous forests; *sal* and bamboos

Distinctive scaled thrush; distinguished from other thrushes by prominent black or buff-tipped feathers; scales on olive-buff upperparts; black patch behind ear-coverts; whitish lores; indistinct malar stripe; dark scaling on whitish underparts, heavier on breast, flanks; sturdy bill and legs. Solitary, or in pairs. Mainly terrestrial feeder, forages in leaf litter. Shy and reclusive; flies to low branches or bushes when disturbed; dips and flares tail like most thrushes.

juvenile

LONG-BILLED THRUSH

Zoothera monticola Turdidae

Size 28 cm

Voice Rattling alarm call. Pensive whistled song *te... e... uw; tew... tew... tew*

Range Uttarakhand to Arunachal Pradesh

Habitat Dense, moist broadleaved evergreen, coniferous, bamboo forests with thick undergrowth, wet ground, streams

Dark, sturdy thrush; distinctive short tail; very long bill with curved upper mandible, hooked at end; upperparts dark grey-brown; dark brown face, dark malar stripe, small, white throat-patch; dense dark spotting on breast; large, dark spots on flanks; less spotting on white belly; brown-and-white-barred vent; strong legs; solitary; shy and reclusive; usually in undergrowth; crepuscular; terrestrial; uses long bill to forage in leaf litter.

DARK-SIDED THRUSH

Zoothera marginata Turdidae

Size 25 cm

Voice Song a thin whistle

Range The Himalayas; NE India

Habitat Dense forests near streams

Rotund, long-billed with rufous-brown upperparts. Sides of dark brown head strongly-patterned; pale, fleshy base to lower mandible; pale lores and black rear patch edged paler; whitish eye-ring; white chin. Underparts paler with bold scaling on breast and flanks; black malar stripe. Short tail; slim, prominent black bill. Wings more rufous-red. Yellowish-brown vent striped with brown. Sexes similar. Juvenile has brighter upperparts with pale shaft streaks and buff tips to wing-coverts. Solitary and crepuscular. Forages on ground amid leaf litter looking for insects. Walks, hops on ground.

TICKELL'S THRUSH

Turdus unicolor Turdidae

Size 21 cm

Voice A 2-noted alarm call; also some chattering calls. Rich song

Range Breeds in the Himalayas, 1,500-2,500 m, east to C Nepal, and Sikkim; winters along foothills east of Kangra, NE, parts of C and E peninsular India

Habitat Open forests, groves

Light ash-grey bird; duller breast and whiter on belly; rufous underwing-coverts in flight. Female olive-brown above; white throat, streaked on sides; tawny flanks and white belly. Small flocks on ground, sometimes along with other thrushes; hops fast on ground, stopping abruptly, as if to check some underground activity; digs worms from under soil; flies into trees when approached too close.

♀

BLACK-BREASTED THRUSH

Turdus dissimilis Turdidae

Size 22 cm

Voice Call a resounding *tup... tup...tup...tup tup...tup...tup...*

Range Resident, NE India

Habitat Breeds in moist, shady broadleaved evergreen forests. In winter, also found in scrub jungles and mangroves

Small, compact thrush. Adult male has black head and breast, grey upperparts, orange upper belly and flanks, and white centre to belly and vent. Female has dark olive-grey upperparts, plain face (lacking supercilium), prominent dark (streaked) malar stripe and dark spotting across olive-grey upper breast, whitish throat (with variable dark streaking) and sub-moustachial stripe; orange lower breast and flanks.

♀

GREY-WINGED BLACKBIRD

Turdus boulboul Turdidae

Size 28 cm

Voice Call a deep *chuck... chuck.* Melodious song

Range Hills from Pakistan to Myanmar

Habitat Mixed broadleaved oak, coniferous forests; edges of forests; clearings

Large, dark thrush with longish tail. Adult male black, with contrasting light grey wing panel; bright orange bill, yellowish eye-ring, legs. Juvenile male has white-edged feathers on belly, vent. Female brown, with less distinct, paler brown wing panel, yellow bill. Juvenile similar to White-collared, but has wing panel rather than wing-bars. Solitary, or in pairs; sometimes, in small winter flocks; fairly shy, but emerges onto forest paths to feed. Arboreal and terrestrial; forages on shrubs, trees, forest floor.

♀

WHITE-COLLARED BLACKBIRD

Turdus albocinctus Turdidae

Size 27 cm

Voice Call a deep *chuck...chuck*. Song a whistled *tchew...tchew, tchew...ee*

Range Hills of Uttarakhand to Myanmar

Habitat Mixed broadleaved, coniferous forests; edges of forests; pastures; clearings

Large, distinctive thrush with pale collar. Adult male black, with white collar extending around throat, upper breast, nape and upper mantle; yellow bill, eye-ring, legs; longish tail; female brown, with pale, faintly streaked collar. Juvenile lacks pale collar; dark brown above, with rufous-streaking; two rufous wing-bars; richer rufous-brown below, with dark spotting, giving a mottled appearance. Solitary, or in pairs; sometimes in winter flocks; shy; forages on forest floor, grassy slopes, trees.

TIBETAN BLACKBIRD

Turdus (merula) maximus Turdidae

♀

Size 26-29 cm

Voice Call a rattling *chak...chak...chak*. Song a mournful, repeated whistle, *piew...piew*

Range NW Himalayas. From Uttarakhand east to Arunachal Pradesh in winter

Habitat Rocky and grassy slopes with dwarf juniper in summer; juniper stands or shrubs in winter

Large, black bird with long tail without yellow orbital-ring. Female even dark brown. Juvenile has rufous-buff underparts with diffuse dark brown barring and spotting, back and rump variably spotted and barred with rufous-buff; crown and mantle tend to be even dark brown (male) or pale brown (female). Larger than Common with longer wings and tail. Usually quite wary, but can be confiding. Nests on ground or low bushes.

COMMON BLACKBIRD

Turdus merula Turdidae

Size 25-28 cm

Voice Calls *chack…chack*. Song not very melodious

Range Breeding visitor to NW Pakistan

Habitat High-altitude rocky slopes, grassy alpine meadows, dwarf juniper scrub, rhododendron scrub

♀

Large, glossy brown-black thrush with prominent yellow bill. Dark crown; narrow, golden-yellow eye-ring. Similar to White-collared but lacks collar. Distinguished from Grey-winged by lack of wing-patch. Female dark brown, with lightly streaked throat and darker bill. Juvenile has paler brown head, rufous underparts; streaked, spotted, barred above and below. In pairs, or small groups when breeding; in small winter flocks with other thrushes; largely, terrestrial feeder.

CHESTNUT THRUSH

Turdus rubrocanus Turdidae

Size 27 cm

Voice Alarm call a *kwik*. Song comprises a series of short phrases, repeated 3-8 times

Range Far W Himalayas. Winters from E Nepal to NE India

Habitat Coniferous and mixed forests in summer; open wooded-areas and orchards in winter

gouldii

rubrocanus

Overall rusty-orange thrush with distinct grey head. Buffish-grey collar; blackish wings and tail; yellow bill and legs. Female duller, but very similar; head and hindneck pale brownish-grey, no distinct collar; wings and tail brown. Juvenile has darker head; more white throat; buff shaft streaking above; dark spotting and barring below; back, rump and uppertail-coverts have rusty-orange cast. Sub-species *gouldii* is a rare winter visitor to the extreme NE.

KESSLER'S THRUSH

Turdus kessleri Turdidae

Size 27 cm

Voice Call a soft *dug...dug*

Range Winter visitor, E Himalayas

Habitat Shrubberies and stands of juniper; potato fields

Largish thrush with distinctive brown-black head. Neck and upper breast also black, creamy-white mantle and lower breast; brown-black tail and wings; darkish vent indistinctly scaled. Female's head pattern similar to male's, but duller; head, neck and breast greyish-brown; brown upper breast and rest of underparts more ginger-brown. Terrestrial and gregarious. Feeds on berries in winter.

GREY-SIDED THRUSH

Turdus feae Turdidae

Size 28 cm

Voice Unreported in the region

Range Globally threatened

Habitat Details unknown. Winters in evergreen forests

Smallish thrush which superficially resembles Eyebrowed. Adult male has rufescent-olive upperparts, crown and ear-coverts. Silver-grey throat; grey lower breast with paler belly and vent. White supercilium and white crescent below eye; silver-grey flanks. Female similar to male, but has white throat, also belly whiter; brown-streaked malar stripe; grey of breast and flanks variably washed with orange-buff. Juvenile similar to female, but has whiter throat and pale tips on primaries and tertials. Feeds on nectar, fruits and berries.

RED-THROATED THRUSH

Turdus ruficollis Turdidae

Largish thrush with even, grey upperparts and wings. Sides of tail reddish-orange, visible in flight. Red supercilium, throat and breast; grey upperparts; whitish underparts; creamy-white belly and vent. Yellow bill with greyish culmen. Female similar to male, but with more whitish-buff throat, black-streaked malar stripe, mottled orange-red breast. Juvenile male similar to adult female, has white-tipped greater coverts and pale-fringed tertials. First-winter female less heavily marked, and has finely streaked breast and flanks; rufous wash to supercilium and throat, and sometimes breast. Gregarious. Often seen with other thrushes. Feeds on ground and low fruit-bearing bushes.

Size 25 cm

Voice Calls include thin see and hard *tack...tack*

Range Winter visitor to the Himalayas, NE India

Habitat Forests; edges of forests; cultivation, pastures with scattered trees

BLACK-THROATED THRUSH

Turdus artogularis Turdidae

Size 26.5 cm

Voice Calls include shrill rattle in alarm and high-pitched squeaky contacts notes

Range Winter visitor, N subcontinent

Habitat Forests; edges of forests; cultivation, pastures with scattered trees

♀

Adult male has grey upperparts and whitish underparts. Black supercilium, throat and breast; yellow bill with greyish culmen. Female similar, but typically has white or buffish throat and black-streaked malar stripe, black gorget of spotting across breast. First-winter has fine white supercilium and white tips to greater coverts and pale-fringed tertials. First-winter male very similar to adult female. First-winter female less heavily marked, with finely streaked breast and flanks. Feeds on ground. Wary, flies into trees when disturbed. Feeds on berries in winter.

EYEBROWED THRUSH

Turdus obscurus Turdidae

Size 23 cm

Voice Call a thin *teseep...teseep.* Also, chatters

Range Locally common winter visitor to hills of NE India and E Nepal. Rare further south in peninsula India, Bangladesh and Sri Lanka. Also occurs in N, E and SE Asia

Habitat Open forests

Medium-sized, orange-and-grey thrush with broad, white supercilium and black lores. Male has small, white patches below eyes, grey head and neck, brownish-grey upperparts. Breast and flanks diagnostic rufous-brown; white belly and vent; lower mandible has yellow cast. Female and immature less grey with blackish-bordered white throat. Small bill with black upper mandible and tip. Feeds on ground on insects, often with other thrushes. Hops. Wary, flushing rapidly into tree canopy.

DUSKY THRUSH

Turdus eunomus Turdidae

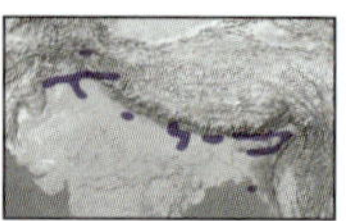

Size 24 cm

Voice Calls include shrill *shrree* and rather harsh *chock...chock*

Range Winter visitor to the Himalayas, NE India

Habitat Open cultivated areas and pastures with scattered trees

Darkish thrush with shades of brown-and-grey in parts. Broad, obvious white supercilium and throat, dark crown and ear-coverts, chestnut-brown wings; rufous-brown mantle with dark feather centres; breast and flanks heavily spotted to form double gorget. Underparts white; dark, scaly breast-band. Female similar to male, but much duller with less distinct marking, but stronger and less prominent supercilium, upperparts greyer, and has duller brown wings. Strong flier. Feeds in open on ground.

FIELDFARE

Turdus pilaris Turdidae

Size 25 cm

Voice Call a hard *shack…shack*, mainly in flight. Also, squeaky tee

Range Very rare vagrant from N Asia. Only one record from Uttar Pradesh

Habitat Open cultivation; pastures, orchards

Large, chestnut-and-grey thrush with blue-grey crown, cheeks, nape and rump; indistinct supercilium; black lores; chestnut-brown mantle. Orange-yellow throat and upper breast strongly streaked with dark brown. White lower breast and belly; grey rump. Orange bill. Sexes similar. Feeds on invertebrates in open, hops on ground. Feeds on berries in winter. Rather shy and flies into trees if alarmed. Seen with other thrushes.

MISTLE THRUSH

Turdus viscivorus Turdidae

Large, pale grey-brown thrush. Brownish rump and yellow-brown lower flanks; dark patch on ear-coverts and breast-sides. Round spots prominent on otherwise evenly pale underparts. Pale underwings and axillaries. Longish brown tail with white tips often visible on outer-tail feathers. Sexes alike. Similar to Scaly and Long-tailed. Feeds on invertebrates on ground and berries, particularly mistletoe, in trees. Usually solitary, or in pairs. Wary, flying high between food sites. Sings from exposed perch. Nests high in trees.

Size 27 cm

Voice Call a harsh rattle, usually in flight. Song mellow and haunting

Range Fairly common breeding resident in N mountains from W Pakistan to W Nepal. Moves lower down in winter. Also occurs in Europe, W, N and C Asia

Habitat Open mountain forests, grasslands and scrubs

SONG THRUSH

Turdus philomelos Turdidae

Size 23 cm

Voice Calls include quiet, but penetrating *silt*, soft *tit* and hard *tchuk*

Range Vagrant

Habitat Thorn scrub in Pakistan

Medium-sized bird (much smaller than Mistle), with warm brown upperparts, buffy-white underparts, and heavily spotted with black, arrow-shaped spots on breast and flanks; white belly; black bill. Underwings rich buff in colour; yellowish bill and legs and feet pink. Sexes similar. Feeds on ground and flies into trees when alarmed.

GREEN COCHOA

Cochoa viridis Turdidae

Size 28 cm

Voice Call a pure, drawn-out monotone whistle, thinner and weaker than that of Purple

Range The Himalayas; NE India

Habitat Dense, moist, broadleaved evergreen forests

Overall green with blue crown and nape. Black eyebrow and lores; dark blue ear-coverts; mantle has faint black scaling; wing has pale blue panel; pale blue tail with black tip. Underparts emerald-green with blue wash on throat and belly. Sexes similar. Female has green at base of secondaries and wing. Secondaries stained yellowish-brown instead of blue. Juvenile like adult, white crown with black scales and tawny spotting; upperparts and underparts also darkly scaled.

PURPLE COCHOA

Cochoa purpurea Turdidae

Size 30 cm

Voice Call a low chuckle. Song a flute-like *peeeee*; also *peeee… you…peeee*

Range Summer visitor. The Himalayas, hills of NE India

Habitat Dense, moist broadleaved evergreen forests

Appears dark in the shade, and colours show only in light. Overall greyish-purple; black mask; silvery-blue crown; grey carpal-patch at base of black wing feathers and prominent wing-patch. Tail silvery-blue with black terminal band. Male has dull purplish-grey secondaries and coverts, body greyish; rufous replaces purple in female. Juvenile has black scaling to crown, indistinct buff streaking and spotting on upperparts, orange-buff underparts with bold, black barring.

RUSTY-BELLIED SHORTWING

Brachypteryx hyperythra Muscicapidae

Size 13 cm

Voice Faster, longer and more musical, high-speed warble consists of rather slurred series of notes, distinctly introduced by 2-spaced notes, *tu…tiu* or *wi…tu*

Range The Himalayas in Nepal and from Darjeeling, West Bengal and Sikkim to Arunachal Pradesh and Assam

Habitat Undergrowth in forests, thick secondary scrub and dense thickets of reeds or bamboos in winter

Plum bird with short tail and small wings. Male has rich orange-chestnut underparts that extend upto throat. Upperparts very dark blue, except for conspicuous short, white eyebrow; male's pale bill turns black when breeding; long, pale pink legs. Female lacks rust-coloured belly, slaty-brown above, dark brown face, pale rufous throat, pale belly. Skulking and inconspicuous. Mainly terrestrial.

WHITE-BROWED SHORTWING

Brachypteryx montana Muscicapidae

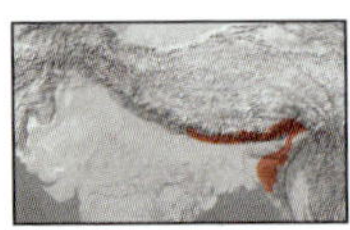

Size 15 cm

Voice Calls include *tak…tak; tt…tt…tt.* Loud warbling song

Range From C Nepal to Arunachal Pradesh

Habitat Damp, mossy forests, undergrowth in forests; near streams; in damp, thickly overgrown gorges

Slightly larger shortwing with long, thin, dark legs and short tail; adult male has distinctive dark blue body, black lores and prominent longish, white supercilium; female has rufous around eyes and forehead; lacks white supercilium; darker brown above, paler below, especially on centre of belly. Immature male like female, but with pale supercilium. Solitary, or in pairs; mainly terrestrial; shy and secretive; usually feeds on damp ground in dense overgrown forest understorey.

GOULD'S SHORTWING

Heteroxenicus stellatus Muscicapidae

Small, round, strikingly-coloured bird with short tail. Adult has black face, bright chestnut upperparts and tail; finely barred, dark slaty-blue-grey underparts with distinctive white triangular spots on belly, flanks, rump. Juvenile duller, streaked rufous above and on breast. Not very shy; often seen in the open and on low, exposed perches; forages on ground in dense undergrowth; not very vocal.

Size 13 cm

Voice Alarm call *tik…tik.* Loud, shrill song consists of *tsi…tsi* notes accelerating into continuous chitter

Range E Uttarakhand to Arunachal Pradesh

Habitat Rocky montane forests above treeline; dwarf rhododendron, juniper scrub; dense undergrowth in moist ravines; forests with fir; bamboos

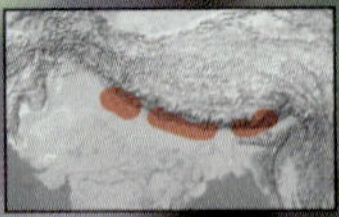

WHITE-BELLIED BLUE ROBIN

Myiomela albiventris Muscicapidae

Size 15 cm

Voice Brief, melodious warbling song of about 10- to 12-notes, with first note alternating up and down and then accelerating into a rapid jumble

Range Restricted to SW Indian hills of S Kerala and Tamil Nadu, south of Palgat Gap

Habitat Thick undergrowth in damp broadleaved forests and secondary growth

Dark, slaty-blue upperparts, black mask and short, whitish supercilium meet above beak; dark lores. Slaty-blue breast graduates to pale grey belly. Long pinkish-purple legs; dark beak. Short tail and wings. Grey flanks and white vent; centre of belly and vent white. Can be confiding. Sings, perches in undergrowth.

LESSER SHORTWING

Brachypteryx leucophris Muscicapidae

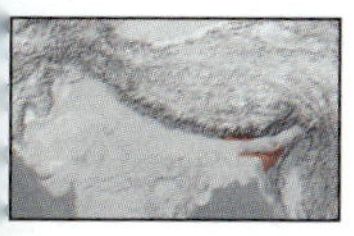

Size 13 cm

Voice Calls include hard *tock… tock* and plaintive whistle

Range The Himalayas; S Assam Hills

Habitat Thick undergrowth in damp broadleaved forests and secondary growth

♀

The Himalayan race *nipalensis*; male grey-blue above, while the race *carolinae*, of the South Assam Hills is brown above. Both races have prominent white supercilium. Pink legs and very short tail. Female has brownish upperparts, white throat and belly. Rare in the Himalayas, but quite easily found in Nagaland and adjoining hills. Keeps to damp undergrowth, in broadleaved forests, often near water.

BLUETHROAT

Luscinia svecica Muscicapidae

Size 15 cm

Voice Calls *tshik…tshik*. Long, varied song

Range Kashmir to Arunachal Pradesh

Habitat Damp scrub, reed beds and cultivation near water

Adult breeding male has greyish-brown upperparts; whitish underparts; bright blue bib with rufous patch in middle, bordered below by narrow black-and-white band and broad rufous band. Non-breeding male similar, but has markings on chin, diffused by pale feather-tips. Female has creamy white throat; bordered below by neck-band of darker streaking and mottling; white moustachial stripe. Juvenile more blackish with buffish spots on back; buff underparts mottled dark brown, giving scaly appearance.

pallidogularis

♀

svecica

cyanecula

abbotti

SIBERIAN RUBYTHROAT

Luscinia calliope Muscicapidae

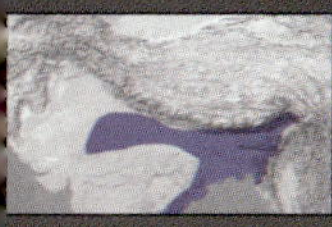

Size 15 cm

Voice Call a *shuk*; ee… *lu*, etc.

Range Uttarakhand to Myanmar

Habitat Dense undergrowth; tall grass, cane, reeds; edges of cultivation

♀

Plumpish, heavy-bodied bird. Breeding male overall olive-brown. Bold, white supercilium and sub-moustachial stripe, edged black; black lores and malar stripe; plain brown rump and tail; ruby-red throat, bordered by thin, black band, varying amounts of grey on breast; greyish-brown underparts; short, unmarked tail. Female uniform brown; buff supercilium, whitish throat, washed grey; grey-brown breast-band. Skulks in dense vegetation; mainly terrestrial; feeds on ground or in low bushes; cocks tail. Feeds singly.

WHITE-TAILED RUBYTHROAT

Luscinia pectoralis Muscicapidae

Size 15 cm

Voice Short, metallic call note; short, harsh alarm note. Rich, shrill song

Range Breeds in the Himalayas, 2,700-4,600 m; winters in N, NE India; winter range not properly known

Habitat Dwarf vegetation, rocky hills in summer. In winter, prefers cultivation, damp ground with grass and bushes

Breeding male has slaty upperparts; white supercilium; white in tail; scarlet chin and throat; jet-black throat-sides, continuing into broad breast-band; white below, greyer on sides. Non-breeding male more brown rather than grey above with scaly, dirty white breast. Female grey-brown above (greyer than Siberian); white chin and throat; greyish breast; white spots on tips of outer-tail. Juvenile male has white tail base and darker head-sides. Solitary; wary, difficult to observe; cocks tail; hops on ground, or makes short dashes; ascends small bush-tops. Breeding male sings all day.

FIRETHROAT

Luscinia pectardens Muscicapidae

Size 15 cm

Voice Call like that of Orange-flanked Bush Robin

Range Vagrant. Arunachal Pradesh, Meghalaya; West Bengal

Habitat Dense bushes, dense woodlands

Medium-sized bird with thin, short bill. Breeding male has slaty-blue upperparts; black forehead and face; white patch on neck-sides; orange throat and breast bordered black; white on base of blackish tail. Non-breeding male has pale underparts with pale blue, rufous and black breast-bands; broad, pale supercilium; tail and upperparts same as breeding male. First-winter male olive-brown above, with slaty-blue back and wing-coverts; tail similar to adult male's, underparts like adult female's.

INDIAN BLUE ROBIN

Luscinia brunnea Muscicapidae

Size 15 cm

Voice Calls include high-pitched *churr* and harsh *tack*... in winter. Trilling song of breeding male, sometimes singing from exposed perch

Range Breeds in the Himalayas, 1,500-3,300 m. Winters in S Western Ghats, Ashambu Hills, and Sri Lanka

Habitat Dense rhododendron, ringal bamboo undergrowth in summer. Evergreen forest undergrowth, coffee estates in winter

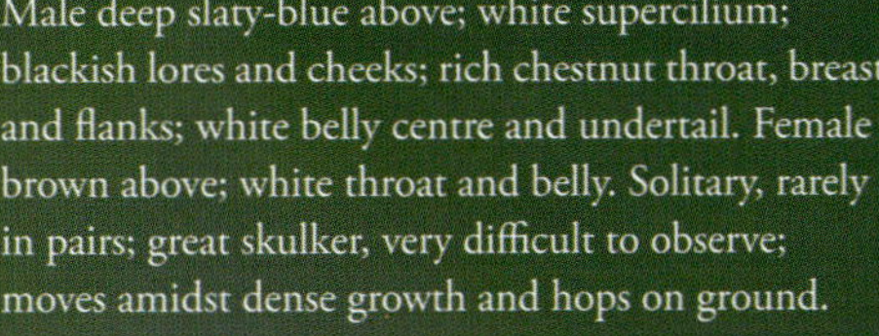

Male deep slaty-blue above; white supercilium; blackish lores and cheeks; rich chestnut throat, breast and flanks; white belly centre and undertail. Female brown above; white throat and belly. Solitary, rarely in pairs; great skulker, very difficult to observe; moves amidst dense growth and hops on ground.

WHITE-BROWED BUSH ROBIN

Tarsiger indicus Muscicapidae

Size 15 cm

Voice Call a churring *trrr*

Range Scarce breeding resident of N hills from Uttarakhand east to Myanmar border. Winters lower down in foothills

Habitat Damp undergrowth of dense forests

♀

Male has slaty-blue face and from forehead to tail with long, white supercilium; yellowish-olive wash to crown; black bill and brown legs; orange throat, breast and flanks. Male similar to Indian Blue but has longer tail with longer supercilium. Much darker above and all orange below. Cheeks black. Female and first-year male have greyish-brown upperparts and orangish-buff underparts and fine, white supercilium. Male displays with drooped wings and flick its tail. Solitary and usually secretive. Sings from small trees. Feeds on invertebrates on ground or in air.

RUFOUS-BREASTED BUSH ROBIN

Tarsiger hyperythrus Muscicapidae

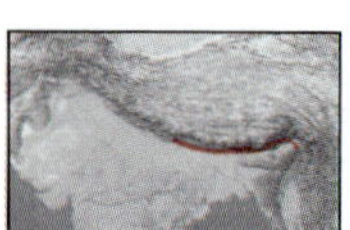

Size 15 cm

Voice Call a *duk...duk...duk...* squeak. Song a lisping warble, *zeew...zee...zwee...zwee*

Range The Himalayas from WC Nepal east to Arunachal Pradesh; winters south to hills of NE India

Habitat Summers in bushes at edges and clearings of dwarf rhododendron, birch forests and in fir-rhododendron forests

♀

Small, blue-and-orange robin. Male dark royal blue above, with blackish face, bright, ultramarine-blue supercilium, shoulder and rump; white undertail-coverts; orange throat, breast and centre of belly. Female olive-brown with bluish cast on tail; no supercilium; olive-brown underparts with rufous wash on flanks. Forages on ground for insects.

GOLDEN BUSH ROBIN

Tarsiger chrysaeus Muscicapidae

♀

Size 15 cm

Voice Calls *tchek...tchek;...trrrr.* High, thin song

Range Hills from Pakistan to Myanmar

Habitat High-altitude dwarf rhododendron and juniper treeline scrub; scattered shrubs on scree-covered slopes; edges of coniferous forests; dense forest undergrowth, bushes, scrubs

Golden-coloured chat. Male has olive-brown crown; distinct bright yellow supercilium; black stripe running through eye to form cheek-patch; golden-yellow scapulars, sides of back and rump; golden-yellow underparts; black-and-golden yellow tail. Female duller yellow-brown above, with indistinct yellow supercilium; paler yellow underparts; long, pale legs. Shy; forages on ground and in low undergrowth, with quick aerial forays.

HIMALAYAN BLUETAIL

Tarsiger (cyanurus) rufilatus Muscicapidae

♀

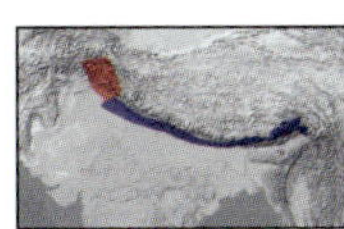

Size 15 cm

Voice Call a deep *tok...tok; weet.* Short, soft song

Range Pakistan to Arunachal Pradesh

Habitat Damp undergrowth in oak, rhododendron, coniferous and evergreen forests

Earlier considered to be a subspecies of the Red-flanked. Longer-tailed chat with diagnostic orange flanks and white throat. Male deep blue above and on breast-sides; brighter, glistening blue forehead, supercilium, shoulder, rump; pale grey-blue underparts; blue tail. Female grey-brown above and on breast-sides; white throat; orange-washed flanks; blue rump, tail. Hunts and forages aerially, on ground. Male often sings from visible forest perch; flares tail, flicks wings.

ORIENTAL MAGPIE ROBIN

Copsychus saularis Muscicapidae

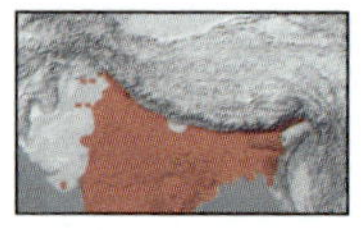

Size 20 cm

Voice Common call a plaintive *sweee…* . One of India's finest songsters; rich, clear song of varying notes and tones; male sings from exposed perches, most frequently between March and June, intermittently year round; also, has harsh *churr* and *chhekh* notes

Range Subcontinent, upto about 1,500 m in the outer Himalayas; absent in extreme W Rajasthan

Habitat Forests; parks; towns

Familiar bird of India. Male glossy blue-black and white; white wing-patch and white in outer-tail distinctive; glossy blue-black throat and breast; white below. Female rich slaty-grey, male black. Solitary, or in pairs, sometimes with other birds in mixed parties; hops on ground, prefers shaded areas. Common about human habitation; when perched, often cocks tail; flicks tail often, especially when making short sallies; active at dusk.

♀

WHITE-RUMPED SHAMA

Copsychus malabaricus Muscicapidae

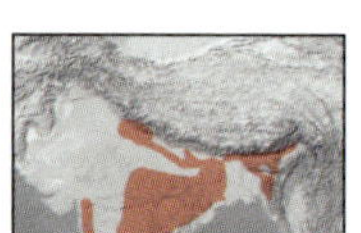

Size 25 cm

Voice Rich songster; melodious, 3- or 4-whistling notes very characteristic. Variety of call notes, including a mix of some harsh notes

Range The Himalayan foothills, the Terai, east of Uttarakhand; NE India; hill forests of Bihar, Odisha, SE Madhya Pradesh, E Maharashtra, south along Eastern Ghats to about Cauvery river; entire Western Ghats

Habitat Forests; bamboos; hill station gardens

Male has glossy black head and back; white rump and sides of graduated tail distinctive; black throat and breast; orange-rufous below. Female grey, male black with shorter tail and duller rufous breast. Arboreal; keeps to shaded areas and foliage, only occasionally emerging in open; launches short sallies.

INDIAN ROBIN

Saxicoloides fulicatus Muscicapidae

Several races in India. Male has dark brown, blackish-brown or glossy blue-back upperbody. Male has white wing-patch; glossy blue-black below; chestnut vent and undertail. Female lacks white in wings; duller grey-brown below. Solitary, or in pairs in open country, and often in and around habitation. Rather suspicious and maintains safe distance between man and itself; hunts on ground, hops or runs in short spurts; when on ground, holds head high and often cocks tail, right upto back, flashing chestnut vent and undertail.

Size 16 cm

Voice Call a long-drawn *sweeeech* or *weeeech*. Warbling song when breeding; also, guttural *charrr...* note

Range Subcontinent, S Himalayan foothills; absent in extreme NE India

Habitat Open country; edges of forests; vicinity of habitation; scrubs

EVERSMANN'S REDSTART

Phoenicurus erythronotus Muscicapidae

Size 16 cm

Voice Warbling song

Range Pakistan and W Himalayas

Habitat Dry hillsides

Grey, black-and-orange chat, larger than most redstarts. Breeding male has grey crown and broad, black face mask, black wings with white bars and patches; fairly mottled orange body, much paler on belly and vent. Brown tail with orange outer feathers. In winter, turns paler and more mottled. Female brown with orange rump and outer-tail and two beige wing-bars.

BLUE-CAPPED REDSTART

Phoenicurus coeruleocephala Muscicapidae

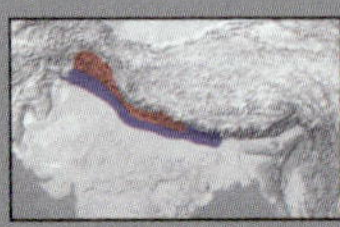

Size 15 cm

Voice Call a soft *tik...tik...tik.* Warbling song

Range Locally common breeding resident in N hills from N Pakistan to Bhutan. Commoner in west. Winters lower down, occasionally moving into N plains as far south as Delhi

Habitat Open forests and scrubs on rocky slopes in summer. Winters in open forests and secondary cover

Adult male has black back, tail, head and breast; white belly and speculum on wing; greyish-blue crown; white belly. Non-breeding male more grey-brown. Female greyish-brown with two buff wing-bars; dark brown tail and chestnut uppertail. Juvenile dark, grey-brown mottled lighter with dark-grey tail and reddish-rufous uppertail; white in wings. Often near water. Feeds on invertebrates on low branches and ground, often dropping from low perch. Shivers and slowly wags tail. Often confiding. Nests on ground.

tricolor

BLACK REDSTART

Phoenicurus ochruros Muscicapidae

♀

Male black above (marked with grey in winter); grey crown and lower back; rufous rump and tail-sides; black throat and breast; rufous below. Female duller brown above; tail similar to male's; dull tawny-brown below. Eastern race *rufiventris* has black crown; common wintering bird of India. Mostly solitary in winter, when common all over India; easy to observe. Perches on overhead wires, poles, rocks and stumps; characteristic shivering of tail and jerky body movements; makes short dashes to ground, soon returning to perch with catch; rather confiding in summer, breeds in houses, under roofs and in wall crevices.

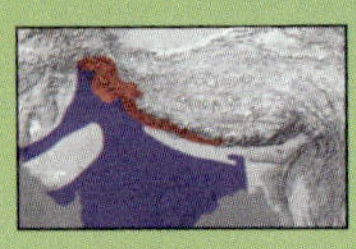

Size 15 cm

Voice Call a squeaking *tictititic...*, often beginning with faint *tsip...* note. Trilling song of breeding male

Range Breeds in the Himalayas, 2,400-5,200m; winters over much of the subcontinent

Habitat Open country; cultivation

HODGSON'S REDSTART

Phoenicurus hodgsoni Muscipidae

Size 15 cm

Voice Calls include rippling *prtt* and harsh *churrr*

Range Locally common winter visitor to N hills from Uttarakhand east to Myanmar border

Habitat Stony riverbeds; scrubs; open woodlands; grasslands; cultivation

Male has grey upperparts except for rufous tail and rump; small, white wing-patch; white forehead; black throat and upper breast; orange underparts. Female overall greyish with rufous tail and vent. Feeds on insects in air and on ground. Behaviour similar to Black's.

♀

WHITE-THROATED REDSTART

Phoenicurus schisticeps Muscicapidae

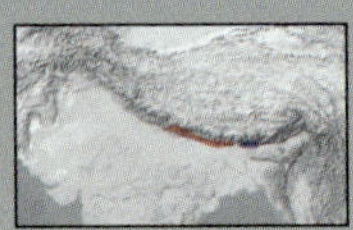

Size 15 cm

Voice Call a drawn-out *zieh*, followed by rattling note. Song undescribed

Range Subject to some altitudinal movements, and winter visitor. Mainly, the Himalayas from W Nepal east to Bhutan

Habitat Summers in open shrubberies on rocky slopes and ridges; also bushes at edges and clearings of open, coniferous and birch forests. Winters in meadows and fallow cultivation and on rocky, bush-covered slopes

♀

Adult male (worn) has blue crown and nape, chin, ear-coverts; mantle black; rufous on scapulars, breast and belly. Adult male (fresh) has rufous fringes to head and upperparts, fringes buff on underparts. Grey-brown on adult female's head and mantle becomes paler on breast, belly buff.

DAURIAN REDSTART

Phoenicurus auroreus Muscicapidae

Size 15 cm

Voice Calls include high-pitched *tseep* or *fit*, scolding *tak* or *teck teck* notes in alarm, rapid rattling *tititik*

Range Summer visitor to the Himalayas from E Sikkim to Arunachal Pradesh, hills of NE India. Winters in foothills

Habitat Sparse, open subalpine, riverine thickets. Also, human settlements upto 2,500 m, breeds between 2,800 and 3,700 m

♀

Adult breeding male pale grey from crown to upper mantle; black lower mantle; large, white wing-patch; rufous rump and uppertail-coverts; rufous tail with dark central rectrices; black scapulars; blackish wings. Rufous underparts; black face, chin and throat. Non-breeding male more brownish-grey from crown to upper mantle; broad, brown fringe on lower mantle, giving scaly appearance, and pale fringing on breast too. Adult female has brown upperparts and paler underparts; smaller wing-patch. Juvenile similar to female but with dark scaling and pale spotting above and below.

BLUE-FRONTED REDSTART

Phoenicurus frontalis Muscicapidae

Size 15 cm

Voice Call a squeaking *tik* or *prik*

Range Altitudinal migrant; breeds in the Himalayas upto 5,300 m. Winters in the Himalayan foothills

Habitat Cultivation; open country; gardens

Male has bright blue forehead with darker blue crown and back; orange-chestnut underparts; rufous rump; orange tail with broad, blackish terminal band and central feathers. Female dark olive-brown; yellowish-orange below; rump and tail as in male; tail pattern diagnostic, to separate it from other female redstarts. Mostly solitary, perched on rocks or bushes; drops to the ground to feed; pumps tail.

GULDENSTADT'S REDSTART

Phoenicurus erythrogastrus Muscicapidae

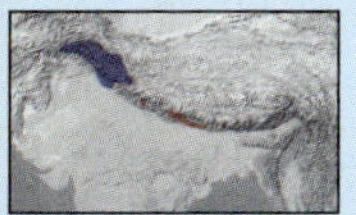

Size 18 cm

Voice Calls include soft *lik* and hard *teek…teek*

Range Locally common breeding resident in N mountains from Pakistan east to Arunachal Pradesh. Winters lower down in foothills

Habitat Stony hillsides, pastures and riverbeds

Big, black, white-and-orange chat with unmarked orange tail. Male has black throat and upperparts with large, white wing-patches and crown. Orange underparts, rump and tail. Female brown above and warm buff below with orange rump and tail. Feeds on invertebrates on ground and through aerial sallies. Perches low. Nests among rocks.

WHITE-BELLIED REDSTART

Hodgsonius phoenicuroides Muscicapidae

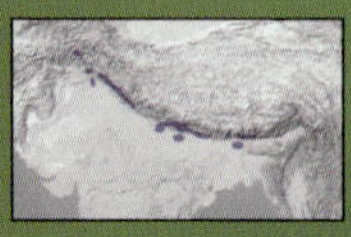

Size 18 cm

Voice Call a grating *croak*. Also, *chack…chack…chack; teuuh…tiyou…tuh*

Range Altitudinal and short-range migrant. The Himalayas from N Pakistan east to Arunachal Pradesh

Habitat Summers in subalpine dwarf birch, rhododendron and juniper; thickets of *Viburnum* and beds of dense, tall herbs in Pakistan

Male overall dark slaty-blue; white belly and vent; rufous sides to base of tail; two white spots on alula. Distinguished from Blue-fronted Robin by white belly, rufous tail-sides and white spots on wing. Female has greenish-brown upperparts; chestnut sides to tail with darker centres, white throat and centre of belly, and reddish-brown flanks and vent. Juvenile similar to female, but spotted above and scaled below.

PLUMBEOUS WATER REDSTART

Rhyacornis fuliginosa Muscicapidae

Size 12 cm

Voice Calls include sharp *kreee…*; also snapping *tzit…tzit*. Rich jingling song of breeding male, infrequently uttered in winter

Range The Himalayas, 800-4,000 m, but mostly 1,000-2,800 m; also breeds south of Brahmaputra River; may descend into foothills, the Terai in winter

Habitat Mountain streams, rivers, rushing torrents

Male has slaty-blue plumage; chestnut tail diagnostic; rufous on lower belly. Female darkish blue-grey-brown above; two spotted wing-bars; white in tail; whitish below, profusely mottled slaty. Juvenile brown, also with white in tail. In pairs on mountain rivers; active, makes short dashes from boulders; moves from boulder to boulder, flying low over roaring waters; tail frequently fanned open and wagged. Hunts late in evening; maintains feeding territories in winter as well as at other times.

WHITE-TAILED ROBIN

Myiomela leucura Muscicapidae

Size 18 cm

Voice Calls include quiet *tuk* and thin whistle. Undulating, rapid song

Range Scarce breeding resident of N hills from Uttarakhand east to Myanmar border. Also, much lower in NE India, Bangladesh. Winters lower down in foothills and rarely in nearby plains

Habitat Damp undergrowth and bamboo clumps in evergreen forests, often near streams or in ravines

Male slaty-blue, with bright blue forehead and shoulders; rufous-chestnut tail and vent; black bill; flesh-coloured legs. Female brown-grey above, with white lower throat-patch and brown breast-band. Long, broad, black tail which it lowers and spreads. Shy, keeping close to ground where it feeds on invertebrates. Flies up into trees if disturbed. Solitary, or in pairs. Nests low down.

WHITE-CAPPED REDSTART

Chaimarrornis leucocephalus Muscicapidae

Adult has glossy black head with white crown and upper nape; black back, wings, chin, throat and breast. Rest of underparts and rump rufous; rufous tail with black terminal band; black underwing-coverts mottled chestnut-orange. Bill, eyes, legs and feet blackish. Perches on stones mid-stream, bobbing body; flicking and fanning wings and tail. Flies low over water.

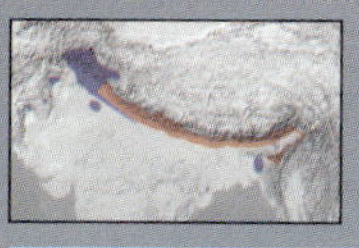

Size 19 cm

Voice Calls include plaintive *tseee* and softer *psst...psst.* Whistling song

Range Common breeding resident to N hills from Pakistan east to Myanmar border. Winters lower down in foothills

Habitat Rocky streams and rivers, fast-flowing water and alpine pastures

BLUE-FRONTED ROBIN

Cinclidium frontale Muscicapidae

Size 19 cm

Voice Call a soft *tch...tchtch...tch*; alarm *schwik*. Mellow song

Range Small patches in N Bengal, Bhutan and Arunachal Pradesh

Habitat Thick dark, damp gullies; dense forest undergrowth; edges of forests

Rare blue robin with long legs and longish, dark, graduated tail. Male deep blue; dark lores, shining blue eyebrow, shoulder; sometimes, blotchy white on lower belly, vent. Female rich dusky brown above, paler below; buff-white throat, centre of belly; brown vent streaked white. Shy, elusive; habits little known; mainly terrestrial; usually seen near ground level in dense forest understoreys. Rarely flies; flight only over very short distances; forages by hopping on ground; characteristic horizontal stance; flares tail.

GRANDALA

Grandala coelicolor Muscicapidae

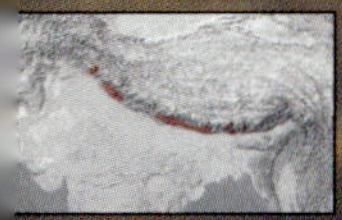

Size 23 cm

Voice Call a sharp *jeeu…jeeu.* Song an extension of this

Range Locally common breeding esident of high mountains from Kashmir east to Arunachal Pradesh. Descends little lower in winter but always remains in mountain zone

Habitat Rocky hillsides and pastures above treeline

Male glossy purplish-blue all over with blackish wings and tail. Female and immature brownish-grey, heavily streaked with white; white patches on wings and bluish wash on rump; exceptionally long wing. Usually in flocks, catching invertebrates on wing or on ground. Also eats berries. Rapid and elegant flight.

LITTLE FORKTAIL

Enicurus scouleri Muscicapidae

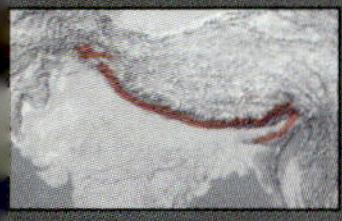

Size 12 cm

Voice Rather silent except a rarely uttered, sharp *tzittzit* call

Range The Himalayas, W to E. Breeds between 1,200-3,700 m; descends to about 300 m in winter

Habitat Rocky mountain streams, waterfalls, small shaded forest puddles

Adult has bluish-black head, nape and upper back; white forehead; blackish-brown wings with broad, white band; white band also across back; white breast and abdomen; dichromatic, slightly forked tail; black rump-patch. Sexes alike. Solitary, or in pairs; energetically moves on moss-covered and wet, slippery rocks; constantly wags and flicks tail; occasionally launches short sallies, but also plunges underwater, dipper style.

BLACK-BACKED FORKTAIL

Enicurus immaculatus Muscicapidae

Medium-sized forktail. Black crown and mantle; broad, white band on forehead extending behind eye; broad white wing-bars; white rump; long, deeply forked black-and-white tail. Black throat, remaining underparts white. Similar to Slaty-backed, but more black and smaller in size.

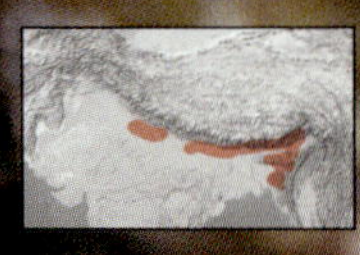

Size 23 cm

Voice Call a short, whistled *tseep…; dew; kurt…see*

Range Foothills from Uttarakhand to Myanmar

Habitat Rushing hill streams in moist tropical forests

Solitary, or in dispersed pairs; forages near water or in rocks at water's edge or mid-stream, occasionally going into water; constantly moves tail up and down; shy; flies along river.

SLATY-BACKED FORKTAIL

Enicurus schistaceus Muscicapidae

Medium-sized forktail with slaty-grey crown and mantle; long, deeply forked black-and-white tail; black throat and wing-coverts; broad, white wing-bars; white rump; narrow, white band across forehead extending behind eye; flesh-pink legs. Juvenile dark brown; adult slaty and has dark streaking on breast. Solitary, or in pairs; always near water; moves restlessly; forages in rocks at water's edge or mid-stream, occasionally going into water; constantly moves tail up and down. Shy.

Size 25 cm

Voice Calls include high-pitched *tsee*; soft *cheet* metallic *teenk*

Range Mountains from Uttarakhand east

Habitat Rocky forested streams

SPOTTED FORKTAIL

Enicurus maculatus Muscicapidae

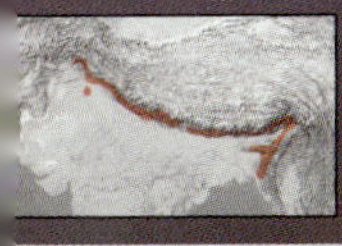

Size 28 cm

Voice Call a shrill, screechy *kree*, mostly in flight; also some shrill, squeaky notes on perch

Range The Himalayas; breeds mostly between 1,200-3,600 m; descends to about 600 m in winter

Habitat Boulder-strewn torrents; forest streams; roadsides

Has white forehead and forecrown; black crown and nape; white-spotted black back; broad, white wing-bar and rump; deeply forked, graduated black-and-white tail; black till breast, white below. Sexes alike. Easily distinguished from other similar-sized forktails in the Himalayas by white-spotted back. Solitary, or in scattered pairs; active, moves on mossy boulders at water's edge or in mid-stream; long, gracefully sways forked tail, almost always kept horizontal.

WHITE-CROWNED FORKTAIL

Enicurus leschenaulti Muscicapidae

Size 28 cm

Voice Call a harsh *scree...scree, chit...chit*. Elaborate, high-pitched whistling song

Range Subject to seasonal movements. The Himalayan foothills from Darjeeling, West Bengal, east to Arunachal Pradesh; hills of NE India

Habitat Fast-flowing streams and rivers in dense, tropical broadleaved evergreen forests

Diagnostic white crown with short crest. Similar to Black-backed but larger, with longer tail. Conspicuous white forehead and forecrown; black throat and breast; unmarked black mantle. Juvenile has brownish-black upperparts, brownish-black throat and breast with white streaking and brown mottling on upper belly, and brown flanks; pink legs. Sometimes seen on rocks mid-stream, constantly flicks tail while foraging.

HODGSON'S BUSHCHAT

Saxicola insignis Muscicapidae

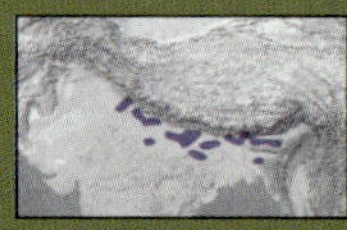

Size 17 cm

Voice Call a metallic *tek…tek*

Range Uttarakhand to Bhutan, Assam

Habitat Dry or wet grasslands, reed beds, cane fields and tamarisks

Largish bushchat with pied upperparts and red-patch on breast. Diagnostic broad, white nuchal-collar on male; white rump. Breeding male has black crown, ear-coverts, mantle, wings and tail; rufous on breast; rufous wash on belly. Female has buff-streaked upperparts; two whitish-buff wing-bars; pale rufous-buff underparts. Solitary, in pairs. Terrestrial hunter. Sometimes dives from perch to catch prey. Upright stance. Territorial in winter.

COMMON STONECHAT

Saxicola torquatus Muscicapidae

Size 13 cm

Voice Call a double-noted *wheet chat.* Soft, trilling song of breeding male in the Himalayas, occasionally in winter grounds

Range Breeds in the Himalayas, 1,500-3,000 m; all over India in winter, except Kerala and much of Tamil Nadu

Habitat Dry, open areas; cultivation; tidal creeks

Medium-sized, black, white and rufous chat. Male black above; white rump, wing-patch and sides of neck and breast; black throat; orange-rufous breast. In winter, black feathers broadly edged buff-rufous-brown. Female rufous-brown above, streaked darker; unmarked yellowish-brown below; white wing-patch and rufous rump. Solitary, or in pairs in open country; perches on small bushes, fence posts and boulders; restless, makes short forays to capture insects, soon returning to perch.

WHITE-TAILED STONECHAT

Saxicola leucurus Muscicapidae

Size 13 cm

Voice Calls include short *pseep* and harder *kek...kek...kek*

Range Local breeding, near-endemic resident in Indus and upper Ganges river systems and the Terai east to Assam, patchily south to N Odisha

Habitat Reed beds and tall grass usually near rivers. Sometimes in adjoining scrubs (often tamarisk) and cultivation. Frequently shares habitat with Common

Small and stocky chat with clearly defined orange breast-patch. Black head; white collar. Dark cinnamon-brown back and wings with white on wing-coverts; dark tail shows white on inner webs of outer-tail feathers. Female very similar to Common but greyer, paler below and with greyish in tail. White in tail visible in flight.

PIED BUSHCHAT

Saxicola caprata Muscicapidae

Size 13 cm

Voice Harsh, 2-noted call serves as contact and alarm. Short, trilling song of breeding male

Range Subcontinent, from outer Himalayas to about 1,500 m

Habitat Open country; scrubs; cultivation; ravines

Breeding male has glossy metallic black plumage; white in wing, rump and belly. Female brown above, paler on lores; darker tail; dull yellow-brown below with rusty wash on breast and belly. Juvenile more grey-brown with yellowish spots and buffy underparts with dark spotting. Solitary, or in pairs; perches on bushes, overhead wires; makes short sallies to prey on ground or carries it to perch; active, sometimes guards feeding territories in winter; flicks and spreads wings.

JERDON'S BUSHCHAT

Saxicola jerdoni Muscicapidae

Size 15 cm

Voice Calls include short, plaintive whistle, higher-pitched than that of other chats, and low *chit...churr, chit...churr*

Range Very rare and local breeding resident. Mainly NE India and Bangladesh; Nepal

Habitat Large areas of elephant grass, grass and reeds along river or channel banks

Uniformly black with glossy blue forehead, crown, nape, lores and upperparts. Silky-white chin and throat. Buff wash on belly and breast. White flank feathers edged grey; dull black remiges; glossy black underwing-coverts; black legs, feet and bill. Female has black forehead and crown with rufous-brown streaking; brownish upperparts and white underparts; greyish-brown underwing-coverts; buffy white undertail-coverts; brown feet and legs. Juvenile male has more brownish upperparts, faintly streaked crown and forehead and greyish buff underparts.

GREY BUSHCHAT

Saxicola ferreus Muscicapidae

Size 15 cm

Voice Call double-noted; also grating *praee*... .Trilling song of male

Range The Himalayas, 1,400-3,500 m; descends into foothills and adjoining plains, including Gangetic plains, in winter

Habitat Open scrub; edges of forests; cultivation

♀

Male dark grey above, streaked black; black mask; white supercilium, wing-patch and outer-tail; white throat and belly; dull grey breast. Female rufous-brown, streaked; rusty rump and outer-tail; white throat; yellow-brown below. Solitary, or in pairs; like other chats, keeps to open country and edges of forests; perches on bush-tops and poles, flits tail often; flies to ground on spotting insects.

RUFOUS-TAILED ROCK THRUSH

Monticola saxatilis Muscicapidae

Size 19 cm

Voice Calls include squeaky *whit* and hard *chak...chak*. Song a quiet extended melody, often in flight

Range Scarce breeder in Balochistan. Winters elsewhere in E Pakistan to Ladakh and occasionally Nepal

Habitat Open, dry, rocky hillsides

♀

Breeding male has bluish-grey head and throat; dark chestnut wings; white patch on back; chestnut underparts and diagnostic, rusty brown tail. Female and winter male dark, scaly brown, paler underparts. Solitary, or in pairs. Shy, but frequently perches on boulders wagging tail. Feeds on ground on insects and seeds. Nests among boulders.

BLUE ROCK THRUSH

Monticola solitarius Muscicapidae

Size 23 cm

Voice Silent in winter. Short, whistling song of breeding male

Range Breeds in the Himalayas, from extreme W to E Nepal; winters from N foothills, NE, S India, throughout the peninsula

Habitat Open, rocky country; cliffs; ravines; ruins; habitation

Male has deep blue plumage; black wings and tail; pale fulvous and black scales more conspicuous in winter; belly whiter in winter. Female duller, grey-brown above; dark shaft-streaks; black barring on rump; dull white below, barred brown. Solitary; has favoured sites, often around habitation; perches on rocks, stumps, rooftops; has rather upright posture; flies on to ground to feed, but sometimes launches short aerial sallies.

CHESTNUT-BELLIED ROCK THRUSH

Monticola rufiventris Muscicapidae

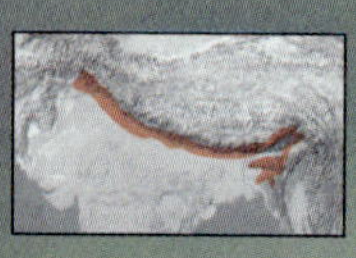

Size 24 cm

Voice Call a harsh rattle. Fluty song

Range The Himalayan forests upto 3,500 m

Habitat Open country, edges of forests, groves on rocky hillsides

Male has deep cobalt-blue head and upperparts with blackish mask; blackish face and head-sides; bright blue rump and uppertail-coverts; rich rufous to maroon belly; dark bluish-black tail. Female dull olive-brown with buff throat and lores; heavy scaling on underparts; distinctive face pattern with eye-ring, dark malar stripe and neck-patch; brown tail edged brownish-grey. Mostly solitary, or seen in pairs; perches upright.

BLUE-CAPPED ROCK THRUSH

Monticola cinclorhynchus Muscicapidae

Size 17 cm

Voice Mostly silent in winter, except for occasional harsh single or 2-noted call. Rich song of breeding male

Range Breeds in the Himalayas, 1,000-2,500 m, sometimes higher; winters in Western Ghats, from Narmada river

Habitat Shaded forests, groves

Male has blue crown and nape; black back; broad stripe through eyes to ear-coverts; blue throat and shoulder-patch; white wing-patch and chestnut rump distinctive; chestnut below throat. Back feathers edged fulvous in winter. Female unmarked olive-brown above; buffy-white below, thickly speckled with dark brown. Female Blue Rock *M. solitarius* grey-brown above, has yellow-brown vent and dull wing-bar. Solitary, or in pairs.

DARK-SIDED FLYCATCHER

Muscicapa sibirica Muscicapidae

Small flycatcher with dark greyish-brown upperparts; streaked across breast, flanks; white throat and centre of belly; large, dark eyes with white eye-ring. Similar to Asian Brown, but has smaller, dark bill, less contrasting eye-ring and lores; darker upperparts and breast-bands and flanks; wings and primary projections longer; head and body slimmer.

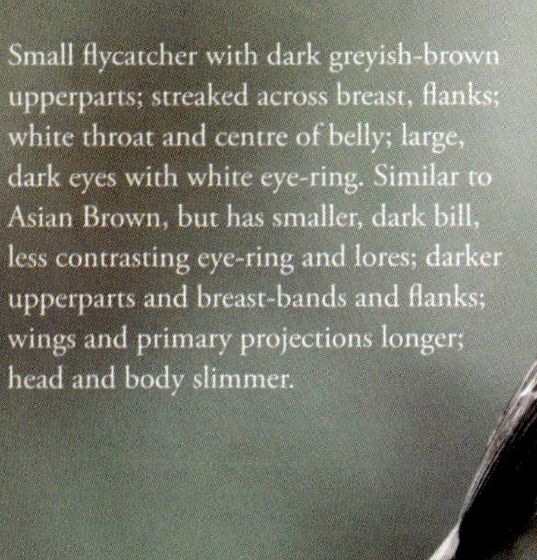

Size 14 cm

Voice Calls *tsee… tsee…tsee*

Range Pakistan to Arunachal Pradesh

Habitat Edges of temperate, or subalpine mixed broadleaved, coniferous forests

ASIAN BROWN FLYCATCHER

Muscicapa dauurica Muscicapidae

Size 13 cm

Voice Call a thin *tzee*. Whistling song

Range Breeding resident of the Himalayan foothills, with several small disjunct populations resident in the hills of C and peninsular India. Widespread winter visitor in the peninsula

Habitat Open forests; groves; gardens; plantations

Nondescript-looking, ashy-brown flycatcher; greyish wash on dirty white breast; short tail; large head with huge eye and prominent eye-ring; pale lores; basal half of lower mandible pale and fleshy; black legs. Sexes alike. Usually solitary; perches upright on lower branches of trees, makes sallies to catch insects and returns to same perch.

RUSTY-TAILED FLYCATCHER

Muscicapa ruficauda Muscicapidae

Size 14 cm

Voice Call a plaintive *peu...peu*. Also, churrs

Range Fairly common endemic breeding summer visitor to N mountains from N Pakistan east to E Nepal. Winters mainly in SW India but widespread passage records from elsewhere in India

Habitat Open forests, clearings and edges

Medium to small-sized flycatcher with flattish head. Warm brown upperparts; dark brownish from throat to breast, whitish belly to vent; large eye; ill-defined supercilium and eye-ring. Rump and notched tail bright rufous. Lower mandible pale orange. Sexes alike. Juvenile dark brownish above with buffy streaks and pale buff-brownish-spotted underparts.

FERRUGINOUS FLYCATCHER

Muscicapa ferruginea Muscicapidae

Size 13 cm

Voice Usually quiet. High-pitched trilling song

Range Scarce and local breeding summer visitor to hills of NE India, E Himalayas from C Nepal. Winters probably in SE Asia

Habitat Dense cover of hill forests

Small to medium-sized flycatcher with large head and short bill. Dark grey head; dark rufous upperparts; white throat and belly; rufous breast and flanks; more orange on rump, tail and on prominent wing-bars. Prominent white eye-rings. Pale legs. Sexes alike. Juvenile spotted rufous-orange. Usually seen solitary, low down in bushes, feeds on insects both in foliage and by aerial sorties. Not shy. Perches in understoreys of forests, flying out to catch insects. Crepuscular and unobtrusive. Nests in moss-covered trees.

SLATY-BACKED FLYCATCHER

Ficedula hodgsonii Muscicapidae

Size 13 cm

Voice Short and abrupt, flute-like meandering song of whistled notes in a rapid, generally descending series: *per...ip...it...u...or... per...ip...it...tu*

Range The Himalayas from WC Nepal east to Arunachal Pradesh; NE India

Habitat Breeds in oak-rhododendron, fir and pine forests; winters in damp broadleaved forests, shrubberies and bamboos

Male deep blue above and bright orange below, whiter belly; black tail has white patches at base. Matt-blue plumage and tail separate from male Cyornis flycatchers. Female olive-brown above and greyish-olive below with poorly-defined whitish throat, lores and eye-ring. Olive-brown uppertail-coverts and tail, distinguished from female Slaty-blue. Confused with female Pale Blue, but smaller and has no rufous to tail. Juvenile has buff spotting on upperparts and dark scaling on buff underparts with whitish throat. First-winter male resembles adult female, often breeds in this plumage.

RUFOUS-GORGETED FLYCATCHER

Ficedula strophiata Muscicapidae

Size 14 cm

Voice Calls include metallic *pink*, harsh *trrt*

Range Uncommon resident in the Himalayas and hills of NE India

Habitat Forest clearings and edges

Male has dark olive-brown upperparts; blackish face and throat; conspicuous white forehead and eyebrow; diagnostic rufous-orange gorget, not always visible; grey breast; white sides to black tail. Female similar but duller, has less distinct eyebrow and gorget. Frequently seen perched quietly in shaded areas or dense canopy. Like all flycatchers, hawks insects but sometimes feeds on ground.

TAIGA FLYCATCHER

Ficedula albicilla Muscicapidae

Size 12 cm

Voice Noisy. Calls include trilled *trrr* and hard *tik…tik*

Range Common winter visitor through most of India, Nepal and Bangladesh. Passage migrant only in Pakistan. Rare in Sri Lanka and extreme S India

Habitat Open wooded country; groves; parks; gardens

Small to medium-sized flycatcher with distinct face pattern; rufous patch on breast strongly demarcated from creamy-buff on lower breast and belly; white patches at base of tail; blackish face; whitish eyebrow. Female overall much duller. Juvenile has rich buff spots above and blackish scales below. Usually solitary, or in pairs. Forages in undergrowth, occasionally on ground. Active but often rather shy. Best located by calls.

KASHMIR FLYCATCHER

Ficedula subrubra Muscicapidae

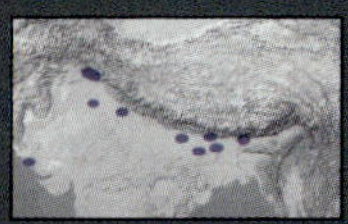

Size 13 cm

Voice Song a short, sweet phrase, *sweet…eat, sweet…eat…didhe*

Range Endemic to the subcontinent. Breeds in NW Himalayas in Neelum valley, Pakistan, Kashmir and Pir Panjal Range, India. Winters in Sri Lanka

Habitat Deciduous forests. Winters in gardens, tea estates and edges of forests

Male has ashy-brown upperparts; deep rufous throat, breast, upper belly and flanks; black-bordered throat and breast; black tail with white panel in outer-tail feathers. Female and first-winter male usually more rufous-orange on throat and breast; grey sides to neck and breast. Juvenile has tail pattern as adult, but has dark brown-spotted upperparts and buffish underparts scaled with dark brown.

WHITE-GORGETED FLYCATCHER

Anthipas monileger Muscicapidae

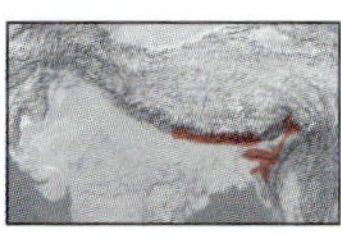

Size 11 cm

Voice Calls include short *tik*, rattle and thin whistle. Wheezy, short song

Range Rare breeding resident from W Nepal east to Arunachal Pradesh. Eastern race rather more frequent in hills of NE India to Myanmar border

Habitat Dense undercover of mountain forests

Small, large-headed, olive-brown flycatcher with short tail. Pristine white throat-patch bordered black. Paler brown underparts. Western race has whitish supercilium, eastern has warm buff. Large head and bill, short tail and pink legs. Sexes alike. Juvenile darker above with pale buff streaks. Feeds on invertebrates on or close to ground. Flycatches and flits tail open but usually shy and difficult to observe. Nests near ground.

SNOWY-BROWED FLYCATCHER

Ficedula hyperythra Muscicapidae

Very small, short-tailed flycatcher with rounded head. Small bill. Male has dark slaty-blue upperparts; short, white supercilium; deep orange from chin to breast, paler below; white patches at base of tail. Female has olive-brown upperparts; rich rusty supercilium, face and breast. Both sexes have pink legs. Feeds on insects unobtrusively on or near ground. Nests in low tree holes.

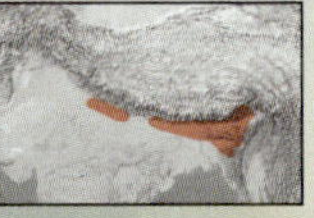

Size 11 cm

Voice Calls include thin, repeated *sip* and *tsit*. Also *sit…si…sii* song

Range Locally common breeding resident in N mountains from E Uttarakhand to Myanmar border. Moves lower down in winter

Habitat Bushy undergrowth of forests, particularly favouring bamboos and ravines

LITTLE PIED FLYCATCHER

Ficedula westermanni Muscicapidae

Size 11 cm

Voice Call a *tweet…*; *churr*. High-pitched song

Range Patchily distributed from Himachal Pradesh to Myanmar

Habitat Broadleaved deciduous and evergreen forests; open woodlands, scrubs, orchards

Tiny flycatcher with very short tail. Male has glossy black upperparts; broad, white supercilium; white wing-bar and white-edged black tail, diagnostic. White underparts, sometimes washed grey. Female has pale greyish-blue and brownish upperparts and greyish-white underparts; reddish-brown cast on uppertail and rump. Female of eastern race *australorientis* has more rufous on rump and tail. Juvenile spotted brown and buff.

ULTRAMARINE FLYCATCHER

Ficedula superciliaris Muscicapidae

Male deep blue above; sides of head, neck and breast, forming broken breast-band; long, white eyebrow; white in tail; white below. Female dull-slaty above and grey-white below. Eastern race *aestigma* lacks white over eye and in tail. Solitary, or in pairs; seen in mixed parties during winter; active, hunts in characteristic flycatcher-style; rarely ventures into open.

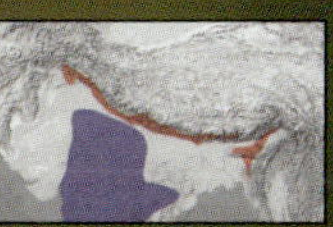

Size 10 cm

Voice Call a faint *tick...tick...* in winter; a *chrrr* alarm note. Three-syllabled song in the Himalayas

Range Breeds in the Himalayas, 1,800-3,200 m. Winters in N and C India, south to Karnataka and N Andhra Pradesh

Habitat Forests; groves; orchards; gardens

SLATY-BLUE FLYCATCHER

Ficedula tricolor Muscicapidae

Size 13 cm

Voice Call a faint *tick...tick*

Range Breeds in the Himalayas, 1,800-2,600 m. Winters in foothills

Habitat Forest undergrowth, reeds, bushes, grass

Male slaty-blue above; greyish-white (The Himalayas) or buff (S Assam hills) below; black mask; white patch at base of black tail. Female has brown upperparts; warm brownish-buff flanks; rufescent rump and tail. Slim, long-tailed flycatcher; usually solitary or in pairs; feeds near ground with tail cocked.

SAPPHIRE FLYCATCHER

Ficedula sapphira Muscicapidae

Size 11 cm

Voice Call a low *tit…it…it… it* rattle, deeper than that of other small flycatchers except Ultramarine; dry, rattled call, *trrrt*

Range NE India, Nepal, Bangladesh

Habitat Moist evergreen broadleaved forests

Small, slim flycatcher. Breeding male has bright, glossy blue crown. Bright blue rump and uppertail-coverts, bright blue upperparts, sides of head, neck and breast; orange throat and breast centre; belly and undertail-coverts white. Crown and mantle of immature and some males brown, sides of head, neck and breast also brownish. Female has olive-brown upperparts and orange throat and breast. Distinguished from female Slaty-backed and Slaty-blue by shorter tail, orange throat and breast, white belly and vent. Juvenile spotted above and scaled on breast.

DULL-BLUE FLYCATCHER

Eumyias sordidus Muscicapidae

Size 15 cm

Voice Call a series of 4- or 5-chip notes. Song a sweet phrase of 6- to 8-notes, often with slide in each note giving a mournful effect

Range Endemic resident in Sri Lanka, common in higher hills

Habitat Edges of forests and well-wooded areas; shady wooded gardens

Adult dull, ashy-blue with brighter blue forehead; greyish-white belly, flanks and undertail-coverts; dark lores and chin bordered pale blue; brownish-grey tail and flight feathers. Sexes alike, but female overall duller. Juvenile has buff spotting and diffuse black scaling on brown upperparts; black scaling on beige throat and breast; wings and tail like adult, but with buff tips to coverts.

VERDITER FLYCATCHER

Eumyias thalassinus Muscicapidae

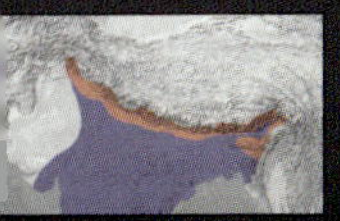

Size 16 cm

Voice Silent in winter, except a rare, faint *chwe*... call. Rich, trilling notes and song during the Himalayan summer

Range The Himalayas, 1,200-3,200 m. Winters in Indian plains, hill forests of C, E and S India

Habitat Open forests; orchards

Male has verditer-blue plumage, darker in wings and tail; black lores. Female duller, greyer overall, has short bill and longish tail. Solitary, or in pairs in winter, sometimes with other birds; restless, flicks tail; rather more noticeable than other flycatchers because of its continuous movement and habit of perching in open-exposed positions, like bare twigs on tree-tops.

juvenile

PALE BLUE FLYCATCHER

Cyornis unicolor Muscicapidae

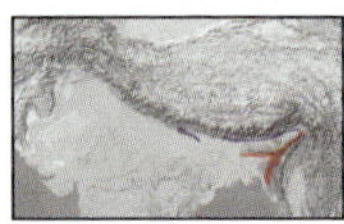

Size 18 cm

Voice Song rich and melodious, loud and thrush-like with descending sequences, *chi..., chuchichu...chuchichu...chucchi*, usually ending with harsh *chizz*

Range The Himalayas in N Uttar Pradesh and from WC Nepal east to Arunachal Pradesh; NE India

Habitat Moist, dense broadleaved forests, bamboos and secondary growth

Similar to the Verditer, but has longer bill and whitish-grey underparts; white vent; vivid blue forecrown and dusky lores. Female pale brown above with reddish-brown uppertail-coverts and tail; greyish underparts. Distinguished by larger size and longer tail, brownish-grey upperparts, and even greyish underparts with greyish-white centre of belly and dark buff undertail-coverts.

HILL BLUE FLYCATCHER

Cyornis banyumas Muscicapidae

Size 15 cm

Voice Calls include hard *tak* and short rattle. Warbling song more complex than Tickell's

Range Rare breeding resident in N mountains from C Nepal east to Myanmar border. Moves lower in winter

Habitat Thick forests

Male very similar to Tickell's but distinguished by sharp demarcation between rufous breast and creamy-white underparts; larger and deeper blue above with more black on cheeks. Female dark brown above with rusty tail and warm buff below. Both have rather long, black bill and pinkish-brown (not black) legs. Juvenile has cinnamon-brown upperparts with buffish spotting. Flycatches. Nests low down.

PALE-CHINNED FLYCATCHER

Cyornis poliogenys Muscicapidae

Size 18 cm

Voice Calls include hard clicks and rattles *tick...tick...*, *etc.* Song a high-pitched series of notes *chee...chee*, *chit...chit...*, etc.

Range C Nepal to Arunachal Pradesh; S Assam Hills

Habitat Bushes, undergrowth, low trees in open broadleaved forests of foothills; open country in the plains

Medium to large-sized, fairly plain-looking flycatcher. Warm brown upperparts; has varying degrees of grey on crown and face depending on the race; buff lores and eye-ring; buff or creamy-white throat; pale rufous-orange breast and flanks, creamy-white belly with pale rufous wash; rufous rump and tail; mostly arboreal; prefers hunting for insects in forest understoreys, sometimes trees, though will also descend to ground.

TICKELL'S BLUE FLYCATCHER

Cyornis tickelliae Muscicapidae

Size 14 cm

Voice Clear, metallic song of 6-notes, sometimes extending to 9 or 10; often uttered in winter too

Range All over India, south roughly of a line from Kutch to W Uttarakhand east along the Terai; absent in extreme N, NW India

Habitat Shaded forests; bamboos; gardens

Male dark indigo-blue above; bright blue on forehead and supercilium; darker, almost appearing black on face-sides; rufous-orange throat and breast; whitish below. Female duller overall. Usually in pairs in shaded areas, often in mixed hunting parties; flits about intermittently or launches short sorties; has favourite perches; often breaks into fluty song.

♀

BLUE-THROATED BLUE FLYCATCHER

Cyornis rubeculoides Muscicapidae

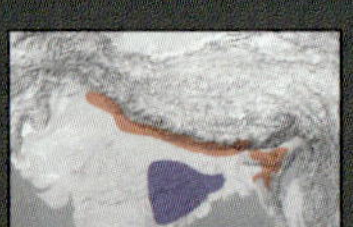

Size 14 cm

Voice Calls include harsh *chrr* and hard *tak…tak*. Rapidly delivered warbling song

Range Locally breeding summer visitor to N hills from N Pakistan east to Myanmar border. Winters in foothills

Habitat Damp forests, particularly overgrown ravines

Small flycatcher with blue throat. Male bright blue; has glossy blue forehead; orange upper breast (sometimes extending onto flanks); white belly to vent. Distinguished from Tickell's by blue throat. Female brown above, more rufous on rump and tail with pale orange throat and upper breast. Lores, belly and vent white. Female Tickell's bluish above. Feeds on invertebrates at lower levels.

♀

RUFOUS-BELLIED NILTAVA

Niltava sundara Muscicapidae

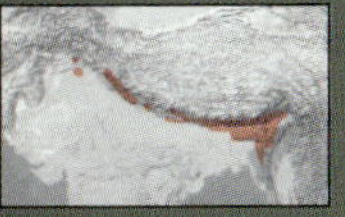

Size 15 cm

Voice Calls include squeaky, churring notes; occasionally sharp *psi...psi;* also some harsh notes and squeaks

Range The Himalayas, NE India; 1,500-3,200 m. Winters in foothills, adjoining plains

Habitat Dense forest undergrowth; bushes

Deep blue and orange niltava. Male has deep purple-blue back and throat; dark blue mask; black forehead; brilliant blue crown, shoulder and rump; chestnut-rufous underbody. Female more olive-brown overall; pale greyish-brown underparts; rufescent tail; white on lower throat diagnostic. Mostly solitary; keeps to undergrowth; highly unobtrusive, seldom seen; often flicks wings like redstart, and bobs body.

VIVID NILTAVA

Niltava vivida Muscicapidae

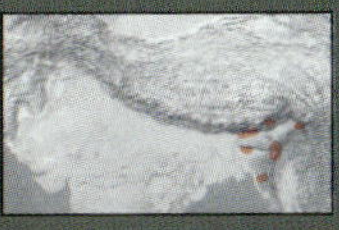

Size 18 cm

Voice Simple, slow song of upto 10 mellow whistles, usually interspersed with scratchier notes, *heu...wee...riu...chrt...trrt...heu...wee...tiu...wee...u*

Range Hills of NE India

Habitat Broadleaved, evergreen and mixed forests

Male cobalt-blue above with blue head and orange below, brighter blue forecrown, rump and tail. Similar to Rufous-bellied, but larger with longer wings, and often has peaked crown. Unlike Rufous-bellied, lacks gleaming blue crown and nape, also, orange of breast extends onto lower throat. Female lacks well-defined oval-shaped patch on lower throat like female Rufous-bellied, and typically has peaked crown. Juvenile as Rufous-bellied, but lacks buff throat-patch. More arboreal and spotted away from dense cover.

SMALL NILTAVA

Niltava macgrigoriae Muscicapidae

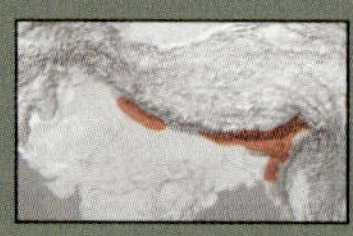

Size 13 cm

Voice Call a high-pitched *see... see; chrrr.* Song *twee...twee-tee...twee*

Range Uttarakhand to Myanmar

Habitat Bushes, undergrowth, paths, forest clearings; lowland reeds, grass jungles

♀

Very small flycatcher, similar to Large, but almost half its size. Male has greyish-blue underparts; very dark blue-black head-sides; glistening pale blue forehead reaching to eye, rump and patch on neck; white vent. Female brown with orangish-brown wings and tail; small, glossy blue neck-patch. Fairly shy, difficult to see; remains hidden in dense foliage of forest understoreys, making occasional aerial sallies for insects; partly crepuscular.

LARGE NILTAVA

Niltava grandis Muscicapidae

Size 21 cm

Voice Call a harsh rattle; nasal *ju... ee*. Song a pleasant whistle *do...remi*

Range C Nepal to Arunachal Pradesh; S Assam Hills

Habitat Dense, moist evergreen forests and streams

♀

Very large flycatcher with dark bill and legs. Male dark blue with black face, chin; slightly crested, has blue crown, shoulder, neck-patches, rump. Female fairly rich brown above; rufous wings, tail; rufous-buff forehead, streaked face; small, buff throat-patch; blue shoulder-patch; pale blue wash on nape, hindcrown; streaked buff-brown underparts. Juvenile rufous-brown; streaked above, scaled below. Almost, totally arboreal; prefers middle, lower storeys in forest interiors; on perch longer during day, hunts more actively in twilight.

PYGMY BLUE FLYCATCHER

Muscicapella hodgsoni Muscicapidae

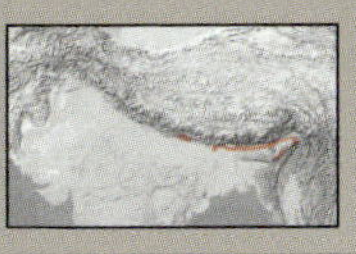

Size 10 cm

Voice Calls include *tchurr...*; weak *tseep...*. Song soft, very high-pitched

Range WC Nepal to Arunachal Pradesh

Habitat Dense, moist broadleaved forests; thick secondary growth

♀

Tiny flycatcher. Male has cobalt-blue upperparts and more vivid, glossy blue crown; bluish-black lores; dark greyish-blue wings and tail and pale orange underparts. Female has olive-brown upperparts; bright orange rump and uppertail; white underparts washed with orange on throat, breast and belly. Distinguished from other flycatchers by tiny size, small, fine bill and short tail. Arboreal; flits restlessly through foliage; often droops wings and cocks tail. Solitary, or in pairs. Prefers middle and lower storeys.

GREY-HEADED CANARY FLYCATCHER

Culicicapa ceylonensis Muscicapidae

Size 9 cm

Voice Vocal. High-pitched 2- or 3-syllabled calls, *whi…chichee… whi…chichee*. Longer, trilling song; also chattering notes

Range Commonly breeds in the Himalayas, 1,500-3,000 m; possibly in some of the hill forests of C India and Eastern Ghats. Common in winter over much of the subcontinent

Habitat Forests, gardens, orchards

Has ashy-grey hood, throat and breast; darker crown; squarish crest; yellow-green back and yellow rump; yellow in browner wings and tail; bright canary-yellow below breast. Sexes alike. Solitary, or in pairs, occasionally several in vicinity, especially in mixed parties; forest bird, typical flycatcher; excitedly flitting about, launching aerial sallies, calling aloud and generally on the move; wherever this bird is, its cheerful unmistakable calls are heard.

BROWN DIPPER

Cinclus pallasii Cinclidae

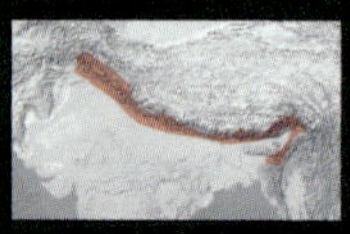

Size 20 cm

Voice Calls *dzit, dzit*. Rich song

Range Mountains throughout the region

Habitat Shallow, fast-flowing, high-altitude rocky streams; mountain lakes

Largish, uniform, dark brown dipper. Small, stocky body; grey-brown mantle, wings and tail; short, stubby tail, often cocked. Brown iris. Sexes alike. Juvenile shows some pale spotting on both upper and underparts. Solitary, in pairs, or small groups. Commonly seen in mountain streams; perches on mid-stream boulders, bobbing up and down; flies low over water; dives and swims underwater, often walking on riverbed; floats downstream briefly on emerging from water. Whirrs wings in display.

ORANGE-BELLIED LEAFBIRD

Chloropsis hardwickii Chloropseidae

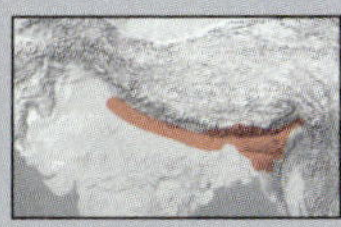

Size 20 cm

Voice Wide variety of harsh and whistling notes; mimics other birds

Range Himachal to the entire NE region

Habitat Broadleaved evergreen, deciduous forests, secondary growth

Dramatically-coloured leafbird with bright orange lower breast and belly. Bright leaf-green back; yellowish-green forehead, crown and nape; broad, iridescent blue moustachial band; blue patch over throat and chest; blue edges to outer wing-coverts, primaries, tail sides; blue shoulder-patches. Female greener; less extensive orange on undersides. Solitary, in pairs or mixed parties; arboreal; usually in canopy or upper forest storeys.

GOLDEN-FRONTED LEAFBIRD

Chloropsis aurifrons Chloropseidae

Size 19 cm

Voice Most common call a drongo or shikra-like *che… chwe*. Noisy; wide assortment of whistling notes, including imitations of several species

Range Upto about 1,600 m in Uttarakhand Himalayas; east to Bihar, Odisha, south along Eastern Ghats and up the Western Ghats and adjoining areas

Habitat Forests

Medium-sized, vivid leaf-green bird. Male has golden-orange forehead; glossy blue 'flash' on shoulder; bluish-black chin and cheeks; black lores; orangish ear-coverts, continuing as loop around blue throat. Female duller. Black chin and throat absent in juvenile; green crown. Usually in pairs; favours canopy. Hunts actively; rather aggressive, and territorial.

YELLOW-VENTED FLOWERPECKER

Dicaeum chrysorrheum Dicaeidae

Size 9 cm

Voice Call a harsh, repeated *tzreep*

Range Common breeding resident in extreme NE India to Myanmar border. Rare in Nepal and Bangladesh

Habitat Canopy of forests and orchard trees

Bright olive-green flowerpecker, heavily streaked; pale yellow underparts. Black moustache; white lores; large, decurved bill; red iris. Dark tail shows white patches; chrome-yellow undertail-coverts; olive-brown wings. Sexes alike. Feeds mainly on *Loranthus* in pairs or singly. Flies strongly, covering considerable distances to favourite feeding trees. Nests high in trees.

YELLOW-BELLIED FLOWERPECKER

Dicaeum melanoxanthum Dicaeidae

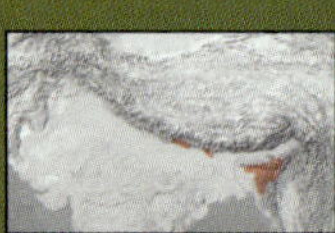

Size 13 cm

Voice Call an agitated *zit… zit…zit…zit*

Range The Himalayas from N Uttar Pradesh and from C Nepal east to Arunachal Pradesh; hills of NE India

Habitat Broadleaved forests, both open forests and clearings, edges of dense forests

Male blackish above with white patch on throat and breast; yellow underparts. Bright red iris. Female duller with olive-brown or olive-grey upperparts; belly and vent pale yellow. Both have white spots at tip of undertail. Juvenile male similar to female, but has brighter yellow underparts. Legge's similar to Yellow-bellied, but smaller, lacks dark sides to breast, and is found only in Sri Lanka.

PLAIN FLOWERPECKER

Dicaeum c minullum Dicaeidae

Size 8 cm

Voice Calls include sharp repeated *chik* and *pseep*, particularly in flight. Extended as song

Range Locally common breeding resident in N foothills from C Nepal east to Myanmar border, parts of Bangladesh, Andaman Islands

Habitat Forest canopy, orchards, gardens and mangroves

Tiny, olive-brown arboreal bird with short, dark, decurved bill. Pale supercilium and lores; yellowish-white underparts. Juvenile has paler bill. Southwestern race darker above and whiter below. Andamans' race greener above and yellowish on belly. Sexes similar. Feeds in pairs or small groups, mainly on *Loranthus* berries. Flies strongly and noisily from site to site over large area. Very lively. Nests high in trees.

PALE-BILLED FLOWERPECKER

Dicaeum erythrorynchos Dicaeidae

Rather plain-looking flowerpecker with olive-brown upperparts and uniform greyish-white underparts; pinkish flesh and yellow-brown, markedly downcurved beak. Sexes alike. Solitary, or two to three birds in canopy; frequents parasitic *Loranthus* and *Viscum;* flits from clump to clump; strictly arboreal, restless; territorial even when feeding.

Size 8 cm

Voice Call a sharp, loud *chik…chik*

Range From E Kangra along foothills to NE India; peninsular India south of a line from W Gujarat to S Bihar

Habitat Light forests, groves

ORANGE-BELLIED FLOWERPECKER

Dicaeum trigonostigma Dicaeidae

Size 9 cm

Voice Call a repeated metallic *zip.* Song a descending *tsi…si…si…si…sew*

Range Local breeding resident restricted to coastal Bangladesh and probably neighbouring parts of India

Habitat Mainly edges of forests, mangroves

Male has bluish-grey head, upper back, wings and tail; darker tail; grey throat and upper breast; orange underparts from lower mantle to rump. Female overall dull olive with dull orange undertail-coverts and belly; greyish throat and breast. Feeds mainly in canopy but also close to ground. Uneven, whirring flight between feeding sites. Very active and confiding.

♀

FIRE-BREASTED FLOWERPECKER

Dicaeum ignipectus Dicaeidae

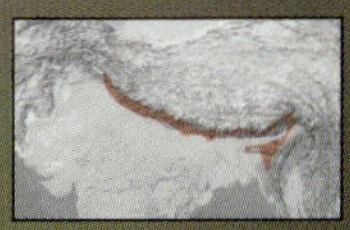

Size 7 cm

Voice Call a sharp, metallic *chip…chip* note. High-pitched, clicking song

Range The Himalayas, Kashmir to extreme E India

Habitat Forests, orchards

Male metallic blue-green-black above; buffy below with scarlet breast-patch and black stripe down centre of lower breast and belly. Female olive-green above, yellowish on rump; bright buff below; flanks and sides tinged olive. Mostly solitary; arboreal and active; flits about in foliage canopy, attending to *Loranthus* clumps; may be encountered in restless, mixed hunting bands of small birds in the Himalayan forests. Nests high in trees.

SCARLET-BACKED FLOWERPECKER

Dicaeum cruentatum Dicaeidae

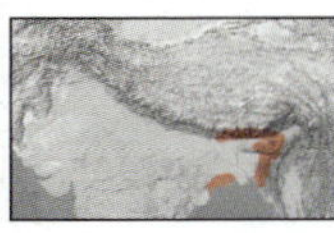

Size 7 cm

Voice Noisy. Call a penetrating *chip…chip*. Song a repeated *tissit…tissit*

Range Scarce breeding resident in N hills from E Nepal (where rare), NE India and Bangladesh

Habitat Open forests, secondary growth and orchards, wherever there is *Loranthus*

Very small flowerpecker; bright red from crown to back. Black head-sides; black cheeks; glossy blue-black upperwing; short, black tail. Greyish-white underparts; darker grey flanks. Longish, slender bill. Female brownish above and buff below with red rump and black tail. Juvenile has hint of red on uppertail-coverts and red bill. Feeds on nectar, berries and insects. Usually solitary, in pairs or small parties. Noisily flies from clump to clump high in canopy. Pouch-shaped nest high up in trees.

RUBY-CHEEKED SUNBIRD

Chalcoparia singalensis Nectariniidae

Size 11 cm

Voice Calls *chwee…eest*

Range Uttarakhand to Arunachal Pradesh; S Assam Hills

Habitat Open broadleaved evergreen forests; secondary growth

Distinctive, medium-sized sunbird with short, rather straight bill, orange throat and breast, yellow over rest of underparts. Male has iridescent emerald green upperparts; deep ruby-red lores and ear-coverts, edged below with purplish moustachial stripe. Female yellowish-olive-green above, with duller orange throat and breast and no ruby cheek; distinguished from other female sunbirds by orange breast, yellow underparts and short bill; more gregarious than other sunbirds; sometimes in small flocks when not breeding; actively forages in foliage in lower half of trees and shrubs.

PURPLE SUNBIRD

Cinnyris asiaticus Nectariniidae

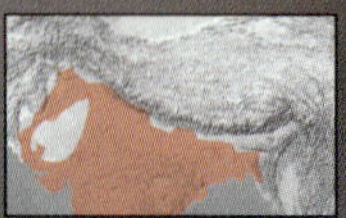

Size 10 cm

Voice Noisier than other sunbirds. Calls include loud *chweet…* notes

Range Subcontinent, south from the Himalayan foothills to about 1,500 m

Habitat Open forests, gardens, groves

Male metallic purple-blue above, and on throat and breast; dark purplish-black belly; narrow, chestnut-maroon band between breast and belly; yellow and scarlet pectoral tufts, normally hidden under wings. Female olive-brown above; pale yellow below (*zeylonica* female has whitish throat). Non-breeding male similar to female but with broad, purple-black stripe down centre of throat to belly. Solitary, or in pairs; important pollinating agent, almost always seen around flowering trees and bushes; displays amazing agility and acrobatic prowess when feeding; sometimes hunts flycatcher-style.

MRS GOULD'S SUNBIRD

Aethopyga gouldiae Nectariniidae

Size Male 15 cm; Female 10 cm

Voice Call a sharp *tzit...tzit*

Range The Himalayas, hills of NE India

Habitat Rhododendrons, forests, gardens, scrubs

♀

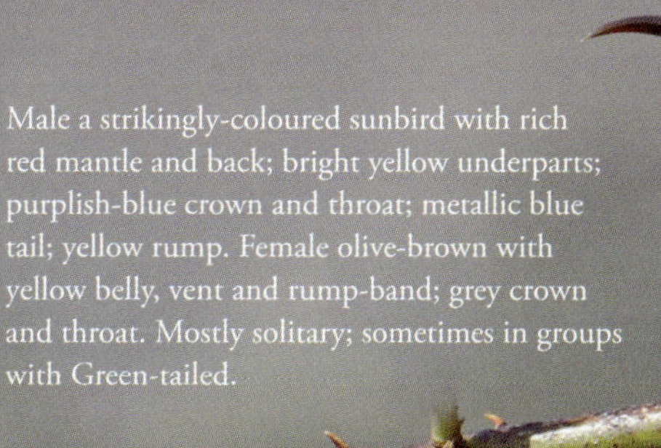

Male a strikingly-coloured sunbird with rich red mantle and back; bright yellow underparts; purplish-blue crown and throat; metallic blue tail; yellow rump. Female olive-brown with yellow belly, vent and rump-band; grey crown and throat. Mostly solitary; sometimes in groups with Green-tailed.

GREEN-TAILED SUNBIRD

Aethopyga nipalensis Nectariniidae

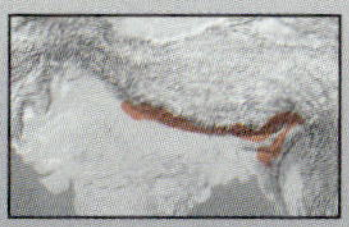

Size Male 14 cm; Female 10 cm

Voice Call a sharp *zig...zig*

Range The Himalayas

Habitat Oak and rhododendron forests, scrubs, gardens

Male has dark metallic blue-green head and nape, bordered by maroon mantle; olive-green back and wings; metallic blue-green tail (appears dark); underparts bright yellow with red-streaked breast; yellow rump not always visible. NW Himalayan race *horsfieldi* has less maroon on mantle. Female olive-green with greyish-olive throat; yellowish-olive on belly; rump slightly yellower than upperparts; pale tail-tips.

♀

BLACK-THROATED SUNBIRD

Aethopyga saturata Nectariniidae

Very dark, mainly black, crimson and greyish-olive sunbird. Distinctive male looks mostly black, with dark, iridescent purple crown, nape, malar stripe, long tail; black throat, breast, face and wings; crimson mantle and sides of neck and throat; underparts greyish-olive. Smaller female has yellow band across back, and no yellow on plain, greyish-olive-green underparts; whitish flanks; ill-defined, pale supercilium around eye; solitary, or in pairs when breeding; normally forages in flowering shrubs, bushes and low branches of trees.

♀

Size Male 15 cm; Female 10 cm

Voice Calls *tzit…tswi…ti…ti…ti…ti*

Range Hills of E Uttarakhand to Myanmar. Moves lower in winter

Habitat Edges of dense forests, scattered bushes, secondary growth, shrubs

CRIMSON SUNBIRD

Aethopyga siparaja Nectariniidae

♀

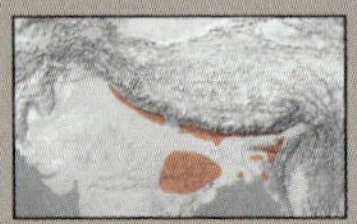

Size Male 15 cm; Female 10 cm

Voice Sharp, clicking call notes. Pleasant chirping song of breeding male (June-August)

Range The Himalayas, hills of NE India. Winters in the Himalayan plains

Habitat Forests, gardens

Male has metallic green crown and long tail; deep crimson back and neck-sides; yellow rump not commonly seen; bright scarlet chin and breast; olive-yellow belly. Female has olive plumage; yellow underparts. Solitary, or in pairs; active gymnast, hanging upside-down and sideways as it probes flowers; also hovers; moves in forests, between tall bushes and canopy.

FIRE-TAILED SUNBIRD

Aethopyga ignicauda Nectariniidae

Larger sunbird with very long, red tail streamers, uppertail-coverts of male distinctive. Male has dark purple cap, face, chin, throat; bright red nape, sides of head, neck, and mantle; yellow band on back; yellow breast and belly have orange wash; paler yellow to greyish flanks, vent; brown wings. Smaller female has olive upperparts with more brown wings; olive-yellow on rump; olive underparts; orange-yellow on centre of belly; typical sunbird; seen in small parties when not breeding.

Size Male 16 cm; Female 11 cm

Voice Calls *zizi…zizizi*

Range High mountains of Himachal Pradesh to Myanmar

Habitat Summers in open fir, pine forests; dwarf rhododendrons, junipers. Winters in broadleaved or mixed forests

LITTLE SPIDERHUNTER

Arachnothera longirostra Nectariniidae

Size 14 cm

Voice Call a high-pitched *chee… chee*. Song a loud *which… which…*, sounding somewhat like ailorbird's

Range Disjunct; found in Western Ghats and Eastern Ghats, foothills from SE Nepal eastwards, E Himalayas and much of NE states

Habitat Forests, secondary growth; nullahs, sholas

Sexes alike. Olive-green above; dark tail, tipped white; greyish-white throat, merging into yellow-white below; orangish pectoral tufts. Very long, curved beak diagnostic. Usually solitary; sometimes two or three birds in vicinity; active, moving considerably between bush and canopy; favours wild banana blossoms, clings upside-down on bracts; long, curved beak especially adapted to nectar diet.

STREAKED SPIDERHUNTER

Arachnothera magna Nectariniidae

Size 18 cm

Voice Calls include harsh chirruping; short *chik* notes

Range E Nepal to Arunachal Pradesh, Bangladesh and Assam

Habitat Wild bananas and dense undergrowth in moist deciduous and evergreen forests; secondary forests

Fairly unmistakable spiderhunter. Distinguished from Little by large size, exceptionally long bill, and streaking; dusky olive above with fine, dark streaking on face and head, broader streaking on mantle; pale, diffused eye-ring; yellowish-white underparts with bold, dark streaking, yellower vent; prominent sturdy pinkish-orange legs. Solitary, or in pairs; sometimes in mixed-species hunting flocks, moving constantly and rapidly through upper storeys of forests.

HOUSE SPARROW

Passer domesticus Passeridae

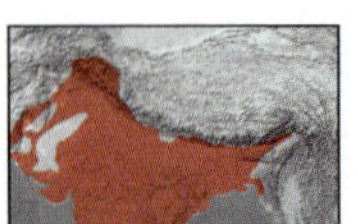

Size 15 cm

Voice Noisy; medley of chirping notes; richer notes of breeding male; double- and triple-brooded

Range Subcontinent, to about 4,000 m in the Himalayas

Habitat Habitation, cultivation

Male has grey crown and rump; chestnut sides of neck and nape; black streaks on chestnut-rufous back; black chin, centre of throat and breast; white ear-coverts. Female dull grey-brown above, streaked darker; dull whitish-brown below. Seen in small parties to large gatherings; mostly commensal on human habitation, feeds and nests in and around habitation, including most crowded localities; also feeds in cultivation; hundreds roost together.

♀

RUSSET SPARROW

Passer rutilans Passeridae

Size 15 cm

Voice Chirping notes *swee…*; Indian Robin-like call

Range The Himalayas; NE India; breeds 1,200-2,600 m, higher to about 4,000 m in NE India; descends in winter

Habitat Cultivation, edges of forests, mountain habitation

Male has rufous-chestnut upperparts streaked black on back; whitish wing-bars; black chin and centre of throat, bordered with dull yellow. Female brown above, streaked darker; pale supercilium and wing-bars; dull ash-yellow below. Gregarious mountain bird; mostly feeds on ground, picking seeds; may associate with other finches; often perches on dry branches and overhead wires.

EURASIAN TREE SPARROW

Passer montanus Passeridae

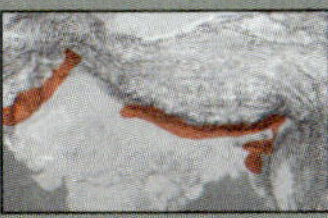

Size 14 cm

Voice Call a *chip…chip; tet…et…et… tsveet*

Range Uttarakhand east to Myanmar; S Assam Hills

Habitat Cities, towns or habitation; cultivation; village groves; orchards

Fairly distinctive sparrow; distinguished from all other *Passer* species by prominent black spots on white ear-coverts, white collar between nape and mantle, cinnamon-chestnut crown; black lores and small throat-patch; darkly streaked, buff-brown upperparts; warm rufous-brown wing panel; two well-defined wing-bars; female slightly paler, with smaller throat and ear-covert-patches; buff-washed flanks; racial variations; gregarious.

WHITE-WINGED SNOWFINCH

Montifringilla nivalis Passeridae

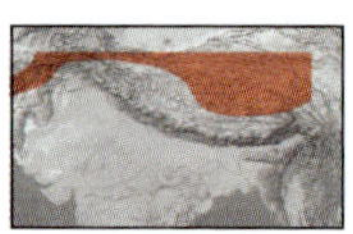

Size 17 cm

Voice Creaky calls. Chattering song, trills

Range Local winter visitor; fairly common in the Gilgit main valley

Habitat Dry stony ground in mountain regions, especially near cliffs

Large, rotund finch with snowy-white underparts and slaty-grey head. Rich brown mantle, scapulars and upper back with pale brown edges to feathers; lower back, rump and uppertail-coverts sooty grey, edged black; long tail with black central feathers and white outer feathers tipped black. Black wings with large, white wing panels, and white-edged black tail seen in flight. Breeding male has more black bill and black bib. Sexes alike. In pairs, or small flocks in breeding and very large flocks outside.

TIBETAN SNOWFINCH

Montifringilla adamsi Passeridae

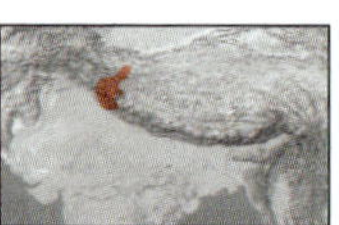

Size 17 cm

Voice Calls include hard *pink… pink* and soft mewing

Range Breeding resident in N Himalayas at higher altitudes above 3,600 m

Habitat High-altitude scrubs, meadows, rocky bushy slopes, hillsides

Sexes alike. Dull grey-brown above with some streaking on back (less pronounced in juvenile and fresh plumage); blackish wings with white-panel in wing-coverts; male has greyish-black bib (not usually seen in female); breeding male has black bill; in flight, shows obvious white wing-patch; white tail with black central feathers and narrow, black terminal band. Gregarious and often seen in large flocks or around human habitation. Runs on ground like a lark. Swift, undulating flight. Courtship flight particularly impressive.

WHITE-RUMPED SNOWFINCH

Onychostruthus taczanowskii Passeridae

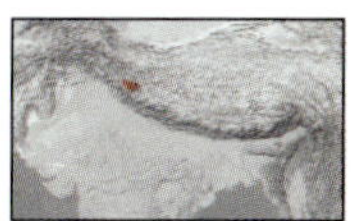

Size 17 cm

Voice Simple, weak song of clipped notes, asthmatic *wheezes* and more pleasant whistles

Range Winter visitor; N Himalayas in Ladakh, N Sikkim and NW Nepal and N India

Habitat Stony plateaux in Tibetan steppe country

Sexes alike. Forehead and supercilium to nape and hindneck whitish-buff; grey crown and nape; black lores become thin, dark eye-stripe behind eye. Pale greyish upperparts, streaked mantle and scapulars; white throat; white on sides of tail and diffused white-panel at base of secondaries and inner primaries. Pale stout. Yellow bill darkly tipped. White rump, conspicuous in flight. Juvenile warmer brown on mantle and wings with buffish breast.

RUFOUS-NECKED SNOWFINCH

Pyrgilauda ruficollis Passeridae

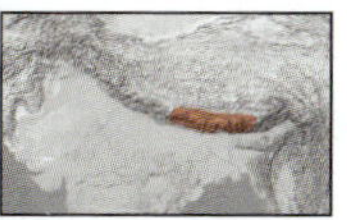

Size 15 cm

Voice Song an erratic repetition of simple sparrow-like notes, *dishu…tchelu…tischu…delu*

Range N Himalayas in N Nepal, N Sikkim and Darjeeling, West Bengal

Habitat Barren, stony Tibetan steppe and grassy plateaux

Distinctive. White face and forehead; black lores; white cheeks with long, dark moustachial stripe; rich chestnut rear ear-coverts, neck-sides. Overall light brown with darker streaks on mantle and scapulars; two prominent white wing-bars. Chin, throat, breast to belly and flanks white. Small, pointed black bill; black legs. Confiding. In small flocks, outside breeding season. Weak flight.

BLANFORD'S SNOWFINCH

Pyrgilauda blanfordi Passeridae

Size 15 cm

Voice Poorly described; flocks give rapid, twittering calls on ground and in flight

Range Tibetan steppe country

Habitat Winter visitor to Pakistan, N Nepal, N Sikkim, near Darjeeling, West Bengal and Ladakh

Sexes alike. Whitish forehead to forecrown; black spur from base of bill to forecrown; black lores; thin eye-stripe across ear-coverts; pale brown supercilium; white cheeks and ear-coverts. Light brown mantle, back and scapulars. Chin, upper throat black; rest of underparts creamy-white. Brown central tail feathers; outer feathers blotched grey with black tips. Dark, conical bill. Juvenile duller with no head pattern. Silent and confiding. Very sparrow-like behaviour. Plainer than juvenile Rufous-necked and has white cheeks.

WHITE-RUMPED MUNIA

Lonchura striata Estrildidae

Size 10 cm

Voice Call a weak up and down twittering

Range Foothills of Uttarakhand to Arunachal Pradesh; Bangladesh

Habitat Light wooded areas, scrubs, fields, grasslands

Slim, dark munia with short, thick, conical beak; dark brown head, throat, upper breast, mantle, wings, tail, vent, with shaft streaking; white patch on lower back; white belly; short, wedge-shaped tail. *Acuticauda* of the Himalayan foothills of N India, Nepal, Bhutan and NE subcontinent has more rufous brown on face, neck, breast. In small family parties when breeding; otherwise, larger flocks; communal rooster; usually associated with other munias and weavers. Forages on ground or on stalks and stems of seed-bearing grass and crops.

ALPINE ACCENTOR

Prunella collaris Prunellidae

juvenile

Size 17 cm

Voice Calls *chirrirrip*. Mellow song

Range High mountains from Pakistan to Arunachal Pradesh

Habitat High-altitude scree, moraine; alpine pastures. Mountain villages in winter

Largest accentor with unmarked grey head, nape, upper mantle, sides of neck and throat, breast, centre of belly; white throat-patch with fine, black barring; thin, pale supercilium mark; buff and brown streaked mantle; black wing-covert panel with white tips; diffused rufous-chestnut streaking on flanks, wings; rufous-chestnut uppertail-coverts; darkly streaked undertail-coverts; forages on ground on rocky or grassy slopes.

ALTAI ACCENTOR

Prunella himalayana Prunellidae

Size 16 cm

Voice Calls *tee…tee*

Range Winter visitor. The Himalayas

Habitat Grassy slopes

Superficially resembles House Sparrow with its back streaked brown, but adult has grey head and red-brown spotting on underparts. Has an insectivore's finely pointed bill. Sexes similar, though male may be contrasted in appearance. Juvenile has more brown head and underparts.

ROBIN ACCENTOR

Prunella rubeculoides Prunellidae

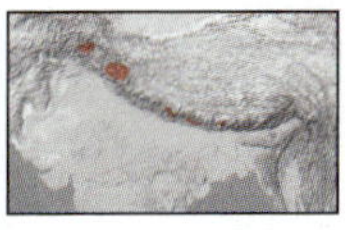

Size 17 cm

Voice Call a sharp trilling note; also, *tszi…tszi…* . Short, chirping song

Range Higher reaches of the Himalayas; breeds 3,200-5,300 m; descends in winter to about 2,000 m, rarely below 1,500 m

Habitat Tibetan facies; damp grass, scrubs; high-altitude habitation

Sexes alike. Pale brown above, streaked darker on back; grey head and throat; two whitish wing-bars; rufous breast and creamy-white belly; streaks on flanks. Flocks in winter, occasionally, along with other accentors, pipits and sparrows; rather tame and confiding around high-altitude habitation; hops on ground; flies into bushes if intruded upon beyond a point.

BROWN ACCENTOR

Prunella fulvescens Prunellidae

Size 15 cm

Voice Call a thin *zit…zit…zit*; also, thin rattle

Range Locally common breeding resident at or above treeline in N mountains from E Pakistan to Nepal. Moves lower in winter

Habitat Montane scrubs. Around fallow and villages in winter

Small, pale brown-and-buff accentor with prominent white supercilium and black cheeks. Crown and upperparts streaked light brown. Rich buff from chin to vent, usually completely unstreaked. Sexes alike. Feeds on ground in pairs or small groups on invertebrates and seeds. Unobtrusive. Nests on or near ground.

RUFOUS-BREASTED ACCENTOR

Prunella strophiata Prunellidae

Size 15 cm

Voice Calls include sharp, trilling notes; also, *twitt…twitt…* . Short, chirping song

Range The Himalayas; breeds between 2,700-5,000 m; descends to about 1,200 m in summer, rarely below 600 m

Habitat Montane scrub, high-altitude habitation; descends lower in winter

Sexes alike. Small chestnut-and-brown accentor; heavily streaked throat; brown-streaked crown and upperparts; orange supercilium with white in front of eyes and buffy-white moustache.

BLACK-THROATED ACCENTOR

Prunella atrogularis Prunellidae

Size 15 cm

Voice Call a soft *trrrt*

Range Locally common winter visitor to foothills of N mountains from E Pakistan to W Nepal

Habitat Bushes, dry scrub and orchards

Small, streaked accentor with black throat, cheeks and crown-sides. Similar to Brown but much brighter and more heavily streaked above and brighter orange-buff below with some streaking. Supercilium and moustache orange-buff. Black throat, sometimes obscured. Sexes alike. Confiding but unobtrusive, although will perch on bush-tops. Feeds on ground, on invertebrates and seeds, in loose groups, often with other passerines.

MAROON-BACKED ACCENTOR

Prunella immaculata Prunellidae

Size 15 cm

Voice Calls *zeh…dzit*

Range Scarce; presumed breeding resident in N mountains from C Nepal east to Arunachal Pradesh. Moves lower in winter

Habitat Ground beneath rhododendrons, coniferous forest undergrowth, edges of forests, nearby cultivation

Small, dark, uniquely-coloured accentor with white iris. Grey head, breast and wing panel with white scaling on crown. Maroon-brown upperparts and belly, darker on wings and tail. Pale legs. Sexes alike. Juvenile heavily streaked. Feeds on invertebrates and seeds on ground. Difficult to observe. Usually in small parties. Nest not known.

CITRINE WAGTAIL

Motacilla citreola Motacillidae

Size 17 cm

Voice Ordinary call note a wheezy *tzzeep*

Range Winter visitor over most of India

Habitat Marshes, wet cultivation, edges of jheels

♀

Grey back; diagnostic yellow head, sides of face, complete underbody; white in dark wings. The race *calcarata* has deep black back and rump; yellow of head may be paler in female; plumage of races often confusing. Sociable, often with other wagtails; shows marked preference for damp areas; sometimes moves on floating vegetation on pond surfaces; either walks cautiously or makes short dashes.

♂ *calcarata*

♂ *calcarata*

♂ *citreola*

YELLOW WAGTAIL

Motacilla flava Motacillidae

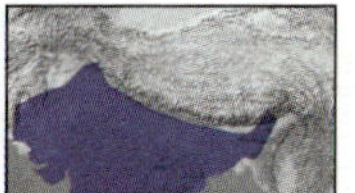

Size 17 cm

Voice Calls include *swee…ip; zhrreep*

Range Lowlands throughout the region. Said to be absent in Bhutan

Habitat Marshy pastures; flooded fields; edges of waterbodies

Very variable, mainly greenish-and-yellow wagtail; many races and hybrids occur; only wagtail with olive-green or brownish mantle, back, and rump (brownish-backed Forest Wagtail has unmistakable wing, breast pattern). Relatively shorter tail; yellow underparts, vent (Citrine has white vent); two wing-bars. Breeding male has greenish-yellow to dark grey crown and ear-coverts. Non-breeding and female brownish with straight, pale supercilium (Citrine has curved); whitish or yellow-washed underparts; very gregarious in winter; less undulating wagtail flight.

beema

lutea

thunbergi

taivana

feldegg

superciliaris

WHITE WAGTAIL

Motacilla alba Motacillidae

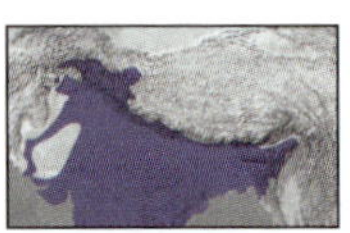

Size 18 cm

Voice Calls include *chee…cheep; cheesik*

Range Throughout the region

Habitat Summers in upland meadows or open areas near streams. Winters in wet fields; often near water

Very variable, black, white and/or grey wagtail; for purposes of ID, races characterised as black-backed or grey-backed; all the several races of White have white foreheads. Breeding bird has extensive black on throat and/or breast. Non-breeding adult generally has white throat; variable wing pattern. Solitary, or in pairs when breeding; sometimes in loose, scattered flocks; communal rooster. Forages on ground; sits prominently on exposed perches; calls while perched, in flight, or on ground.

alba

baicalensis

alboides

personata

dukhunensis

ocularis

leucopsis

WHITE-BROWED WAGTAIL

Motacilla maderaspatensis Motacillidae

Size 21 cm

Voice Call a sharp *tzizit* or *cheezit*. . . . Pleasant whistling song of breeding male

Range Most of India; south of the Himalayan foothills to about 1,200 m; only resident wagtail in the Indian plains, breeding upto 2,000 m in peninsula mountains

Habitat Rocky streams, rivers, ponds, tanks; may enter wet cultivation

Black above; prominent white supercilium and large wing-band; black throat and breast; white below. Female usually more brown, male black. Mostly in pairs, though small parties may feed together in winter; bird of flowing waters, especially fond of rock-strewn rivers. Feeds at edges of water, frequently wags tail; also rides on ferry boats plying rivers.

GREY WAGTAIL

Motacilla cinerea Motacillidae

Size 19 cm

Voice Call a sharp *tzitsi*. . ., uttered on the wing. Pleasant song and display flight of breeding male

Range Breeds in the Himalayas, from N Balochistan east to Nepal, 1,200-4,300 m; winters from foothills south throughout India

Habitat Rocky mountain streams in summer. Open areas, forest clearings, watersides in winter

breeding

Breeding male grey above with white supercilium; brownish wings with yellow-white band; yellow-green at base of tail; blackish tail with white outer-tail feathers; black throat and white malar stripe; yellow below. Wintering male and female have whitish throat (sometimes mottled black in breeding female); paler yellow below. Mostly solitary, or in pairs; typical wagtail, feeds on ground, incessantly wags tail; settles on house roofs and overhead wires.

BLYTH'S PIPIT

Anthus godlewskii Motacillidae

Size 17 cm

Voice Calls include buzzing *spzeeu* and *chup…chup*

Range Probably widespread and fairly common winter visitor to most of Indian plains, but identification problems make status uncertain. Very rare in Pakistan and Sri Lanka; rare in Bangladesh and Nepal

Habitat Short, open grasslands, cultivation, fallow and marshes; similar to Paddyfield's, wetter than Tawny and drier than Richard's, although all four can occur together

Similar to Richard's, but has shorter bill, tail, legs and hind claws; also, more buff below. Adult has squared centres to median coverts. Penultimate outer-tail feathers have white edges. Powerful flight. Feeds in loose groups, on ground, on insects and seeds. Can be rather furtive.

TREE PIPIT

Anthus trivialis Motacillidae

Size 15 cm

Voice Call a sibilant, piercing *beeze*, usually louder than Olive-backed's. Loud trilling song

Range Local breeding summer visitor to N mountains from Pakistan to Himachal Pradesh. Winters widely in lowlands except extreme S and E India. Commonest in N and C areas. Vagrant to Bangladesh. Unknown in Sri Lanka

Habitat Breeds on grassy mountain slopes. Winters in open wooded areas, cultivation and village margins with trees

haringtoni

trivialis

Small, brown pipit, heavily streaked above, especially crown, though rump plain. Buffish edgings to wing feathers and buff-washed breast and flanks, white belly. Indistinct whitish lores and supercilium. Sometimes shows white spots on ear-coverts. Pink legs and bill base. Horizontal stance.

OLIVE-BACKED PIPIT

Anthus hodgsoni Motacillidae

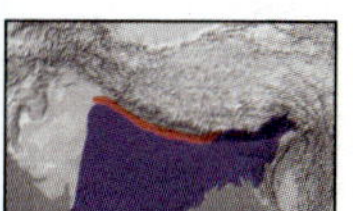

Size 15 cm

Voice Call a faint *tseep*... . Lark-like song of breeding male

Range Breeds in the Himalayas, east from W Himachal Pradesh; above 2,700 m, to timberline; winters in foothills and almost across India, except arid NW, Kutch

Habitat Forests, grassy slopes

Sexes alike. Olive-brown above, streaked dark brown; dull white supercilium, two wing-bars; pale buff-white below, profusely streaked dark brown on entire breast and flanks. Gregarious in winter; spends considerable time on ground, runs briskly; if disturbed, flies with *tseep*... calls into trees; descends in few minutes.

ROSY PIPIT

Anthus roseatus Motacillidae

Size 15 cm

Voice Call a short, thin *seep*... *seep*

Range Common breeding summer visitor to N mountains from Pakistan east to Arunachal Pradesh. Winters in N plains south to Rajasthan, Odisha and Bangladesh

Habitat Breeds in high-altitude meadows. Winters in marshes and damp cultivation

In non-breeding, plumage has heavy, black streaks on greyish-olive upperparts and heavily streaked breast. Prominent buff supercilium, white eye-ring, black eye-stripe and moustache. Greenish-olive wash to wing feather edges. Light pinkish wash on underparts when breeding. Similar to Red-throated.

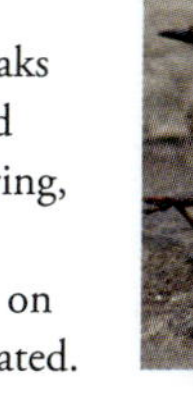

UPLAND PIPIT

Anthus sylvanus Motacillidae

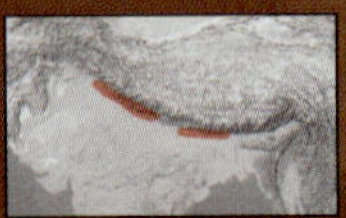

Size 17 cm

Voice Calls include short *chirp* and *zip...zip*. Double whistling song *wee...chee...wee...chee*

Range Locally common breeding resident in N foothills from Pakistan east to West Bengal, including Nepal. Moves lower down in winter

Habitat Open woodlands, scrubby grassy slopes and abandoned cultivation

Large, heavily streaked pipit with short, broad bill. Dark buff or grey-brown with very heavy, blackish streaking on upperparts and breast. Prominent buff supercilium, blackish lores and moustache. Pink legs. Thin, pointed tail feathers. Flicks tail. Feeds solitary or in pairs, on invertebrates and seeds on ground. Often rather furtive but will perch prominently, particularly when singing.

COMMON CHAFFINCH

Fringilla coelebs Fringillidae

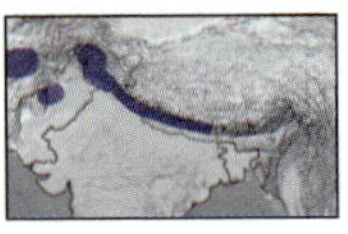

Size 16 cm

Voice Calls *chink*. Strong voice

Range Rare winter visitor to hills of Pakistan and N India

Habitat Open woodlands

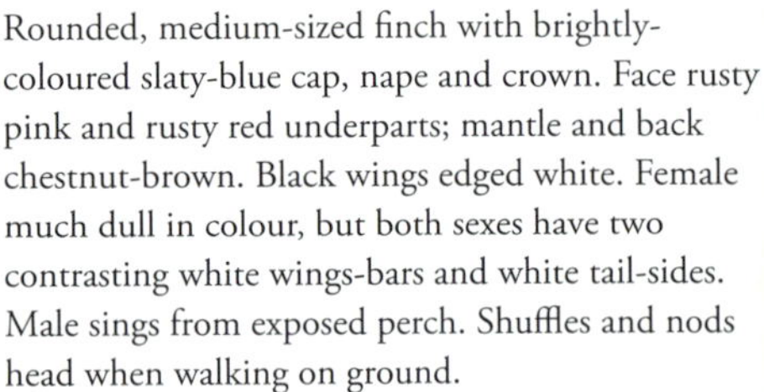

Rounded, medium-sized finch with brightly-coloured slaty-blue cap, nape and crown. Face rusty pink and rusty red underparts; mantle and back chestnut-brown. Black wings edged white. Female much dull in colour, but both sexes have two contrasting white wings-bars and white tail-sides. Male sings from exposed perch. Shuffles and nods head when walking on ground.

♀

BRAMBLING

Fringilla montifringilla Fringillidae

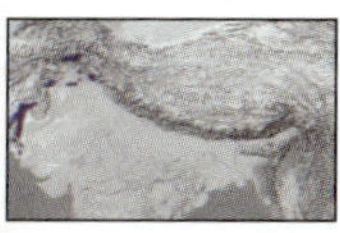

Size 16 cm

Voice Call a loud *zweee*

Range Rare winter visitor to hills of Pakistan and N India

Habitat High-altitude fields

Distinctive-looking bird, particularly in breeding. Black head, nape, cheeks, mantle and upper back; rusty orange scapulars; sooty-grey uppertail-coverts; orange breast and white belly. Jet-black tail. Female similar to non-breeding male but more brown rather than black. In pairs, or small parties. Strong, undulating flight. Feeds on ground, but makes frequent forays into trees.

RED-FRONTED SERIN

Serinus pusillus Fringillidae

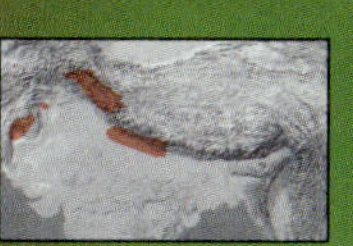

Size 12 cm

Voice Pleasant twittering *chrr… chrr*; faint *tree…tree…* call note

Range W Himalayas, extreme west to Uttarakhand

Habitat Rocky, bush-covered mountainsides

juvenile

Small finch with bright scarlet-orange forehead. Blackish-grey crown; buffy back streaked dark; yellow-orange rump and shoulder; yellow wing edges and whitish wing-bars; sooty-brown underparts; dull yellow-buff belly and flanks, streaked brown. Female similar, but has duller and smaller patch of red on forehead. Gregarious and active; feeds on flower-heads and on ground; drinks and bathes often; spends considerable time in bushes and low trees.

TIBETAN SERIN

Serinus thibetanus Fringillidae

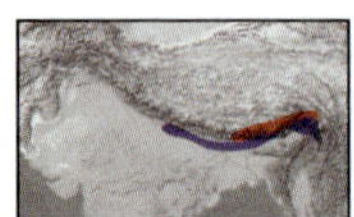

Size 12 cm

Voice Call a wheezy *twang*

Range C and E Himalayas

Habitat Temperate forests

Adult male has bright olive crown, olive-greenish upperparts, yellow underparts, yellowish-green rump, yellow supercilium and border behind ear-coverts. Wing and tail feathers broadly differentiated by yellowish-green colour. Female has black streaking on darker greyish-green upperparts, more clearly defined wing-bars and paler, yellowish throat and black-flanked breast with streaking. Juvenile duller green, tinged brownish-buff on upperparts, with duller rump, buff fringes to greater coverts and heavily streaked underparts.

EURASIAN SISKIN

Carduelis spinus Fringillidae

Size 12 cm

Voice Call a wheezy *toolee*

Range Vagrant to Nepal and N India

Habitat Coniferous forests

Male black from forehead to hindcrown with long, yellow supercilium beginning above eye and extending behind ear-coverts and neck-sides. Narrow, black eye-stripe; olive-green lores, cheeks and ear-coverts. Lower nape, back mantle and scapulars, deep olive-green; bright yellow rump. Short, notched tail. Black median coverts broadly-tipped with greenish-yellow; greater coverts also black-tipped, pale green. Underparts yellow around chin and breast turning greenish towards belly. Female overall greenish-brown; duller supercilium; heavily streaked upperparts and dull yellow underparts. Gregarious. In mixed feeding parties with other finches. Undulating flight. Feeds high in trees.

BLACK-HEADED GREENFINCH

Carduelis ambigua Fringillidae

Size 12 cm

Voice Call a thin, high-pitched, metallic twitter

Range NE Arunachal Pradesh

Habitat High-altitude fields

Male has diagnostic black head and yellow base to primaries and secondaries forming broad panel across wing; dull greenish nape and mantle; greenish rump and grey uppertail-coverts; yellow sides to base of tail. Underparts olive-green, mottled yellow towards throat; pale belly and thighs; pale yellow undertail-coverts. Female has brownish-grey crown and mantle, with indistinct dark streaking; grey ear-coverts. Juvenile overall buff-brown and darkly streaked; bright yellow in wings and yellow underparts streaked brown.

YELLOW-BREASTED GREENFINCH

Carduelis spinoides Fringillidae

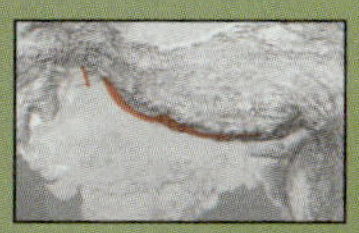

Size 14 cm

Voice Noisy. Calls include *tzweee…* and *weeee…chu.* Also twitters and extends calls into song, often uttered in flight

Range Locally common breeding resident in N mountains from Pakistan to Myanmar border. Moves lower down in winter

Habitat Edges of forests, cultivation, meadows, gardens and scrubs

Medium-sized finch with bright yellow forehead, lores and stout, pink bill; yellow supercilium extends below eye and around cheeks; greenish-black sub-moustachial stripe. Upperparts blackish-brown with olive-brown mantle. Yellow bars on wings, rump and base of tail. Female duller. Prefers trees. In small flocks. Feeds on seeds, berries and sometimes insects. Active and sometimes confiding. Undulating flight. Nests in trees.

EUROPEAN GOLDFINCH

Carduelis carduelis Fringillidae

Size 13 cm

Voice Ordinary call note a somewhat liquid *witwit…witwit…*

Range The Himalayas, extreme west to around C Nepal

Habitat Open coniferous forests, orchards, cultivation, scrubs

juvenile

Distinctive-looking bird with bright crimson forehead; black lores; greyish-brown upperparts with large, white rump-patch; black-and-yellow wings striking, at rest and in flight. Sexes alike. Juvenile has streaked upperparts. Sociable; flock size ranges from four to several dozen together, sometimes along with other finches; forages on ground; also attends to flower-heads; undulating, somewhat dancing flight.

TWITE

Carduelis flavirostris Fringillidae

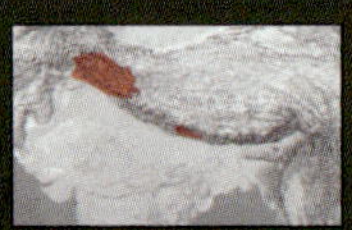

Size 13 cm

Voice Calls include nasal, drawn-out *tweet* and twittering *ditoo…di…dowit*

Range Locally common breeding resident from N Pakistan east to N Nepal. Moves lower down in winter

Habitat Dry, open, montane, stony plateaux and scrubby slopes above treeline

Medium-sized bird with dark brown crown and forehead; plain, buff supercilium and face. Streaked brown upperparts, breast and flanks; pinkish rump; whitish wing-bars and whitish edges to flight and tail feathers. Often spotted in flocks mixed with other passerines; undulating, erratic flight. Deeply notched tail. Feeds on ground on seeds and invertebrates. Often in flocks with other ground feeders. Nests low down. Perches on rocks and low bushes.

EURASIAN LINNET

Carduelis cannabina Fringillidae

Size 13 cm

Voice Call a dry *teet...eet... eet...eet*

Range Erratic winter visitor to N Pakistan and Kashmir hills. Vagrant elsewhere in N India and Nepal

Habitat Open stony country and fallow

Male has crimson forehead and creamy-beige lower forehead. Grey face, head and neck; cinnamon-brown back and scapulars; back and rump paler; black uppertail-coverts have whitish tips; deeply notched tail, pale creamy chin and breast streaked brown; crimson breast in breeding season. Female grey-brown, streaked brown with greyer head; creamy-white rump. Feeds on ground on seeds and invertebrates; perches on bushes and trees. In flocks with other seed-eaters. Fast, undulating flight.

PLAIN MOUNTAIN FINCH

Leucosticte nemoricola Fringillidae

Grey-brown upperparts streaked dark brown; greyer on rump; pale-buffy bar and markings in dark brown wings; dull grey-brown below, streaked more brown on breast-sides and flanks. Finches with plenty of white in wings, and generally found in the high Tibetan country of the Himalayas, are snowfinches. Sexes alike. Gregarious; good-sized flocks on ground, amidst stones; sometimes associates with other finches and buntings; calls often when feeding.

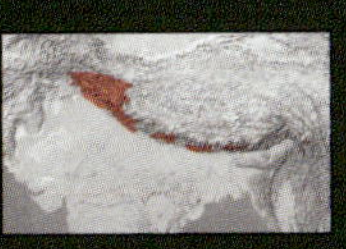

Size 15 cm

Voice Twittering and chattering notes, rather Sparrow-like in tone; calls frequently

Range High Himalayas, breeds between 3,200-4,800 m (above timberline); descends in winter, occasionally to as low as 1,000 m

Habitat Open meadows, dwarf scrub, cultivation

BRANDT'S MOUNTAIN FINCH

Leucosticte brandti Fringillidae

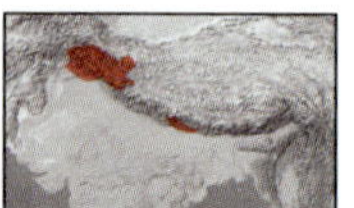

Size 18 cm

Voice Call a *twitt...twitt...twee... ti...ti...it...peek...peek.* Also, *churrs*

Range Locally common breeding resident in N mountains from N Pakistan east to Sikkim. Moves lower down in winter

Habitat Stony slopes and montane meadows, favours edges of snowmelt

Male has sooty grey forehead and crown with grey nape and ash-brown mantle. Upperparts a mix of shades from dark grey to brown; tail tipped whitish; rump washed pink. Underparts pale grey graduating to buff around belly. In non-breeding season, head more brown. Female similar to male, but duller. Juvenile paler with dark wing edging. In pairs, or flocks. Feeds on seeds and invertebrates.

SPECTACLED FINCH

Callacanthis burtoni Fringillidae

Size 18 cm

Voice Call a loud whistle

Range Resident; the Himalayas

Habitat Open mixed forests

♀

Reddish-brown bird with diagnostic broad, red or yellow around eye. Male has red forehead and lores; crown, nape and neck-sides finely streaked with grey; black wings have distinct white tips. Ash-brown chin; black throat, mottled scarlet towards breast. Female more olive-brown with paler head with yellow 'spectacles', olive-brown mantle, and buffish-brown underparts with yellowish wash to breast. Juvenile has buff eye-patch. In pairs, or small flocks; shy, keeps to undergrowth.

MONGOLIAN FINCH

Eremopsaltria mongolica Fringillidae

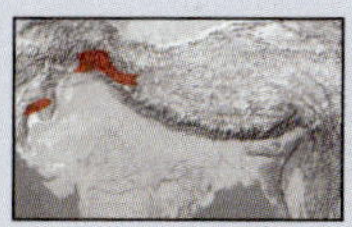

Size 15 cm

Voice Call a loud, liquid *djou*. Measured *do mi sol mi* song

Range Locally common breeding resident in N Pakistan and Ladakh. Moves lower down and, rarely, east to Nepal in winter. Rather nomadic

Habitat Dry stony and gravely hillsides

♀

Plain-looking, medium-sized finch with stout, yellow bill. Forehead and upper crown sandy grey-brown; pale beige eye-ring; faded pink lores and supercilium. Upperparts streaked beige; black-edged pink and white in wings and tail. Black eyes and brown legs. Breeding male has pink supercilium and flanks. Female has pale buff supercilium and underparts. Feeds on seeds on ground and low growth. Usually in pairs, or small parties. Confiding. Strong, bounding flight, particularly to water sources. Nests on ground.

BLANFORD'S ROSEFINCH

Carpodacus rubescens Fringillidae

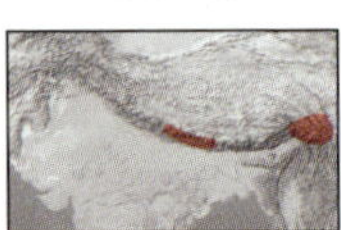

Size 15 cm

Voice Calls *sip...sip*

Range C and E Himalayas

Habitat Meadows in mixed forests

Male has bright crimson head and deeper crimson upperparts. Unstreaked, pinkish-red underparts; crimson double wing-bars; dusky lores; chin, throat and lower breast lighter pinkish-red; rump and uppertail-coverts reddish-crimson with slightly paler edges. Dark brown tail with crimson edging, slightly notched. Female has reddish-brown crown; unstreaked underparts and plain khaki-brown upperparts. Juvenile similar to female. Feeds on ground.

DARK-BREASTED ROSEFINCH

Carpodacus nipalensis Fringillidae

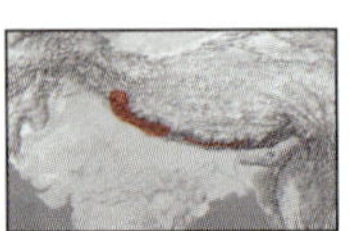

Size 17 cm

Voice Twittering, churring, monotonous chipping song

Range Kashmir to Arunachal Pradesh

Habitat Oak, rhododendrons, fir forests; alpine pastures, shrubberies; grassy slopes; clearings; fields

♀

Dark rosefinch with brown upperparts washed with crimson; slender bill; dark brownish-maroon mantle, wings, flanks, breast-band, rump; broad eye-stripe; rose-pink forehead, forecrown, supercilium, throat, belly; diffusely streaked mantle; pale scaling on undertail-coverts. Female darker than most female rosefinches; unstreaked underparts; two buffish wing-bars, tips to tertials; paler throat; normally lacks supercilium; streaked mantle. In pairs, or small flocks. Feeds on ground, bushes, trees; wary.

BEAUTIFUL ROSEFINCH

Carpodacus pulcherrimus Fringillidae

Size 14 cm

Voice Calls *trip, trillip* or *cheet cheet*

Range Very local breeding resident in N mountains from Uttarakhand east to Arunachal Pradesh (where the only recent Indian records come from). Common in Nepal. Moves lower down in winter

Habitat Scrubs, above treeline in summer. Often near cultivation in winter

Medium-sized rosefinch with broad, pale pink supercilium. Pinkish-brown upperparts darkly streaked; upper forehead, nape and crown greyish-streaked with dark brown; dark eye-stripe and dark brown around base of pale bill; pink, unstreaked rump. Female has heavily brown-streaked white underparts. Feeds on seeds and buds on ground or in low bushes. In small groups, or pairs. Sits quietly, especially after being disturbed. Nests low down.

♀

COMMON ROSEFINCH

Carpodacus erythrinus Fringillidae

Size 15 cm

Voice Call a double-noted, questioning, *twee…ee*. Rather quiet in winter. Pleasant song of upto 8 notes; may sing before departure from wintering grounds

Range Breeds in the Himalayas, 2,700-4,000 m; winters over most of India

Habitat Cultivation, open forests, gardens, bushes

♀

non-breeding

Grey-brown finch streaked red. Bright red head and breast; dark eye-stripe; brown wing panel washed crimson; rump and underbody crimson, fading into dull rose-white belly; brown, notched tail. Female buff-brown above, streaked dark; two pale wing-bars; dull buff below, streaked, except on belly. In small flocks; feeds on bushes and crops; often descends to ground; associates with other birds.

breeding

PINK-BROWED ROSEFINCH

Carpodacus rodochroa Fringillidae

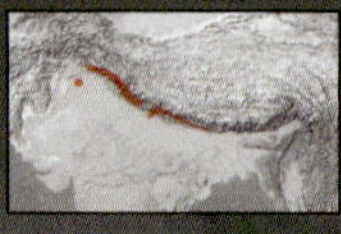

Size 15 cm

Voice Calls include *swe…eet perle* and *chew…eee*

Range Locally common breeding resident in N mountains from N Pakistan east to Nepal. Moves lower down in winter

Habitat Open forests and scrubs. Winters in oak forests and scrubs, sometimes near villages

Bright pink rosefinch with distinct broad, pink supercilium. Male has dark-streaked, pinkish-brown upperparts; unstreaked, reddish-brown crown with pink wing-bars. Dark crimson-brown eye-stripe; pink rump. Underparts uniformly dark pink with indistinct streaking. Female has whitish supercilium; heavily streaked rusty-buff, above and below; whitish throat streaked brown, unstreaked rump. In small flocks in non-breeding season. Forages in low bushes or on ground.

♀

DARK-RUMPED ROSEFINCH

Carpodacus edwardsii Fringillidae

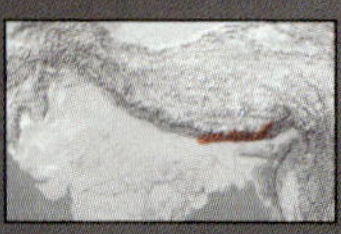

Size 17 cm

Voice Calls include sharp *twink* and *chreewee*

Range Scarce breeding resident in N mountains from C Nepal east to Arunachal Pradesh. Moves lower down in winter

Habitat Montane scrubs

♀

Male has dark brown forehead, crown and nape; distinct pink supercilium; dark pink lores; pale pink cheeks and lower ear-coverts; indistinct pink wing-bars and reddish-brown lower breast-band; brown rump; dark brown tail, slightly notched. Female paler and more streaked below with buff wing-bars. Solitary, in pairs or small parties. Skulks; shy. Feeds on rhododendrons, bushes close to ground, on seeds and nectar. Nest not known.

THREE-BANDED ROSEFINCH

Carpodacus trifasciatus Fringillidae

Size 20 cm

Voice Unknown

Range Vagrant

Habitat Temperate forests

Male has white forehead edged crimson, dark grey, red-tinged upperparts; red rump, black tail and wings. Sides of neck, crown and nape very dark, almost black. Cheeks, lores and ear-coverts black with crimson edges; throat and chin brownish-black; darkish wing panel with white wing-bars. Female overall deep grey, streaked with black; yellowish-brown throat. Underparts, breast and flanks white. Black tail. Juvenile similar to adult female but overall darker brown. Feeds on ground, mostly on seeds and in bushes. Seen hopping on ground.

SPOT-WINGED ROSEFINCH

Carpodacus rodopeplus Fringillidae

Size 16 cm

Voice Calls include *chirp* and *schwee*

Range Very local breeding resident in N mountains from Himachal Pradesh east to Arunachal Pradesh. Rare in India, less so in Nepal

Habitat Rhododendron shrubs and meadows, bamboo thickets in winter

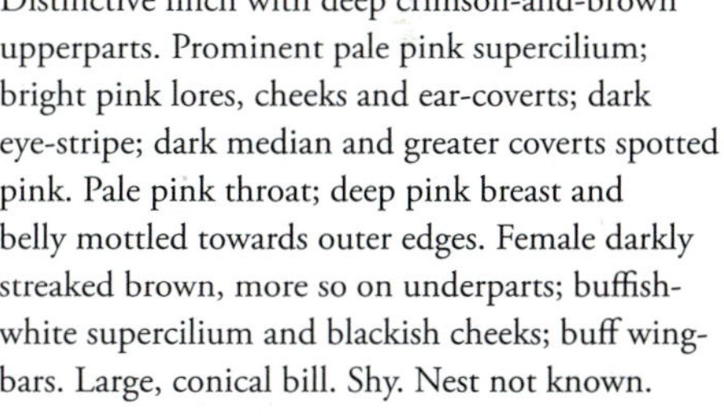

Distinctive finch with deep crimson-and-brown upperparts. Prominent pale pink supercilium; bright pink lores, cheeks and ear-coverts; dark eye-stripe; dark median and greater coverts spotted pink. Pale pink throat; deep pink breast and belly mottled towards outer edges. Female darkly streaked brown, more so on underparts; buffish-white supercilium and blackish cheeks; buff wing-bars. Large, conical bill. Shy. Nest not known.

♀

WHITE-BROWED ROSEFINCH

Carpodacus thura Fringillidae

Size 17 cm

Voice Calls often when feeding on ground, a fairly loud *pupuepipi*…

Range The Himalayas, breeds at 3,000-4,000 m; winters to about 1,800 m

Habitat Treeline forests, fir, juniper, rhododendrons; open mountainsides and bushes in winter

Male rich brown above, streaked blackish; pink-and-white forehead and deep pink supercilium; dark eye-stripe; rose-pink rump and double wing-bars. Underparts uniformly pale pink; brownish flanks. Female streaked brown; broad, whitish supercilium and single wing-bar; yellow rump; buffy below, streaked. White in supercilium easily identifies this species. In small flocks, either by themselves or with other finches; mostly feeds on ground, but settles on bushes and small trees.

♀

RED-MANTLED ROSEFINCH

Carpodacus rhodochlamys Fringillidae

Size 18 cm

Voice Calls include *wheezy… quwee* and sharp *wir*

Range Locally common breeding resident in N mountains from W Pakistan east to Uttarakhand. Moves lower down in winter

Habitat Dry montane forests and shrubs

♀

Largish finch with greyish-brown washed pink upperparts and indistinct streaking. Upper forehead and crown deep pink; broad, rose-pink supercilium. Underparts white-streaked pink. Female ash-brown and heavily streaked. Both sexes have strong, pale bill. Feeds mainly on or near ground on seeds, berries and buds. Solitary, in pairs or small flocks. Confiding. Powerful, undulating flight.

GREAT ROSEFINCH

Carpodacus rubicilla Fringillidae

Size 19 cm

Voice Varied calls, including a drawn-out *weeep* and *twink*

Range Generally scarce breeding resident in N mountains from N Pakistan east to Sikkim. Moves lower down in winter

Habitat Dry, rocky and bushy mountainous country

Large-billed rosefinch. Male has crimson-red forehead, crown, lores, cheeks, nape and ear-coverts, streaked or spotted white and pale pink; pale brown tinged with crimson back and mantle with mild streaking; deep pink rump; notched tail darker brown. Chin and throat crimson; rest of underparts pale with crimson wash and spotted. Female pale brown-grey, finely streaked, darker red and brown. Juvenile similar to female, but more sandy-brown. Solitary, in pairs or in small flocks, often with other rosefinches, feeds on ground on seeds and berries. Strong, undulating flight. Nests on ground.

STREAKED ROSEFINCH

Carpodacus rubicilloides Fringillidae

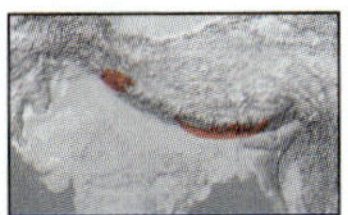

Size 19 cm

Voice Calls include *twink…sip* and *doid…doid*

Range Locally common breeding resident in N mountains

Habitat Dry stony country

Large-billed rosefinch. Bright crimson face; forehead and crown less deep pink-crimson, finely streaked; nape, lores, cheeks and ear-coverts bright crimson. Back and mantle brown-washed with crimson; pink rump; dark brown notched tail. Female overall grey-brown, streaked darker. Solitary, in pairs or small flocks. Feeds on ground on seeds.

RED-FRONTED ROSEFINCH

Carpodacus puniceus Fringillidae

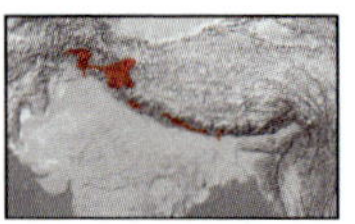

Size 20 cm

Voice Call a cheerful *wistle*

Range The Himalayas

Habitat High-altitude slopes, above treeline, rock screes, cliffs and meadows

Large, brown high-altitude finch. Red forehead extends above eye; crown, nape and mantle brown with streaks; short supercilium; chin, breast and rump also crimson; lower breast slightly duller crimson; brown belly streaked with black; notched dark brown tail with lighter brown edging; dark brown wing panels; pink undertail-coverts. Female similar to male, but slightly smaller and olive-brown, with narrower and paler supercilium. In small flocks; fairly approachable but wary, flying into trees when disturbed. Hops on ground foraging for seeds.

CRIMSON-BROWED FINCH

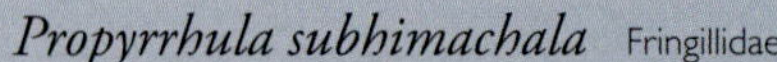

Propyrrhula subhimachala Fringillidae

Size 19-20 cm

Voice Calls include pleasant chirping; warbling

Range Patchily from Nepal to Bhutan. Rarer East

Habitat Montane shrubberies, dense undergrowth in open forests

Large, stocky, overall grey-brown finch. Bright crimson forehead and throat; upper breast crimson, mottled pink-and-white; dark eye-stripe; red rump and unstreaked, greyish belly, smallish bill and long tail. Female has olive-yellow forehead, brow and breast; streaked grey throat, grey face, nape, belly and greenish-brown upperparts. Solitary, or in pairs when breeding; shy and quiet; forages in bushes, moving slowly in undergrowth.

SCARLET FINCH

Haematospiza sipahi Fringillidae

Size 18 cm

Voice Call a pleasant *tu...wee; quee...i...eu*

Range Uttarakhand to Arunachal Pradesh

Habitat Coniferous, oak forests; streamsides, ravines, clearings

Bright scarlet bird from head to uppertail. Slightly brown from lower forehead to lores; dark wings and tail edged scarlet; short, square-ended tail edged dark red. Large, strong bill with upper and lower mandible curving towards tip. Female has olive-green upperparts with dark scaling on crown, nape, mantle and finer scaling on throat and breast; greyish underparts; rump bright yellow. Juvenile male similar to female, but overall more brownish with orange rump. Solitary, in pairs or small flocks; vocal; forages on ground, in bushes and canopy levels.

♀

RED CROSSBILL

Loxia curvirostra Fringillidae

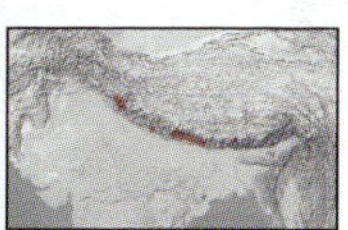

Size 16 cm

Voice Noisy. Call a distinctive *chip... chip*

Range Scarce and erratic visitor or breeding resident in N mountains from N Pakistan east to Bhutan

Habitat Coniferous forests

Medium-sized bird with large head and crossed mandibles. Red head and nape, cheeks and ear-coverts (varies to orange-red); brown lores. Upperparts duller brown, mottled darker. Upperwings washed red; bright red-pink rump; wings edged reddish. Female dull greenish-brown with yellower rump and darker wings and tail. Juvenile heavily streaked and mandibles not crossed. Feeds noisily on seeds of cones high in canopy. In small flocks. Restless with bounding flight. Frequently drinks out of pools. Nests colonially.

♀

BROWN BULLFINCH

Pyrrhula nipalensis Fringillidae

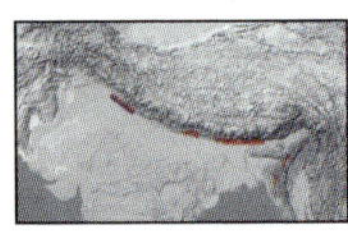

Size 17 cm

Voice Call a mellow *per…lee*

Range Resident with small altitudinal movements. The Himalayas

Habitat Dense moist forests or thick undergrowth in fir, oak and rhododendron forests

Smallish bullfinch with ash-brown back, head, nape and breast, mottled darker. Forehead, lores, and edge of chin edged grey-black; dark patch surrounding eye; white cheek. Thick, short, dark grey bill. Centre of belly white and undertail-coverts; black wings with ash-brown bars; deeply notched, black tail. White rump seen in flight. Female very similar to male, but with small, whitish-yellow wing edgings. In pairs, or small flocks. Confiding.

ORANGE BULLFINCH

Pyrrhula aurantiaca Fringillidae

Size 14 cm

Voice Call a rising *tew or tewtya*

Range Local endemic breeding resident in N mountains from N Pakistan east to Uttarakhand

Habitat Open coniferous forests

Distinctive orange-and-black finch. Male has black forehead, lores, upper cheek and chin; rich orange crown, mantle and back; white base to uppertail-coverts; white rump and vent; broad, orange wing-bars; thick, stubby bill. Female has lighter orange-and-grey head. Similar to Red-headed but has smaller and yellow rather than grey mantle. Juvenile similar to adult female, but crown and forehead more tawny-brown. Feeds singly, in pairs or groups. Nests low in trees.

RED-HEADED BULLFINCH

Pyrrhula erythrocephala Fringillidae

Size 17 cm

Voice Call a single or double-noted *pheu...pheu...*

Range The Himalayas, Kashmir to extreme E India; breeds at 2,400-4,000 m; descends in winter to about 1,200 m

Habitat Forests, bushes

Exotically-coloured finch. Male has black around base of beak and eye; brick-red crown; grey back; white rump; glossy purple-black wings; forked tail; black chin; rusty red below; ash-white belly. Female similar to male, but has olive-yellow crown; grey-brown back and underbody. Seen in small parties, occasionally with other birds; feeds in low bushes, sometimes on ground; rather quiet and secretive.

GREY-HEADED BULLFINCH

Pyrrhula erythaca Fringillidae

Size 17 cm

Voice Call a soft *soo...ee* or *poo...ee*

Range Resident, subject to altitudinal movements. Darjeeling Himalayan Hill region, West Bengal, east to Arunachal Pradesh

Habitat Coniferous, rhododendron forests

Male has black forehead, lores and chin. Dove-grey back, head and nape; rusty orange breast; black wings and tail. Greater coverts have broad, pale grey tips, greyish-white wing-bar and white rump conspicuous in flight. Female brown below, darker grey on head and nape. Feeds on seeds and cones, and usually found in small flocks in winter.

WHITE-WINGED GROSBEAK

Mycerobas carnipes Fringillidae

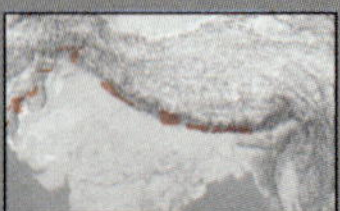

Size 22 cm

Voice Loud 3- or 4-noted calls, usually from tree-tops; harsh note sometimes

Range The Himalayas, extreme W to E India; breeds at 1,500-4,000 m, but mostly above 2,500 m, even in winter. *M melanozanthos* descends much lower in winter

Habitat Dwarf juniper above timberline; high forests; may be seen in bamboos and pine during winter

Sooty black grosbeak with long tail. Male black above, on throat and breast; olive-yellow rump, belly and wing spots; larger, white wing-patch. Square-ended tail. Female brownish-grey, male black; streaks on ear-coverts. Juvenile similar to adult female, but more brown than black and parts of wing olive-yellow and tipped. Seen in small flocks, often with other grosbeaks; active and noisy; mostly feeds in higher branches.

♀

BLACK-AND-YELLOW GROSBEAK

Mycerobas icterioides Fringillidae

Size 22 cm

Voice Call a loud 2- or 3-noted *whistle*. Familiar bird call of W Himalayas; loud *chuck…chuck* note when feeding. Rich song of male. Rather noisy

Range W Himalayas up to C Nepal

Habitat Mountain forests

♀

Male has black head, throat, wings, tail and thighs; yellow collar, back and underbody below breast; thick, finch-like bill. Female grey above with buff rump and belly. Seen in small parties in tall coniferous forests; also feeds on ground and bushes, but spends considerable time in higher branches, where it is difficult to spot.

COLLARED GROSBEAK

Mycerobas affinis Fringillidae

Size 22 cm

Voice Noisy. Calls include ringing *ki…ki…ki…kiw* and *pip…pip…pip…pip…ugh*

Range Locally common breeding resident in N mountains from Himachal Pradesh to Arunachal Pradesh. Moves lower down in winter

Habitat Similar to Black and Yellow's, though also found in mixed forests

Large grosbeak with glossy black crown and throat. Hindneck and sides of lower neck bright golden-yellow, creating a collar. Rest of upperparts black; tail black with glossy black central feathers. Underparts golden-yellow. Female has grey head, greenish-grey upperparts and greenish-yellow underparts. Nest not known.

SPOT-WINGED GROSBEAK

Mycerobas melanozanthos Fringillidae

Size 22 cm

Voice Call a *teew…teew; krrrk*

Range Pakistan to Myanmar

Habitat Mixed broadleaved and coniferous forests

Large finch with very large, stout bill, and relatively short tail; white spots on greater wing-coverts, secondaries, tertials. Male has greyish-black hood, mantle, tail, rump, including nape and throat; breast, belly, vent bright yellow; black on flanks. Female heavily streaked on yellow upper and underparts, with dark eye- and malar stripe; yellow supercilium; white-spotted dark wings. In pairs, or fairly large groups; feeds at all levels, usually on fruiting trees; strong bill used for opening fruit stones for kernels.

♀

GOLD-NAPED FINCH

Pyrrhoplectes epauletta Fringillidae

Size 15 cm

Voice Call a *fuweet; teeew…; pi… pi…pi…pi*

Range Nepal to Arunachal Pradesh

Habitat Dense forests, undergrowth in oak, rhododendrons, bamboos; edges of forests

Small, distinctive finch, almost completely black except for bright yellow-orange crown, wing, nape and white edges to tertials. Short, dark bill. Female has olive-yellow crown, nape and face. Upperparts grey and rufous; black wings; pinkish-orange underparts. Juvenile similar to adult female, but duller. Solitary, in pairs when breeding; sometimes in winter mixed-species flocks; forages at lower levels, within bushes or on ground; quiet and inconspicuous.

♀

CRESTED BUNTING

Melophus lathami Emberizidae

Size 15 cm

Voice Call a faint *chip*… . Pleasant, though somewhat monotonous song of breeding male

Range Resident in India, from the outer Himalayas to about 1,800 m

Habitat Open, bush and rock-covered mountainsides, open country; sometimes also cultivation

juvenile

Glossy black bunting with long, pointed crest and chestnut wings and tail. Female also crested; olive-brown above, streaked darker; rufous in wings; buffy-yellow below, darkly streaked on breast; darkish moustachial stripe. Juvenile overall duller with streaked upperparts. In small flocks, often spread wide over an area; feeds on ground, paths, meadows and tar roads, especially along mountainsides; perches on ruins, walls, stones and low bushes.

YELLOWHAMMER

Emberiza citrinella Emberizidae

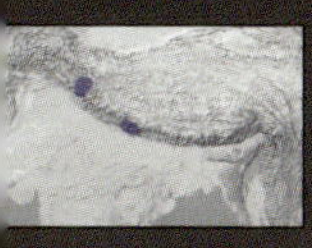

Size 17 cm

Voice Call a *tzik*. Wheezing song

Range Vagrant or rare winter visitor to N India and Nepal

Habitat Upland fallow and stubble fields or scrubs

Has distinct yellow head and underparts. Plain face; narrow, black streak above supercilium and blackish ear-coverts. Rufous breast darker towards wings. Olive-brown mantle streaked brown-black; streaked flanks; white in outer-tail feathers. Upperparts streaked brown; plain rump. Female also heavily streaked with yellow head. Sometimes interbreeds with Pine. Juvenile much duller with less yellow, pale yellow underparts and less distinct streaking. Nests on ground beneath shrubs. Gregarious. Seen in flocks of hundreds.

PINE BUNTING

Emberiza leucocephalos Emberizidae

Size 17 cm

Voice Call a *pit…*, *trp* or *dzee*

Range Fairly common but erratic winter visitor to N hills from E Balochistan. Very scarce in E India

Habitat Hill cultivation

Identified by distinct head patterning. White crown and cheeks edged black; narrow, lateral crown-stripe; broad chestnut-brown supercilium; rufous-brown scapulars boldly streaked with black; rufous-mottled breast and white belly. Female has dark moustache; pale spot on rear cheeks; streaking on chestnut-brown upperparts, rufous rump and underparts; white outer-tail feathers. Rather shy. Feeds in flocks on seeds on ground. Nests on ground in shallow depressions. Seen in large flocks with other buntings and finches.

ROCK BUNTING

Emberiza cia Emberizidae

Size 16 cm

Voice Squeaky *tsip…tsip…* note; calls often. Common bird call of W Himalayas. Squeaky song of several notes

Range The entire Himalayas between 1,500-4,200 m; most common in W Himalayas; winters in foothills

Habitat Grassy, rocky hillsides in open forests; cultivation, scrubs

Male has blue-grey head with prominent black lateral stripes. Black eye-stripe, lores and moustachial stripe; whitish supercilium and cheeks; pale chestnut-brown back, streaked dark. Unmarked rump; white outer sides of dark tail distinct; blue-grey throat and breast; rufous-chestnut below. Female duller. Solitary, or in small parties; active and restless; mostly feeds on ground, meadows, paths and roads; flicks tail often; regularly settles on bushes and trees.

GODLEWSKI'S BUNTING

mberiza godlewskii Emberizidae

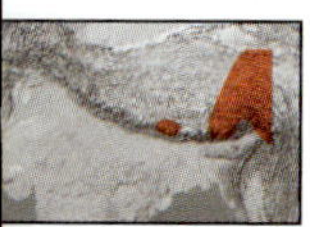

Size 16 cm

Voice Unknown

Range N Arunachal Pradesh

Habitat Dry slopes with bushes d rocks

Largish bunting with grey head, neck, and breast. Prominent chestnut-brown lateral crown-stripes; black moustachial stripe. Grey breast sharply separated from rufous belly. Underparts and rump have buff. Back streaked orange-and-black. Black tail with some orange above and white below. Beak black above and pale below. Legs and feet light pink.

WHITE-CAPPED BUNTING

mberiza stewarti Emberizidae

Size 15 cm

Voice Call a faint but sharp *tsit*… or *chit*… note

Range Breeds in W Himalayas, treme west to Uttarakhand, 1,500-3,500 m; winters in W malayan foothills, and over extensive parts of W and India, south to Maharashtra

bitat Open, grass-covered, rocky hillsides, scrubs

ale has pale grey top of head; black eye-stripe; whitish eeks; blackish supercilium; black chin and upper roat distinctive; chestnut back and rump; white ter-tail; white breast with chestnut gorget below; dull lvous below, chestnut flanks. Female lacks black-and-ite head pattern of male; brown above, streaked; fous-chestnut rump; fulvous-buff below with rufous east. Seen in small flocks, often with other buntings d finches; feeds on ground; rests in bushes and trees.

CHESTNUT-EARED BUNTING

Emberiza fucata Emberizidae

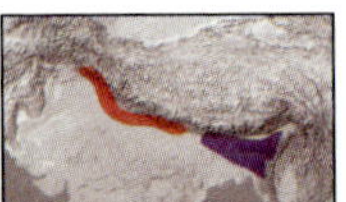

Size 16 cm

Voice Calls include loud *pzik…,* and *chutt*

Range Uncommon breeding resident in N hills from N Pakistan east to C Nepal. Winters in nearby foothills and plains

Habitat Rocky, grassy and bushy hillsides

Large bunting with distinctive chestnut cheeks and lower breast. Grey mottled crown and nape; creamy-white throat and upper breast; black moustache extends to upper breast forming a bro gorget of spots; buffish flanks and belly. Upperpar buff, heavily streaked russet; rufous rump; white outer-tail feathers. Female very dull and more brown. Nests in dry patches in marshy lands. Nev seen in large flocks.

ELLOW-BREASTED BUNTING

mberiza aureola Emberizidae

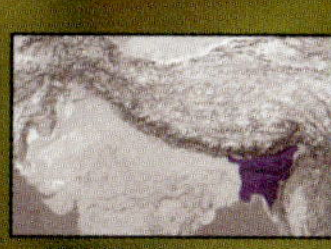

Size 15 cm

Voice Calls *tzip...tzip*

Range Common winter visitor to plains of Nepal, NE India and Bangladesh. Rare further W India

Habitat Cultivation and grasslands, often near wetlands

Chestnut brown-and-yellow bunting with diagnostic bright yellow chin, throat and belly. Breeding plumage male dark chestnut-brown above with striking white wing-bars. Face and throat black; chestnut collar. Non-breeding male paler and more streaked with dusky cheeks. Female similar but with black-edged pale cheeks and no breast-bar. Feeds on seeds, inconspicuously on ground, usually in large flocks. Confiding. Perches in trees and bushes when disturbed.

ITTLE BUNTING

mberiza pusilla Emberizidae

Size 13 cm

Voice Call a clicking *zik*

Range Nepal to Arunachal Pradesh

abitat Grass, stubble, fields, orchards, gardens

ny bunting with a small, pointed bill and rufous-chestnut face. eeding male has rufous-chestnut crown-stripe; dark blackish-own lateral crown-stripes; rufous-chestnut face; pale eye-ring; oad, buffish-white sub-moustachial stripe curving around hind ear-covert stripe; dark brown malar stripe; buffish-white in and throat; dark streaking on rufescent-brown upperparts; o pale wing-bars; whitish underparts with prominent streaking breast and flanks. Seen in small parties; forages on ground; es into bushes or trees when flushed.

RED-HEADED BUNTING

Emberiza bruniceps Emberizidae

Size 17 cm

Voice Call a high-pitched *tzeett...*

Range Common winter visitor over most of the country, south of the Himalayas; absent in extreme south and along E coastal regions

Habitat Open cultivated areas

Male has rufous-chestnut crown, throat, breast; olive-yellow back streaked blackish; unmarked yellow underparts and rump; whitish wing-bars; yellow neck-sides, underbody below breast. Female pale-brown above, has yellowish rump. Highly gregarious winter visitor; appears in huge numbers, frequently along with Black-headed; causes considerable damage to crops.

CHESTNUT BUNTING

Emberiza rutila Emberizidae

Size 15 cm

Voice Call a short *zick*

Range S Assam Hills

Habitat Rice fields, forest clearings, open forests

Fairly small bunting with uniformly chestnut-brown head, breast and upperparts; yellow belly; primary coverts, primaries and secondaries brown; dusky streaking on flanks; short, pointed tail. Brownish bill and pale brown tarsus. Breeding male has bright chestnut-brown upperparts and head. Yellow breast and belly with streaks on sides. Female mostly dull brown with dark streaks above, while underparts pale yellow; rufous rump; buffish throat. Feeds on ground, flees into trees when disturbed. Relatively shy.

BLACK-FACED BUNTING

Emberiza spodocephala Emberizidae

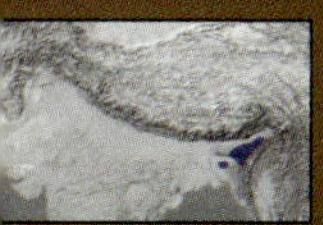

Size 15 cm

Voice Calls *zit…; sip…; zii*

Range Nepal to Arunachal Pradesh

Habitat Tall grass, stubble, fields, paddy fields

Distinctive small bunting with greyish-olive-green head; black lores and chin; pale brown mantle streaked black; grey-brown lesser coverts; median coverts brown-black-tipped buff; grey-brown greater coverts tipped pale buff. Unstreaked grey rump. Upperparts pale yellow; white on outer-tail feathers. Female and non-breeding male have duller head with yellowish supercilium; yellowish sub-moustachial stripe around ear-coverts; yellowish throat; streaked breast; olive rump. Solitary, in pairs, or small flocks; normally feeds on ground. Shy.

ACKNOWLEDGEMENTS

The authors and Om Books International would like to thank the following photographers for so generously contributing their photographs. If any names have inadvertently been omitted, please contact us at biks.grewal@gmail.com and we will rectify it in the next edition.

A D Wilson CC
A P Zaibin
A V Prassana
Aameesh Patel
Abhay Kewat
Abhilash Arjunan
Abhinash Dhal
Abhishek Das
Abhishek Varma
Abrar Ahmed
Adesh Shivkar
Adrain Pingstone CC
Agnij Sur
Akshay Charegaonkar
Aleksey Levashkin
Alka Vaidya
Amano Samarpan
Amar Jyoti Saikia
Ameya Joshi
Amish Patel
Amit Gupta
Amit Thakurta
Anand Arya
Anand Israel
Ananda Bannerjee
Ananta Singh
Anantha Murthy
Andre Karwath CC
Andrea Trepte CC
Anirban Chatterjee
Ankur Patel
Antony Grossy
Anuj Gande
Anup Dutt
Anushree Bhattacharya
Arka Sarkar
Arpit Bansal
Arpit Deomurari
Ashish Imamdar
Ashok Chaudhary
Atanu Mondal
Ateeb Hussain
Atul Jain
Avinash Adappa
Avinash Khemka
Barsha Gogoi
Bhanu Singh
Bharat Rughani
Bhaskar Das
Bhavita Toliya
Bhilhotra Dips
Bijoy KI
Biju P B
Bikram Grewal
Bishan Monappa
Biswapriya Rahut
Bjorn Johansson
Brian Patteson
Chandima Jayaweera
Charles J Sharp CC
Charles Lam CC
Chewang Bonpo
Phempu Lhasung
Chinmay Rahane
Clement M Francis
Dant Mante CC
Dave Curtis CC
David Iliff CC
Debapratim Saha
Deboshree Gogoi
Deepak Sahu
Devashish Deb
Devindra Dadhwal
Devojit Deb
Devon Pike CC
Dhananjay Joshi
Dhanu Paran
Dhanushka Senadheera
Dharuman Nanjan
Dhritiman Hore
Dhritiman Mukkerjee
Dibyendu Ash
Dileep Kumar Pushpangadhan
Dipaknkar Ghosh
Dolly L Bhardwaj
Donna Dewhurst CC
Dr Tanmoy Das
Dr Vaibhav
Dr. Nagraj
Duncan Wright CC
Dushyant Prashar
Eash Hoskote
Esha Munshi
Falguna Shah
Francis C Franklin CC
Francis Yap CC
Frank Schulenburg CC
Frankie Chu CC
Franky Boy CC
Ganesh Adhikari
Garima Bhatia
Gaurav Bhatnagar
Gaurav Deshmukh
Gaurav Kataria
Gaurika Wijeratne
Gayathri and Mansoor
Gertrud and Helmut Denzau
Girish Ketkar
Gopal Chandra Rao
Gopi Sundar
Gopinath Kollur
Gunjan Arora
Gurum Eklaya
Guruprasad Kambar
Gururaj Moorching
Hardik Pala
Harish Narasimhamurty
Harmenn Ningthoucha
Harshvardhan
HB Varun
Hilary Chambers CC
Hiyashi Haka CC
Igor Karyakin

ngo Waschkies
M Garg CC
ainy Maria Kurikose
ames Eaton
ames Merrill
ames Perdue CC
an W van Besten
ason L Buberal CC
aysukh Parekh
erry Strzelecki CC
ignesh
itendra Bhatia
J Harrison CC
oanna Van Gruisen
ohn and Jemi Holmes
ugul Tiwari
yotendra Thakuri
yotimoy Dev,
Ramesh
Uschel Gurung
allol Mukkerjee
alyan Varma
arthik R
artik Patel
edar Potnis
im Rogers CC
im Yip Ho CC
oshy Koshy
shounish Shankar Ray
ulashekara Chakravarthy
uldeep Shukla
unan Naik
J Tim CC
ieven De Temmerman
I Savitha Ravi
lahesh Reddy
laitreyee Das
lanjeet Jadeja
lanjula Mathur
lanoj Sharma
larjolein De Weirdt
lasood Hussain
laurice van Bruggen CC
IC Sajin
ID Imran
leg Roy Choudhury
legna Bannerjee
lichael J Braid CC
Misha Desai
Mital Patel
Mitash Biswas
Mohamed Mothi
Mohan Munivenkatapa
Mohanram Kemparaju
Mousumi Datta
MV Shreeram
N Shiva Kumar
Nandhini Raveendaran
Narbir Singh Kalhon
Natalia Parlina and Christan Orden
Navendu Lad
Nayan Khanolkar
Nikhil Bhopale
Nikhil Devasar
Nilay Desai
Ninaad Kulkarni
Niraj Mistry
Niranjan Sant
Nirmala Sridhar
Nitin Bhardwaj
Nitin Srinivasamurthy
Olivier Klein CC
Otto Pfister
Panchami Manoo Ukil
Paramanand Chikane
Parashuram Lad
Partha Sen
Parvinder S Anand
Pema Bhutia
Peter Kaestner
Porag Jyoti Phukan
Prabhakar Manjunath
Prakash Ramakrishnan
Pranesh Kodancha
Pranjal J Saikia
Prasad Basavaraj
Prashant Kotian
Prashant Poojary
Prassana Parab
Prosenjit Singa Deo
Puja Sharma
Pushpal Goswami
R K Pai
R Kartik
Raghavendra M
Rahul Sachdeva
Raj Kamal Phukan
Raj Phukan
Rajeev Kumar
Rajesh Dhareshwar
Rajesh Panwar
Rajneesh Suvarna
Rakesh Kalra
Ramakrishna Prakash
Ramanan RR
Ramesh Anantharaman
Ramki Sreenivasan
Ranand Israel
Ranjan Barthakur
Ranjan K Das
Rathika Ramasami
Ratna Ghosh
Ravi Chand
Ravindar Musalcol
Rayees Rahman
Remi Bigonneau CC
Rohit Naniwadekar
Rohit Sant
Ron Knight CC
Ronald Haldar
Roon Bhuyan
Roshan Kamath
Rosy Chaudhary
S Krishnamurthy
S N Ragavendra
S Rajeshkumar
Saandip Nandagudi
Saandip Nandangudi
Sachin Rai
Salim Ali
Sameer Khan
Saminathan Babu
Saminathan Babu
Samyak Kaninde
Samyak Kaninde
Sangameshwar Ghattargi
Sanjay Dutt Tiwari
Santosh Gujjar
Sarthak Awhad
SarwanDeep Singh
Satish Chettri Kutwal
Satisha Sarakki
Satyendra Sharma

Savio Fonseca
Savitha Ravi
Sayan U Choudhury
Shahnawaz Khan
Sharad Agrawal
Sharad Sridhar
Shashank Dalvi
Shiva Shankar
Shiva Shankar
Shreya Singha Roy
Shyam Ghate
Sidharth Bramhankar
Sidharth Damle
Simon Cook CC
Sitara Kartikeyan
Solomon Sampath Kumar
Soma Jha
Sonu Anand
Sonu Arora
Soumayjit Nandy
Steve Ryan CC
Subharanjan Sen
Subharghaya Das
Subhasis Roy
Suboranjan Sen
Subramaniam Mani
Subranangshu Ghosh
Subroto Sanyal
Sudeep Dhatre
Sudhir Garg
Sudhir Shivaraman
Sudipto Roy
Sugata Goswami
Sujan Chatterjee
Sumit Das
Sumit K Sen
Supriya Dam
Supriya Das
Supriyo Samanta
Surendra Chouhan
Suresh K Rathod
Suresh Kamath
Suru Nair
Susan Myers
Sushmita
Swethadri Doraiswamy
T Saburaj
Tapas Misra
Tejinder Singh Rawal
Tejus Naik
Tim Loseby
Udayan Borthakur
Udayan Rao Pawar,
Umesh Srinivasan
Urmil Jhaveri
Uttan Mahata
Vaibhav Dalal
Vaibhav Deshmukh
Vaibhav Mishra
Vaidehi Gunjal
Venu Gopal
Vijay Anand Ishmavel
Vijay Cavale
Vijay Sachan
Vijay Sethi
Vishvatej Nair
Vishwatej Pawar
Vitraag Shah
Vivek Tiwari
VK Gupta
Waler Siegmund CC
Yoav Perelmen
Yograj Jadeja

Hundreds of birdwatchers, photographers and friends helped in the creation of this book. We are specially grateful to the following for providing advice and friendship: Ajay Mago, Bittu Sahgal, Hemlata Pradhan , Krishna Kumari, Lavanya Khare, Meena Subramaniam, Om Mago, Prakash Muduli, Panchami Manoo Ukil, Prosenjit Singa Deo, Raghuvir Khare, Ramki Sreenivasan, Ranjan K Das, Rayika Sen, Rohan Chakravarty, Rohit Chakravarty, Samiha Grewal and Sanjay Mago.

Special thanks to Alpana Khare for all help.

Above all, we would like to thank Neeraj Aggarwal, Ajmal Nayab Siddiqui and Raj Kishore Beck—for designing this book; and Ipshita Mitra and Dipa Chaudhuri for treating *Birds of the Himalayas* as their own.

BIBLIOGRAPHY

Ali, S. (1960) *A Picture Book of Sikkim Birds.* Gangtok : Government of Sikkim.

Ali, S. (1962) *The Birds of Sikkim*. Delhi: OUP.

Ali, S. & Ripley, D. (1964-74) *Handbook of the Birds of India & Pakistan* (Vols. 1-10). Bombay: OUP.

Ali, S. & Futehally, L. (1967) *Common Birds*. New Delhi: NBT.

Ali, S. (1968) *Common Indian Birds, A Picture Album*. New Delhi: NBT.

Ali, S. (1969) *Birds of Kerala*. Madras: OUP.

Ali, S. & Ripley, D. (1983) *A Pictorial Guide to the Birds of the Indian Subcontinent*. Bombay: OUP.

Ali, S. (1996) *The Book of Indian Birds*. (14th ed.) New Delhi: BNHS & OUP.

Ali, S., Biswas, B. & Ripley, D. (1996) *Birds of Bhutan*. Calcutta: ZSI.

Bates, R.S.P. & Lowther, E.H.N. (1952) *Breeding Birds of Kashmir*. Bombay: OUP.

Beebe, W. (1927, 1994) *Pheasant Jungles*. Reading: WPA.

Besten, J, W den. (2004) *Birds of Kangra, Dharmsala*: Moonpeak Publishers.

Choudhury, A. (2001) *Birds of Assam*, Guwahati: Gibbon Books.

Choudhury, A. (2006) *A Pocket Guide to the Birds of Arunachal Pradesh*, Guwahati: The Rhino Foundation.

Choudhury, A. (2003) *A Pocket Guide to the Birds of Nagaland*, Guwahati: Gibbon Books.

Dewar, D. (1915) *Birds of the Indian Hills*. London: The Bodley Head.

Dewar, D. (1923) *Himalayan and Kashmiri Birds*. London: J. Lane.

Finn, F. (1920) *How to Know the Indian Waders*. Calcutta: Thacker, Spink & Co.

Fleming, R.L. Sr. & Fleming, R. Jr. (1970) *Birds of Kathmandu and Surrounding Hills Kathmandu*: Jore Ganesh Press.

Fleming, R.L. Sr. et al. (1984) *Birds of Nepal: With reference to Kashmir and Sikkim*. Nepal: Nature Himalayas.

Gould, J. (1832) *A Century of Birds from the Himalayan Mountains*. London: Published by the author.

Grewal, B. (1995) *Birds of the Indian Subcontinent*. Hong Kong: *The Guidebook Company Limited*.

Grewal, B. (1995, 2008) *Birds of the India & Nepal*. London: New Holland.

Grewal, B. (1998) *A Photographic Guide to the Birds of the Himalayas*. London: New Holland.

Grewal, B., Pfister, O. & Harvey, B. (2002) *A Photographic Guide to the Birds of India, and the Indian Subcontinent including Pakistan, Nepal, Bhutan, Bangladesh, Sri Lanka and the Maldives*, Singapore: Periplus.

Grewal, B., Sen S. & Sreenivasan. (2012) *Birds of Nagaland*, Kohima: Nagaland Govt.

Grewal, B., Sen S. & Sreenivasan. (2012) A Companion to the *Birds of Nagaland*, Kohima: Nagaland Govt.

Grimmet, R. Inskipp, T., & Inskipp, C. (1998) *Birds of the Indian Subcontinent*. UK: A&C Black.

Grimmet, R. Inskipp, T., & Inskipp, C. (1999) *Field Guide to the Birds of Bhutan*; UK: A&C Black.

Grimmet, R. Inskipp, T., & Inskipp, C. (2017) *Field Guide to the Birds of Nepal*; UK: A&C Black.

Inskipp, C. (1988) *A Birdwatchers' Guide to Nepal*. England: Prion.

Inskipp, T. & Inskipp, C. (1991) *A Guide to the Birds of Nepal*. London: Christopher Helm.

Inskipp, C. & Inskipp, T. (undated) *An Introduction to Birdwatching in Bhutan. Thimpu*, Bhutan: WWF.

Jones, A.E. (undated) *The Common Birds of Simla. Simla:* Liddell's Printing Works.

Lister, M.D. (1954) *A Contribution to the Ornithology of the Darjeeling Area*. Bombay: BNHS.

Mackintosh, L.J. (1915) *Birds of Darjeeling and India*: Part I. Calcutta: J.N. Banerjee & Son.

Naoroji, R (2006) *Birds of Prey of the Indian Subcontinent*, London: Christopher Helm.

Pfister, O. (2004) *Birds and Mammals of Ladakh*. New Delhi: OUP.

Pittie, A. (2010) *Birds in Books*. New Delhi: Permanent Black.

Rasmussen, P. & Anderton, J. (2005) *Birds of South Asia: The Ripley Guide*, Barcelona: Lynx Editions.

Ripley, D. (1952) *Search for the Spiny Babbler*. Boston: Houghton Mifflin.

Shrestha, T.K. (1998) *The Spiny Babbler, An Endemic Bird of Nepal (?)*

Vaurie, Charles. (1972) *Tibet and its Birds*. London: H.F. & G. Witherby Ltd.

Whistler, Hugh. (1928) *Popular Handbook of Indian Birds*. London: Gurney and Jackson.

SOUND GUIDES

Barucha, E. (1999) *Indian Bird Calls*, Bombay: BNHS.

Breil, F., & Roche, J.C. (2000) *Birding in India and Nepal*. Sittelle Editions.

Connop, S. (1993) *Birdsongs of Nepal*. New York: Turaco.

Connop, S. (1995) *Birdsongs of the Himalayas*. Toronto: Turaco.

DESCRIPTIVE PARTS OF A BIRD

A GLOSSARY OF ORNITHOLOGICAL TERMS

Aberrant Abnormal or unusual

Accidental Vagrant

Adult Mature, Capable of breeding

Aerial Making use of the open sky

Allopatric Relating to two or more related species whose range do not overlap

Altitudinal migrant Moving between high mountains and lower foothills

Altricial Blind and helpless when hatched

Apical Outer extremities, particularly of the tail

Aquatic Living on or in water

Arboreal Living in trees

Ashy Greyish Colour

Axillaries Underwing feathers at the base of the wings, forming 'armpits'

Back Loosely applied to the mantle scapulars and rump

Banyan Type of fig tree

Barring 'Sideway' lines such as on tail or breast

Basal Innermost extremities, particularly of the tail or bill

Bheel Shallow lake or wetland

Biosphere The part of earth that is inhabited by life

Biotope Area of uniform environment, flora and fauna

Bristles Sensory feathers near beak

Brood Young hatched from a single clutch

Brood Parasitism Depositing of eggs by one species in the nest of an another

Buff Yellowish white with a hint of pale brown

Bund Man-made mud embankment

Canopy Leafy foliage of treetops

Cap Upper part of head

Carpal Bend of a closed wing, sometimes called shoulder

Casque Growth above bill of hornbills

Cere Patch of bare skin on upper base of bill of raptors

Cheek Term loosely applied to sides of head, below the eye or on ear-coverts

Chevrons V-shaped contrasting marks on wings or bands across breast

Cinnamon Light yellowish-brown colour

Clutch Complete set of eggs laid by a single female

Collar Distinctive band of colour that encircles or partly encircles the neck

Colonial Roosting or nesting in groups

Confiding Not shy

Commensal Living together with man for mutual benefit

Coverts Small feathers on wings and base of tail

Covey Small group of partridges and allied species

Crepuscular Active at dusk (twilight) and dawn

Crest Extended feathers on head

Crop Pouch-like enlargement of gullet in some birds where food is partially digested

Crown Upper part of head

Crown-stripe Distinct line from forehead along centre of crown

Cryptic Hidden - having protective colouring and/ or behaviour

Culmen Ridge on upper mandible of bill

Cursorial Ground running

Deciduous Trees that shed their leaves annually

Decurved Curving downwards

Diagnostic Sufficient to identify a species or sub-species

Dimorphic Having two forms of plumage

Distal Terminal or the outer end

Diurnal Active during daytime

Down Small soft feathers close to body of chicks

Drake Male duck

Drumming Rhythmic territorial hammering on trees by woodpeckers

Duars Forested areas south of eastern Himalayas

Ear-coverts Feathers covering the ear opening. Often distinctly coloured

Ear tufts Feathers protruding near ears

Echolocate Navigate by sound

Eclipse Plumage New dull plumage after breeding season, especially in ducks

Endemic Indigenous and confined to a place

Endangered Species facing high risk of extinction

Eurasian Of both Europe and Asia

Evergreen Forests that always have leaves

Eye-ring Contrasting ring around the eye

Eye-stripe Stripe through eye

Extinct No longer in existence

Extirpated Locally extinct

Extralimital Not existing in the region

Facial Disc Heart-shaped arrangement of feathers as in some owls and harriers

Fallow Cultivated land after cultivation and before ploughing

Family Specified group of genera

Forage Search for food

Ferruginous Rusty-brown colour

Feral Escaped, and living and breeding in the wild

Filoplume Hair-like feathers like in breeding egrets

Flank Side of body

Fledged Having just acquired feathers and ready to leave nest

Fledglings Young birds which have just acquired feathers

Flight feathers Primary and secondary wing feathers

Flushed When disturbed into flight at close quarters

Foreneck The lower throat

Form Sub-species

Frons Forehead

Frugivorous Fruit-eating

Fulvous Brownish-yellow
Game birds Pheasants, partridges and allied species
Gape Basal part of the beak (mainly for young birds and raptors)
Genera Plural of genus
Genus Group of related species
Ghats Hills parallel to the east and west coast of India
Gorget Band across upper chest
Granivorous Grain-eating
Gregarious Sociable living in communities or flocks
Gular pouch Loose area of skin extending from throat as in pelicans and hornbills
Gular stripe Narrow and often dark stripe running down from the centre of throat
Guttural From the throat
Hackles Long and pointed neck feathers
Hawking Capturing insects in flight
Hepatic Rust or liver coloured plumage phase, mainly in female cuckoos
Hood Dark-coloured head and throat
Hunting party Group of birds usually of different species, seeking food
Hybridisation Cross-breeding between two different species
Immature Plumage phases prior to adult
Incubate Giving warmth for eggs to hatch
Iris Coloured eye membrane surrounding pupil
Irruption Mass movement of a population from one place to another
Jheel Shallow lake or wetland
Jizz Essence or striking characteristics of a species;
Juvenile Immature bird immediately after leaving nest
Lamellae Small stiff comb-like membrane on inner edge of bill used for sieving food
Lanceolate Lance-shaped. Slim and pointed
Lantana Invasive aggressive shrub introduced to the region
Leading edge Front edge of wing
Lek Sociable courtship gatherings
Lobe Fleshy extensions to side-edges of toes of some birds
Local Unevenly distributed with a region
Loranthus Parasitical bush that grows on tress and frequented by flowerpeckers
Lores Area between eye and bill base
Lump Treatment of one or more forms previously treated as distinct species as race of a single species
Malar Stripe on side of throat
Mandible Each of the two parts of bill
Mangrove Coastal salt-resistant trees or bushes
Mantle Back, between wings
Mask Dark plumage round eye and ear-coverts
Mesial Stripe Central throat stripe
Migration Seasonal movement between distant places
Mirror White spots in wing-tips, mainly of gulls
Monotypic Of a single form with no subspecies
Montane Pertaining to mountains
Monsoon Rainy season in India
Morph One of several distinct types of plumage in the same species
Moult Seasonal shedding of plumage
Nail Hook on tip of upper mandible
Nape Back of neck
Nares Nostril openings
Necklace Narrow line round neck
Nictitating Membrane Transparent fold of skin forming a third eyelid
Nidicolous Chicks that remain in nests for a long duration after hatching
Nidifugous Chicks that leave the nests soon after hatching
Nidification Relating to nests or nesting
Nocturnal Active at night
Nomadic Species without specific territory except when breeding
Nominate First sub-species to be formally named
Non-passerine All order of birds except for Passerines
Notch Indentations in outline of feathers, wing or tail
Nuchal Crest Crest along back of neck
Nullah Dry or wet stream bed or ditch
Nuptial Plumage Breeding plumage
Ocelli Brightly-coloured 'eye-like' spots as on peacocks
Occipital Back of head
Oology Study of bird's eggs
Orbital ring Narrow ring of skin or feathers round the eye
Order Group of related families
Paddy-fields Rice fields often flooded
Paleartic Old world and arctic zone
Parasitic Deriving sustenance or taking advantage of others, like cuckoos laying eggs in other bird's nest
Passerines Perching and song birds
Pectoral Breast area
Pelagic Ocean-going
Pellet Indigested material regurgitated by owls
Phase Colour form of a species
Pied Black and white
Plumage Feathers of a bird
Plumes Long, showy feathers, acquired during the breeding season
Polyandrous Female having more than one mate
Polygamous Male with more than one mate
Polymorphic Taking several forms
Postocular Area behind the eye
Precocial Young hatched sighted and down-covered, e.g. ducklings
Predator Who feeds on other birds or animals
Primaries Outer flight feathers in wing
Race Sub-species

Rachis Central shaft of a feather
Range Geographical area or areas inhabited by a species
Raptors Birds of prey and vultures, excluding owls
Record Published, or otherwise broadcast, occurrence
Rectrices Tail feathers
Remiges The primaries and secondaries combined
Rictal Around the bill
Resident Non-migratory and breeding in same place
Riparian Along creeks, streams, rivers and waterways
Roost Resting or sleeping space
Rufescent Inclining to redness
Rufous Reddish brown
Rump Lower back
Sal Dominant tree of North Indian forests
Sallies Short flights and returning to perch as in bee-eaters and flycatchers
Salt pans Shallow reservoirs for drying out salt
Savanna Open flat land with grass and scattered bushes
Sedentary Staying in the same area throughout the year
Scalloped Curved markings on edges of feathers
Scapulars Feathers along edge of mantle
Scrape Shallow depression made by birds to serve as nest
Secondaries Inner wing feathers
Sedentary Confined with a particular area
Shaft Central stem of a feather, often hidden
Shank Bare parts of a leg
Sholas Small forests in SW Indian valleys
Shoulder Where the wing meets the body
Shorebird Long-legged bird living near water
Skins Bird specimens prepared for scientific studies
Skulker Bird that mostly remains within vegetation cover
Slaty Dull bluish-grey
Soar Rising flight on still extending wings using thermals
Speculum Area of colour on secondary feathers of wings
Streamers Long extensions to feathers, usually of tail
Spangles Distinctive white or shimmering spots in plumage
Species Groups of birds reproductively isolated from other such groups
Speculum Shiny, colourful patch on secondary feathers of the wing of some ducks
Storey Level of the tree or forest
Spur Sharp horny growth on legs of some birds
Straw Pale yellow colour
Streaks 'Lengthwise' lines on breasts or tail
Streamers Long extension of tail feathers
Striated Marked with fine streaks
Sooty Blackish colour
Sub-adult Immature moulting into adult plumage
Sub-montane Hills below highest mountains
Sub-song Subdued version of normal territorial song
Sub-species Distinct form that does not have specific status
Sub-terminal Band Broad band on outer part of feather
Supercilia Plural of supercilium
Supercilium Streak above eye
Symbiotic Interdependence between different species
Tail Streamers Elongated ribbon-like tail feathers
Talons Strong sharp claws used to seize or kill prey
Tank Water reservoir
Tarsus Lower part of a bird's legs
Taxonomy Science of classifying organisms
Teak Dominant tree of South Indian forests
Terai Alluvial strech of land south of the Himalayas
Terminal band Broad band on tip of feather or tail
Terrestrial Living on the ground
Tertials Innermost wing coverts, often covering secondaries
Totipalmate All four toes connected to a single web
Trailing edge Rear edge of wing
Underparts Under surface of a bird from throat to vent
Underwing Undersurface of a wing including the linings and flight feathers
Upperparts Upper surface of a bird including wings, back and tail
Upperstorey Canopy of a tree
Vagrant Accidental, irregular
Vent Undertail area
Ventral Undersurface of body
Vermiculations Wavy (worm-like) markings
Vinaceous Red wine coloured warm pink
Vocal mimicry Imitating the sounds of other birds
Waders Shorebirds. Usually, the smaller, long-legged waterbirds
Washed Suffused with a particular colour
Wattle Bare skin, often coloured, on part of head
Web Skin stretched between toes
Wildfowl Ducks and geese
Wing-bar visible line of colour at tip on wing-coverts
Wing-coverts Small feathers on wing at base of primaries and secondaries
Wing-span Length from one wing tip to the other when fully extended
Winter plumage Plumage seen during the non-breeding winter months
Zygodactylous Having two toes directed forward and two backwards

Himalayan Monal

CHECKLIST: BIRDS OF HIMALAYAN HIDEAWAY AND ENVIRONS

nglish Name	Scientific Name	Alternative Name(s)
nseriformes (Anatidae)		
ommon Merganser	*Mergus merganser*	Goosander
uddy Shelduck	*Tadorna ferruginea*	Brahminy Duck
ed-crested Pochard	*Netta rufina*	
ommon Pochard	*Aythya ferina*	
ufted Duck	*Aythya fuligula*	Tufted Pochard
orthern Shoveler	*Spatula clypeata*	
adwall	*Mareca strepera*	
urasian Wigeon	*Mareca penelope*	
ndian Spot-billed Duck	*Anas poecilorhyncha*	Spotbill Duck (incl. A. zonorhyncha)
allard	*Anas platyrhynchos*	
orthern Pintail	*Anas acuta*	
ommon Teal	*Anas crecca*	Green-winged Teal, Eurasian Teal
alliformes (Phasianidae)		
ommon Hill Partridge	*Arborophila torqueola*	Hill Partridge
alliformes (Phasianidae)		
ufous-throated Hill Partridge	*Arborophila rufogularis*	Rufous-throated Partridge
lack Francolin	*Francolinus francolinus*	Black Partridge
ed Junglefowl	*Gallus gallus*	
alij Pheasant	*Lophura leucomelanos*	Kaleej Pheasant
olumbiformes (Columbidae)		
ock Pigeon	*Columba livia*	Rock Dove, Blue Rock Pigeon
riental Turtle Dove	*Streptopelia orientalis*	Rufous Turtle Dove
urasian Collared Dove	*Streptopelia decaocto*	Indian Ring Dove
ed Collared Dove	*Streptopelia tranquebarica*	Red Turtle Dove
potted Dove	*Streptopelia chinensis*	[Western Spotted Dove, Eastern Spotted Dove]
aughing Dove	*Streptopelia senegalensis*	Little Brown Dove, Senegal Dove
ellow-legged Green Pigeon	*Treron phoenicopterus*	Yellow-footed Green Pigeon
in-tailed Green Pigeon	*Treron apicauda*	
edge-tailed Green Pigeon	*Treron sphenurus*	Kokla
merald Dove	*Chalcophaps indica*	
aprimulgiformes (Caprimulgidae)		
rey Nightjar	*Caprimulgus indicus*	[Jungle Nightjar/Indian Jungle Nightjar]
arge-tailed Nightjar	*Caprimulgus macrurus*	Long-tailed Nightjar (incl. C. atripennis & C. andamanicus)
aprimulgiformes (Apodidae)		
rested Treeswift	*Hemiprocne coronata*	
imalayan Swiftlet	*Aerodramus brevirostris*	
sian Palm Swift	*Cypsiurus balasiensis*	
lpine Swift	*Tachymarptis melba*	
epal House Swift	*Apus nipalensis*	
ndian House Swift	*Apus affinis*	Little Swift, House Swift (incl. A. nipalensis)
uculiformes (Cuculidae)		
reater Coucal	*Centropus sinensis*	Crow-pheasant; [Andaman Coucal]
ied Cuckoo	*Clamator jacobinus*	Pied Crested Cuckoo, Jacobin Cuckoo
sian Koel	*Eudynamys scolopaceus*	Common Koel
rey-bellied Cuckoo	*Cacomantis passerinus*	Indian Plaintive Cuckoo
rongo Cuckoo	*Surniculus lugubris*	[Fork-tailed Drongo Cuckoo, Square-tailed Drongo Cuckoo]
arge Hawk Cuckoo	*Hierococcyx sparverioides*	
ommon Hawk Cuckoo	*Hierococcyx varius*	Brainfever Bird
ndian Cuckoo	*Cuculus micropterus*	
ommon Cuckoo	*Cuculus canorus*	Eurasian Cuckoo
imalayan Cuckoo	*Cuculus saturatus*	Oriental Cuckoo (incl. C. optatus)
esser Cuckoo	*Cuculus poliocephalus*	Small Cuckoo
elecaniformes (Ardeidae)		
lack-crowned Night Heron	*Nycticorax nycticorax*	

English Name	Scientific Name	Alternative Name(s)
Striated Heron	*Butorides striata*	Little Green Heron
Indian Pond Heron	*Ardeola grayii*	Paddybird
Cattle Egret	*Bubulcus ibis*	
Grey Heron	*Ardea cinerea*	
Intermediate Egret	*Ardea intermedia*	Median Egret, Smaller Egret
Little Egret	*Egretta garzetta*	
Pelecaniformes (Phalacrocoracidae)		
Little Cormorant	*Microcarbo niger*	
Great Cormorant	*Phalacrocorax carbo*	Large Cormorant
Indian Cormorant	*Phalacrocorax fuscicollis*	Indian Shag
Pelecaniformes (Anhingidae)		
Oriental Darter	*Anhinga melanogaster*	Snake-bird
Charadriiformes (Recurvirostridae)		
Black-winged Stilt	*Himantopus himantopus*	[White-headed Stilt, Pied Stilt]
Charadriiformes (Charadriidae)		
Little Ringed Plover	*Charadrius dubius*	
Kentish Plover	*Charadrius alexandrinus*	[White-faced Plover]
River Lapwing	*Vanellus duvaucelii*	Spur-winged Lapwing/Spur-winged Plover (with V. spinosus)
Grey-headed Lapwing	*Vanellus cinereus*	
Red-wattled Lapwing	*Vanellus indicus*	
Charadriiformes (Scolopacidae)		
Temminck's Stint	*Calidris temminckii*	
Little Stint	*Calidris minuta*	
Pintail Snipe	*Gallinago stenura*	
Common Snipe	*Gallinago gallinago*	Fantail Snipe
Terek Sandpiper	*Xenus cinereus*	
Common Sandpiper	*Actitis hypoleucos*	
Green Sandpiper	*Tringa ochropus*	
Spotted Redshank	*Tringa erythropus*	Dusky Redshank
Common Greenshank	*Tringa nebularia*	Greenshank
Common Redshank	*Tringa totanus*	
Wood Sandpiper	*Tringa glareola*	Spotted Sandpiper
Accipitriformes (Pandionidae)		
Osprey	*Pandion haliaetus*	
Black-winged Kite	*Elanus caeruleus*	Black-shouldered Kite
Oriental Honey Buzzard	*Pernis ptilorhynchus*	Crested Honey Buzzard
Bearded Vulture	*Gypaetus barbatus*	Lammergeier
Crested Serpent Eagle	*Spilornis cheela*	[Central Nicobar Serpent Eagle]
Himalayan Vulture	*Gyps himalayensis*	Himalayan Griffon
Mountain Hawk Eagle	*Nisaetus nipalensis*	[Legge's Hawk Eagle, Hodgson's Hawk Eagle]
Changeable Hawk Eagle	*Nisaetus cirrhatus*	[Crested Hawk Eagle]
Rufous-bellied Eagle	*Lophotriorchis kienerii*	Rufous-bellied Hawk Eagle
Black Eagle	*Ictinaetus malaiensis*	
Tawny Eagle	*Aquila rapax*	
Steppe Eagle	*Aquila nipalensis*	
Shikra	*Accipiter badius*	
Besra	*Accipiter virgatus*	
Eurasian Sparrowhawk	*Accipiter nisus*	
Northern Goshawk	*Accipiter gentilis*	
Pallas's Fish Eagle	*Haliaeetus leucoryphus*	Ring-tailed Fishing Eagle
Grey-headed Fish Eagle	*Icthyophaga ichthyaetus*	Grey-headed Fishing Eagle
Black Kite	*Milvus migrans*	Pariah Kite, Black-eared Kite M. m. lineatus
White-eyed Buzzard	*Butastur teesa*	White-eyed Buzzard Eagle
Himalayan Buzzard	*Buteo refectus*	
Collared Owlet	*Glaucidium brodiei*	Collared Pygmy Owlet
Asian Barred Owlet	*Glaucidium cuculoides*	Barred Owlet
Jungle Owlet	*Glaucidium radiatum*	Barred Jungle Owlet
Spotted Owlet	*Athene brama*	
Mountain Scops Owl	*Otus spilocephalus*	Spotted Scops Owl
Collared Scops Owl	*Otus bakkamoena*	[Indian Scops Owl]
Indian Eagle Owl	*Bubo bengalensis*	Rock Eagle-Owl

nglish Name	Scientific Name	Alternative Name(s)
ucerotiformes (Bucerotidae)		
reat Hornbill	*Buceros bicornis*	Great Pied Hornbill, Great Indian Hornbill
riental Pied Hornbill	*Anthracoceros albirostris*	Indian Pied Hornbill
ndian Grey Hornbill	*Ocyceros birostris*	Common Grey Hornbill
ucerotiformes (Upupidae)		
ommon Hoopoe	*Upupa epops*	Eurasian Hoopoe
iciformes (Picidae)		
urasian Wryneck	*Jynx torquilla*	Wryneck, Northern Wryneck
peckled Piculet	*Picumnus innominatus*	
Iimalayan Golden-backed Woodpecker	*Dinopium shorii*	Himalayan Flameback, Himalayan Golden-backed Three-toed Woodpecker
esser Golden-backed Woodpecker	*Dinopium benghalense*	Black-rumped Flameback
ufous Woodpecker	*Micropternus brachyurus*	
ireater Yellow-naped Woodpecker	*Chrysophlegma flavinucha*	Greater Yellownape, Yellow-naped Woodpecker
esser Yellow-naped Woodpecker	*Picus chlorolophus*	Lesser Yellownape, Small Yellow-naped Woodpecker
irey-headed Woodpecker	*Picus canus*	Grey-faced Woodpecker, Black-naped Green Woodpecker
caly-bellied Woodpecker	*Picus squamatus*	Scaly-bellied Green Woodpecker, Large Scaly-bellied Green Woodpecker
ireater Golden-backed Woodpecker	*Chrysocolaptes lucidus*	[Greater Flameback, Large Golden-backed Woodpecker, Malabar Flameback]
irey-capped Pygmy Woodpecker	*Dendrocopos canicapillus*	Grey-crowned Pygmy Woodpecker
ulvous-breasted Pied Woodpecker	*Dendrocopos macei*	Fulvous-breasted Woodpecker; [Spot-breasted Woodpecker, Freckle-breasted Woodpecker]
rown-fronted Pied Woodpecker	*Dendrocopos auriceps*	Brown-fronted Woodpecker
Iimalayan Pied Woodpecker	*Dendrocopos himalayensis*	Himalayan Woodpecker
iciformes (Ramphastidae)		
ireat Barbet	*Psilopogon virens*	Great Hill Barbet, Hill Barbet
rown-headed Barbet	*Psilopogon zeylanicus*	Large Green Barbet
ineated Barbet	*Psilopogon lineatus*	
lue-throated Barbet	*Psilopogon asiaticus*	
oppersmith Barbet	*Psilopogon haemacephalus*	Crimson-breasted Barbet
oraciiformes (Meropidae)		
lue-bearded Bee-eater	*Nyctyornis athertoni*	
ireen Bee-eater	*Merops orientalis*	Small Green Bee-eater, Little Green Bee-eater
hestnut-headed Bee-eater	*Merops leschenaulti*	
oraciiformes (Coraciidae)		
ndian Roller	*Coracias benghalensis*	[Indochinese Roller]
ollarbird	*Eurystomus orientalis*	Broad-billed Roller
oraciiformes (Alcedinidae)		
ommon Kingfisher	*Alcedo atthis*	Small Blue Kingfisher
rested Kingfisher	*Megaceryle lugubris*	Himalayan Pied Kingfisher
ied Kingfisher	*Ceryle rudis*	Lesser Pied Kingfisher
tork-billed Kingfisher	*Pelargopsis capensis*	Brown-headed Stork-billed Kingfisher
Vhite-throated Kingfisher	*Halcyon smyrnensis*	White-breasted Kingfisher
alconiformes (Falconidae)		
ommon Kestrel	*Falco tinnunculus*	Eurasian Kestrel
ed-necked Falcon	*Falco chicquera*	Red-headed Falcon, Red-headed Merlin
eregrine Falcon	*Falco peregrinus*	Shaheen Falcon F. p. peregrinator; [Barbary Falcon]
sittaciformes (Psittaculidae)		
laty-headed Parakeet	*Psittacula himalayana*	Himalayan Parakeet, Himalayan Slaty-headed Parakeet
Plum-headed Parakeet	*Psittacula cyanocephala*	Blossom-headed Parakeet
Alexandrine Parakeet	*Psittacula eupatria*	Large Indian Parakeet
Rose-ringed Parakeet	*Psittacula krameri*	
Passeriformes (Eurylaimidae)		
Long-tailed Broadbill	*Psarisomus dalhousiae*	
Passeriformes (Campephagidae)		
Small Minivet	*Pericrocotus cinnamomeus*	
Long-tailed Minivet	*Pericrocotus ethologus*	
Scarlet Minivet	*Pericrocotus flammeus*	[Orange Minivet]

English Name	Scientific Name	Alternative Name(s)
Rosy Minivet	*Pericrocotus roseus*	
Large Cuckooshrike	*Coracina javensis*	
Black-winged Cuckooshrike	*Lalage melaschistos*	Dark Grey Cuckooshrike
Passeriformes (Vireonidae)		
Himalayan Shrike-babbler	*Pteruthius ripleyi*	
Green Shrike-babbler	*Pteruthius xanthochlorus*	
Passeriformes (Oriolidae)		
Maroon Oriole	*Oriolus traillii*	
Black-hooded Oriole	*Oriolus xanthornus*	Black-headed Oriole
Indian Golden Oriole	*Oriolus kundoo*	
Passeriformes (Artamidae)		
Ashy Woodswallow	*Artamus fuscus*	Ashy Swallow-shrike
Passeriformes (Vangidae)		
Bar-winged Flycatcher-shrike	*Hemipus picatus*	Pied Flycatcher-shrike
Common Woodshrike	*Tephrodornis pondicerianus*	
Passeriformes (Aegithinidae)		
Common Iora	*Aegithina tiphia*	
Passeriformes (Dicruridae)		
Black Drongo	*Dicrurus macrocercus*	
Ashy Drongo	*Dicrurus leucophaeus*	Grey Drongo
Bronzed Drongo	*Dicrurus aeneus*	
Hair-crested Drongo	*Dicrurus hottentottus*	Spangled Drongo
Greater Racket-tailed Drongo	*Dicrurus paradiseus*	
Passeriformes (Rhipiduridae)		
White-browed Fantail	*Rhipidura aureola*	White-browed Fantail-flycatcher
White-throated Fantail	*Rhipidura albicollis*	White-throated Fantail-flycatcher; [White-spotted Fantail, Spot-breasted Fantail]
Passeriformes (Laniidae)		
Bay-backed Shrike	*Lanius vittatus*	
Long-tailed Shrike	*Lanius schach*	Rufous-backed Shrike
Grey-backed Shrike	*Lanius tephronotus*	Tibetan Shrike
Passeriformes (Corvidae)		
Rufous Treepie	*Dendrocitta vagabunda*	Indian Treepie
Red-billed Blue Magpie	*Urocissa erythroryncha*	Blue Magpie
Common Green Magpie	*Cissa chinensis*	
Eurasian Jay	*Garrulus glandarius*	Red-crowned Jay
Black-headed Jay	*Garrulus lanceolatus*	Black-throated Jay
House Crow	*Corvus splendens*	
Large-billed Crow	*Corvus macrorhynchos*	[Jungle Crow, Indian Jungle Crow, Eastern Jungle Crow]
Passeriformes (Monarchidae)		
Black-naped Monarch	*Hypothymis azurea*	Black-naped Monarch Flycatcher, Black-naped Flycatcher
Indian Paradise-flycatcher	*Terpsiphone paradisi*	Asian Paradise-flycatcher (incl. T. affinis)
Passeriformes (Dicaeidae)		
Pale-billed Flowerpecker	*Dicaeum erythrorhynchos*	Tickell's Flowerpecker
Plain Flowerpecker	*Dicaeum concolor*	[Andaman Flowerpecker, Nilgiri Flowerpecker]
Fire-breasted Flowerpecker	*Dicaeum ignipectus*	
Passeriformes (Nectariniidae)		
Purple Sunbird	*Cinnyris asiaticus*	
Fire-tailed Sunbird	*Aethopyga ignicauda*	Fire-tailed Yellow-backed Sunbird
Black-throated Sunbird	*Aethopyga saturata*	Black-breasted Sunbird
Green-tailed Sunbird	*Aethopyga nipalensis*	Nepal Yellow-backed Sunbird
Mrs Gould's Sunbird	*Aethopyga gouldiae*	
Crimson Sunbird	*Aethopyga siparaja*	Yellow-backed Sunbird (incl. A. vigorsii)
Golden-fronted Leafbird	*Chloropsis aurifrons*	Gold-fronted Chloropsis, Golden-fronted Chloropsis
Orange-bellied Leafbird	*Chloropsis hardwickii*	Orange-bellied Chloropsis
Passeriformes (Ploceidae)		
Baya Weaver	*Ploceus philippinus*	Indian Baya
Passeriformes (Estrildidae)		
Indian Silverbill	*Euodice malabarica*	White-throated Munia

English Name	Scientific Name	Alternative Name(s)
Scaly-breasted Munia	*Lonchura punctulata*	Spotted Munia
Passeriformes (Passeridae)		
House Sparrow	*Passer domesticus*	
Russet Sparrow	*Passer cinnamomeus*	Cinnamon Tree Sparrow, Cinnamon Sparrow
Eurasian Tree Sparrow	*Passer montanus*	Tree Sparrow
Passeriformes (Motacillidae)		
Tree Pipit	*Anthus trivialis*	Eurasian Tree Pipit
Olive-backed Pipit	*Anthus hodgsoni*	Indian Tree Pipit
Rosy Pipit	*Anthus roseatus*	Vinaceous-breasted Pipit
Upland Pipit	*Anthus sylvanus*	
Western Yellow Wagtail	*Motacilla flava*	
Grey Wagtail	*Motacilla cinerea*	
Citrine Wagtail	*Motacilla citreola*	Yellow-headed Wagtail
White-browed Wagtail	*Motacilla maderaspatensis*	Large Pied Wagtail
White Wagtail	*Motacilla alba*	Pied Wagtail
Passeriformes (Fringillidae)		
Common Rosefinch	*Erythrina erythrina*	
Red-headed Bullfinch	*Pyrrhula erythrocephala*	
Plain Mountain Finch	*Leucosticte nemoricola*	Plain-coloured Mountain Finch, Hodgson's Mountain Finch
Yellow-breasted Greenfinch	*Chloris spinoides*	Himalayan Greenfinch
European Goldfinch	*Carduelis carduelis*	
Fire-fronted Serin	*Serinus pusillus*	Red-fronted Serin, Gold-fronted Finch
Passeriformes (Emberizidae)		
Crested Bunting	*Melophus lathami*	
Red-headed Bunting	*Granativora bruniceps*	
Godlewski's Bunting	*Emberiza godlewskii*	
Passeriformes (Stenostiridae)		
Yellow-bellied Fairy-fantail	*Chelidorhynx hypoxanthus*	Yellow-bellied Fantail, Yellow-bellied Fantail-flycatcher
Grey-headed Canary-flycatcher	*Culicicapa ceylonensis*	Grey-headed Flycatcher
Passeriformes (Paridae)		
Yellow-browed Tit	*Sylviparus modestus*	
Coal Tit	*Periparus ater*	Spot-winged Tit/Crested Black Tit P. [a.] melanolophus
Rufous-naped Tit	*Periparus rufonuchalis*	Black-breasted Tit, Dark-grey Tit, Simla Black Tit
Rufous-vented Tit	*Periparus rubidiventris*	Rufous-bellied Crested Tit, Black Crested Tit
Green-backed Tit	*Parus monticolus*	
Cinereous Tit	*Parus cinereus*	Grey Tit/Great Tit (with P. major)
Black-lored Tit	*Machlolophus xanthogenys*	Yellow-cheeked Tit (incl. M. spilonotus); [Indian Tit, Indian Black-lored Tit, Himalayan Black-lored Tit, Black-lored Yellow Tit]
Passeriformes (Alaudidae)		
Sand Lark	*Alaudala raytal*	Indian Short-toed Lark
Passeriformes (Cisticolidae)		
Hill Prinia	*Prinia atrogularis*	Black-throated Hill Warbler; [Black-throated Prinia]
Grey-breasted Prinia	*Prinia hodgsonii*	Franklin's Wren Warbler, Ashy-grey Wren Warbler
Yellow-bellied Prinia	*Prinia flaviventris*	Yellow-bellied Wren Warbler
Ashy Prinia	*Prinia socialis*	Ashy Wren Warbler
Common Tailorbird	*Orthotomus sutorius*	
Passeriformes (Locustellidae)		
West Himalayan Bush Warbler	*Locustella kashmirensis*	
Passeriformes (Pnoepygidae)		
Nepal Wren Babbler	*Pnoepyga immaculata*	Immaculate Cupwing
Pygmy Wren Babbler	*Pnoepyga pusilla*	Brown Wren Babbler, Pygmy Cupwing
Passeriformes (Hirundinidae)		
Northern House Martin	*Delichon urbicum*	Common House Martin, European House Martin
Asian House Martin	*Delichon dasypus*	
Nepal House Martin	*Delichon nipalense*	
Streak-throated Swallow	*Petrochelidon fluvicola*	Indian Cliff Swallow

English Name	Scientific Name	Alternative Name(s)
Red-rumped Swallow	*Cecropis daurica*	Striated Swallow (incl. C. striolata)
Wire-tailed Swallow	*Hirundo smithii*	
Barn Swallow	*Hirundo rustica*	Common Swallow
Eurasian Crag Martin	*Ptyonoprogne rupestris*	Crag Martin
Dusky Crag Martin	*Ptyonoprogne concolor*	
Sand Martin	*Riparia riparia*	Collared Sand Martin (incl. R. diluta), Bank Swallow, Common Sand Martin
Passeriformes (Pycnonotidae)		
Ashy Bulbul	*Hemixos flavala*	Brown-eared Bulbul
Mountain Bulbul	*Ixos mcclellandii*	Rufous-bellied Bulbul
Black Bulbul	*Hypsipetes leucocephalus*	[Square-tailed Bulbul, Himalayan Black Bulbul]
Black-crested Bulbul	*Pycnonotus melanicterus*	[Flame-throated Bulbul, Ruby-throated Bulbul]
Red-whiskered Bulbul	*Pycnonotus jocosus*	
Himalayan Bulbul	*Pycnonotus leucogenis*	White-cheeked Bulbul (incl. P. leucotis)
Red-vented Bulbul	*Pycnonotus cafer*	
Passeriformes (Phylloscopidae)		
Hume's Leaf Warbler	*Abrornis humei*	Hume's Warbler, Mandelli's Leaf Warbler A. [h.] mandellii
Lemon-rumped Warbler	*Abrornis chloronotus*	Pale-rumped Warbler, Pallas's Leaf Warbler (with A. proregulus)
Smoky Warbler	*Phylloscopus fuligiventer*	Smoky Leaf Warbler
Sulphur-bellied Warbler	*Phylloscopus griseolus*	Olivaceous Leaf warbler
Tickell's Leaf Warbler	*Phylloscopus affinis*	
White-spectacled Warbler	*Seicercus affinis*	Allied Flycatcher Warbler, White-spectacled Leaf Warbler
Grey-crowned Warbler	*Seicercus tephrocephalus*	Grey-crowned Leaf Warbler
Whistler's Warbler	*Seicercus whistleri*	Whistler's Leaf Warbler
Greenish Leaf Warbler	*Seicercus trochiloides*	
Grey-hooded Leaf Warbler	*Seicercus xanthoschistos*	Grey-headed Flycatcher Warbler
Passeriformes (Scotocercidae)		
Chestnut-headed Tesia	*Cettia castaneocoronata*	Chestnut-headed Ground Warbler
Black-faced Warbler	*Abroscopus schisticeps*	Black-faced Flycatcher Warbler
Brownish-flanked Bush Warbler	*Horornis fortipes*	Strong-footed Bush Warbler, Brown-flanked Bush Warbler
Passeriformes (Aegithalidae)		
Black-throated Tit	*Aegithalos concinnus*	Black-throated Bushtit; [Red-headed Tit]
Passeriformes (Sylviidae)		
Yellow-eyed Babbler	*Chrysomma sinense*	
Passeriformes (Zosteropidae)		
Stripe-throated Yuhina	*Yuhina gularis*	
Whiskered Yuhina	*Yuhina flavicollis*	Yellow-naped Yuhina
Oriental White-eye	*Zosterops palpebrosus*	
Passeriformes (Timaliidae)		
Slender-billed Scimitar Babbler	*Pomatorhinus superciliaris*	
White-browed Scimitar Babbler	*Pomatorhinus schisticeps*	Slaty-headed Scimitar Babbler (incl. P. horsfieldii)
Passeriformes (Pellorneidae)		
White-hooded Babbler	*Gampsorhynchus rufulus*	White-headed Shrike Babbler
Rusty-capped Fulvetta	*Schoeniparus dubius*	Rufous-headed Tit Babbler
Rufous-throated Fulvetta	*Schoeniparus rufogularis*	Red-throated Tit Babbler
Yellow-throated Fulvetta	*Schoeniparus cinereus*	Dusky Green Tit Babbler, Yellow-throated Tit Babbler
Rufous-winged Fulvetta	*Schoeniparus castaneceps*	Chestnut-headed Tit Babbler
Long-tailed Grass Babbler	*Laticilla burnesii*	Rufous-vented Prinia L. [b.] burnesii, Swamp Prinia L. [b.] cinerascens
Spot-throated Babbler	*Pellorneum albiventre*	Brown Babbler
Buff-breasted Babbler	*Trichastoma tickelli*	Tickell's Babbler
Abbott's Babbler	*Malacocincla abbotti*	
Streaked Wren Babbler	*Turdinus brevicaudatus*	
Eyebrowed Wren Babbler	*Napothera epilepidota*	Small Wren Babbler
Long-billed Wren Babbler	*Rimator malacoptilus*	
Passeriformes (Leiothrichidae)		
Nepal Tit Babbler	*Alcippe nipalensis*	Nepal Fulvetta, Nepal Quaker Babbler

English Name	Scientific Name	Alternative Name(s)
Jungle Babbler	*Turdoides striata*	
White-crested Laughingthrush	*Garrulax leucolophus*	
White-throated Laughingthrush	*Garrulax albogularis*	
Streaked Laughingthrush	*Trochalopteron lineatum*	[Bhutan Laughingthrush]
Variegated Laughingthrush	*Trochalopteron variegatum*	
Chestnut-crowned Laughingthrush	*Trochalopteron erythrocephalum*	Red-headed Laughingthrush; [Assam Laughingthrush]
Red-billed Leiothrix	*Leiothrix lutea*	
Red-tailed Minla	*Minla ignotincta*	
Blue-winged Minla	*Siva cyanouroptera*	Blue-winged Siva
Chestnut-tailed Minla	*Chrysominla strigula*	Bar-throated Siva, Bar-throated Minla
Passeriformes (Regulidae)		
Goldcrest	*Regulus regulus*	
Passeriformes (Certhiidae)		
Bar-tailed Treecreeper	*Certhia himalayana*	Himalayan Treecreeper
Passeriformes (Sittidae)		
White-tailed Nuthatch	*Sitta himalayensis*	
Velvet-fronted Nuthatch	*Sitta frontalis*	
Wallcreeper	*Tichodroma muraria*	
Passeriformes (Sturnidae)		
Asian Pied Starling	*Gracupica contra*	Pied Myna
Brahminy Starling	*Sturnia pagodarum*	Black-headed Myna, Brahminy Myna
Chestnut-tailed Starling	*Sturnia malabarica*	Grey-headed Myna; [Malabar Starling, Malabar White-headed Starling]
Common Myna	*Acridotheres tristis*	Indian Myna
Bank Myna	*Acridotheres ginginianus*	
Jungle Myna	*Acridotheres fuscus*	
Spot-winged Starling	*Saroglossa spilopterus*	Spotted-winged Stare
Passeriformes (Cinclidae)		
Brown Dipper	*Cinclus pallasii*	
Passeriformes (Muscicapidae)		
Indian Robin	*Saxicoloides fulicatus*	Indian Black Robin
Oriental Magpie Robin	*Copsychus saularis*	
White-rumped Shama	*Kittacincla malabarica*	[Andaman Shama]
Dark-sided Flycatcher	*Muscicapa sibirica*	Sooty Flycatcher
Rusty-tailed Flycatcher	*Muscicapa ruficauda*	Rufous-tailed Flycatcher
Ferruginous Flycatcher	*Muscicapa ferruginea*	
Tickell's Blue Flycatcher	*Cyornis tickelliae*	Tickell's Red-breasted Blue Flycatcher
Blue-throated Flycatcher	*Cyornis rubeculoides*	Blue-throated Blue Flycatcher
Rufous-bellied Niltava	*Niltava sundara*	
Small Niltava	*Niltava macgrigoriae*	
Verditer Flycatcher	*Eumyias thalassinus*	
Bluethroat	*Luscinia svecica*	
Little Forktail	*Enicurus scouleri*	
Black-backed Forktail	*Enicurus immaculatus*	
Slaty-backed Forktail	*Enicurus schistaceus*	
Spotted Forktail	*Enicurus maculatus*	
Blue Whistling Thrush	*Myophonus caeruleus*	
White-tailed Rubythroat	*Calliope pectoralis*	Himalayan Rubythroat
Siberian Rubythroat	*Calliope calliope*	Rubythroat
Golden Bush Robin	*Tarsiger chrysaeus*	
Himalayan Bush Robin	*Tarsiger rufilatus*	Orange-flanked Bush Robin (with T. cyanurus), Himalayan Bluetail, Himalayan Red-flanked Bush Robin
Red-breasted Flycatcher	*Ficedula parva*	
Taiga Flycatcher	*Ficedula albicilla*	Red-throated Flycatcher
Rufous-gorgeted Flycatcher	*Ficedula strophiata*	Orange-gorgeted Flycatcher
Ultramarine Flycatcher	*Ficedula superciliaris*	White-browed Blue Flycatcher F. s. superciliaris, Little Blue-and-white Flycatcher F. s. aestigma
Slaty-blue Flycatcher	*Ficedula tricolor*	
Slaty-backed Flycatcher	*Ficedula sordida*	Rusty-breasted Blue Flycatcher
Blue-fronted Redstart	*Adelura frontalis*	

English Name	Scientific Name	Alternative Name(s)
Plumbeous Water Redstart	*Rhyacornis fuliginosa*	Plumbeous Redstart
White-capped Water Redstart	*Chaimarrornis leucocephalus*	River Chat, White-capped Redstart
Black Redstart	*Phoenicurus ochruros*	
Blue-capped Rock Thrush	*Monticola cinclorhyncha*	Blue-headed Rock Thrush
Chestnut-bellied Rock Thrush	*Monticola rufiventris*	
Blue Rock Thrush	*Monticola solitarius*	[Asian Rock Thrush]
Siberian Stonechat	*Saxicola maurus*	Collared Bushchat, Eastern Stonechat, Commo Stonechat (with S. torquatus)
Pied Bushchat	*Saxicola caprata*	
Grey Bushchat	*Saxicola ferreus*	Dark-grey Bushchat
Passeriformes (Turdidae)		
Long-tailed Thrush	*Zoothera dixoni*	Long-tailed Mountain Thrush
Himalayan Forest Thrush	*Zoothera salimalii*	
Long-billed Thrush	*Zoothera monticola*	Large Brown Thrush, Long-billed Ground Thrus
Scaly Thrush	*Zoothera dauma*	Scaly Mountain Thrush, Small-billed Mountain Thrush/Small-billed Scaly Thrush Z. d. dauma; [Nilgiri Thrush]
Orange-headed Thrush	*Geokichla citrina*	Orange-headed Ground Thrush, White-throatec Ground Thrush G. c. cyanota
Mistle Thrush	*Turdus viscivorus*	
Grey-winged Blackbird	*Turdus boulboul*	
Indian Blackbird	*Turdus simillimus*	
Tickell's Thrush	*Turdus unicolor*	
White-collared Blackbird	*Turdus albocinctus*	
Black-throated Thrush	*Turdus atrogularis*	

INDEX